'QUEEN'
OF THE
MARA

'QUEEN' OF THE MARA

PETAL

DAVID DRUMMOND GM. CPM(G). MID.

WITH A FOREWORD BY
DR DAPHNE SHELDRICK MBE MBS

Matador
9 De Montfort Mews
Leicester LE1 7FW, UK
Tel: (+44) 116 255 9311 / 9312
Email: books@troubador.co.uk
Web: www.troubador.co.uk/matador

ISBN 1 905237 25 1

Cover photograph: © Angie Scott, courtesy Nature Picture Library Bristol (NPL – 1097329)

Typeset in 11pt Stempel Garamond by Troubador Publishing Ltd, Leicester, UK

Matador is an imprint of Troubador Publishing Ltd
Printed and Bound by The Cromwell Press

1958–1996

Dedicated to my Daughter
Heather

"The best kind of friend is someone
you can sit on a porch and swing with,
never say a word and then walk away
feeling it was the best conversation
you've ever had.

It is true that we don't know what we have
until we lose it.

You were my best friend.

CONTENTS

THE BEGINNING

This true and incredible story of a mother cheetah and her family unfolds in the heart of the great Maasai Mara Game Reserve in Kenya. Nature's unforgiving principles had decreed their mother would not survive.

No one could have foretold the terrible tragedy that was to lie in wait for the mother and her five little cheetah cubs.

Born free in the wilds and destined to die, nobody visualised that fate would intervene and provide a foster father to help the cubs fulfill their natural lives.

The orphans lives' became intertwined with a human whom they came to accept, trust and protect as one of their own. They introduced him to their adventures and taught him to understand the ways of their kind in the wild.

This remarkable account made famous by a wild orphaned 'Queen' cheetah named Petal is dramatically described and illustrated in detail over a period of 16 years. Their adopted foster-father, David Drummond, is a well-known Kenyan Conservationist, Safari Operator and Honorary Game Warden.

Petal's offspring, surviving by their natural instincts, live and roam wild in the Mara. By some genetic quirk they continue to recognise the Queen's foster-father and welcome him each time he visits them in their chosen territories.

Born to be wild!
Hopeless, Hackles, Whispers, Petal and Prickles I vowed these little cubs would
not be left to die.

ABOUT THE AUTHOR

David Drummond was born in Kenya of Scottish stock whose ancestors for centuries, farmed the fertile lands of Perthshire and the sheep-covered hills of the Midlothian borders.

David was brought up on a cattle ranch in Kenya where the milling herds of wildlife and cattle grazed side-by-side. The predators preyed on their stock and the wildlife day and night.

The seeds of the out-doors and the adventures they offered were implanted in David at an early age. The knowledge of the country and its peoples became second nature to him. He spoke their languages and understood their mind-set.

It was not surprising that Mother Nature presented this Taurean with a unique opportunity by introducing him to her wild animal kingdom. Above all she taught him to trust one of her wild predators with his life.

As his cousin, I felt very privileged to be invited to Kenya to witness the beginning of this incredible adventure. Over the years I followed the progress of his bold experiment with keen interest. His enthusiasm and understanding of all things wild will surely lead to a successful ending. Future research will benefit from this exciting breakthrough and by following along these lines the formula will provide the key to a new hands-on approach in bridging the communication gap between wild free range cheetahs in their protected areas, and humans. The cheetah, a beautiful intelligent and endangered predator of the African savanna, must never be permitted to fade into extinction.

Here is a man who stands his ground in the face of adversity. The sign of the Zodiac had blessed him with a will to survive through to a full and charmed life. His adventures documented in a best seller 'Bwana Drum' that describes him as a courageous, sensitive and intelligent individual who won acclaim as one of the most commended and highly decorated under-cover men who pioneered the anti-guerrilla-warfare techniques that brought the Kenya Emergency to an early end.

Andrew Brown (1925-2000)
Chief Superintendent
Lothian and Borders Constabulary

FOREWORD

In my time, I have hand-reared most wild African species, from elephants to field mice, and many of them, except the Big Cats, although I know many other people that have handled these magnificent predators. Cheetahs are perhaps, not only the most beautiful, but also the most mysterious of all. In truth, they are really the Adam and Eve of the Animal Kingdom, each sharing genes that reach back through millennia to a common pair of ancestors. Although officially classified as "Cat", they are part "Dog", and anyone who has known and loved their domestic cat or dog, will understand that these beautiful, graceful and gentle predators have the traits of both in abundance. Those fortunate people who can put aside the mistaken and arrogant belief that the human "animal" is superior to others that share the planet with us, and who have been blessed by exposure to the natural world, and been rewarded by an acquired empathy for its wondrous wild inhabitants, have breached the barriers that segregate the human animals from the natural animal world. By earning the trust of a totally wild creature who can sense that empathy by mysterious means, they are rewarded by a friendship and a love that is selfless and complete, given by a being that shares with us humans many emotional traits. David Drummond is one such person who possesses that rare ability, and whose long and intimate relationship with the cheetahs of the Maasai Mara is now graphically described in this book. Here, I think it is fitting to quote a passage taken from *The Outermost House* by Henry Beston:

> *We need another and a wiser and perhaps a more mystical concept of animals. Remote from universal Nature, and living by complicated artifice, man in civilization surveys the creatures through the glass of his knowledge and sees thereby a feather magnified and the whole image in distortion. We patronize them for their incompleteness, for their tragic fate of having taken form so far below ourselves. And therein we err, and greatly err. For the animal shall not be measured by man. In a world older and more complete than ours, they move finished and complete, gifted with extensions of the senses we have lost or never attained, living by voices we cannot hear. They are not brethren, they are not underlings; they are other nations, caught with ourselves in the net of life and time, fellow prisoners of the splendour and travail of the earth.*

Dr Daphne Sheidrick MBE MBS
1992 UNEP Global 500 Laureat
Winner of the 2003 BBC Lifetime Achievement Award

ACKNOWLEDGEMENTS

My sincere admiration must go to the computer wizards who typed and retyped this manuscript several times over without complaint:

Carmel Milon and Wendy Hubble

Patrick Hamilton, Anne and Tommy Richardson for all their efforts in assisting me to select the best photographs from many hundreds for inclusion in this book.

A very special thank-you must go to my wife, Hilary, who has persevered with me through all of my computer rage outbursts from the very start of this project to its final publication. without her dogged support this impossible adventure would never have seen the light of day.

A percentage of the proceeds of this book has been donated
to The Oxford Radford Clinic Leukemia CMML Research Fund.
Registered Charity No. 1057259

PHOTO CREDITS

This is dedicated to all of 'Petal's friends' who sent me their photos and shared these experiences on safari with us. Their 'masterpieces' and many more have added colour and authenticity to this book. I am most grateful for their contributions in bringing this story to life. They are:

Margaret Ardell   'Petal' Queen of the Mara
                                 The Five Little Cheetahs
                                 Prickles' wound almost healed
                                 Petal made her move

The late Andrew Brown   Jean and Tom Somerville

Theresa Sorgen-Blazer   Her outstretched paw

Dave Drummond   'Kamonde' The Hunter-gatherer
                                 Prickles' life hangs by a thread
                                 Prickles' wound almost healed
                                 Summer had come and Petal had vanished in the night
                                 Kibet with the bird-watchers
                                 Bad weather ahead
                                 The King Cheetah
                                 Full moon over the Aitongs
                                 Mankind and Nature at one
                                 Home-made inflatable
                                 Breakfast in the bush
                                 Farewell Jamie
                                 'Mbwa Mwitu'
                                 The poachers' hideout
                                 A spitting cobra strikes
                                 Six months later
                                 A very lucky cheetah
                                 Petal in her den

Teaching the boys to hunt
The five cheetahs hunting in the acacia
'Buzz off'
Petal's Prince
Sitting with Astra
Walking with Petal and the two cubs
An hour later
Petal's walk-about
Scamp always up to mischief
Petal walking her territorial boundaries
First encounter with Astra and cubs
Sprite lies injured
Petal walked at Sprite's pace
Petal's antics

Herbert Spitz   Looking towards the dead croc
Adventure camp

David Stanley   Snared leopard

Fiona Walthall   All hell let loose
Order and calm restored

Esther Wolf   The Introduction – Getting to know Astra
Petal always takes the lead

PROLOGUE

How must it have been for my parents, buoyed by the excitement and spirit of adventure, to break away from the land of their birth with little knowledge of the dangers of wild, untamed Africa awaiting them? The fear of the unknown, let alone planning a family, must surely be how 'the courage of one's convictions' came to be defined and translated as to 'nerve one's self to a venture'.

Their journey began through the Bay of Biscay and the clear blue waters of the Mediterranean, onwards through the Suez Canal that permitted circumvention of the Continent of Africa, sailing onwards past the Great Pyramids and calling in at Port Said. Here the 'Gully Gully Man', by sleight-of-hand, made wondrous magic on board ship to the delight of even the youngest children. To me it was a matter of which came first, the chicken or the egg. The bum-boats jostled along the ship's side at anchor offshore selling their brightly coloured leather ware and copper trinkets. The jovial, turbaned trader winched the article tied to a rope up the ship's side to the buyer. Some heartless buyers often left their bartering to the last minute as the ship set sail with the bum-boats still tied to its stern. Bartering is a soulless art – some win, some lose.

I remember those awe-inspiring trips when, as a boy, my father took leave to visit family and friends in their native Scotland. For I, born and bred in Africa, found great pleasure at the sight of snow and of course snowball fights ensued, fought out to the last against my long suffering cousins; they always taking the brunt of my enthusiasm with good humour.

The little village of Fowlis Wester is where my parents and the generations before them had toiled the fields and upheld the Christian faith amongst this small community. The cemetery bears witness well into the 17th century that many of the family have been buried there, where the ashes of my 98-year-old father now lie. A man whose courage I always admired; he had no fear of man, nor tempest – but of God. I was proud to have his genes within the spirit of my makeup, for I would have wished to have no other. Yet in my upbringing I had to endure his terrible wrath as he gradually moulded me into his replica. In later years I came to question his method of the harsh discipline he dispensed.

The resultant effects manifested in me a strong desire to beat the stuffing out of any bruiser who remotely showed any signs of becoming the school bully. Whether he was bigger or fatter than I made little difference. It took half the senior form to drag me off one unfortunate victim. The classroom furniture took a terrible beating. The bulldog in me would not let go until the bully was silenced.

At the young age of fourteen, the teachers of my secondary school, The Prince of Wales school in Kenya, realised something 'short of a handful' had appeared in their midst.

My excessive energy and mischievous humour was looked upon with bated breath. It was not long before the Head-teacher, whose complexion matched the colour of his pink pyjamas; one Saturday morning found his pyjamas locked at full mast flying from the Quadrangle flagpole. As if this embarrassment was not enough, the clock tower bell that solemnly struck at each hour to remind us of the long hours of day and short nights was silenced.

Access to the tower was gained by climbing up a fifty-foot drainpipe. By placing several pairs of rugby socks around the bell hammer, I threw a spanner into the start of the timetable for that day.

This schoolboy prank earned me a thorough tanning. It necessitated the local Fire Brigade to remove the pyjamas from the flagpole and the rugby socks from around the bell hammer. I was sorely reminded by each stroke of the cane delivered by a somewhat overly pink Headmaster that the punishment being meted out to me was not for the prank, but for negligence and my total stupidity.

I had overlooked the very clue that did not require a detective to trace the culprit - the socks bore my name label so fastidiously sewn on all my school-wear by my caring mother.

This was learning 'the hard way'. I realized that any further pranks, whether they were of my making or not, the finger of suspicion would always point at me. Throughout my life I never had any inclination to shoulder the blame for others' misdeeds. The boarding school was for boys only, so the need to knuckle under and transform played heavily on my mind.

As a student I was very mediocre and applied just enough academic effort to scrape through my exams. My real interests lay in every sporting ball game including hockey and cricket, the Cadet force, boxing and music. I played hard, earned my school colours and my prefectship. At the age of seventeen, I still had no clues as to what my future choice of career would be. I had grown up in the outdoors, the call of the wild having been nurtured on my parents' cattle ranch. Nature had already planted her seed in me at an early age, and in later years, her wondrous way was to fulfill my life's wildest dreams.

Anything mechanical, be it driven or static, became second nature for me to handle. The hammer, the saw and the need to design and construct had already surfaced in me at an early age. I also had a flair for drawing.

My end of school term reports pointed to a career as an architect. The ingredients were apparently there, so in my final year my interests favoured the drawing board not art. My sights were now set.

I left school having completed my sixth grade education, equivalent to the first year at university, and commenced my apprenticeship in the building trade in Kenya, with a large UK based firm, as a student quantity surveyor. Molem's construction company had large building contracts in Kenya. For several years I worked in their head office in Nairobi under the tutelage of a qualified quantity surveyor, after which I was attached to the practical side of construction under the experienced eye of their senior works foreman. I found the work interesting and rewarding. My father, and particularly my uncle, who was also a qualified surveyor and foreman in the trade, had already taught me the initial hands-on basics during my school holidays.

The political signs of unrest amongst the indigenous Kenya tribes brought forth a sense of foreboding that preceded the rumblings of much deeper dissatisfaction.

In 1952 the bubble burst. My Police Reserve call-up papers arrived and my chosen career and apprenticeship were suddenly in tatters. An uprising against the British Colonial Government was in the making. Kenya was about to be plunged into Civil War. I remembered my Cadet Force training and the need to serve King and Country. I had not truly visualised the depths to which this pending uprising would go.

My qualifications were already in place. They had come well wrapped in the natural process of a home-grown product that understood the mind and could speak the common language of the indigenous people. I had indeed been born an African. I was well versed in the ways of bush craft, tried and tested. I loved exploring and following the wild animal tracks. Life in the mountain forests had become second nature to me.

In my childhood an old Kikuyu forest hunter-gatherer taught me how I could live off the fruits and trappings of nature's bounty. He taught me the ways of the wild animals, the call of the honey birds, the art of forward tracking using that second sight or sixth sense to recognise that which trod immediately before me and the danger that could lie in wait along the path of my choice. His teachings stood me in good stead for the years to come.

It was here that the first seeds of the outdoors were planted in my mind. He taught me

Kamonde
My wise old hunter-gatherer friend of no fixed abode.
Nature was his friend and poachers his sworn enemies.

to speak his tribal language fluently and I came to understand some of the many common languages spoken by the indigenous people, also the ways of the wild animals and poachers and how to track their movements.

I treasured his wise counsel 'measure each step with care, my son, and you will be blessed with a long and adventurous life'.

I always looked forward to my school holidays. Living as I did, on a large cattle ranch, there was always plenty to do to keep my active mind in trim.

Much of my daily routine was to make and mend, mechanical or otherwise. The long hours of work to earn my pocket money was never boring. I was permitted to play the occasional game of cricket or rugby for the local sports club, but in the main my yearning to be with my hunter-gather friend, Kamonde, was ever present.

I wanted to be with nature – there was so much to learn. My father was always keen that I should accept responsibility from an early age.

I recall, in my early youth, my first real tests came in my school holidays in many unexpected forms. I was to cheat death by a whisker many times in the months and years to come.

Petal's antics
Petal captured the hearts of her admirers.

CHAPTER 1

THE CHARGING BUFFALO

DRUMVALE Cattle Ranch situated some 20 miles east of Nairobi grew Napier grass, a semi-drought resistant cattle fodder often mistaken at first glance as sugar cane. It must have been 'hell' for the hand cutters—the fine hairs would find their way down the back of your neck and then dig into every crevasse of your body! The 'itch' is worse than torture! The best cure I know to remove it is to apply sellotape and 'rrrip' it off! Your screams of agony will be heard for miles, but it's worth it.

The grass is cut by hand, carted away, placed in an underground silo-pit and then compressed. The heat ferments the cane stem and sabre-like leaves. After several months it is processed through a 'chaff cutter' and fed to the milking stock in times of drought. The cows will run a mile for it, especially if laced with molasses! Their milk yield remains steady throughout the dry period. The dairy farmer is happy, so are his cows, albeit a little tipsy.

Napier grass grows well in low-lying swamp areas close to floodwater channels or rivers—when mixed with sugar cane it presents an almost impenetrable barrier.

Several old short-tempered bull buffaloes, evicted from their herd, had taken up residence in the 300-acre area of Napier grass and objected to cutters demolishing their 'patch'.

Sooner or later the inevitable happened—the head cutter was attacked and badly gored and his gang promptly went on strike.

The Game Department was contacted and agreed to send a professional hunter to come and rid us of the menace. He arrived in due course, but swallowed hard when shown the thick and almost impenetrable Napier grass.

This was not what Bousfield had expected, but not to be outdone he called for human reinforcements. His plan 'A' was to send in beaters banging empty tin cans with home-made drumsticks! I wasn't surprised when they said no! Their plan 'A' was to stand around the perimeter and beat their tins!

Bousfield vetoed this idea as it would only alert the buffalo bulls and push them deeper into their patch; it would also put the buffalo on their 'ambush' guard. "What would be the next move?" I asked.

The Game Department's control officer was an experienced and well-known white hunter. His plan 'B' surprised me even more! He said, "I need a couple of your adult Dachshund dogs". My sister was into breeding these sausage like dogs and had half a dozen yappers around the house. "But surely," I said, "they are just lapdogs, no more than yap dogs". Bousfield smiled. "Come with me—you will see!"

Here I was, a 17 year old fearless youth ready for the hunt—with zero experience in big game hunting let alone hunting buffalo, the most feared of all—in thick Napier grass! Oh boy, I was about to be taught the lesson of my life. I was confident in handling a rifle even at that age and could hold my own with my seniors at shooting. On several occasions I had used my father's gun to cull hippos that were destroying the lucerne (cattle fodder) near the river. A dozen hippos can graze and clear an area of many acres of lucerne and more in one night, right down to the very roots. They are quick to learn and move down river if their leader is despatched. That was the depth of my big game shooting experience!

Armed with my father's .375 rifle, two fat Dachshunds—who could do with roller skates to keep their under carriage off the ground—and a crazy big game hunter carrying a rifle that surely, from the size of its ammunition, would blast away even the sturdiest of elephants, let alone a buffalo, we set off! How could things possibly go wrong?

The two dogs were bundled into the back of his Land rover pickup complaining bitterly that their pecking order, when travelling anywhere, must always be on the lap of their mistress and until such time as this was understood by all concerned, they would continue to bark incessantly, behaving like lunatics. Although they already had pride of place in our family home, I had little time for them! Their demands were ignored and off we drove down to the river.

By this time the African bush telegraph had been hard at work, we had many spectators, not just a few, but some sixty men, women and children, all eager to see the 'buffalo kill'. They looked in disbelief as we disembarked from the Land rover. We attempted to remove the two Dachshunds, who had now turned into snarling and snapping demons, angrily refusing to get out or be lifted from the rear of the pickup. This was their way of telling us their pride had been truly dented. Our spectators were now in fits of laughter.

Bousfield looked amused. I was about to say, "I told you so." (After all, who in their right mind would believe these two insane low slung sausages would ever, by any stretch of ones wildest imagination, be of any use to us in hunting down one of Africa's most dangerous animals?) My sister and mother were away for the day delivering fresh farm eggs to the city market. Father, surprisingly had nodded his approval that I participate in this hunting madness; as for the 'Daxies' two less out of six, to my mind, would not go amiss! If anything worse than death happened to them I would have to accept total responsibility and be man enough to bear the full brunt of my sister's wrath. These bandy legged creatures were free range, untrained and did not know the meaning of the words 'heel', 'sit', or 'leash'.

My being condemned to the doghouse already appeared to be more than just a possibility. Danger had not even entered my mind. Bousfield summoned Bongie, the head cutter and tractor driver, and gave him instructions to search for the biggest, most recent and best looking buffalo dropping he could find and bring it to the vehicle.

Bongie was also the farm comedian; among his other skills he was a self taught farm tractor driver with several spectacular credits to his name; namely parking the one and only farm tractor down a newly completed twenty foot deep uncapped pit latrine. Later on there was another incident that would have impressed any stuntman.

Bongie uprooted the wooden uprights supporting a twenty-five foot high corrugated iron service tank that provided the family home with water, pumped from a nearby borehole, by attaching a four-inch belt to the tractor drive shaft; a simple piece of bush engineering brilliance known only to Bongie. He had successfully carried out this job without mishap over several years. It was one of those days from hell that convinced Bongie the devil himself had entered the soul of his ancient tractor! Probably due to old age, the large rear metal drive-wheel mysteriously exploded and punctured the tractor wheel sending large chunks of rubber in all directions. Bongie's rocket-like departure from the seat of this mechanical 'devil' released the foot brake! The four supporting posts were uprooted as the tractor lurched forward—the rest of the story is history.

A somewhat shaken tractor driver appeared later and surveyed the damage from a distance and concluded the situation was decidedly unhealthy. The mangled heap of metal that was once a tank was just too much for him to stomach, let alone the thought of the dusting down he was sure to receive from the 'boss'. Bongie decided to go AWOL (desert!). I was able to persuade him with a simple-minded solution—that if he put bees wax in his ears he would only hear the bees buzzing and not the cussing and blinding that he was about to receive from my father.

When the 'boss' returned from the city he surveyed the heap, said not a word, turned around and walked away! The next day a brand new 1000-gallon tank (guaranteed for ten years) replaced the rusting old tank that had miraculously contained the farm water supplies and fulfilled its purpose without a leak for fifteen years. Bongie somehow kept his job and gave many years of accident-prone service! He became a faithful and willing member of the Drumvale demolition squad. There is a saying in Africa; "It is wise to employ the devil you know"!

Bongie had organised the beaters to search along the Napier grass perimeter for a suitable buffalo dropping as he put it, "for presentation to the gods". He, like I, had not immediately questioned the reason for this odd request from the hunter, though it had crossed my mind that maybe Bousfield was about to smear the dogs and both of us with the buffalo shit! A 'pad' was located and we drove to the spot. I recall that buffalo are short-sighted animals and have a highly developed sense of smell; somehow it made sense and so to the amusement of all we plastered the smelly stuff on our boots and leggings.

The two Dachshunds were electrified—their demeanour and appearance changed as if by a flick of a switch. They were no longer the snapping dogs of the previous half-hour, allowing themselves to be picked up out of the rear of the vehicle. Without any further encouragement from us they ran straight into the tall Napier grass. The hunt was on. "What do we do now?" I asked. "Lets wait a while and listen" Bousfield replied. I was now very impressed. "They had never shown this hunting aspect ever before" I said; Bousfield replied, "My boy, they are the best buffalo hunters you can find for this type of work. It's all built in—it's carried in their genes, it's instinctive; they need no training and they will track through the undergrowth like rats". Bousfield continued, "They pick up the scent of the buffalo then follow it and when they find them they will bark like never before!" I am even more impressed, this is unbelievable!

I now realised the reason for the wry smile the white hunter had just given me. He had it all worked out long ago. "Why the buffalo dung smeared on my nice polished leggings"? I asked. Bousfield replied, "That's to mix your body odour with theirs."

Bousfield continued, "The dogs will keep barking whilst continuing to snap at the heels of the buffalo, there is nothing more frustrating for a buffalo. That is when we move in quietly and follow their direction—if the wind is right it's our lucky day—if not we could be dead meat".

For a moment time stood still. All the onlookers were willing the dogs on and not a sound; not even a cough came from the spectators nearby. Bousfield was testing the direction of the wind, should the dogs find the buffalo we could then enter from down wind. "Come in the back door," as he put it. In these few minutes I was seeing, first hand, years of professional hunter experience enacted before my very eyes. What would my newly found hunter-gatherer African friend say if he were here? Suddenly the Napier grass parted; out came this huge buffalo a short distance from me. Strangely, there was no barking from the dogs; where were they?

The buffalo's appearance and disappearance was so quick I had no time to shoot as it vanished into the green wall of Napier grass. Seconds later, the dogs appeared, puffing and panting as if to say, "We did our job what the heck happened to you lot"? The dogs hesitated to take up the trail once more. Our quarry was still standing, silent, and dangerously close by.

The unexpected happened. The buffalo had shown himself for a fleeting second and caught us totally off guard. Bousfield was keen to follow but the dogs body language was signalling caution—they were now in charge and aware of their responsibility. We began to move in quietly step-by-step, keeping our eyes on the two dark forms of the dogs moving ahead of us.

After some fifty yards of very slow and stealthy progress, the dogs stopped—they were listening intently. Blackie, the lead male, had lifted his foreleg in a stance that was almost a point. Bousfield placed his index finger to his lips, (the sign to keep absolutely quiet), then rotated his finger in circles indicating 'It's somewhere here'. Was it the buffalo I could smell? Or was it...?

My heart was thumping from the adrenalin rush—then the Napier grass suddenly parted behind me—the buffalo had ambushed us! He had waited to let us pass and was coming in the back door like a steam engine; he had sprung his trap and now we became the hunted. As I half turned to shoot I lost my balance and fell backwards onto the wall of Napier grass. I pulled the trigger, but dammit—I had forgotten to take off the safety catch!

In the next second, the buffalo's horn hooked into the underside of my legging and tossed me some six feet into the air, still holding onto my rifle. The beast now charged forward towards Bousfield and the dogs. On the way down the thick stems of the Napier grass cushioned my fall. The dogs were now nipping at the attacker's heels, distracting his attention. I heard two shots in quick succession and it was all over. Bousfield came over to where I lay dazed. He was concerned that I may have been badly injured. The only injury was to my pride—I had been very lucky. It certainly was my lucky day; today I learned my number one lesson the hard way. I almost lost my 'crown jewels'.

Bongie now took charge of the situation. There would be celebrations and buffalo steak on the menu tonight. The farm labourers would soon descend upon the carcass to cut their best steaks. Bousfield now believed that having dispatched the lead buffalo, his companions would move out to other pastures. Several months passed and no other incidents occurred—his assumption was correct. The dogs were now waiting patiently for our return to the Land rover, proud in the knowledge that they had played their part. I was now converted. Both took pride of place on my lap as we drove back to the farmhouse. They could do nothing wrong in my book and they knew it.

Bousfield's parting words were "Dave, if you ever hunt buffalo, for whatever reason, watch your back; they are masters of cunning". "How could I ever forget?" I said. Sadly these were the last words I spoke to him. Ironically a month later, he was tragically killed at a railway crossing in fog, at a little town called Karatina. His Land rover slammed into a single steam engine freewheeling on a downhill gradient. Bousfield was caught unawares in the early hours of the morning – this silent killer took his life.

My father was impressed with the story of the hunt, and even congratulated the dogs! Their pecking order by now had reached dizzy proportions amongst their fellow companions. Father and I had decided not to disclose the events of this day to the returning household management. The unapproved use of my sister's star breeding studs in such a dangerous and stupid escapade would have started a riot in the house. Docile temperaments were not part of this dysfunctional family's makeup; though mother was the perfect saint at pouring oil on all troubled waters. My regular rebellions against my sister's desire for total supervision over me did not endear me to her. I was the rebel in the family who could not wait to untie the apron strings and flee the cuckoo's nest early in life.

It was not until a few days later when the two self-styled 'musketeers' decided life was getting too dull, (after their recent experiences). They were now trusted and tried professional hunters with status in the family hierarchy. The two dogs considered they had served their apprenticeship and were free to go buffalo hunting any time without a human armed escort! Both were not missed after having a hearty breakfast, the day passed and evening came. Their 'special' bowl of dogs' dinner remained untouched—Panic stations!

I instinctively knew it was time to distance myself from my sister's searchings and head for the river and the Napier grass. Darkness had set in, not the best time for the pooches to get lost in such thick undergrowth! I called several times and I heard their bark some distance away. Sound travels far on the night air; I was certain it was coming from over the river.

The only way to get to them safely would be to drive down river and cross over at 'Stinky bridge'; a bridge at which my elder brother had once misjudged his crossing! He missed the bridge and drove the pickup into the river; the problem was the vehicle was carrying the farm milk production to the Nairobi milk depot. Thankfully, this special commodity was contained in watertight sealed cans and held firm. Though no contents were delivered into the river, several were unaccounted for initially but finally were retrieved beached further down stream, none the worse for wear after their travels.

My father's account of my brother's incident is unprintable; for days after he was heard muttering out loud the first principles of Murphy's Law. "Anything that can go wrong will go wrong, don't let him touch anything!" he said. "But Dad" replied my brother, "Murphy was an optimist wasn't he?"

Bongie had volunteered to come with me to the river, remembering he was also party to the secret. Bongie had realised my plight and we agreed to keep total silence on the matter.

The possibility of the 'cat being let out of the bag' was very real and the 'punishment' I would receive from my sister would surely not be less than a thousand tongue-lashings! The thought did not bear thinking about. The Daxies, on seeing the approaching lights came to the Land rover and presented themselves with that look of total innocence, as little children would do after being caught misbehaving!

The worst was to come; both had attempted to cross the river. Stinky bridge had not been christened without good reason; effluent and sewage from an up-river village was undoubtedly the cause of their pong! 'Oh sh-t!' was all my brother could say on my arrival back at the ranch house. He too, could relate to his missed approach that landed him in the same river and coming out smelling of roses. His was an understatement! I tried to clean up the dogs to make them smell like roses, even going to great lengths by pouring my sister's expensive perfume over them was to no avail—the game was up. The whiplash tongue never stopped—from thereon the mad house became hell!

Weeks later, I had a frightening encounter with an eighteen foot python in the bush whilst out shooting for the pot. The python was duly skinned and in the hopes of presenting a 'peace offering' I had a taxidermist cure the skin. My pavement side, Asian shoemaker, old man 'Pitamba', made up a pair of elegant shoes and handbag from the skin. I presented these to my sister. When she opened the box I had neatly wrapped in Christmas paper; all of her prize pedigree dogs took off at high speed and refused point blank to come anywhere near her. Inbred instincts of the fear of the 'sausage dog swallowing reptile' had sent her pets into orbit. The shoes and handbag were returned to me with a firm "get rid of them, burn them, do anything, but now!" Not to be outdone, I put them up for sale at the town auction and, with the proceeds, bought myself a pair of binoculars that have survived to this day.

It was about two months after my encounter with the buffalo in the Napier grass and stocks of farm labour meat supplies were running low. At certain times of the month father would carry out a game count of the gazelles and decide what number should be culled on the farm. It was my responsibility to carry out the culling—two gazelles per day, selected from younger males out of the non-breeding bachelor coalition. They would be despatched then skinned and placed in the cold room. The cropping would continue for five days. Occasionally older females well past their prime and sell-by date would complete the numbers required.

I used a rifle with a fitted silencer accurate and effective up to about one hundred yards— the soft crack of the shot would not alarm other wild animals in the vicinity.

My Maasai water bearer always accompanied me on foot with his bow and arrow; we would stalk the gazelle to within fifty or sixty yards. The thick long grass gave sufficient cover to crawl forward unseen. My usual dress was khaki shorts and shirt, boots with leggings and a battered old khaki bush hat. Father was a good shot and insisted that my aim be on the mark; he would not tolerate any slapdash marksmanship and personally issued me with the exact amount of ammunition to do the job. On occasions he would inspect the carcass and take me to task over a misplaced shot; similarly if the ammunition count did not tally with the quota after the five days were up—please explain! I therefore made sure that my aim and hunting skills were perfected and unless I could despatch the animal without any pain and suffering I would not shoot. My concentration, whilst stalking and crawling forward through the long grass towards the gazelles, was so focused that I overlooked to scan the all important area of ground a few feet ahead and to the side of me. Seconds later I saw the mottled black and khaki outline of what I instinctively knew was a very large python curled ready to accept any prey that wandered into its coil, including me. My first reaction was to stand up and shout for my Maasai bearer, who was some twenty yards away, lying low in the grass behind me. In that split second of time I knew I was in serious trouble. I felt the python grip me like a vice, around my knees and ankles and I was about to topple as in a rugby tackle. Seconds later Ole Kaparo was running towards me, he had drawn his simi—a razor sharp two-sided blade almost fifteen inches long. He saw my predicament and his bush craft instincts knew where to attack. Goliath's Achilles tendon is its tail end when hooked into a clump of grass, the python's anchor and vice-like crush starts from there. He hacked viciously at this point like a chaff cutter; the snake released its grip and raised its head snapping at the air around it. A very shaky shot from me found its mark and the terrifying moment was over. I still have nightmares to this day about the incident.

Kaparo was sent to the farmstead a mile away to arrange a wheelbarrow and more hands to help lift and transport the monster. When laid out on the ground the serpent measured 17 feet 6 inches from head to tail with a girth the size of my calf. The rest of the story you already know about—my sister was still twittering about the shoes and handbag because her 'dawgs' were never the same afterwards and had quit breeding! Unbeknown to her some mischief-maker had put bromide in their dinner bowls. Now I wonder who would have done such a thing!

Soon I found myself in the midst of guerrilla 'hit and run' tactics and the rooting out of many fanatical gangsters from the dense forests. I came to realise that war does not determine who is right or wrong. War only determines who is left. This war was about shedding the yoke of colonialism in Kenya. Many died on both sides in the name of freedom and those that are now left after almost 40 years of self-government in Kenya have yet to reap the fruits of their endeavours.

Kenya, once considered a role model for republics in the making, had found that their party politics, greed, corruption and insecurity had eroded all that they had fought for. The past rule of law determined by the Colonial Government did not seem so bad after all in a country whose people were once law abiding.

The air crash that changed my inner self and my life

A miracle—both pilot and myself, although badly injured, survived this horrendous crash. We had been sent to locate a police sergeant who went berserk after shooting dead all of his police station colleagues. He was armed with a sub-machine gun and had taken to the bush. In our low approach the pilot misjudged his height and collided with a sixty-foot radio pylon and we crashed into the ground at over two hundred miles an hour. (The mentally disturbed policeman took his own life.)

These front-line years of "do or die" in this war and the loss of my close police special force colleagues had a profound effect on my outlook on life. A horrendous plane crash on active duty resulted in several years of hospitalisation in England. Without modern day counseling I suffered unsociable withdrawal symptoms. I had forgotten how to laugh—that carefree, happy-go-lucky feeling had left me.

Facial plastic surgery and pain had moulded a new person and a new face. I shuddered when I saw, after months of darkness, the faces of the World War II Battle of Britain pilots still undergoing plastic surgery reconstruction at the famous Queen Victoria Hospital, East Grinsteads.

They too had won their fight, but the price they paid was so very high. Every one of them fought like tigers for their country—their courage must never be forgotten.

My boyhood years matured quickly. The hardening effects of prolonged pain had set in. At twenty-four years of age, I was the youngest Chief Inspector in the Special Branch of the Kenya Police Force and my return to duty was to be minutely scrutinized by my superiors.

They questioned whether I had lost that quality of purpose so essential to view my continued career as a challenge, to overcome the fear of flying and whether I had regained my gamesmanship and marksmanship? Did I still possess that clear and calculated approach necessary in times of emergencies? Those were the capabilities I had been blessed with in the past, which always stood me in good stead at my promotion interviews. I knew to succeed again I must meet them head on.

There was little time to reflect. I had to take control of the beast that almost cost me my life. I learned to fly, recurring double vision was laser corrected and my eyesight was restored. I was able to compete with world-class marksmen. I played tennis, hockey and rugby—the pleasures of my youth had returned.

I remembered the wise words of my old hunter-gatherer and mentor "Measure each step with caution, my son, along your chosen path and listen to the sixth sense that nature has given you. You will be rewarded with a long, successful and interesting life." I had regained control of my inner self as before.

My career in the security field progressed and soon, at 30 years old, I was promoted to the senior ranks. This was my reward. Early retirement from this disciplined service was offered, as Kenya's independence grew closer.

My security background was ideally suited to the transfer that took me into the vast and specialised role of airline security—the future looked ominous. The beginnings of political hijackings, the suicide bombers and their religious beliefs were taking hold in an attempt to destroy and plunge the rest of the world into the abyss of chaos.

Our world will never be the same, but we shall learn to live with it in order to root out this evil and punish it in the manner it deserves.

For me a decade passed in which the foundations of International Airline Security were set. Other airlines throughout the world prepared themselves, albeit a little slowly.

There was little doubt that stringent methods of protection both in the air and on the ground would develop at an unprecedented rate.

The traveling public reacted accordingly and air travel suffered its worst fears. Some airlines went out of business overnight and security in the air and on the ground became paramount—I had chosen the right field.

Ten years later one of the world's respected and successful African airlines, East African Airways, fell foul to the axe of Independence. The flagship of the East African Community of Kenya, Tanzania and Uganda, which the airline represented, was dissolved.

My post as a Kenyan-born citizen was Africanised!

The commercial field of charter flying tourists to the Kenyan and Tanzanian Game Parks was booming. I held a full twin-engine commercial pilot's rating for this profession and for the next seven years my introduction to every game park in Kenya was exciting. As seen from the air and the ground another interest had developed—another door had opened. I loved my flying job, particularly in connection with wildlife and tourism.

The path I had chosen had its moments of fear and great pleasure. Yet the beast that once almost cost me my life was to revisit me.

Unexpectedly at 10,000 feet, the single engine of my aircraft stopped with a loud bang over the treacherous Taita Hills Range. My French passengers easily interpreted the 'Mayday' distress call that I made to the world around me – they were terrified. There was one difference in my favour; I had control of the beast this time.

I knew my height and the 'wind beneath my wings' would allow me to glide in search of a landing place.

My instructor, an ex-Battle of Britain Spitfire pilot, had taught me well. He had explained the principles of a 'flying brick' — with calculated care the aircraft really could be made to glide a long way; after all this was Africa and there were miles and miles of nothing but bush!

My passengers and I walked away from that aircraft unscathed. Standing aside, I knew that I had tamed the beast.

The time had come to move on, the path ahead for me was clear. My apprenticeship in the ways of tourism had fueled my desire to go it alone and set up a photographic safari company and fly my own clientele. I had made many contacts. All that was required was to establish a luxury tented camp and introduce my clientele to the real Africa, not the canned tourism of tourist minibuses, and to seek a place out in the wilds of the Maasai Mara, off the beaten tracks, commune with nature and put into practice all the wise teachings of my hunter-gatherer friend.

It is true that when one door closes at the end of a chapter in one's life, another surely opens. It was also true to say that this new and exciting career was to be the most rewarding in my life. "Listen to the sixth sense nature has given you, my son, you will be rewarded".

The voice of that old man of the bush was talking to me!

Safely down on *terra firma*
We walked away from this aircraft unscathed.

CHAPTER 2

KENYA SAFARIS

THE next months and years progressed in successfully establishing a name in the competitive field of personalised photographic wildlife safaris under canvas. This true story of a mother cheetah and her cubs unfolds in the heart of the great Maasai Mara Game Reserve in Kenya.

No one could have known the tragedy that was to lie in wait for this little family. Nature's unforgiving principles had decreed they would not survive to roam the vast plains of the Mara. Nobody could have visualised that fate would step in and provide the key to fulfill their wild adventure.

Their birthplace was in a well-concealed outcrop of rock overlooking the 'Paradise Valley'. As the days and nights passed, so mother and cubs thrived. Their lair was impenetrable and each time mum went off to hunt far and wide the little ones were shuttled into their hideaway, safe and secure, until mother came home.

One may ask where was dad all this time. Well, like all good cheetah males he and his brother were away pollinating other flowers in their vast territorial area, which seemed to stretch from the Northern Serengeti through and into every corner of North Mara.

Few cheetah mothers can boast a one hundred percent no-casualty upbringing of their offspring, but the unexpected happened.

A mother and her five four-month old cheetah cubs left their home to seek out and explore the greener pastures of their 'estate'. The cubs became more adventurous, bolder and stronger as the months went by. The tourist observation pressure did not really seem to bother them. It all looked just too good. The harsh reality of survival in the animal kingdom brings home the inescapable fact that 'Leo does eat Bambi' and when it happens in the cold light of day, before ones very eyes, even the hardiest find they can still shed a tear for the unfortunate victim.

At first light in the rising mist of the dawn, after a night when the heavens opened all the taps, mother and cubs stumbled into a crouched and waiting lioness. The lioness had a litter of four cubs just a week old and was in the process of translocating the last one to drier ground. Mother cheetah, in her frenzy to save her cubs from certain death, leapt in front of the lioness to draw its attention away from her fleeing babes; for that momentary second her life or death plan had worked, but in her attempt to leap away from the big cat she slipped in the treacherous black cotton soil. It was too late by a hair's breadth. Claws from the outstretched paw of the lioness sank deep into her flank and it was all over.

I watched horror-struck—I could do nothing! The stream ahead of the steep rock strewn bank and me was impassable. I found myself choked up with emotion and unable to speak.

There was no sign of movement from the slain cheetah mother and no doubt in my mind that she was dead. The lioness had bitten deep into her back and neck. I watched distressed and frustrated at this helpless situation.

I vowed that the cubs would not be left to die. They were still too young to even consider the thought of hunting for themselves and dependent on their mother for food. I pondered this situation for a moment. The lioness had moved off without retrieving her cub. Somewhere in the grass was another potential orphan.

I realised I was not alone in my grief when I heard a gentle sobbing from behind me; my numbed mind remembered I was on safari with clients, showing them the wonders of nature! Suddenly we had all been catapulted speechless into a scene as dramatic as one could ever observe.

Word was despatched urgently to the Senior Game Warden at Keekorok Headquarters to search his soul—nature had played its part. Was it right that man should intervene? After all, the law of the wild dictates Nature should be left to take its course—which is man's teaching. Much of our off track thinking is at the root and ruination of our ecosystems and wildlife. There were those who wanted to step in, dart and capture the cheetah cubs and confine them to a life of imprisonment. Who are they to decide on such a sentence? I waited, the hours dragged by—would there be an answer?

Deep down I prayed that the Warden would not let the cubs die. At dusk the order came through to his Rangers, "free range, feed them". That was the best tonic for my tortured mind—I knew it would work. The cynics and the so-called professionals said it was total madness.

I wrote the following text to the Chief Game Warden and the Director of Wildlife and Conservation at the time, Doctor Perez Olindo. "I wish to compliment you on your practical decision and application in taking care of the five nine month old cheetah cubs that were orphaned. I personally believe in your idea of open range feeding, spacing the days to implant the idea that they must think about hunting for themselves.

My observations and encouragement are purely in support of your programme and I believe your efforts will be rewarded by a satisfactory conclusion, barring determined predator intervention. I shall continue to take a personal interest in the project and will keep you informed of their progress."

And so the cubs lived happily ever afterwards? Not so! What happened to number five? One day he just vanished. I had a gut feeling that something was at odds. My trusted sixth sense was telling me number five was not a casualty of nature.

The remaining four cheetah cubs, three males and a female, became inured to the pressures of tourist game viewing, they even explored the exterior and sometimes mischievously the interior of occupied tourist vehicles, much to the dismay and fear of the occupants. Such was their evacuation that I found my stifled mirth was stimulating. I needed

I noticed Prickles was getting thin and listless, each day he became weaker and weaker.

a booster; my batteries were in need of charging!

Then suddenly two months after the fateful day, cheetah number five rejoined the party! I was mystified; no cheetah cub could survive two months alone in the bush at nine months of age! I checked my video film of the original five cubs, was it really number five? Yes, the tail markings, the face and the chest markings were similar, but very clearly he was slightly bigger than the rest and was developing an early muscular frame—the makings of a fine animal. I sensed it would not be long before he became the lead male in this young coalition.

My safari visits to the Mara occurred weekly; I was blessed with more observation time than most. I gave the now adults each a name—something that my mind could identify them by. 'Petal' fitted the female; 'Prickles' a male whose coat seemed prickly and often stood on end; the larger of the males was named appropriately 'Hackles'; 'Hopeless' was another male who never seemed to get anything right—poor fellow, he was always instrumental in blowing the hunt which Petal had tried to set up for them. The final male was named 'Whispers' for he mouthed his calls with no sound; at least nothing my hearing could pick up—yet the others could hear his call.

A trip to my audiogram specialist confirmed my hearing was still above standard. It was found that Whispers, and this was later established, was calling outside and above my human audio range.

So, the tourists had their money's worth and the cheetahs behaved amiably and amicably.

Their range began to lengthen, and then expand to forty kilometres by about ten kilometres. Their hunting skills improved. Petal continued as their leader and 'think machine'.

At seventeen months the boys found their puberty exciting, much to the annoyance of Petal. She must surely soon be due for her first oestrus and might well leave the family any day. To lose their one and only 'cook' could be a disaster for the boys! However, to reflect for a short while on a miracle that really did happen.

I noticed Prickles was getting thin and listless. Each day he became weaker and weaker, there was something drastically wrong. I watched—I followed. We were in an area east of the Olaro Orok Ridge, away from the normal range of intense daily tourist activity. Their diet was mainly African hare. Prickles was not participating or eating. He was dying slowly and painfully.

It was time to blow the panic whistle once more. A message was sent to the Director of Wildlife for veterinary assistance. The Kenya Wildlife Service Headquarters then contacted Doctor Dieter Roettcher. I flew to Nairobi to collect him, I was relieved that some possible help was on its way and we flew back to the Mara together.

I had not met or had the pleasure of his acquaintance before but I felt confident in the knowledge that if anything could be done, Dieter might just save the day. I had heard that his hands and his heart were for the wildlife of this country. He was acknowledged as one of the top wildlife veterinarians in Kenya. Much, indeed most, if not all of his wildlife work for the Wildlife Service of Kenya was voluntary and unpaid.

Dieter's diagnosis was immediate. In layman's language it was "a mechanical blockage in the intestines, probably due to hair balls; a common and often fatal complaint in dogs and cats". Prickles was in desperate straits and there was nothing else to do but to operate there and then. The Game Rangers nodded their approval. The chances of Prickles' survival were less than 50/50; infection, peritonitis and half a dozen other 'secondaries' could still take his life away. Dieter set to work.

The Rangers and I watched fascinated—his expertise was obvious. I marvelled at the dexterity of his hands. There was no 'get me this or hand me that', he had placed everything to hand—the operating table was God's earth. If Prickles were to survive his post-operative care, my attention to him in the wild could run into days. I remembered my vow; it was now or never. I had to help him and I was fully prepared to do so.

Dieter was in deep concentration. I noticed he had hardly said a word. I checked my watch; it was one-and-a-half hours since the anaesthetic and the first incision had been made. Storm clouds were gathering in the East, it would not be long before the heavens opened. We prepared a makeshift shelter and shortly after, the first drops heralded the approaching storm. Dieter was now stitching up and tying the final knots. Ten rock hard hairballs, the size of golf balls, lay beside Prickles as evidence of his pain and suffering.

The Rangers were motivated and fired with enthusiasm, they too were keen and so we planned the next three days and nights on a roster system.

Dieter stood up, staggered and wiped the perspiration from his forehead—the strain of the last hours had sapped his energy. It really had been a race against the clock. The golden

There was nothing else to do but operate there and then. The operating table was God's earth.
Prickles' life was hanging by a thread!

shades from the evening sunset had faded and the storm was upon us — Dieter had to catch a
6 p.m. flight back to Nairobi. It was to be a long night of vigil for us; Corporal Daniel and I
would probably take turns. Prickles had slowly recovered from his anaesthetic, and in
preparation I had already placed some sacks around his body with a light rainproof canvas
over him to keep in the warmth. He dozed fitfully and occasionally called softly into the
night. I sensed his companions were not too far away and were probably camped down close
by.

A pride of lions and a hyaena pack passed by on their nightly prowl. Prickles sensed their
proximity but was comforted and relaxed by my presence. Our patient occasionally lapped
water offered to him from a 'karai'. Prickles was fighting for his life. I felt a bond had
developed between us – this wild animal had accepted me as his helper and for this I was very
grateful.

The dawn seemed a long way off. It was 4 a.m. and bitterly cold. Prickles, I sensed, was

Prickles was not partaking in any chases — he preferred to stroll up and join the melee at his own pace. The four fit cheetahs realised that their brother Prickles had been very sick. They stayed close to him and never strayed too far from his sight.

listening intently—he could hear something that I could not. I strained my ears; there was nothing that I could distinguish out of the ordinary, but I knew instinctively that we were not alone. Corporal Daniel was cat-napping in the Landcruiser parked some ten feet away.

Prickles, with head up, was peering groggily into the dark a few feet from me. I shone my torch for a second and there, almost within touching distance, was Whispers. Prickles attempted to stand—I helped to steady him. There is no doubt in my mind that Whispers had been sent to collect his pal. I was overjoyed.

The first fingers of the African dawn were clawing up into the sky and its rays provided just sufficient light for me to make out forms in the fading darkness. I tapped a signal quietly on the vehicle body and both the Ranger and I peered astonished at the two outlines disappearing into the dawn light. To me it was a miracle—Prickles was making a determined effort to survive.

We followed at a distance, using night vision binoculars and there, some fifty yards away from where Prickles had his operation, were the four cheetahs waiting. Prickles was checked over and over by them—he seemed genuinely pleased to be back with his siblings.

The dawn came and went and the family group sought refuge from the burning sun in a clump of bushes. Prickles spent most of the day sleeping off his anaesthetic effects and drank copious amounts of water from his 'karai', while allowing his siblings to share his bowl. The heat of the day passed uneventfully—apart from a bus-load of noisy tourists who were ignorant of recent happenings.

The group of cheetahs appeared content to settle down for the night. Meantime, a caring Manager from Buffalo Camp saw and realised our plight and brought us hot coffee, biscuits and buns—a very welcome gesture to two starving conservationists.

Everything seemed set for a quiet vigil and a night's catnapping for me. It was Corporal Daniel's turn to keep wide-awake. At midnight a pack of ten hyaenas came to investigate our Landcruiser and I found my trusty fire extinguisher very handy, it worked a treat, the hyaenas took off in one direction and…. the cheetahs in another!

Prickles had steadied up remarkably and seemed capable of walking purposefully. The next hour, walking with the aid of night vision binoculars, we were able to locate and follow the group at a distance of some fifty yards without too much trouble. We covered about three kilometres in distance through a wooded copse and here they stayed for the next four days, never straying too far from Prickles. His recovery was extraordinary!

The Game Rangers took turns to range feed the group every second day and I was relieved when Prickles took his first small meal after three days. His strength slowly returned and their wanderings became more purposeful—the group began to hunt again. Prickles, gently flexing his muscles but not partaking in any chases, preferred to stroll up and join them at his own pace. Fifteen days passed and the wound appeared almost closed. the twenty or so stitches were beginning to fray—I had visions of the incision coming apart and depositing the whole of Prickles' 'plumbing' on the ground!

Dieter answered our call and flew into the Mara. He removed the stitches, applied a hefty

Prickles
Fifteen days later the wound appeared almost healed.

dose of antibiotics via a syringe douche into the drain hole and pronounced Prickles over the worst. The Rangers and I were overjoyed. Tour drivers and their clients appeared from nowhere to join in our happy state. I realised then just how many people, who valued wildlife, had been holding their fingers crossed for Prickles—it was a memorable moment shared with much handshaking and backslapping. Prickles and Whispers formed an inseparable friendship with each other and my reward was the recognition by the group of their total trust and acceptance, without fear of either Corporal Daniel or myself.

I sensed the day was coming close when the group would finally split up. Petal, the female and 'chief cook' would soon depart and attend to her natural instincts of preserving her species. Here would lie a possible clue to number five, Hackles. Was he ever part of the original 'family'? If he were, Petal would not choose him, or other male member of the family, as her first mate. The next few weeks, as the group approached their eighteen months'

I recall the many safaris when the family of five cheetahs and I hunted together.

birthday, would tell another story. One thing I know for certain is that Prickles and Whispers will roam the Mara together as brothers to propagate their species.

I realised I had successfully completed the unusual task of teaching these young cheetahs how to hunt on a 'no touch' basis. I had walked and stalked with them and stayed out for days and nights in an area well away from the pressures of Maasai cattle and tourists. They soon picked up the art and by fourteen months old, were proficient enough to be sent solo. The story continues to unfold—the little group lives on and each day they carve another niche into the cheetah history of North Mara.

From Petal I began to sense and recognise signs of irritation and frustration in the boys' presence though I was totally accepted as their foster-father. Petal seemed reluctant to continue as their 'think machine'—was she trying to tell me something? I concentrated and pondered on her moods. What could this be? Might it be the first signs of the parting of their ways that I had inwardly hoped would never happen? I chose to stay the night.

The Aitong hills in North Mara, on Christmas Day, and succeeding days, for as long as I can remember, are blessed with the heaviest downpours of rain for the year. The following day I awakened to a fresh crisp dawn. I looked up to scattered high cirrus clouds that reflected a golden wash over the rolling plains of Mara. I had spent the night in the back of my truck, rolled up in a blanket.

The cheetah family was still close by, snuggled up to each other to ward off the dawn chill; it would only be moments before they would rise and stretch in the warmth of this magnificent sunrise. I poured a cup of tea from a thermos and ate a biscuit to dampen the approaching pangs of my usual pre-breakfast hunger. Wake-up time for the cheetahs was due. I walked over to where the spotted bundles lay and was quick to notice that Petal was not there. My heart sank. In my panic, I began to mimic the practised and perfected cheetah birdlike whistle calls that Petal knew and would never fail to react to warmly. Nothing stirred, not even the birds; in this unusual early morning silence I knew that the dreaded parting of the ways had arrived.

Petal had chosen and timed it well. It was New Year's Day; the sun was shining and the high cirrus clouds had disappeared to reveal a deep, fresh, clean blue African sky. Summer had come and Petal had vanished in the night.

My loyalties were in a jumble—was it my duty to follow suit and quietly leave the boys to their own destiny? The answer to Petal's restlessness was now clear. I turned away and walked back quietly to the truck. My mind was numb but my subconscious was in control. I, too, must leave the boys—would that be Petal's wish? It was time for them to grow up and fend for themselves. I drove a distance of some one hundred yards to higher ground where I stopped. I desperately needed to think for a moment—was this the end of our wonderful and incredible relationship? A lump in my throat signalled the onset of tears that rolled freely down my cheeks. I raised my binoculars; inwardly wanting to share their moment of realisation of Petal's parting—but only from a distance. It was no good; I could only distinguish a blur. Was it Nature's way of saying to me "let it be, let it be"?

I drove around aimlessly for hours knowing not where to look for Petal. At midday I

Prickles, Hopeless, Whispers and Hackles
I was quick to notice Petal was not there. Petal had vanished in the night.

must return to camp and prepare to fly back to Nairobi. I had promised to return home for New Year's Day to participate in those traditional festivities with my close friends. My thoughts were far from eating left over Christmas turkey and plum pudding. I must also plan to return to Mara as soon as possible, and seek out Petal once again. I left word with tour drivers in the area to send me information, via the 'bush telegraph', should Petal or the boys be seen anywhere.

At home the office work dragged on and Christmas pudding continued to remind me of its presence. The bush telegraph remained silent—no news was bad news. The call of the wild was beckoning me—was it Petal sending out her signals for help? Days later I was back in Mara, but no one had any concrete news of Petal. There were some confused reports of sightings from tour drivers in transit, but on further questioning I dismissed these reports as inaccurate. I searched far and wide but each day produced a blank, and for me, more depression.

Maasai herdsmen were approached for information. I showed them colour prints of the family. In every case this produced total disbelief that a human being would be permitted to socialise with 'Ol-waru-lo-lasho', the 'one that eats calves'. They wondered what medicine I was using. "Was it possible to do the same with lions?" they asked. Although their questions were genuine, I knew their underlying motives to be more sinister.

Much still needs to be done to educate some Maasai—indeed the world—that wildlife is a precious heritage which, once destroyed, will never return.

The David Sheldrick Wildlife Trust once quoted this passage from Wallace Stignor, Professor at Stanford University. I passionately believe in it and each day I preach its wholesome truth.

"Something will have gone out of us as humans if we ever let the remaining wilderness be destroyed, if we permit the last virgin forests to be turned into comic books and cigarette cases; if we drive the few remaining members of the wild species into zoos or to extinction; if we pollute the last clear air and dirty the last clean streams and push our paved roads through the last of the wilderness, so that never again will people be free in their own country from the noise, the exhausts, the stench of human and automotive waste, so that never again can we have the chance to see ourselves as single, separate, vertical and individual in this world and as part of the environment of trees and rocks and soil, brother to the other animals, part of the natural world, and competent to belong in it. We simply need that wild country available to us, even if we never do more than drive to its edge and look in, for it can be a means of reassuring ourselves of our sanity as creatures and part of the geography of hope".

My hope is that the 'Friends of Conservation', an organisation with offices in England, the United States of America and Kenya, will continue to financially support the efforts in making the Maasai Mara a better and safer place for our wild animals to live in, and at the same time educate those people who now hold the vast Mara savannah in trust for the children of tomorrow.

My search for Petal and the boys was in vain. Every inch of ground within some three hundred square miles was covered—with no trace and not a word, I began to have doubts. Could it be that the boys or Petal might have fallen to the lethal arrows of poachers or their snares?

I concentrated on seeking out information from the local Maasai on the movement and hideouts of meat poachers. 'Friends of Conservation' assisted me with funds for rewards to informers and soon the picture became clear that some poachers were still around despite earlier arrests. Information was passed to the Game Warden and Police. More snares were located and uprooted.

Petal had become the centrepiece of attention. Tourists were flocking into the Mara to see the Queen. These were dangerous and difficult times for her.

Donations from tourists and well-wishers came pouring in, paid in cash, in the field, and these funds were channelled into the F.O.C. in Nairobi to obtain, when necessary, the services of a Veterinary Surgeon and to have him flown into the Mara if there was a dire emergency.

The camp staff were looking forward to their Christmas break. It was important and necessary they too were given time off to be with their families in their Reserves. The camp would be taken down and stored in steel containers.

My reward was soon to come and can only be described as an incredible happening. Petal, by some quirk of her intuition, came to my camp on the very morning I was to leave

Petal drank water from her 'karai' and seemed content to rest and sleep deeply in my presence.

Her outstretched paw was her signal for me to touch.

She had made this pilgrimage—how could I leave her now?

for Nairobi and Australia. I wept tears of joy—my camp staff shared this very touching moment with me. They had endured my wrath and frustration since my parting with the cheetahs.

Petal had come a long way; she was healthy, but tired and footsore. I could only repeat to her, in a gentle kind whisper, "Where have you been? You have come home!" Not that she would have understood my mutterings, but her eyes suddenly lit up at the sound of our 'cheetah whistle'—I could have hugged her but my 'no stroke' policy came to the fore. Her outstretched paw was her signal for me to touch and, with a thankful prayer from me to her maker, we were once again happily reunited.

The crew had struck camp and were patiently waiting for the convoy to proceed. How could I leave Petal now? She had made this pilgrimage—drawn by some instinct of survival that we humans lost centuries ago in our quest to wipe ourselves from the face of this planet.

I gave the 'thumbs up' signal for the camp lorry containing all the camp equipment, and an escort Landcruiser, to proceed—I would catch up later. The journey to Nairobi promised to be an eight-hour nightmare of potholes, diversions and broken springs!

Petal wakened to the noise of the departing vehicles, stretched and wandered into the

For three hours we sat together – she was tired, heealthy but footsore.

now empty campsite. I followed to watch—she knew where my tent had been sited. No doubt her sense of smell led her to this as my occasional early morning bladder required defuelling urgently close by—when all other bushes seemed to move or were just too far away for safety! Petal, I knew, sensed my departure was imminent and was content to let me go.

Four hours later I rejoined the convoy at the town of Narok. The journey back to Nairobi was uneventful. The convoy had done well to come through unscathed and I was pleased. The one hundred kilometres passed quickly for me. I couldn't remember clearly the bone-jarring sector to Narok—my mind had been working overtime on other things. It gave me time to think back to those last moments prior to leaving camp.

Had Petal brought me a memorable Christmas present? Might she be in early pregnancy? That possibility could not be discounted – but where had she been?

Australia beckoned. The time had come to make a flying visit to see my retired father living out the eve of his days in another country that still offers boundless opportunities for the young and adventurous.

CHAPTER 3

MAN-EATING LIONS

I N those early days in Kenya my father earned his pennies working on the engineering train that paved the way for the 'iron snake' from Mombasa to the shores of Lake Victoria. Mother, too, played her humble part as cook and bottle washer in the railroad 'caboose'. A firewood stove was all that she had to cook on and the daily comforts were nothing to write home about. Life was not easy for them in those pioneering days of man-eaters and malaria. Mother was the family 'rock', her loving care towards her children and her determination and strength to prevail over all the difficult times, was beyond the call of any wife.

Their meagre savings were invested in land and Strathearn Dairy was born. In the years that followed milk was push-carted to Nairobi and delivery was made to the customers' door. My parents' hard work was rewarded. As Nairobi expanded it swallowed up Strathearn Dairy, pushing the farming lands further to the East. Later their new venture, Drumvale Cattle Ranch, became a role model for post-independent Kenya.

As it had for Petal, tragedy struck when I was beginning to appreciate my mother's exceptional affinity towards her youngest offspring. She could read my mind better than I and vividly foretold my path through life, as would a clairvoyant. Her passing and later that of my young daughter Heather from cancer left a deep sadness in me that refuses to go away.

Yet here was Petal helping me to bridge the gap in a way that only animals can do for humans. Was it the wish of those two departed souls making that sadness more bearable for me?

With the loss of my mother, father sold Drumvale Estate and tried to settle back into his native Scotland—sadly he found that many friends of his generation had passed on. His boundless energy, drive, and determination to live to a hundred, was overwhelming and exhausting for those nearest and dearest to him. At the age of sixty-seven he remarried and emigrated to Australia. Finally his long and interesting life came to a peaceful end in that faraway land of sunshine—it was indeed the end of an era—just two years short of his target!

My visit to Australia was therapeutic. I was introduced to many different species of wildlife. It seemed to me that Noah's Ark had off-loaded part of her strange cargo onto a continent whose evolution clock had missed a millennium beat or two in time. It was then that I realised the country of my birth, Kenya, and wild Africa contained everything I could wish for.

The incredible incident I describe in this chapter occurred just before my Christmas break spent in Nairobi.

I returned to my beloved Mara to seek out Petal and was heartened to hear that during my Christmas absence she had been seen near our vacated camp. I searched every nook and cranny for signs or sightings of her—the days and nights dragged on. Why was the whole world hiding Petal from me?

My search widened and to my joy I found, resting on a hillock over-looking their old training ground, none other than Hackles, Hopeless, Whispers and Prickles! They had developed into powerful, sleek, muscular beasts, though Prickles appeared thin. Might they have forgotten their foster-father? I remembered Petal's 'karai' and plastic water-can were in the front cradle of my Landcruiser that normally housed the spare petrol can. If I were to drive within twenty metres of them and pour water into the now battered tin bowl, might this just trigger their memory of our times together?

I believe in being a 'constant factor'—always appearing in khaki colour dress, khaki bush hat and brown bush boots, for specific body recognition. Petal relaxed in my presence when I wore this 'garb' but dressed in anything else she would examine me with caution and suspicion. This presentation was my trump card; would it work with the boys?

I stepped out of the vehicle and made our cheetah whistle call. It was Hackles who reacted first. He quickly sat up, head low, then arched his back and growled with hackles raised. My heart rate quickened – was he about to attack me?

Hackles' standard procedure with me for as long as I could remember required that he should always be treated with respect and caution. He became aggressive on eye contact with me—I was careful to avoid this with practised submissive body language—looking away and appearing disinterested. This ploy had worked on previous occasions—it seemed to calm the situation and reinstate him at the head of the 'pecking order'- but it was Prickles who broke the ice. Without hesitation Prickles walked directly towards me. I promptly missed the 'karai' and poured the water down the front of my trouser leg! This was much to the amusement of my trusted friend the Maasai Ranger, Corporal Daniel was my low profile bodyguard and seldom left the vehicle.

Prickles was confident in his approach and the others followed him to investigate. The sight of pouring water from the plastic can was like manna from heaven to the four thirsty cats. I held my stance in an outwardly relaxed style with the bowl on the ground at my feet. The boys lapped slowly, occasionally looking up at me with a quick glance and checking warily behind and around themselves, returning to the bowl once again to quench their thirst. Prickles took the opportunity to sniff my trouser leg and boots, then the front wheel and bumper of my vehicle and finally, satisfied that all was his, promptly sprayed, (marked), my front fender with urine. This was his signal of acceptance. I was pleased his operation scar had healed well and was covered with new hair. Whispers, Hopeless and Hackles, each in turn carefully inspected the vehicle tyres but surprisingly they did not 'over mark' the front fender or me!

My presence did not upset them, and the group finally wandered off to lie in the shade

Teaching the boys the first principles of hunting as a group.

of a nearby acacia tree, leaving me weak-kneed, to ponder more about the male cheetahs' routine of spray marking. I pictured the six weeks with Petal on the East Olarok plains— teaching the boys the first principles of hunting for themselves and how to seek out African hares in the clumps of sour grass and acacia that proliferated the area. When a chase occurred I was left far behind, bewildered and lost as to which direction they might finally have ended their run. My cheetah calls made no distance in competing with the wayward wind that gently blew amongst the whistling thorns. I sat, sometimes up to an hour, waiting patiently for their return but it was always Petal and Prickles who came to seek me out.

During these anxious hours of watching and waiting I noticed Petal's inbound track always routed via my defuelling spots. This prompted the comment from Corporal Daniel that I definitely needed a brake on my bladder! My continuous water intake and anti-dehydration soluble mineral sachets, kept my system well activated and in tune with the temperatures that soared at midday and early afternoon. My active 'defuelling system' was playing an important part in assisting Petal in tracing my movements and whereabouts.

In this way I 'mark' Petal's post boxes—these are her favourite trees which she routinely visits on her wanderings. Often, I have found her waiting patiently for me under their shade, after having left my calling card days previously.

Petal's post-boxes
These are her favourite trees that she visits on her wanderings.

I have often found her waiting patiently for me having left my
'calling card' days previously.

Prickles' last safari
Hopeless, Hackles, Prickles and Whispers had spent the night near camp

This photograph was taken soon after they set off early the following morning. By dusk they had a covered a distance of some fifteen miles, heading South towards the Serengeti. They returned two months later escorting a very sick Prickles back home to die. The old problem of the blockage in his intestinal tract had returned. My pleas to give him another chance were vetoed by the Director of Wildlife. Prickles was defective and would otherwise have been weeded out by Nature when this condition first occurred. Much as I tried to offer Prickles an alternative 'Granny's cure' by placing a mixture of petroleum jelly and glycerine on his fur, which he liked and regularly licked off—the blockage remained solidly stuck in his small intestine. Prickles moved away from his brothers; he became weak and listless again. He probably fell to the jaws of the clean-up squad. For me, it was a bitter pill to swallow but I realised I must concede to Nature's rules.

Cheetahs pick up a wealth of information on their species from these 'mail boxes'. Who has passed by and when, and by casting around at the foot of the other nearby trees, establish in which direction they might have gone.

The four cheetahs moved into their familiar childhood training ground—an area of some one hundred square kilometres. From their actions they appeared not to be looking for Petal, neither 'marking territory' nor posting calling cards.

The cheetahs' larder here has always been sparse, though good harvests of African hare abound and much of the two weeks they spent hunting in this area was specifically on this diet. I remembered that this was where Prickle's digestive system had first shown signs of imperfection that subsequently led to his intestinal blockage. The vet's warning rang loud and clear again; hairball blockages could recur in Prickles if his digestion was faulty. But where was Petal? There were still no reports of sightings from anyone. I was mystified and doubts began to eat away at my inner fears. Was she still alive? I cast out the frightening thought that she might not be.

News had just come through to me, via the Mara's information grapevine that Corporal Daniel was on the list for posting to another area in South Mara. This was disastrous news, a shuffle that appeared designed to frustrate any form of continuity in conservation! Someone at Narok Council H.Q. was shuffling all the cards again and I felt I was about to be dealt a Joker for a replacement.

A strong understanding of mutual trust had built up between Daniel and myself; our years of bush work together had honed our senses to perfection. His judgements were calculated and usually correct. Ranger Daniel would be a very difficult man to replace.

To make matters worse, there were reports from Maasai friends that meat poachers were operating again along the northern stretches of the Mara River. I felt an inner sense of panic as I lifted my hand in a farewell salute to this man who shared with me my hopes for the future of wildlife conservation in the Mara. We had spent many hours together protecting our cheetah family and the other wild animals of the North Mara from harm.

Corporal Daniel's parting words to me were: "At full moon our cheetahs (Ol-waru-lo-lasho) will walk many miles. They will come to visit you soon and bring news of Petal". I prayed inwardly that his intuition would be right.

As I watched the Land Rover and distant dust cloud disappear southwards towards Rhino Ridge, I felt a gentle hand on my shoulder. I turned to see the smiling face of a tall middle aged Maasai Ranger. He introduced himself as Corporal Daniel's replacement. I was relieved. This was no 'Joker'. The hand that shuffled the cards had dealt me an Ace in Sergeant James. He required no introduction to me or to our cheetah family. Daniel had briefed him well. Maybe turbulent times were in store for the poachers of North Mara?

During the next three days to full moon the weather was expected to remain clear. Thereafter, heavy rain could follow. Petal's ninety days gestation period since my Christmas break was almost complete. Maybe she had found her den by now in which to have her babies and would lie low for the next three weeks, close to water from where short quick forages for food could be made; then return hurriedly to her den to protect her cubs.

I realised all of this was pure conjecture on my part! I had no proof Petal was pregnant, but my telepathic mind was willing her to be. I so wanted her to have a family!

I was glad to remain in Mara with my clients to continue our search for Petal along the watercourses, looking closely at the spots where gazelles were plentiful; we investigated all the likely places she might have chosen to make her den.

The nights approaching full moon are cool and unusually silent. Most nocturnal

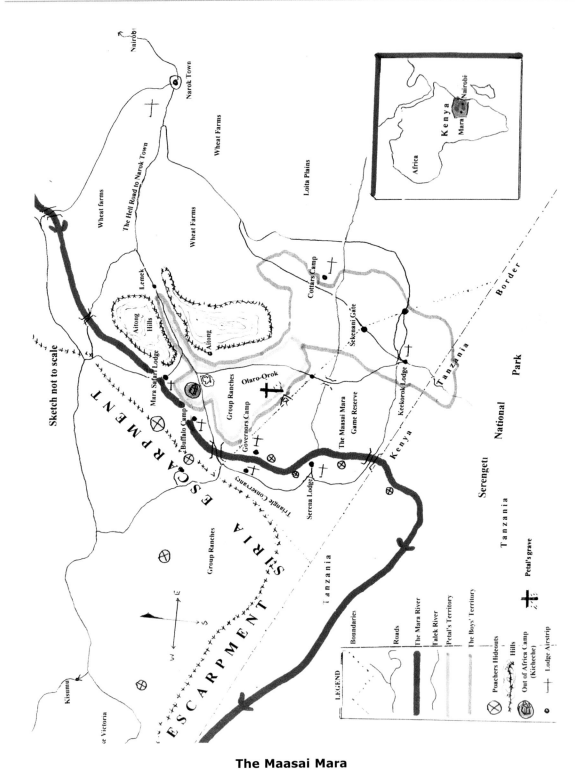

The Maasai Mara
showing the cheetahs' territories, the Out of Africa Camp and Petal's grave.

predators turn to their exceptional night-distance vision during this phase and seldom communicate their whereabouts as they often do when in total darkness.

It was a still clear moonlight night. The full moon cast a yellow wash over the landscape. Back at camp we had decided to take an early hot shower to freshen up after sitting out the day on a high vantage point, watching the body language of the Thompson's gazelles and the ever alert Topi, grazing peacefully below us in an area which, a week previously, had been set alight by Maasai cattle herders. The first heavy storm had over night turned the charred remains of a cool grass 'burn' into a carpet of green and succulent shoots.

Many plains game head for these areas and their attendant predators usually follow to take up their positions by lying low in the gullies during the day in preparation for the night's hunting.

CHAPTER 4
INTRODUCTION TO A WILD CHEETAH

THE months prior to my Christmas break and flying visit to Australia, my close relationship with Petal continued to develop her understanding that my presence with her was more than just providing security.

Petal began to show an unusual interest in our association with each other and in the birdlike whistle of the cheetah species. Petal was wild; there was no doubt about that as she shied from noisy tourist vehicles and distanced herself from Maasai herdsmen.

There appeared to be an added willingness on her part to continue with our contact, as evidenced by her call in reply to mine, and the ease with which she sprang onto my vehicle and allowed herself to be closely examined without physical contact.

We often walked for hours, with Petal leading the way as pathfinder. I trusted her complete sense of in-built awareness in deciphering the level of danger that may lie in wait along her chosen path. She too had been well tutored by the gene of instinct which had now matured within her makeup. She was obviously taking my personal security into consideration.

It was on one of these daylight outings that we came across an unfamiliar wild female cheetah. Under normal circumstances, if family recognition could not be established, each would slink away in opposite directions. In this case this did not happen. Petal's body language was not threatening—it took me several minutes to realise why the normal aggression of territorial dominance was lacking—the newcomer could be carrying Petal's family bloodline! What followed next was totally unexpected. To my mind this was the breakthrough and the key given to me by Petal to establish a rapport with unrelated wild cheetahs.

Petal seemed to have the air of authority. For the wild cheetah, my presence with Petal was clearly cause for fear; totally mystified the cheetah flattened her body into the short grass and took stock of this odd situation.

It was time for me to retreat slowly to a vantage-point where I could view and listen to any happenings. My binoculars would give me a clear picture of the situation unfolding before me. Petal's high pitched whine was loud and assertive as she moved slowly forward, her long slender tail held into the contour of the sleek underside of her body. This stance fascinated me; it was not that Petal was about to flee with her tail between her legs but her outward body language was one of dominance in control.

Petal moved forward cautiously, ears back, head and shoulders held high. The intruding cheetah was nervously holding her ground, without a movement, her eyes fixed on Petal with no sign of aggression. Was the submissive cheetah slowly blinking? Yes, it was all beginning to make sense, a new female cheetah had entered Petal's territory and was now requesting acceptance into that territory. Her markings were not 'family'. Petal was towering over her now; her whining had ceased. It dawned on me that this trespasser could be pregnant—Petal was sniffing her posterior. I instinctively knew that assumption was correct, and further it could be within the bounds of possibility that the newcomer may have been mated by one of Petal's brothers and that Nature's way had conveyed this information to Petal in the scenting. I had read and studied many cheetah research 'observations'—none had developed the key I now possessed. Here was a wild cheetah, free from any chains of confinement and human dependence, communicating her every sense by bridging the gap between animal and man.

Purist scientists may scoff at my humanist interpretations of this behaviour. They would be within their rights to do so, for their pattern of scientific progress towards discovery must stick to certain guidelines that shy away from any form of suggestion that wild animals cannot relate to a human's feelings. This to my mind is off track.

Man's best friends, the dogs and cats within our own homes, albeit domesticated, can show a remarkable understanding and concern for their mentors and masters. Indeed they have a body language and feelings that one day we humans may come to understand, bear a similarity to our own. Petal was walking towards me, occasionally looking back at the spotted shape still in the grass. Should I walk forward to greet her? I had guessed correctly that she would head towards the shade of another tree a short distance ahead of me closing the distance to some fifteen metres from her new friend.

I took the opportunity to walk forward with half an eye on our visitor, hoping that my presence would not send her slinking away to disappear into the undergrowth. Both Petal and I reached our chosen trees simultaneously.

Our visitor was fascinated. She moved cautiously to a short clump of sour grass left untouched by other grazing animals and peered through the cluster, watching our every move. I got the feeling she may have watched us previously from a concealed distance and observed Petal and I taking our regular walk together—this may have provided her with the instinct that this human presented no danger.

I realised I must not transmit any vibes that could be mistaken for aggression though I was tempted to stretch out my hand and touch Petal to show the other cheetah that a physical bond existed between Petal and her human friend. Was it our unusual relationship that had placed Petal onto a higher plane than others of her kind?

Cheetahs have been known since early times to have placed their trust in man. I remember clearly the two cheetahs retained by Emperor Haile Selassie. They had the run of his palace; both were females from the same litter brought in from the wild at a young age. They were there not for the sport of Kings, but displayed as status symbols. Their proud beauty and aloofness attracted much admiration from Princes, Princesses, and other visiting dignitaries.

Petal had dozed off fitfully, her tail lying across my outstretched legs. I was sitting uncomfortably with my back supported against the tree.

For the next half-hour the flies that play hide and seek in Petal's fur provided some distraction for me. I carried in my pocket a small tin of environmentally friendly pyrethrum powder dispensed by twisting the top to expose the minute holes; then shaking a fine shower of powder that would penetrate into those parts of her fur where these pestiferous blood sucking insects were gorging themselves. Their resultant scurrying and rapid departure flight gave her respite from their constant and irritating pinpricks. On reflection, could my relationship with Petal really have placed her onto a higher plane? I was beginning to think so; the next hour was to confirm that my thinking was not entirely off track.

The sun was almost directly overhead. Temperatures rise rapidly on the Equator, more so when cloud cover is sparse. The naked eye can soon detect the shimmer where the rising heat of the day on the windless plain produces a mirage, and with it an optical illusion. A shimmer of water suddenly appears—the distant herd of zebras disappears. Nature's camouflage was washing the waterless plains signalling the time for siesta when most plains game seek shade at midday. I noticed our visitor was restless and hyperventilating, a sure sign the heat of the day without shade was now too much for her. In those preceding minutes before she stood up I had given her a name, for that show of courage I had witnessed moments before had made her part of my 'family'.

The name 'Astra' fitted perfectly. It was a simple name that bore no relationship to Planet Earth. This was an occasion requiring a special name to confirm her identity in film and in my mind's eye. Every cheetah, whether male or female, is different in form and markings. One has to recognise the subtle differences in their build and spotted makeup. I prefer to record the cheek, the chest, and the inside foreleg markings. The rings on the tail provide the family tree recognition.

Astra, with head low, was hesitatingly approaching the shade area of our tree. Petal was sound asleep and breathing heavily. I turned my head away to avoid eye contact with Astra by taking up a disinterested pose. My buttocks had long numbed—my uncomfortable posture and blood supply had deserted my posterior—that tingling feeling was torturing my mind. I had not envisaged or planned for this situation. The excruciating pain made it absolutely essential that I adjust my position.

The last thing I wanted was for Petal to wake up with a start as this could have a disastrous result in unnerving 'Astra' and making her bolt for the bushes; all the good work Petal had done in bringing a situation of trust and calm into the 'introduction' would be lost. Any future attempts might not come so easy; confidence once lost takes patience and perseverance to restore and this perfect opportunity might not present itself again.

Firstly, I must remove Petal's tail from across my legs to waken her. Momentarily, she lifted her head and looked around; in those few seconds Petal had surveyed all her surroundings including a momentary glance at Astra. Cheetahs appear to have that owl like capability of rotating their gaze through almost two hundred and seventy degrees! Having now satisfied herself that nothing untoward was afoot she stretched out once again to sleep. Here was my opportunity to move to the outer circle of the shade. Astra held her ground and

The introduction – getting to know Astra
Petal, unconcerned, continued to attend to her grooming.

although still very alert had used the body language from Petal that all was well. I stood for several minutes experiencing the blessed relief of circulation returning to my rear end. I was now able to radio call the Sun-trekker mobile caravan to come in closer.

Kibet, my patient and experienced African safari driver, had been watching all the happenings from a distance, and was elated for he, like myself, realised that one big step had been made in communicating with a wild cheetah. Petal in her own natural way had succeeded in providing the key to my first introduction. Her tactics had made sense to me. Inwardly bursting with excitement I must not make sudden outward or awkward body movements—Astra still had me under close surveillance. Both cheetahs paid little attention to the arrival of the camper van. Kibet had brought the vehicle in slowly and quietly. I marvelled that he was always fully in tune with the sensitivity of the moment and in this case paid specific attention to light and photographic detail. He parked the vehicle within ten metres of the tree and switched off the engine. I was then able to proceed directly to the campervan from where I could observe both cheetahs in comfort.

Astra must have come across from the Mara Game Reserve; she was obviously accustomed to tourist vehicles. Another plus for me in this equation.

Both Petal and Astra had become aware of a group of Maasai women who were in transit on route to the market place, held every Saturday in the village of Aitong. Traders from distant northern agricultural holdings brought in maize meal, millet, and vegetables. The diet of the Maasai is changing slowly over to more conventional foods. The women had seen the cheetahs and realised the necessity to give them a wide birth.

Once the colourful pageant was out of sight I planned to dismount from the camper, van, taking care to avoid making any furtive movements, and to walk confidently and diagonally across towards the resting cheetahs. Both cheetahs were still alert watching the women disappear into the distance. I had briefed Kibet of my intentions. Petal I sensed would act as my anchor.

Phase two of getting to know Astra was about to commence. Kibet would take the pictures and the rest was up to me. Petal, I hoped would continue to do her bit. I sat down at the outer edge of the shade looking into the distance, avoiding any direct eye contact with Astra. Petal with her back to me was unconcerned; that was good. Astra was growling quietly, trying instinctively to alert Petal to danger. Petal still unconcerned continued to attend to her grooming. That too was good for me.

I prayed inwardly for Astra not to bolt; confident she would not attack me. Had I been dealing with a male seeking to mate Petal, the probability of attack or at least a show of severe aggression would be certain. My belief was that, by moving to and from the caravan, Astra would see that my body language and my proximity to her was not a threat. In due course I would bring out Petal's 'karai' and the white plastic five-litre water container that on a hot day always encouraged Petal to quench her thirst. Would Astra observe and then partake—the next half-hour would tell. I placed the karai near Petal and poured the water out of the container. The sound of running water has several effects, for me it triggers an unconscious signal that my bladder is in urgent need to defuel, and for Petal the need to tank up. Petal took the initiative to drink first – then Astra followed after Petal.

I walked towards another tree; after all I too must leave my calling card and add confusion to any male cheetah that wished to mark his territorial mating ground. I often took time away from Petal to follow her brothers and plot their markings on my home-made map of Petal's territory. There was no doubt they too signalled their presence in this way to her, and to other female cheetahs coming into oestrus that a choice of partner is around and available.

Kibet was sitting patiently in the driving cab. Although equipped with a chemical toilet the caravan did not have an internal access from the cab to the rear portion—being a dismountable and drive away. Access to the caravan body itself was through the rear outside entrance door.

The Suntrekker is designed to fit on most one tonne, four-by-four pickups, an amazingly simple to handle all-terrain vehicle. If Kibet were to get out from the cab, the whole effort to establish Petal's and Astra's trust in me alone would collapse. Similarly to try and introduce another human to them at this or any future stage could have long term complications in identifying friend or foe. It was for this reason that I remained a constant factor in dress.

Whistling my practised and trusted imitation cheetah call that Petal, since her childhood, always answered to, I announced my approach. All of this I attribute to her intelligent understanding of my human attempt to communicate with her. It was necessary to spend quality time with Petal.

Safaris took up much of my thinking time; also attending to organisational matters at camp, but with forward planning I was able to arrange time off with Petal. My VHF pocket radio was crackling, Kibet or the camp wanted to contact me, being some distance away I had missed seeing Petal jump onto Kibet's vehicle bonnet. It was customary for her to do this on occasions; however Kibet's voice over the radio seemed more excited than his usual cool calm and collected self. All I could hear was him saying, "She's peeing on my windscreen – Woi" (wow), what extraordinary behaviour this was! To add further insult to injury, "She has dumped her calling card as well. What do I do now?" said Kibet in a not so very amused tone. I could not contain my mirth and laughed out aloud.

Kibet had instinctively pressed the windscreen washer squirt button which also activated the wipers. This surprised Petal who took a quantum leap into mid-air and, as all cats have that built in capability, she landed square on all fours almost on top of Astra. Panic reigned for a few fleeting seconds as both cheetahs bolted for the undergrowth.

I walked back to the caravan, not knowing quite what to say. Should I chastise Kibet for his folly? The look on his face said it all; he was not amused. In Swahili he retorted "Hii paka ni jangirri", translated politely "this is a crazy mixed up cat!"

Kibet, for the past half-hour, had painfully avoided having to attend to nature's call for fear of disrupting the whole show, but now Petal had committed the final insult on his vehicle and he was damned if he was going to suffer any longer. Kibet quietly walked away from the caravan and true to his inconspicuous manner disappeared from my view. A few minutes later he returned. His dry sense of humour never failed to amuse me. With a wry smile he pronounced that Petal, not to be out-done, had christened the caravan "**Pottyloo**"—how true this was! I figured it would be highly unlikely that we would get so close to these two cats for some time to come. There was no point in hanging around; Petal was not answering my cheetah call, it was best we return to camp. I would come back towards evening time alone and possibly stay the night. It was full moon. Meantime I must try and make light of the incident for Kibet's sake.

En route to camp we met up with a minibus full of Japanese tourists. The driver stopped and asked if we had seen any cheetahs. Kibet, still wearing that same embarrassed look, said "yes" and pointed to the object on the bonnet, whereupon the African driver to my great surprise spoke to his passengers in fluent Japanese; whatever he said had an instant effect— cameras were drawn en-masse. **At** this point Kibet's foot hit the gas pedal; being photographed with Petal's 'dump' was just too much. There had been enough embarrassment for one day. I could sense his concern at the ragging he would get from the camp staff—they were always keen to hear about each day's adventure – particularly Andrew. Would Kibet have the courage to recount the incident?

Kibet was a good raconteur and well respected by all the staff and within the tour industry. Few experts could match his knowledge in ornithology; he had learned his trade from the legendary ornithologist, Don Turner, with whom he had worked in the early stages of his career as an apprentice tour-escort specialising in that field.

At the wheel he was always careful in the extreme and never once in his 15 years of service with me did he ever fail to get through to camp single-handed. Nightmare roads, mud, slush, rain and tempest never seemed to cause him or his passengers any anxiety. Kibet was popular, with an endearing nature; patience too was another of his virtues.

Darkness was falling and the glorious African sunset was about to say goodnight to the rising full moon.

This period of sunset occurs at about 6.30 to 6.45 p.m.—a regular evening occurrence on the Equator. This was a hallowed time for Petal, she would sit and watch the fireball disappear to somewhere down-under, its golden light blazing in her eyes; not a flicker, not a whisper, not a movement, almost as if she was transfixed by the spectacle that makes we humans stand and stare in total silence admiring its beauty each to his own thoughts. I often wondered what Petal was thinking at times like this? I believe it was her prayer time, a time to thank her maker—as I do for this precious life.

The caravan was always revitalled and ready for any night stop. To ease matters the camp cook had prepared a ready-cooked portable meal that only required heating. My turnaround at camp was quick, as I was eager to look for both of the traumatised cheetahs. Kibet would be left to tell his story in graphic detail whilst I carried his prize card still stuck to the bonnet of the Landcruiser. Inwardly I knew I would be expected to act as postman the following day to seek out others of Petal's kind.

Petal was now dictating the shots but first I must find her. The situation could end up by tail-chasing each other in the dark in ever increasing circles. It would be best if I positioned myself within two to three hundred yards of where Astra and she had taken to the bushes.

The full moon had already risen through the first quarter of its arc in the night sky providing good visibility for the naked eye to a distance of approximately seventy metres. My night binoculars absorb light from the stars and moon. Two pencil batteries power them and when switched on, the night becomes a different world bathed in an eerie pale green colour. Prolonged viewing can bring on a slight headache when operated in excess of twenty-minute intervals. I felt confident that I would detect any movement within three to four hundred yards covering a full circle around me.

The African night can get very cold; I was thankful that the caravan had a hatch in its roof from which I could comfortably view. Now it was a matter of patience. I could hear a single lion grunting in the distance and made a mental note of its position—hoping inwardly it would not come my way, then there was the short positioning call of a hyaena advertising his or her whereabouts to its mate, a nearby flutter of wings and a night-jar whistled it's mating call. Jackals barked far off, their call brought towards me on the gentle night breeze. I was tuning in to my surroundings, thankful to have taken care of my hearing and eyesight in my youth.

I often ask myself how the children of today will cope with tomorrow on a planet that has gone crazy with noise. Earplugs and sunglasses are part of my valuable possessions—particularly so when I visit the big city with my clients. Busy restaurants, noisy night-clubs, coloured lights flashing out of unison sends my brain into a scrambled mess. Noisy motorbikes, vehicles belching smoke, they call it 'back to civilisation', no thank you! Here, around me is peace and tranquillity—I couldn't be happier with my life. How unbearable it would be to become hard of hearing caused by one's own stupid neglect. Our eyes are so precious and failing to care for them, due to insufficient protection from the sun and disco dance halls, supposedly enjoying ourselves in this make-believe world that we now live in, is asking for trouble in the future.

The moon was high in the sky; the magical hour of midnight had long passed. The antelopes and gazelles were resting quietly, some catnapping, a sign that suggests there are no predators close by. I too am beginning to wilt; it's time to shut down for the night and hope that the early morning will bring some contact with Petal.

I was feeling a little depressed. No answering call came from Petal, except a light moment when a night-jar mistook my whistle for a courting call. Was it a male or female? I asked myself—remembering the shrill and mimicked night-jar calls that were used in the forests by the freedom fighters announcing their approach to their forest hideout after a night out of murder and plunder. A low short whistle gave the 'all clear'. I was never sure whether it was the female or male that used that call. Kibet would know; I must ask him in the morning. Still wearing my clothes I wrapped my sleeping bag around me and fell asleep. I recalled sleeping in the bush one night, with Petal nearby, when it poured heavens hard—my sleeping bag proved not to be waterproof. Our 'passions' were somewhat dampened!

Nights out under the stars with my spotted girlfriend had become commonplace. Sometimes Kibet would not be able to get to me with the caravan due to flood and impassable terrain. NASA, with its many spin-offs from its explorations had invented a space blanket—

an ultra light full sized cover made from what appeared to be an aluminium cloth on the one side and, when hung like an awning, reflected the sun off the bright surface, giving shade and cool. When wrapped around me, inside out, the aluminium acted as an insulator and retained my body heat—very effective and comfortable during the coldest of nights. The reverse side was waterproof—problem solved. It weighed only sixteen ounces and fitted neatly into my waterproof backpack.

Everything in that pack had to be ultra light, including 'compo rations', the standard American army front-line rations. Need I say more? I could eat like a king. Cigar shaped smokeless weatherproof kindling, when lit, would help to heat up my tinned rations. A balanced diet of all the necessary mineral and vitamin requirements would see me through a week of trekking; water purification tablets that fizzed were also very important. Petal was always fascinated by the effervescing bubbles!

Sometimes we travelled through waterless country so I had to be careful to ration my water intake. Petal had the sense to avoid travelling between 11 a.m. and 4 p.m., these being the peak temperatures on the Equator. Her body system after 'tanking up', seemed to hold her fluid far better than myself. Each time I drank copious amounts of water it had the effect of encouraging me to instantly defuel, thus losing out on the retention of necessary minerals and energy. I found that regularly sipping small quantities of water, balanced with my level of dehydration, retained my energy. I am very susceptible to heat exhaustion and avoid the problem by taking regular re-hydration salts.

The night in the camper had been uneventful. I slept fitfully, often waking and subconsciously listening for Petals call that never came.

The first shafts of the dawn light were clawing up into the sky; time for a quick brew-up and some cornflakes for breakfast.

Petal would be out in the open curled up alone against the early morning cold. So would Astra. The time for Petal's usual morning walkabout would coincide with the heat generated by the direct rays from the rising sun that takes the chill out of the air and soaks up the morning patches of ground frost that lie like sheets of glass in the valleys.

Kibet would be expecting my radio call within the next hour to brief him regarding my plans for the day.

Clients were due to fly into camp in three day's time. I therefore had two full days and another night out before having to switch my concentration to prepare for their arrival.

Today I would require Kibet to assist me to search around in the hopes of locating either Petal or Astra. He had good instincts coupled with patience and thoroughness. Without my even calling for him he arrived in one of the safari Land Cruisers prepared for a long day's outing. My plan was to leave the caravan on a nearby high point safely locked up with Petal's calling card still on the bonnet.

Tour drivers from nearby lodges would always head for my vehicle knowing that Petal or possibly other cheetahs could be with me or close by. This saved them valuable search-time on their short, before-breakfast, early morning game viewing drives—all the more eyes to help Kibet and me locate Petal.

The 'Hawk Eye'
Kibet had amazing eyesight. Walking with the bird watchers.

Should any drivers locate cheetahs they co-operated by flashing their headlights towards us and we would reciprocate. Kibet and I took turns to drive; two experienced pairs of eyes looking ahead concentrating on avoiding pot-holes and solid rocks that are guaranteed to appear too late to avoid—they always occur just when the drivers' eyes wander away from forward-looking vision! The resultant unexpected emergency stop could easily catapult one or both of us through the windscreen, let alone the resulting bump on the head that in seconds feels the size of a golf ball. The jar and damage to one's spinal column will surely re-visit you in later years! Another pair of eyes is good insurance against these painful accidents.

Out on the plain, a distance of some four hundred yards away, an Impala male had suddenly frozen in his stance head held high looking intensely and directly ahead. Kibet called 'stop'. Might the Impala have spotted a predator; could it be a lion or cheetah? I switched off the engine to allow Kibet a steady platform. I too adjusted my wide-angle binoculars and carefully followed the direction of the Impala's gaze. His harem of females was still heads down and grazing—his body language had yet to be transmitted to them. Could it be another male Impala trespassing on his turf? If so he would lower his head and move forward to challenge the intruder, if not, and a predator was sighted, he would snort an alarm whereupon all his females would instantly stop grazing and, with heads up, close ranks and face the direction of the threat. The male Impala had still not pressed the panic button. I hardly dared breathe—something was about to happen—he moved forward a few steps, and then in total unison the females scattered and reformed into a tight group.

The alarm had been raised. All heads turned to look in the same direction as their leader, towards a clump of bushes. Not a word came from Kibet. There was always a healthy keenness between us to be 'first spot'. "Pengine-ni-chui" Kibet whispered in Swahili (translated means "Maybe it's a leopard.")

A leopard was always a prize find on any game viewing drive for a tourist driver. Up on the hill some vehicles were circling the caravan; many camera flashes suggested Petals calling card was once again being well photographed!

Kibet's one syllable conversation with the Japanese-speaking tour driver the previous evening must have been well broadcast! I flashed my lights to distract their attention and to bring them to us in order that their wanderings would not disturb the impending action currently being kept in focus by Kibet. He had still not identified the predator or its place of hiding. Having already flashed my headlights, I suggested to Kibet that we should hold fast until the tour vehicles arrived. Each tour company has their own distinctive colours which were easily recognisable from a distance—ours was forest green and brown and blended with the background. I was banking on my ruse working; that the tour vehicles would be keen to come straight to my call and not see the body language signs the Impalas were showing.

Many tour drivers have little time for the art of watching and waiting. Their clients become impatient and the pressure of 'delivering' is ever present. Many times I have been rewarded by patience. The waiting was worth it. I suggested we move closer—Kibet agreed. The Impala herd was still transfixed and taking no notice of our approach. Sure enough, there was a cheetah quietly relaxing in the shade of a clump of bushes. The cheetah was none other than Astra, close to the area where the previous day's debacle had put Kibet through an emotional mangle. Within the hour Astra disappeared. A full three months passed before she returned with her little cubs.

Petal too had not been seen for almost the same period of time since introducing me to Astra. Despite our constant searching within Petal's territory not a whisper had come through to me on the 'Bush Telegraph'. I was mystified and concerned—dismissing the idea they could be together. I had never known related or unrelated females in the company of each other wandering outside their territorial limits except as singles looking for a mate.

Some clients were due to arrive by road for an overnight stay, so Kibet and I returned to camp to prepare a welcome for them. Their long and tiring journey had taken up much of the day—the roads were dusty and pot-holed and the going was slow, so the remainder of the day was put to good use in rest and repair.

Dinner had been served and consumed in style, when Kibet came to tell me that Sergeant James had arrived with news from Corporal Daniel. Daniel had been on an anti-poaching foot patrol that morning, some twenty miles south of us, when he came across Petal's three brothers. According to Daniel they were in good shape. He also sent his good wishes and to remind me it was full moon!

James had called in to tell me Petal had been spotted at dusk this evening by a Mara River Camp driver. She was seen heading in our direction along the 'mikono moja' track. Mikono moja in Swahili is 'one hand' – a code word used by tour drivers that specifically refers to an elephant track that runs North and South through the middle of the Koiyaki Group Ranch. A cheer went up from our visitors, echoed by the kitchen staff! Petal was alive and well. James didn't know whether she was pregnant or not – only that she was alone, with no male in tow—this was encouraging news.

Corporal Daniel was almost right. "At full moon the boys will bring you news of Petal". His prediction was not far wrong—if he had said "James" his prophecy would have been written into the cheetah history books.

James was on his way to Narok, a hundred kilometres away; he would probably reach there at about midnight. We gave him and each of his three crew members, a thermos of hot soup and a loaf of Andrew's newly baked bread and off they went as happy as sand boys.

"Kibet" I said "At first light tomorrow we will set off to Muguu Moja". Kibet cautioned, "It's full moon Boss, she will not be sleeping tonight; by dawn maybe she will be close by". Kibet's intuition had merit. "Let's go to Euphorbia Hill and wait there. Andrew can bring the breakfast in the Bush Baby" – our new name for the 'Pottyloo camper'. "Good, thinking Kibet", I said. "Great, we'll do just that!" I could see Kibet was as excited as myself, though seldom does he show his inner feelings.

Early to bed and early to rise. The night was quiet and the moon full—of course! Our clients slept well.

It was 6 a.m. Tea and biscuits were being served at the campfire and now, buoyed by the thought of finding Petal at last, we set off at 6.30 a.m. on the dot. Kibet had taken the lead: today was to be his day. Hell or high water – we MUST find Petal!

We had tracked south towards Euphorbia Hill passing by a group of hyaenas on the way back to their dens; they too had feasted well.

A small herd of elephants could be seen moving with purpose across the plains about five hundred yards distant, when we spotted a group of young Thompson's gazelle 'pronking' (a stiff-legged bouncing display of jumping side-to-side)—this youthful exuberance suggested the first rain was in the air.

We parked on the hill and dismounted from our vehicles. The plan was to search the low-lying area with our binoculars, along the same principles as Kibet and I had used the previous day. Each one of the ten of us would take a sector of 30 to 35 degrees, making a full circle 'observation' platform.

Soon there were shouts of "there, there", "where, where?" All were false alarms and proved to be moving bushes! Kibet was undeterred with all these amateur red-herring calls: nothing was going to distract his attention. He moved away some fifty yards from the group and sat down on a rock. Minutes later he called "I see her!" and pointed; we all zoomed our binoculars in the direction and for a full minute no movement or anything resembling a cheetah could be seen. "And she is coming our way!" he said excitedly.

Then, as if by one command everyone shouted "I see her, I see her". There was no doubt Petal had the Euphorbia Hill in her sights. It would be nice to have her join us for breakfast! Kibet, in his usual considerate and thoughtful way, suggested we should go and greet her and welcome her back 'home' with a 'karai' of water—she would be thirsty. The area and watercourses had dried up and everyone and everything, including the wildlife, was thirsting for rain.

We drove towards Petal and stopped; I hurriedly placed the 'karai' on the ground and poured the water into it. Petal's last fifty yards were taken up in a canter. It was a happy occasion for everyone – including myself. I was overjoyed at being reunited with her though I could see she was not pregnant. This moment of joy overpowered my inner disappointment, but where had she been? This spotted sphinx had vanished into thin air for almost three

Without further warning she jumped onto my vehicle bonnet and lay down, looking back at me through the windscreen.

months! I marvelled at her slim and sleek body, so graceful, clean and tidy.

Kibet's face was a picture "Abandon ship! Breakfast is on its way to Euphorbia Hill," he said. Everyone piled into his vehicle and off they went, leaving Petal to rest in safety and in peace. Our plan had worked perfectly, with all due respects going to Kibet. He was our 'star' today!

I elected to remain behind with Petal to make her feel I had not abandoned her. This was my opportunity to inspect her at close range for signs of sarcoptic mange. I was also looking for signs or any clues as to what had kept her away for so long, a false pregnancy or looking for a mate? Once again, was there any early sign of pregnancy? Am I getting paranoid about her state? Might she be barren?

Petal was content and happy to have me sit on the front mudguard close by her. I muttered away to her in a gentle voice—talking about nothing in particular. I just wanted her to hear my voice again. After about half an hour she chose to move onto the top of the vehicle and fall asleep in the upturned padded roof-hatch cover. It made a comfortable mattress for her.

I walked slowly towards where the breakfast caravan had been parked some two hundred yards away and joined my clients for a hearty breakfast; our morning adventure was complete. The five-minute walk back to the breakfast site was completed in deep thought; my gut feeling was that Petal had come into or had just come out of oestrus.

Observation of her movements over the next few days would tell me a story. Irritability, marking her post boxes, my windscreen – all are pointers towards a pre-oestrus build-up. It was a matter of 'wait and see'. Kibet was offering cautious optimism and nothing more—just "pengine" (maybe)!

My thoughts momentarily turned to Astra. She too had not been seen since our last fleeting glimpse of her before Christmas. The incident which occurred at the 'introduction' earlier, was still a party piece story among the camp crew when the camper was named 'Pottyloo' by Kibet!

We now had one vehicle out of service, abandoned because one special cheetah had commandeered it for herself, no time limit had been set to recover it and nobody had the heart to chase her off. She deserved peace and security; nothing would or could harm her 'on top'—and she knew it!

After breakfast was completed and all the 9 o'clock ablutions attended to, Andrew, Kibet and the 'Breakfast Camp Crew' returned to camp with the trailer and Bush Baby (alias Pottyloo!). The clients were due to return to Nairobi this afternoon on the scheduled 4 p.m. flight. The airline crew had a short duty-leg the following morning to Dar-es-Salaam, and back to Nairobi, followed by an overnight stay, returning on the long haul duty flight the next day, to Switzerland.

Meantime I took over Kibet's vehicle and he returned with the spare one that was always on standby at camp in case of a breakdown.

Our 'abandoned ship' caused much hilarity and laughter from passing tourist vehicles. I heard their drivers laid on a story that its occupants had 'toroka'd' ('run away') because this wild cheetah had hijacked it—it was the truth!

Both vehicles and their occupants continued on their game viewing drives with Kibet and Patrick, the reserve driver. I stayed with Petal and gave impromptu wildlife lectures to passing tourists who came to visit. Everybody was told to 'shush' (be quiet) take their pictures and come back to me under 'my tree' some one hundred yards away; Petal must not be disturbed.

My clients passed by at around 1 o'clock on their way to camp for lunch, and pack their bags for transfer to the airfield. They had seen most of the Big Five except leopard, and were in a happy mood.

Off they went, waving goodbye, promising to come back sometime and bring their parents and families. Petal had unwittingly become my full-time unpaid 'advertising manager'.

I called the camp mechanic to bring out 'Bush Baby'. My intention was to stay the night with Petal. The mechanic could take the now 'spare' vehicle back to camp for maintenance work. Provided, of course, her 'ladyship' would oblige and hand us back our 'abandoned ship'.

Dusk was approaching and soon Petal's prayer time would wake her—she had not stirred the whole day. At sunset, sure enough, she was awake and watching when the camper arrived—sundown was upon us. Petal dismounted and walked the hundred yards to Bush Baby conveniently parked for her in our favourite spot on Euphorbia Hill.

She seemed not to be too hungry—her tiredness was evident. This beautiful cat had travelled a long way. From where, I wondered?

I decided to try out the red film cover for the portable spotlight and pick out a few hares or an unwary gazelle in the darkness for Petal to chase after. I had not long to wait when her supper arrived in the form of a spring hare, a swift hopping mini-kangaroo-like creature not much bigger than an African hare. It is a vegetarian and mostly nocturnal but easy prey for a cheetah that can 'see' in the dark under artificial red-light conditions. Petal did not require any night-time training – we had done this all before. The meal seemed to satisfy her requirements but she drank a considerable amount of water which suggested the effect of dehydration, after her long safari, was still bothering her system.

Petal chose to return to the camper and climbed on top. It was her favourite 'room at the top' for the night. I heated up my ready-made dinner and hit the mattress. It was only then that I realised I was totally 'bushed'- a safari operator's slang for being one click short of exhaustion—my day had been full to overflowing. Tomorrow was another day. What would it hold for me I wondered?

I was still sound asleep when Kibet arrived. It was just getting light – about 6.15 a.m., when I heard a vehicle draw up. He had come to tell me that Base had called by radio to say an unexpected booking of five airline crew (maybe more), would arrive on the morning's flight—this had put a spanner in the works. He would meet and greet them and explain that I was with Petal, and awaiting their arrival in due course. The rest of the day would be left to fate and the cook!

This was a one-night, two-day special request safari from out of the blue. Andrew took the news in his stride.

The back-up aircraft
Stormy weather and bad visibility, particularly during the November rains, can
be a pilot's nightmare.

As usual Petal had 'dumped' on the bonnet of my vehicle before her night out on top; she had attended to her ablutions as I had done. My comfortable bush thunder box on Euphorbia Hill was now almost a permanent fixture.

Kibet eyed the calling card with some amusement; I think he was getting used to the idea and the reasons for it. He knew I would be expected to play 'postman' and make a tour around Petal's territory to spread the 'news' to her subjects. "The Queen is looking for her Prince!" Might this be the message contained in her scat on the pottyloo bonnet?

Another message had since come through to the camp from home base in Nairobi, to prepare for an extra two or three additions to the safari, pending seat availability on the incoming flight to the Mara—the outgoing aircrew had done their 'public relations' well!

Sudden last minute additions and subtractions can cause logistical problems with inbound and outbound seats for last minute stand-by passengers. The new arrangements would require another vehicle and driver.

What comes in has to go out; everyone must fly together both incoming and outgoing—this is the bottom line for my aircrew clients. Sometimes there are extra seats on the scheduled flight into the Mara, but no extra seats out the next day and to call in the emergency aircraft for only a couple of passengers would eat into the profits, which are marginal at times.

I have the responsibility to ensure they all get back to Nairobi for obvious reasons. An

MD11 Swissair jet airliner sitting on the tarmac at Nairobi Airport, without a crew, would spell disaster for me—no more crew safaris! This is the reason I have a back-up 10-seat aircraft on standby in Nairobi for any such emergencies, including bad weather.

Kibet was anxious I should accompany him to meet and greet the incoming group and to brief the pilots to arrange their flight planning accordingly—he was right.

The plan, once again, was to abandon 'Pottyloo' to Petal. Kibet and I would travel back to camp, pick up the spare vehicle and meet the clients. Off we went, leaving Petal in charge of Bush Baby (a new name for the Suntrekker campervan).

As usual the Air Kenya flight was on time; we had nine 'in-comers' and only five seats available for this group to fly out the next day! The pilots gave me their word—nobody would be left behind tomorrow. They too, understood my whole reputation was on the 'line'. I accepted their word, comfortable in the knowledge that I had my own back-up aircraft on standby in Nairobi.

Nine flight attendants, all females, disembarked. I asked, "Where are the men!" "Golf" replied one—enough said!

Once again they were a happy crew, so interested in everything. It is such a joy to have people like this on safari. I was very lucky and the envy of many—and getting paid for it!

Andrew would be in his element again—more pictures for the 'lads back home' in his Reserve.

Everything was ship-shape on our arrival back at camp. There is a camp introduction routine – the do's and don'ts and what to do if a 'don't' comes into camp! This is a humorous lecture on all things creepy! There is much nervous laughter. Is David our guide and saviour really serious? It's all good fun and sets the mood for the next twenty-four hours.

The time is 10.30 a.m. and half the morning has gone. There is no chance to have lunch in the bush today—Petal has occupied the 'meals on wheels' vehicle (Bushbaby) on Euphorbia Hill. Lunch will be in camp. Andrew is relieved.

We set off and our first stop will be to visit Petal. I drive and Kibet sits with me up front; Patrick will take the second vehicle and follow us in convoy.

CHAPTER 5
A PRINCE ARRIVES

A few minutes out from camp, Kibet called 'stop'! He had seen a movement in some bushes ahead. "Is it a cheetah? Could it be Petal? Had she followed us to camp?" I asked. "No", he said. "Was it Astra?" I queried.

Kibet was mumbling to himself still focusing his binoculars, then in a surprised tone he said "It's a male cheetah—he's big!", "You must be joking" I retorted. "Haki-ya-mungu (on Gods truth) take a look" he said. There was no doubt about it, here was a fine looking male, big in stature with a kind face, his markings were not 'family', and he was not one of the boys. I had never seen him before. My mind was racing ahead; could this be Astra's or Petal's mate?

There was one way to get confirmation: bring the caravan and Petal's postcard to him— but not Petal. Cheetah males can become quite vicious and often beat their female partners into submission prior to copulating, particularly so if the males are coalition partners. A female cheetah does not necessarily have to be in oestrus, for I have seen Petal's brothers making forcible advances to her and she has fought them off in a manner that suggested incest was not part of her make up. We arrived at the caravan.

I took these moments to update everyone on the developments over the past two days. The Queen's Prince had arrived! A perfect love story was about to unfold and we were all going to play matchmaker—my clients were ecstatic.

Petal had just dismounted from the caravan top and was resting under a nearby tree; she had tourists for company. I was able to pass on the information and whereabouts of the new male cheetah and asked the drivers to give us a few minutes to revisit him alone. The tourists were quite happy to stay a while with Petal: my driving away with her calling card again on the bonnet caused some amusement.

Kibet was picking up on the trend of my thinking; our route back would resemble an egg and spoon race. It was not going to be easy keeping Petal's calling card on the bonnet! The terrain was through a rocky outcrop; yards before we arrived the 'egg' rolled off onto the front plate housing the spare wheel where it came to rest. Best let it be I thought—would the new-found male pick up the scent? Time would tell.

I positioned upwind from our newcomer and received an immediate reaction. Sniffing the air and following his nose he came straight to the spare tyre, placed his forelegs onto it and then, to my astonishment, came around to my side and looked up directly at me as if to say, "Where is she?"

Petal's Prince checking out her 'perfume'!

I was excited; he made as if to place his paws on the running board but held back—it would have brought us face to face. There was no aggression; this was an unusually calm cheetah!

Our eye contact continued for almost thirty seconds; all I could think of was to chirp several quick cheetah calls. He appeared to understand but made no reply having satisfied himself that I had no aggression towards him and he lay down close to the caravan.

Kibet had positioned his vehicle close by me and was busy concentrating on taking photographs for the record: the tourists were now on their way towards us. The Impalas had moved away—still alert to the presence of a predator in their area.

I was now in a position to mentally note the cheetah's markings, particularly the tip of his tail. A thin wisp of a fine white tail-ring not seen in any of Petal's brothers was a tell-tale indication that he was not 'family' and had come from far off, possibly the vast Serengeti Game Reserve. He seemed to be accustomed to vehicles, so within the space of several days a suitable name had to be found for Petal's Prince.

Kibet had drawn alongside me and we were able to exchange observations and agreed that our newly found friend was not one of Petal's brothers. Whether he was to be Astra's or Petal's mate we would have to wait and see? Now we must name this handsome male.

Without further ado, our new cool, calm and collected male was christened 'Namibia'. In

To my astonishment Namibia
came directly to my side of
the vehicle and looked up at
me as if to say 'Where is she?'

the back of my mind something was beginning to make sense. Had Namibia followed Petal's scent? Was this the answer to her long absence, and now she was bringing him into her territory? Namibia's approach towards me was out of character for any wild cheetah—let alone a male.

I am sure Namibia was still hoping, in his mind, that I would miraculously deliver a mate to him—the scent was still distracting him; presumably it was that recently left by Petal on the bonnet whilst entertaining the tourists a half hour or so ago. The tourists had already left to seek other delights en route to their respective lodges, where a hearty breakfast was awaiting them.

Kibet would stay with Namibia. I decided to return to Petal's resting place some four hundred yards away and within sight from where Namibia was. Maybe if Petal investigated the 'Portaloo' fender she would pick up his scent—her reaction would be worth noting. A 'karai' of water placed on the ground near the front fender might entice her to the vehicle. I poured the water in the accustomed style taking care not to overdo the supply.

The water attracted her interest and she came to drink; there was just sufficient in the bowl to quench her thirst and as predicted she lifted her head and began sniffing the spare wheel, gradually moving to where Namibia had placed his paws on the fender. Petal obviously recognised his scent. Had they met during the previous night? I didn't think so; she seemed to have a genuine alertness and leapt onto the bonnet, then sat on her haunches and from this raised position focused into the distance to where Kibet had parked. I noticed Kibet had moved his earlier position to more open ground and through my binoculars I could clearly see Namibia. The radio crackled—it was Kibet. Namibia had apparently disturbed and caught a fawn left behind in hiding by a mother in the Impala group; some were grazing but most were very alert and looking at the cheetah from a safe distance. The ball was now in Petal's court; would she slink away or would she position herself closer and be seen? The custom in this chauvinistic human world of ours dictates that the male shall be the suitor, although it may now be changing for the female human gender in today's liberated state! The attraction of the dominant male in the animal world is irresistible to the female and that is the way it will remain for Nature decreed the biggest and the best will survive, that is if man permits them to do so.

Petal had moved a little closer to Namibia closing the distance to about one hundred yards. Now it is a matter of patience, just waiting and watching their every move. I was aware that Petal was occasionally glancing over towards the tour vehicles coursing over the savannah; like me she was making a mental note of where a cluster of vehicles had stopped. Was it possible they had found lions?

A cheetah is blessed with long sight—we humans are blessed with binoculars—the resultant equation balances out between Petal and myself. I know where to find the lions; she knows how to avoid them. At night I have the advantage of my night vision binoculars; she has the advantage of smell. Science believes the cat has more than one hundred times the sensory smell and visual acuity of a human; how this is measured is beyond me but I believe it to be true. The sun has almost set in the west; this is Petals moment of prayer and nothing must disturb her as its golden wash falls gently over the Mara. That aura of red and gold never ceases to impress me—these moments are magic. Much as I would wish to join Petal I must stay in the vehicle. My presence outside the vehicle may be spotted and cause Namibia some anxiety if he were looking our way. Nightfall was upon us; the crickets were in communication with each other—their high pitched chirpings bring a sense of security at night to any animal that seeks to sleep or cat-nap. They are the sentries of the night; beware if their chirping ceases—danger is near at hand.

It is important for me to stay with Petal and send Kibet back to camp with the clients for hot showers and freshen up. They too wanted to stay out late with me but unbeknown to them we had a surprise treat—the camp crew had arranged a 'dinner under the stars' for them.

Tables, chairs, tablecloths, kerosene lamps and all the necessities had already been positioned and laid in place. The spare camp vehicle, trailer, the bush mechanic and two camp crew had set this up out in the bush at sundown, a mile from camp.

Back at camp Kibet announced the surprise—a dinner under the stars at full moon and a possible honeymoon in the making was just too romantic for words! It was a sell-out! I too, would join them for dinner.

Petal would have to give up 'Bush Baby' for a few hours. She could use the spare vehicle to rest on as a replacement safe platform.

Her camper was then hijacked and taken to the dinner site for use as Andrew's kitchen. All the meals were served on trays from the caravan window and handed to several waiters dressed in white uniforms—tonight it was 'waiter service'! The air crew were delighted at being treated in the same way as they would serve their passengers—it became an evening of teasing and joyous laughter. I was very proud of my camp crew—they had provided the surprise dinner. The camp crew and clients returned to camp for the night leaving me with Petal and Bushbaby.

The moon is now well up into the African night. The caravan lurches slightly and I hear padded paws land softly on the bonnet—Petal has come to rest a while –this is my chance to quietly move out and around to her, chirping softly to warn her of my presence.

Our meeting must be short – 'a kiss in the dark'- and a few loving words. There is always a thrill in the softness of love, especially if it is stolen! These are golden moments for me even if only pictured in my mind. I sense Petal's excitement. Namibia is not too far away so I must return to the caravan where I can sit and wait, listening to the crickets and their night sounds. Petal is restless and keeps shifting her position on the bonnet. She must hunt soon; two days and two nights have passed since her last meal. Was she expecting me to accompany her on another night walk and give her support?

Cheetahs hunt during the day, preferably early morning or evening just at sunset; though when tourists' viewing is at its peak many streetwise predators will hunt when the plains are clear of tourist vans. Much of the action usually occurs when tourists are back at their lodge, having their breakfast, lunch, or enjoying an afternoon siesta.

The experienced safari campers take breakfast and a picnic lunch and stay out for the day; a breed that prefers to watch and wait and not disturb. Their patience and understanding is usually rewarded. Most understand the rules of nature and they are a pleasure to be with. I have made many loyal and good friends, sharing in their delight at Petal's acceptance of them. Many unsuspecting tourists come close to heart failure and dive for the floorboards when a wild cheetah jumps on the bonnet of their vehicle. Petal senses this and quickly departs from her observation perch; the startled tourists are happy and relieved. Another dinnertime story with all the trimmings will be told time and again on their return home.

I feel torn as to whether I should go outside once more, taking with me my night binoculars and backpack including the fire extinguisher—but common sense prevails. The Prince enticed by his Princess's perfume seemed not to fear my presence or the caravan; he also appeared to be in a receptive mood after my communication with him earlier in the day.

I must not interfere in Petal's love life. Females like most humans, are very selective about whom they choose to be their suitors. It was getting late—time to have a sandwich and night-cap from the hot thermos—but no cooking. Too many confusing smells would waft around and attract the scavengers of the night—the last thing I wanted to happen.

I stretched out on my bed still in my safari clothes, boots and all. I fell into a deep sleep having promised myself it would only be a short cat-nap; a state of semi-suspension of sleep which with practice becomes second nature in the wild. Any slight sound or movement and immediately I would awaken and be ready to react.

I became aware of a constant cheetah chirping interspersed with a low short growl. The calls were very close and their direction kept changing as if slowly circling the caravan. Was this Petal calling me, giving me a signal she wished to go hunting with me? I hoped not. I looked through the small window that faced into the cab and from where I could see the front of the Landcruiser.

Petal was still there on the bonnet lying in a prone position watching the goings on. I moved over to the large sliding side windows of the caravan and saw it was Namibia; it was he who was calling. Great, so far so good. I was thrilled; Petal was giving the impression of aloofness and a display of disinterested body language. She could be in oestrus—though I had seen no tell tale signs except some restlessness and her habit of urinating on the windscreen. Could this be interpreted as marking for a male, possibly the early stages of oestrus?

I was inwardly willing her to step down from her perch—that was all she had to do. Namibia was still chirping and circling. His little growl was not one of anger; on the contrary it had a rather comforting and seductive sound to it.

In humans this pleasant growl supersedes the suggestive and embarrassing male 'wolf whistle' that in my opinion does not produce the required reaction in women! Petal stirred and sat up on her haunches. "That's right my girl" I muttered, "safety first, sit on it"! She was hoping for an opportunity to escape; looking around checking for a departure route and waiting until Namibia was around the back of the caravan out of sight, then she took off at high speed—playing hard to get!

Namibia was quick off the mark—this was what he had planned for, clever chap. Had he lain down close by within Petal's sight, who knows, Petal might not have made a move off the bonnet.

I grabbed my night binoculars and fire extinguisher and dismounted, taking care to lock the door. I followed the pair at a safe distance, strapping on the head cradle, and switching on the power; the binoculars turned night into day! Namibia was still chirping and making his courting growl having caught up with Petal. She was leading him a little dance by making short teasing hide and seek disappearing acts, darting into the bushes and out again, not really intent on making a determined high-speed getaway!

I made a mental note as to the direction and bearing we were heading in relation to the caravan. For safety I always carried a small luminous compass on a wrist strap, an essential piece of equipment that indicates you are 'on track' and not walking in circles.

On a dark, star-less, cloudy night with no reference points, particularly if it's pouring with rain and forward visibility is down to zero, the word 'lost' slots easily into the subconscious mind. Vertigo is not just confined to the vertical plane, but can present itself in the horizontal; the mind's giro compass can tumble very easily in the pitch-black night. Have you ever had that sensation of your foot stepping into space when there is no eye contact with the ground? Totally blind people without a feeler, agree it is one of their most feared 'off balance' sensations. Similarly, stepping down and finding nothing to hold onto is a disaster waiting to happen.

The Prince was still singing his love song—if only he would change his tune. "How long is this going on for?" I asked myself. Every yard forward on foot for me meant another yard back in distance. In time, an hour out adds another hour back, there has to be a cut off point. I decided on one hour out then about turn. It was midnight. The caravan was now behind me to the west. We had been travelling east towards the steep slopes of the Aitong hills some five kilometres away.

Yes, she was taking him to the hills; there they could spend their three-day honeymoon in undisturbed peace. The terrain was too steep for tourist vehicles and Maasai cattle and sheep. I returned to the caravan. It was now 2 a.m.; I was exhausted after the long uneventful walk back and drive to camp. My plan for the following day was to search the area from where I left off; I might just see Petal before she took to the hills.

Morning came early! I had not slept too well. On my walk back to the caravan last night I skirted around where the pride of lions had been seen at dusk. Petal and her Prince may have done the same.

CHAPTER 6
MAASAI WARRIORS

MAASAI herders from the surrounding ranches are not permitted to graze their cattle within the boundaries of the protected Mara Game Reserve. This restriction gives the predators more freedom to hunt during the day and provides visitors the opportunity to view the lions, leopards and hyaenas hunting in their natural state. These predators pose a threat within the Game Reserve to the timid cheetahs, either when hunting or eating at their kill. Often the cheetahs lose their hard-earned dinner to these predators. The cheetahs tend to migrate to the group ranches where they know their enemies prefer to seek cover and lie low during the day, hiding from the Maasai and their herds. The cheetahs are aware there is less predator harassment on the ranches where they can select their quarry, usually antelopes and gazelles, that prefer the short regularly grazed grasses on the group ranch plains and surrounding hills.

I made it known to the cattle herders that it was in their future interests not to harm the cheetahs. The herders had become interested onlookers keen to find out what medicine I was using to permit my close association with the dumas (cheetahs).

My presence in the field gave these young warriors an interest. I always carried clean drinking water for them; surprisingly they never seemed to carry water. I often picked them up and sat them on the front of the vehicle and drove towards the lions. These escapades provided a real buzz for them adding a little bit of excitement to their day. These trips gave them a close up view of the lions and in return for this they provided me with information on the whereabouts of the dumas.

Lions react nervously to the distinct smell of Maasai Moran. It is important these warriors are carried only in the back of my tourist game-viewing vehicle and never in or on the caravan. Petal would definitely disown me if she sensed, by smell, her human escort associated with Maasai. If I did I earned myself a disdainful look from her that penetrated through to my soul making me feel unclean and unworthy of sitting close to a Princess!

Predators, in particular lions, cheetahs, hyaenas and leopards, have a built-in gene that triggers alarm and caution; I see this often whilst out game viewing. When watching Maasai walking at a distance across the plains with spears glinting in the sun, one can observe these predators giving them their constant and undivided attention until well out of sight.

I once witnessed a thirty-strong Maasai Moran lion hunt. The warriors had surrounded a lone adult female that had taken refuge in a rocky outcrop: Her crime was being alone.

Driven by the pangs of hunger she had killed and partly eaten a yearling calf, which had strayed from its herd. This was dangerous but easy prey for her. Unfortunately it was the domesticated property of a Maasai! She had killed on his land. Yes she had committed her crime outside the 'protected area', an area which man had set aside for himself and forbidden her or others of her kin to feel free to act out their lives in accordance with the laws of nature. The lioness died a horrible and painful death; in her fight for her life she clawed a terrible disfigurement on the Maasai Moran that finally speared her. To this day his gruesome facial scars bear witness to her fearsome fight—he was lucky to survive.

I was returning to camp one afternoon having delivered my clients to a nearby airstrip for their flight back to Nairobi, inwardly relieved they had been spared this terrible scene— the wonderful memories of their time in the Mara would have been totally shattered. I also felt sick to my stomach, but sensed if I drove past the incident, showing no concern for their wounded, it would not be long before I would pay the price of their scorn and possibly face instant eviction. I was, after all, a paying tenant on a campsite on their land!

I drove across to the highly excited group knowing I would be required to provide first aid beyond my capability and training. The nearest medical clinic was at Lemek some fifty kilometres away; I could see the deep claw lacerations into the side of the warrior's face, others were on his chest and shoulder. Surprisingly there were no teeth marks, but he was bleeding profusely; time was of the essence as early shock could set in.

In my first aid sachet I had a roll of cotton wool, plenty of bandages and a very effective disinfectant. I bandaged and bound him up like a mummy and rolled him into a blanket. Others with minor cuts and scratches possibly self inflicted in their initial charge toward the lioness were insisting their wounds be bandaged as well to show to those back home they too had participated in the kill. Lion killing or lion hunting is still practised as part of the Maasai tradition; thankfully it is no longer a sport in the Maasai Mara. To kill a lion single-handed permits the warrior to wear the stamp of a courageous supremo. He will have first choice of any maiden's hand in marriage and receives status perks as a true Morani (warrior).

The Maasai Mara Game Reserve is the inalienable heritage of the Maasai. They have now formed their adjacent areas into group ranches with stakeholders as their management.

The Reserve or 'protected' area is under the management of the Narok Maasai Mara County Council. Years of mismanagement and misappropriation of tourist revenue by those in authority has brought the protected wildlife sanctuary to the brink of collapse.

There are changes for the better taking place however. Perception of a 'Mara conservancy' has taken root where management has been leased from the Transmara County Council. There are moves afoot to import experienced wildlife management personnel. I am optimistic.

There is some controversy raging over apportionment of the tourist entry takings. Political greed and intrigue over motive is rife, but the proof of transparency and rehabilitation by good management will be seen as a role model.

An enormous amount of goodwill must come from all sides for this scheme to be successful. The group ranches, where cattle and sheep have always been their tradition, have pledged their support to establish conservation areas within their ranches solely for wildlife and to rid the area of mushrooming and unsightly shanty villages that have no place in this pristine wilderness.

The future of the Mara and the wildlife within it will not survive if these pledges are not honoured. The cheetah population, in particular, is in serious decline due to the loss of their habitat and pressure from an increase in domestic stock — a result of revenue distributed to ranch stakeholders from tourism.

The average Maasai still prefers to see his investment in cattle. Only when disease strikes and wipes out their stock do they begin to see the folly of their ways. Once upon a time they were pastoralists, continually on the move following the rain to graze their stock on greener pastures. Now they have to consider a new venture — into tourism; a fickle source of revenue that follows the trend of the world's economy. This bigger picture will be hard for them to understand. It has its downsides when tourism and travel falls prey to insecurity. Kenya has had more than its fair share of undue adverse publicity, much of it in the overseas press. I have often wondered about the true purpose of this sensationally charged journalism directed at Kenya.

The local Maasai and conservationists are becoming increasingly vocal and claim that the Kenya Wildlife Act is completely out of date. It presently bestows ownership of wildlife on the Government and dispossesses the rightful owners, the communities which, like the Maasai, coexist with the wildlife.

The current law in force treats communities as a potential menace to wildlife; the fact is, though this may be true in many cases, how can the landowners be blamed if they do not directly benefit from the wildlife on their lands? For our precious wildlife to survive they must be of economic benefit to the people who coexist with them. Ownership of the wildlife outside the parks and protected areas must revert to the local communities.

There is urgent need for more neighbourly co-operation within the newly formed group ranches bordering these reserves and game parks. They are becoming popular for visitor viewing and will take the pressure off the reserves and parks. Local participation and visitor income will provide the incentive to discourage illegal poaching. Game reserves and their administrators may well become a luxury of the past for the councils running them seem incapable of doing so; the takings are just too much temptation for the greedy and those who prefer to get rich quickly.

Objection to administration by outsiders other than their indigenous fellow men could be the undoing of a brave attempt at controlled conservation in the Mara. Conservation and wildlife authorities in South Africa have offered financial assistance and expertise. This would go a long way towards assisting in the future overall conservation plan for the Mara.

I have always been keen to investigate whether the king cheetah existed in the Mara at some time in the distant past. I believe it did. The question why it is no longer seen is perplexing. I visited De Wildts Cheetah Research Station in South Africa soon after this phenomenon occurred.

I still believe the king cheetah had a place in the pyramid of the cheetah's evolution. Now

The King Cheetah!

This dramatic pattern might suggest that it would be less conspicuous as a forest dweller.

that molecular science has come into being, possibly somewhere along the line it may give man a key to another window into halting the cheetah's slide into extinction. Many scientists and researchers thought at the time, that Nature in her wisdom, had produced a new species from a spotted cheetah—but later came to the conclusion it was as the result of a single recessive gene carried by both parents that made this possible.

The King Cheetah's beauty holds us all in awe at the colour scheme nature has given it.

Today it is seldom seen in the wilds from where it once existed. The coat of this fine animal has a dramatic and different colour pattern from that of other cheetahs. There was great excitement at the De Wildts Cheetah Breeding Station situated west of Pretoria in the northern foothills of the Magaliesberg Mountains when a single King Cheetah cub was born from a common spotted cheetah.

De Wildts had been given the key by Nature's way to breed this most beautifully marked animal. Their captive programme continued its success by keeping track of the gene carrier's bloodline and over the years more King Cheetahs have been born.

It is well documented that captive cheetahs when returned to the wild do not survive in areas where wild cheetahs are present. There is one experiment waiting in the wings; that of using a spotted fostered wild mother, like Petal, to accept a young King Cheetah or other spotted orphaned cub or cubs of similar age to her own.

With careful husbandry this natural process, I know, would work. The purest behaviourists scoffed at my suggestion; their remarks bore the markings of derailed thinking. Introducing an aberration into the system was frowned upon! King Cheetahs had been sighted in the wild in Zimbabwe, Zambia, Kruger Park and Mozambique. I was once shown a piece of skin by an old Maasai honey hunter in the Loita Hills of the Mara. His father, he claims, found this animal in a snare and despatched it—believing it to be a young leopard. Much of the hair on the skin, I noticed, had been rubbed away over time—it had served as an underside cover in his cradle-like bed. The old boy was not prepared to part with this piece of jaded looking family heirloom, but having examined it closely it could well have been the pelt of a King Cheetah.

The Loita is distributed with well-wooded and open forest glades; more suited to the leopard. What caught my eye were the clear cut black stripes either side of the long spinal ridge that suggested at least another melanistic variant. Who was to say that King Cheetahs never inhabited the Mara at one time or another? The hard line of science was again, to my thinking, too negative and unyielding not to sanction this experiment of reintroducing the King Cheetah to Kenya's Maasai Mara. Petal was the 'key'. In a few years this valuable 'tool' would be past her prime and in the process of losing her instincts of motherhood.

Retirement comes early in the life of a female cheetah; conception wanes after the third or fourth litters. Longevity depends on health and a good deal of luck in the art of survival. Sarcoptic mange, a common debilitating disease in cheetahs unless treated early, becomes a constant drain on their stamina—it can also kill.

I have often found, while out after sundown living rough with Petal each in the others company resting or catnapping, when our sentries the crickets suddenly stop their chirpings that we both awaken simultaneously ears tuned to our surroundings. I seldom if ever carry a rifle; I trust implicitly in my small powerful pressurised fire extinguisher—the heaviest item in my backpack. This piece of equipment has proved its worth many times over though Petal finds it terrifying when used in anger. She has come to accept that it is part of my defence system. Petal and I have often battled male lions, a lioness with cubs objecting to our transit through their territory, buffalo, elephants and a spitting cobra at close range. Could I have survived without this unusual piece of scaremongery? I doubt it!

Countless hyaenas to our amusement have been startled out of their wits by the thick white jet mixed with a touch of ammonia that travels a good twenty yards at high speed when fired at the aggressor. This calls for quick and accurate reactions on my part. Petal at the very first sight of this object has long taken off into the sticks leaving me to face the adversary. At close quarters this extinguisher is an extremely effective tool and has also been used effectively against poachers. The principle behind not carrying a rifle is that I trust my tried and tested survival instincts. The risk factor of encountering an 'ambush' is effectively reduced if the senses are in tune with the surroundings as one tracks along.

Wild animal droppings and spoor all tell an instant tale of how recently which animal had passed. Look ahead for the path the animal is taking and your mind will assimilate and draw the picture of the unseen around you. Take note of the direction of the wind, stop and listen, scent the smell in the air and listen to the birds, particularly oxpeckers for they signal the presence of buffalo, my most feared wild animal. Avoid thick bush; skirt around it. Elephants can be noisy when feeding in forested areas. Their communication rumblings during the day and night are certain give-aways, but when on the move they are the silent giants of the night; their padded feet cushion the sound of their passing, almost inaudible to the human ear even at close quarters.

Carry a rifle and your courage and confidence is bolstered. Remember fear is the best medicine for survival. If one has no fear then over confidence will soon lead you to your maker. The natural reaction is to shoot, that is what the rifle is for; you shoot—your shot is slightly off the vital mark and that animal is now wounded and crazed!

Unless you are a professional with years of experience the chances are you or someone with you will soon die. Show me a professional hunter who claims he has no fear! There are none, they are all dead. A wounded wild animal can be terrifying and very dangerous.

The radio.com crackled. It was Kibet reporting his arrival at the airstrip and enquiring my whereabouts. I briefed him about the pride of lions and the route we should take back to camp. I informed him there was no sign of Petal or Namibia and believed they may have skirted the lion area. The presence of these lions might have put a stop to Namibia's constant chirpings and I hoped he would be wise enough to know that his amorous conversation with his bride could attract unwanted attention. This is when some cheetah males can be caught off guard; so engrossed are they in their songs of love that caution and safety is thrown to the winds. Petal's level head would have steered them clear, though I sensed she had not yet reached the hills.

Now I must head for the airstrip keeping an eye open and picturing in my mind the various locations of the surrounding wildlife. On my return the repositioning of the wildlife, the distance moved and their body language might suggest the presence of a predator in the area. I felt Astra could not be too far away. I listened and could hear the distant droning of an approaching aircraft; it is a clear blue sky today and the air temperatures are rising. Our clients will have had a bumpy flight from Nairobi. All that is left is for the Captain or his co-pilot to make a safe landing. Kibet has been busy checking the airstrip for ant-bear holes; they appear overnight, are difficult for the pilot to avoid and can spell disaster for any aircraft undercarriage. Wildlife must be chased well clear of the runway and aircraft will not land until the 'ground staff' have cleared the approach. Several low-level runs over the airstrip during the wildebeest migration are not uncommon.

Passengers often get a memorable birds-eye view of one of the greatest spectacles of wildlife migration on earth moving north and flooding into Kenya's Maasai Mara from the vast Serengeti plains in Tanzania. The migration arrives most years in mid-July and departs south again in mid-October. This is high tourist season and prime time to visit the Mara.

Flying in the DC.3 is a special treat for my airline clients. A little bit of the Captain's 'personal touch' goes a long way; he is a long-standing friend and often communicates with me on our air to ground radio when overhead and when I'm in the bush walking with Petal. They are always concerned knowing that my airline crew must get back to base on time, no matter what the weather. Never once did these superb Air Kenya pilots ever fail me. On many occasions I thought the storms in the vicinity would defeat them as dark was setting in and with no runway lights except our own Landcruiser headlights at both ends of the runway to guide them in. This was their only visual aid to landing in heavy rain—somehow they always made it!

The DC.3 had touched down and was now taxiing towards us, its twin engines making a confident popping sound as the rich mixture applied on the approach to landing burns off under pressure in the cylinders. These are nostalgic sounds to the ears of any pilot who has flown this reliable aircraft.

My clients disembark. Captain Ian Cowie gives me the thumb-in-mouth sign from the cockpit; this sign indicates there is mail and camp food supplies on board for me. My clients are a young crew, two men and six ladies. It always amazes me that it's the hostesses who are the ones with get up and go; always full of spirit and ready for any adventure!

Some of the men come along as 'chaperones' or could it be the other way around? Everything, including today's weather has the makings of a pleasant and friendly two-night three-day safari. Kibet has placed their baggage near the vehicle. Safari duffel bags are easy to stack and fit snugly into the luggage compartment. Everyone is responsible to ensure their bag is loaded into the vehicle. Four passengers are carried in each vehicle specially constructed with open-sided bodies and canvas pull-downs on one side and sliding windows on the other. There are two spacious roof hatches large enough to accommodate two standing persons comfortably. The sides of the hatches are well padded with foam to absorb any bruising from sudden stops—very important where ladies are concerned!

We drive alongside the runway and chase away any nearby wildlife; finally turning around and signalling with or headlights towards the pilot—this is the 'all clear' for take off. Headlights left on high beam with hazard lights flashing indicates 'no go'. It is an unwritten law and out of courtesy that we always wait until the aircraft takes off and becomes fully airborne. It is a thrilling sound when a DC.3 passes directly overhead with engines at full throttle.

Now is the time for checking out cameras—'what no film?' How often this happens!

Everyone is fired up with great expectations and now the really hard work starts for me. My nights out with Petal and me sleeping in the camper have not been wasted; a picture has formed in my mind and I know where to look for the various prides and single lions;

Full moon over the Aitong Hills (above). Petal's brothers check out a static postbox whilst others check out my mobile postbox (left).

When the moon is full mankind and Nature are as one.
Its phases dictate a pattern of life beyond our understanding.

and where the zebra and wildebeest are grazing—these are the likely places that the 'daylight' lion hunts will take place, mostly during early morning or late evening. A moonlight night also has added advantages for all the predators. During full moon the herds tend to graze rather than rest and they move unwittingly into the traps set by the lions. When walking with Petal I prefer the black starlit nights when the predators call out their hunting positions after dusk and before dawn. During full moon the African night can be silent and dangerous.

When the moon is full—mankind and nature are at one. Its phases dictate a pattern of life in ways beyond our comprehension, exacting a primordial rhythm on all earth's living things. Tonight the moon will be late in rising; the early evenings will be as dark as pitch, alive with the sounds of the African wilds.

We set off along the Mara River; groups of hippopotamus in mid-stream grunt their disapproval at our presence—their loud protests never fail to amuse visitors.

There is constant competition among the bulls, each jealously guarding their stretch of river. At night near camp, male hippos fighting for dominance and control over their grazing rights can be an adrenalin pumping experience for guests and staff. Terrible wounds are frequently inflicted on each other by their large tusks, which protrude like forklifts! These tusks can impale and with one chomp can sever a human in two from jaws which when opened, resemble a mechanical grab. Some say a hippo is more dangerous to man than a buffalo! Everyone is entitled to their own opinion! Always be careful when standing on the shoulder of the river bank when observing these huge aquatic mammals; be alert for should the bank cave in under the weight of the group the consequences to any one or all toppling into the river is unthinkable—the chances of survival are almost nil.

I remember a sickening and terrifying moment when a middle aged woman on safari with me and part of a group of ten were standing on the river bank edge. My inner lights were flashing danger. I asked everyone to step back a little and as I spoke this lady had an epileptic fit, lost her balance and fell forward. Kibet was standing closest to her, by some miracle of his split second reaction he grabbed at her khaki bush jacket belt. Both were now suspended for that fleeting second in mid fall. Several others and I grabbed at Kibet and between us our chain link pulled both of them to the side of the bank. We hauled them up; my immediate task was to prize open her mouth with a twig; place her on her front and slap her back hard; my concern was that she might swallow her tongue and choke. I was disturbed that I knew nothing in advance of her medical problem, she had made no mention of it on her confidential medical sheet which every client must complete, for when in my care I take their lives in my hands.

Decisions are made by me where the red line is and how close to this is safe. This incident was a perfect example of how one can be caught out; in the excitement of the mornings outing she had forgotten to take her medication—that simple mistake nearly cost Kibet his life.

Leaving the hippos to continue their snortings we embarked once more to look for 'mamba' the Swahili word for crocodile. Mamba can also refer in Swahili to the mamba snake, black or green; both are deadly and the Mara has its fair share of them. I'm a great believer in taking along a snake catcher—a member of the camp crew. He is our tent attendant once employed by Jonathan Leakey the famous herpetologist. Between him and the 'securicor', (the banded mongoose) they do an excellent job in camp. To my mind these people and the mongoose are a breed of their own; outstanding in detecting the presence of snakes in forested areas. On one short game viewing walk of less than a kilometre our 'snook spotter' caught several species ranging from 'the ten minute and you're dead' type, if bitten, to the harmless thin green tree snake.

Never once could I say, "There's one"! It was embarrassing to admit I could not see even one and to be told "there it is a few feet away looking at you". This was enough to make me turn cold, feel decidedly uneasy and ready to put as much distance as possible between 'it' and flee with the rest of the group.

I have an inbuilt fear of snakes, and believe most sane people have; simply because we have no idea whether they are poisonous or not! I personally take the easy way out by believing all snakes are deadly. Use the fire extinguisher, light the taper, squirt and run is my policy! In my youth my father taught me never to pick up corrugated iron sheets that had lain on the ground, stacked or singly for any length of time. Sure enough when the pieces were moved there was a snake coiled up ready to strike. In those early days I had not invented the fire extinguisher method of self-protection, but in later years many opportunities availed themselves to test out the effectiveness and to my surprise when fired in the direction of the snake's head caused it immediate and temporary blindness. Those fleeting seconds would provide the opportunity to either kill it or do the next best thing—get out of its way. Yes, once bitten no wonder I became twice shy!

Crocodiles are the next on our sightseeing agenda. The Mara River flows westwards and finally into Lake Victoria, home to some of the world's largest crocs. They are monsters!

My parents often took trips on the lake steamer; it was part of the Kenya Railways network to inaccessible places. As children we would enjoy the night train to Kisumu and then take the steamer up to Lake 'Namasagali' and beyond. I remember clearly an old man called 'Katembo'—he was from the Luyha tribe that lives on the lake shore—a fisherman by trade who had his own tourist attraction. The steamer anchored offshore and Katembo would paddle his dugout to the ship, collect his fee from the onlookers and paddle back to shore, then in a loud booming voice he would call out the name of this incredibly huge crocodile "Temboo". "Tembo-o-o". He claimed the reptile was over a hundred years old. Then out of the water this monster would appear, dragging its huge frame up the gently sloping bank to within a few feet of him. Large chunks of meat were thrown into this monster's open jaws— it was like feeding a furnace; the beast had no teeth and swallowed whole each carefully measured chunk—bones and all.

Years later I recall reading a scientific experiment at a zoo in the USA; they force fed an elephant that had lost the last of its seven ten-year cycle of new teeth, rendering it toothless after eighty years of age. It was claimed she had reached her century; I guess the crocodile's longevity was due to the same factor. These true stories fascinated my visitors.

Crocodiles remain high on my list of dangerous reptiles. Petal and I have seen them moving territory across country a fair distance from any river. Hippos also trek across land at night but must seek shade during the day to avoid life-threatening sunburn. We walked along the river path and circled back around its oxbow—Kibet had already inflated the compact three-man dinghy at the river's narrowest point to allow us to cross back to where we had disembarked from the vehicle. With the wild stories of hippos, crocs and snakes still fresh in our tourists' minds, we boated across the river by hauling on a rope fixed to a stump on the opposite side; this made for more excitement and a shorter way rather than the hour-long walk back along the same route. There are several hours of daylight left to cruise around the foothills in the hopes of finding Petal and Namibia, her Prince. The news is already out that the Queen has left for her 'honeymoon' in the hills of Aitong. This thought conjures up different fantasies in each of our minds for it is something very special, very private, and very beautiful. It provides a kick-start for the future and pleasant memories for human couples. Love is one of the most powerful forces presented to us by our maker; it bonds us to our mate, to our offspring and to our parents. We humans would like to believe the same is true in the wild animal world—but there is a difference!

The cheetah male in the wild has one duty, that is to procreate, and the female bears his children. Her sole duty is to rear and protect his protégé and defend them with claw and fang. After copulation the father deserts her to pollinate other flowers in his territory; establishing himself as the worthy bearer of his genes. The male has little to do with the upbringing of his offspring. Nature in her wisdom will know when his time is up; another king will come to town to try and unseat him. He knows his time is short; he must keep busy—this is the way of the cat family in the wild! Time was marching on and we still had to visit the hills where Petal was last seen heading towards and to check the small copse of leleshwa where I had left the lions dozing under a tree. Despite our searchings we saw no sign of the courting couple. We headed for Euphorbia Hill.

Nyundu, our mechanic, had driven and positioned the camper and trailer from camp accompanied by Andrew the cook and waiter; both had dressed up in their white uniforms to await us in this area. Folding tables, camp chairs, white tablecloths and soft drinks were set up in readiness for our arrival. The all-important toilet and canvas wash basins for the ladies and a separate one for the gents were placed out of sight. The view from this very pleasant cool and comfortable premier site overlooked the lion copse.

On our arrival at Euphorbia Hill named for is proliferation of the monkey puzzle type cactus trees, we were greeted by our camp comedian, Andrew, the cook, acting out the part of Aladdin and his magic lamp. "Your wish is my command" he says proudly, bowing towards the spotless tablecloth neatly set out with silverware, crockery and chairs to seat all ten of us.

This unexpected surprise lunch treat in the middle of nowhere set the mood and the safari off to a good start. Lunch was delicious, no flies, no dust, just clean cool fresh air all to the sound of music—not the tape-recorded stuff; but the birds—they were happy and singing their hearts out for us as they knew their reward would soon come—Andrew would attend to that with the crumbs from his delicious oven baked bread.

After resting a while it was time to head for camp some ten minutes drive to a large copse that housed ten spacious mosquito proofed tents each containing two single beds with toilet and shower attached. Bed boards are an important option, (it is amazing how many people demand these), together with high density foam mattresses, sheets and pillows, including that essential warm blanket that is not too heavy but just right. There are large side window flaps that can be zipped up to ones liking; all planned to give a good night's sleep. This is 'camp walkabout time', where clients can familiarise themselves with their surroundings.

An afternoon rest is encouraged, either in a hammock or a deck chair, even a mattress can be laid out on the lawn. No creepy crawlies here! A spray of eco-friendly liquid pyrethrum across the lawn lasts for several weeks keeping away unwanted biting insects and mosquitoes.

Four o'clock is teatime; an English tradition of Kenyan tea and a choice of pancakes, scones and Swiss rolls, with cream for the non-calorific minded—all baked and presented by Andrew from his magic tin trunk.

At five o'clock it is time for the wheels to start turning once again, the afternoon heat has cooled—this is the time the wildlife ventures out from shaded resting places.

The predators are awake and planning their tactics, for they are hoping that dinner will not elude them again tonight; their prey instinctively knows where the lions are during the day, but when darkness falls the plains game are at their mercy.

As the African sun dips gently down towards the horizon, there is that mesmerising half-hour of the red and gold wash which flares up from the western sky; the zebras and the wildebeest then distance themselves from the forest clumps that hide their enemies. The night will bring a life or death game of hide and seek. For the plains game the night is long and the constant vigil becomes tiring for the zebra stallions constantly guarding their female herds. The wildebeest bulls have spent much of the day exhausting their energy cavorting and snorting their challenges to possible male intruders of their kind who show the slightest intent of luring any frolicking female from their cluster.

The clients are keen to see the lions but there is still clear soft light for photographing giraffe, elephant and buffalo against the setting sun. A herd of some fifteen female elephants with young can be seen moving slowly through a nearby swamp heading our way; they will pass close to us and hopefully will be unconcerned by our presence. A huge male is in attendance at the rear of the group flapping his ears in a mock charge at us as he passes by— he is enormous; his frame towers above us. My clients have been briefed; the Landcruiser motor is switched off; at the sign of any abnormal aggressive behaviour from him towards us I will hit the starter button. This always produces the right reaction, surprised at the noise he backs off trumpeting loudly, we too back off; this immediate manoeuvre satisfies his macho status and telegraphs our body language to him that we have understood and obeyed his command. Elephants will charge head on and can severely damage a vehicle by ramming their tusks through the radiator or side; it takes but one push to roll the vehicle over onto its side.

An experienced safari driver first senses the mood of the group and must instinctively identify the matriarch or the dominant bull. By reading their body language he then knows the limits to which he can proceed towards them with safety. I prefer to pick my spot ahead of a moving group with my back to the light and let them decide their track. This method usually provides head-on photography both for video and still cameras. There is something more dramatic about a photo other than just taking pictures of elephants from the side or of their rear ends. If the elephants are comfortable with your presence they will pass close by; the thrill of finding one's self right in the middle of the herd and being accepted by them as part of the furniture is a humbling experience to be remembered.

This is what game parks and reserves are about; generally the wildlife is visitor oriented. There are rules designed to protect the environment from degradation and the wildlife from undue harassment. The 'do's and don'ts' are being strictly enforced within the game parks. Getting too close to wildlife is now frowned upon with spot fines for transgressions.

Long-running digital video recorders with plenty of zoom, good binoculars and a telescopic camera lens are a recommended part of safari equipment in these modern times.

It is now 6.30 p.m. on the equator and the last moment of the African sun has disappeared; the high cirrus cloud reflects its rippled orange effect upward from the horizon.

This is the time to visit the lion pride; they will be on the move fanning out from the day's resting-place and hopefully their cubs will be with them. The reflection on the clouds provides a wonderful colour backdrop for any amateur photographer to just select the lever to automatic and let the camera do the figuring out; avoiding if possible the flash that an automatic selection can produce, if the light is too low. I am not a professional photographer but can boast many pictures that have won acclaim just by correct backlight positioning and letting the camera do the rest.

The lions are still where I expected them to be; I am surprised at the total count of seventeen which is more than I had first envisaged but better still, they were moving in the direction of our camp! Not good news for Andrew but good news for our visitors. Picture taking completed we relaxed and viewed the lions from a distance through binoculars. It was important now to leave them alone and not disturb their plans for the night; the cubs could do with a square meal and with the wind into their faces and their body language suggesting their hunt could be successful—there is purpose in their minds. I took a wide circuit down wind of them and move towards our camp making sure our lingering human smell and diesel fumes did not pollute their acute powers of smell. Lions, like other cats, have good sensitive light absorbing cells but it is the leopard that possesses the amazing ability to see in the dark, better than most other diurnal predators.

We arrived back at camp to find an inviting log fire awaiting us. A hot shower followed by drinks with cashew nuts and salted crisps brings us all together to chat about the days adventures. Dinner is served early under the stars, roast potatoes, roast chicken with the stuffing of herbs and mint with 'posho' (an African maize meal dumpling) served with delicious gravy, chopped onions, freshly cooked vegetables and peas. Andrew's home-made newly baked bread and rolls with a touch of garlic all go towards making a delicious meal; choice wines are also available for the discerning. There is a selection of sweets; crème caramel with a sauce of Andrew's recipe which is 'secret to him alone'! Sherry trifle with cream and custard is always a treat for those from the continent—it never fails to satisfy. I seldom interfere with the menu; Andrew plans it all including the vegetarian dishes. After dinner we retire to the camp-fire; the clear cloudless African night displaying its sparkling jewels in the sky has no comparison—this is paradise!

The scene is now set for an evening's sing-along, from story telling to an African music and dance jig acted out by the camp staff. Their instruments are home-made; necessity is the mother of invention here—a comb and paper, a ribbed soda bottle stroked with a steel knife sharpener makes good rasping sounds; a bucket with a taught goat skin cover improvises as an excellent tom-tom drum; a string bow pressed firmly on a hollow wooden box when strummed omits a base sound just like the real thing; several glass tumblers filled with varying levels of water tapped with a fork, plus a sprinkling of the true African rhythm hummed in unison, produces a catchy foot-tapping tune. I am always ready to encourage our visitors to participate. The staff enjoy the hilarious uninhibited solo visitor performances particularly those that depict the days major moments of fear and laughter experienced out in the wild. The 'ants in your pants' jig is always a winner.

The lions are quiet; a sign that they are still hunting. Soon they will announce their success by roaring in unison. This is their signal for their handsome king to come and feast. Midnight is an hour away—a time when everyone should be in bed. Adrenalin rushes, fresh air and recounting the day's events, soon brings on the need for a good night's sleep. The years in the bush have tuned my body time clock—sometimes I wonder why there is the necessity to carry a timepiece! Few Maasai are the proud owners of a watch but ask them the time of day and they will look at you with a sly grin knowing you are testing their bush clock. A quick glance at the sun's position in the equator sky and their shadow on the ground provides their estimate to within half an hour of accurate time.

What is half an hour or an hour in their lifestyle—no stress—no hurry, what cannot be done today can always be done tomorrow.

In contrast our western lifestyle and culture has regulated our daily activities to be driven by time. Somewhere in my makeup I am thankful to have been born free with a distaste for crowded cities with the rush of traffic, people always in a hurry with no time for themselves to unwind, while their body clock urges them on faster and faster towards a heart attack and early grave.

I now understand why my subconscious mind drove me to stop the school clock for a few hours just so that I could watch the pitiful chaos that followed. How easy it was to put a spanner in the works of human time, yet without it what a chaotic and muddled world it would be. I trust in my body clock to waken me and seldom do I use an alarm. Nature's time clock is considered the seventh sense that can be imprinted into the subconscious mind.

Before retiring for the night, everyone is briefed on the morning's activities. Clients are advised they will receive, tea, biscuits and a wake up call at 5.00 a.m., departure will be 6.00 a.m. sharp. Bush lunches or maybe dinners out under the stars are always announced each morning. These exciting feeding times depend on the activities planned for the day. Most importantly, Andrew the cook is briefed on the times with regular updates from me. Radio contact from the field keeps him happy and us from ruined meals.

I am awakened by a grunt close by my tent situated on the outer perimeter of the camp settings. If it were a leopard, I would have heard a cough or a rasping sound as in hand-sawing wood, but I know the sound I really heard in my subconscious sleep was that of a lioness gently calling her cubs. My guess is that it must be about 3.00 a.m. when most other humans are in their deepest sleep—there is no danger. I lie wide-awake listening intently, the night is still and cold, the crickets have long gone to sleep and so has the Maasai night watch! Let him be, he may soon get a rude awakening for his sins!

There is activity outside. The lioness could have positioned her cubs in a thicket near my tent prior to participating in a hunt and has now come back to fetch them—dinner must not be too far away. There has been no roaring to call for big daddy yet; the ladies will feed their offspring and themselves first, for when their father arrives he will take all.

It is now 5.00 a.m. and I am dozing; wake-up call is only half an hour away though I sense there will be no need for this. I hear footsteps—Morani the Maasai watchman, has come to my tent, I call his name gently before he even speaks; he acknowledges and tells me the lions are feeding some one hundred yards away from camp. The kill was made about an hour ago—that fits into the jigsaw in my mind. "Soon they will call," he says. I am pleased Morani has not been asleep—he like me had tuned into the situation. Morani is told to stoke up the camp-fire. I shall be along and will join him there in ten minutes; meanwhile he should awaken the kitchen staff and stoke the hot water boiler ready for distribution to the wash buckets outside the tents.

It is now 5.30 a.m. and I am still hoping the pride will roar to signal their position to others before retiring to the nearby forest after their meal. As if planned the still moments before the dawn erupt into a nerve tingling reverberating cacophony of sound that no one in their right mind could sleep through. Our wake up call has arrived spot on time.

For the uninitiated the sound of lions roaring in unison, then followed by their out of step crescendo is frightening. 'Close' is an under statement, it is as if the show is right in camp. I walk the length of the camp tents announcing "Time to get up". "You're joking," they say; I continue "Wakey-wakey, rise and shine". Hot water is poured into their verandah buckets and this act alone triggers that 'get up and go' feeling. I announce "Tea and biscuits will be served at the camp fire in five minutes"!

The African dawn is less than a half-hour away. It's a wonderful sight to behold as we board our vehicles; viewing hatches open with drivers at the ready. There are no 'tail end Charlies' this morning. Everyone is in top gear and ready to go thanks to Leo's early wake up call. Prior to departure I check my list of priorities. Number 1—very important that each vehicle carries a full two-pack toilet roll—one for the men and one for the ladies. Visitors need only ask, for there are several 'sit-me-downs' positioned at strategic places within 'get me there in a hurry' distance. There is nothing worse than when nature calls miles from the camp. Don't panic, we have our own private thunder boxes tucked away neatly in the bushes. There could be unexpected surprises—one wag wrote on the underside of the toilet lid in black felt pen 'After fright please return and clean up your mess'!

We arrived at the lion kill to see not just one wildebeest but two had met their maker.

One had been completely devoured and the other partly eaten. Most of the eleven large adult females had gorged themselves and were flat on their backs with paws in the air. The remaining two sub-adult males were still feasting on the second; the four little cubs, about three months old, were being cuffed and bullied by their cousins for being out of pecking order! There was much squealing and growling from the four little chaps, calling for their mother to come and restore order and oblige by opening up more tender parts to breakfast upon.

At this young age most lion cubs have been weaned and this is a difficult time for them if the kill is some distance away. The whole pride will participate in protecting the carcass from other predators until the cubs arrive.

Mysteriously the King of Beasts is not here, yet he was seen resting with the pride the previous day. I can only think he must be in hot pursuit of a female in season; it is seldom that there would be any other good reason for Leo to miss out on his second preference—food.

We are now alone with the lions and enjoy watching their unruly table manners! I will 'trade' our find should we meet up with another safari driver later on. I need to update my information on the whereabouts of other interesting subjects, such as cheetahs or mating lions! Our radio communication is not tuned into other lodge-based tourist vehicles, which tend to charge around from one sighting to another in a cloud of dust. My powerful binoculars can pick them out at a distance and I am usually able to distinguish the animal they have surrounded. There is no hurry to join them; let them be and when satisfied they too will leave their 'find' for us to view in undisturbed privacy.

In the distance I can see a cluster of lodge tourist vehicles surrounding a clump of bushes, not too far from where the pride of lions was resting yesterday. I guess this could be the father of the cubs we are presently watching. It appears he has more important business to attend to and would now be otherwise engaged, food being the last thought on his mind for the next three or four days! Eventually, hunger will drive them both not so much to hunt themselves but to take advantage of the pride's capability of providing a meal within reasonable walking distance. The King must save his energy over the next five-day honeymoon. Finally the copulation peaks at the rate of one mount every fifteen minutes—the male is at the mercy of the female's whim—she dictates 'when'. How often have the male members of my group laughed out loud, no doubt they are relating in their minds to the look of complete exhaustion on the King of Beast's face which clearly says "Oh no, not again"! With all due respect he always makes the effort on demand!

I shall not forget one mating incident that occurred and was witnessed by several middle aged married couples from the United States. Their aircraft pickup was delayed by bad weather out of Nairobi and so we had an hour to spare. A safari driver had called at the airfield to check on the estimated time of arrival of the aircraft. Over my air-to-ground radio-com I could speak with any pilot in the area and obtain the information he required.

In exchange for this information the driver mentioned the presence of mating lions not too distant from the airstrip. With time in our favour we drove off in the direction he pointed—we soon found the spot. The male was a young short-maned four-year-old Mara lion; inexperienced and totally out of his depth in the ways of making love—or so we thought!

To my surprise his partner was a mature lioness almost twice his age. We all came to the unanimous conclusion that he was having his first lesson from her in this age-old art. Little did we realise that this 'hot shot' had another much younger piece of snippet hidden out of sight of the senior lioness behind a large bush some forty yards away. This came to light when, having dismounted her, he strutted off in that direction. It was clear that he had been back and forth several times before. Whilst he was out of sight the streetwise lady took a short walk and peered around the bush to see what this other attraction was. We instinctively knew that the scene before us was about to erupt into a real 'domestic' of great proportions. Her immediate reaction to inflict grievous bodily harm upon the young couple was overruled by her maturity and cunning. She returned to her bed and waited for this two-timer. Expectancy was at its peak; my clients were quivering with excitement. 'Hot Shot' strolled up to her once again and she made to crouch as in normal acceptance; in fact her positioning was so that she could deliver the knock out punch that connected full blast to the side of his face. The impact was such that the force of the blow catapulted him through the air onto his back. It could have been a re-enactment of a bedroom scene taken from the movie 'Revenge is Sweet'—the seething boxtress then strolled off flicking her tail in total disgust. The punishment had been painfully dispensed and our flattened gigolo could only holler for her forgiveness. My clients were in hysterics and almost sick with laughter. "Let that be a lesson dear husbands, the law of the jungle will prevail in our homes from now onwards"! Such was the good-humoured banter between husbands and wives—women's liberation had come of age today! Andrew the cook would have sold his treasured magic tin trunk to have witnessed this 'affair' for inclusion in his next comic act.

The new dawn had given way to shards of sunlight that pierced the eastern sky; soon its heat would dry off the morning dew. From this position I could see the Maasai cattle herders moving their cattle out of their corrals for the leisurely trek across the plains to the nearest watering hole. Lions on seeing this will retreat into cover for the rest of the day.

It was time for us to move along to the high point 'look out'. Petal must be out there somewhere! If we could only find her it would make the safari a memorable one for all of us. I must meet once more with her to hold a picture in my mind for the period I would be away. My instinct was telling me to head for Euphorbia Hill. I had heard from the lodge drivers that a female leopard and her two semi-adult cubs could often be seen at this time of the morning lying high up in the acacia trees. This vantage-point provided mother and her family with a shady look-out post over the plains below; an ideal cover to watch unwary gazelles grazing close to their offspring hidden in the grass.

Many a tour driver has passed by these acacia trees; indeed they have parked under them only to find themselves and their clients staring directly into the eyes of a leopard hidden in total camouflage amongst the foliage above them! To avoid this frightening experience it is wise to first focus on the tree from a short distance away through binoculars and look for the tell-tale signs of what appears like a thin dislodged branch hanging three to four feet vertically down from the underside of the foliage. The chances are almost certain this could be the tail of a leopard; also take a closer look around any branch forks high up in the underside of the canopy; you may sometimes find the leopard's dinner cunningly fixed in the fork out of harms way—there the carcass will stay to be dined upon at leisure.

From our present position with the lions I noticed Kibet had his binoculars firmly fixed on one of the acacia trees. He glanced directly across at me with a look that I knew suggested we move in that direction. He obviously had seen something that required closer inspection—Kibet then moved forward. Radio communications between us is kept to the absolute minimum except when we are traversing in different areas and out of sight of each other. A quick flash of headlights when in sight of the other would suggest a find of some interest; lights full on would be read as 'Please make urgent radio contact with me when the moment is right', meaning 'Don't let the whole world hear the message—move away if you have other company'. These are our visual codes. Both Kibet and I prefer to separate on our game drives; the habit of following the leader, as many do, has little purpose! It is fun for the clients to talk about what they saw and what was missed when we meet up. There is always a little vying for 'top cat' between Kibet and I; this I encourage for I have every respect for his quiet and thorough bush knowledge. He knows too, should he slacken his grip for one moment, his mentor will smile a knowing 'crocodile smile' that maybe it's time he should visit an optician! I too am kept on the ball.

At the end of the day I often admit a little defeat by saying, "Well done Kibet. That was super 'sana', top class". It always gave me great pleasure to see his smile and his knowing look which said it all "One up for me today boss"!

Kibet was now stationary on the hill; I was preparing to move when the radio-com crackled. What he had spotted was in fact a fresh carcass of an adult female gazelle hanging in the fork of one of the acacia trees. There was no sign of the leopard but a small portion of the kill had been eaten suggesting the killer was nearby—would I care to join him in the search?

I had heard a few tummy rumbles issuing from my clients which indicated that breakfast time and that 8 o'clock feeling was soon approaching for some. Leopards are difficult to find and if located score top of the 'Big Five' list. This opportunity to see one must not be missed and moving in too close would send it deeper into hiding. I knew the layout of the area, the grass was short, but there were islands of thick, tall swamp-grass and for sure it would be in hiding there. If we waited at a distance and watched our patience might well be rewarded. Kibet agrees; this could be a long wait but my inner sense told me that 'chui' (the Swahili word for leopard), would also be having tummy rumbles and like us, be ready for breakfast. I radio-called camp and Andrew the cook answered—always happy to oblige. I gave him two options; the first, being so close to camp we could arrive in ten minutes or less; have breakfast—that would take a good hour or more—then dash out once again. The second option that seemed a better bet, was for the camp mechanic to hook up the covered trailer, which carried all the necessary folding tables and camp chairs to the caravan that already contained all the necessary plates and utensils, and bring it to us.

"No problem" was Andrew's reply "I will bring breakfast to feed ten people as well as Kibet and yourself. The camp staff need exercise, they are getting fat"! Andrew was ready for a challenge; sudden requests like this could ruin any cooks day, but the previous day's lunch had confirmed that eating out in style was definitely a popular idea which received instant approval from our visitors. Breakfast today would be in the 'bush', with a chance to get out of the vehicles and stretch legs. There was an ideal spot I knew of some three hundred yards downwind amongst a cluster of leleshwa bushes that overlooked the leopard's larder and very importantly a convenient and secluded toilet within a short distance out of view of everybody. Each of us would take turns to monitor the tree; all that we required now was for the breakfast caravan to arrive.

I suggested that should this beautiful beast appear we would hold back and let it settle in the tree. The timing to move quietly forward in our respective vehicles would be critical, bearing in mind that if he or she was unaccustomed to vehicles the chances of a close up snap would be slim. Leopards are very shy in daylight and our only hope would be to enjoy the sight through our binoculars. Some of the video camcorders also had excellent zooming quality. The lodge tour vehicles, unaware of our find, would be heading home soon taking their clients for their breakfast and hopefully then we would have the place to ourselves. I could see Kibet willing the leopard to appear. This would be the 'ace' of the day for him; he was not alone—if there were such a thing as communal will-power then this little group of ours would not fail him.

Kibet pointed to a moving cloud of dust coming from the direction of camp. Andrew and his team were on their way. Kibet flashed his lights towards them; the signal was returned acknowledging that our whereabouts had been noted—breakfast was on its way! Soon we were all helping to off load tables and camp chairs and setting up the site in the shadiest spot we could find. Andrew was busy in the caravan attending to his three-burner gas stove and grill. On the menu was bacon and eggs, scrambled egg, omelette, boiled egg, toast and cereals, orange or apple juice or grapefruit, even bananas—everyone to their own order and tastes. A bush breakfast is always great fun; the two mess tent waiters were dressed in their white uniforms, which provided the right ambience to the five star silver-service. Cameras clicked and videos whirred, each photo and film would take its place in the archives of their owners' homes and minds. These are the pleasant reminders that bring back memories of happy days once shared on safari with good friends.

The best of Kenyan coffee and tea does not go unnoticed; for many it always tastes better in the bush. If one carries coffee in personal baggage overseas be sure the smell of coffee will attract the drug sniffer-dogs like bees to honey! If push came to shove I suppose coffee could legally be classed as a drug—which it is! I wish I were a cartoonist I could draw the hilarious picture I see in my mind. I've often noticed Petal's nostrils pleasurably twitching from the aromatic odours of coffee wafting out of my thermos flask while on our short walkabouts. When in her company I am careful to avoid scented soaps, particularly after-shave that sends her into fits of sneezing. Thank goodness I don't suffer from hay fever or we would both make a miserable pair.

Breakfast had gone down well. Andrew was congratulated for his outstanding efforts; job offers for his services were jokingly pledged by the clients although he was unsure how his magic 'trunk' would cook in their arctic conditions overseas! However he was willing to try, "But would his future employer be able to accommodate and feed his three wives and twelve children" he asked? Few visitors realise that behind the scenes African polygamy is part of their pension in kind and the more children there are the better, in order to contribute to the family coffers, help plant and care for their half acre vegetable patch back in their Reserve. Surviving by hand to mouth is an art in itself; having a secure job and a considerate and caring employer begets loyalty. Many domestic employers are Kenyans like myself. Engage one employee and you take on another ten mouths to feed, plus their medical needs—the strain on the exchequer can be considerable.

Our watchful 'leopard' roster had fallen by the wayside. The object of the initial exercise had been temporarily shelved. It was now time to reinstate the lookout system and check out the surrounding scenery with our binoculars. I was not surprised when Kibet announced he could see several tails hanging down from the acacia tree that held the carcass and was sure he was not seeing double. Ten pairs of binoculars zoomed onto the subject—there was no doubt about it, two distinct tails could be seen hanging down—our spotted friends were having their breakfast! How long had they been there? Kibet was the last to check some fifteen minutes previously but saw nothing; now it was a matter of moving forwards slowly by stages in our vehicles. The stalk was on; we must remember to close our viewing hatches when coming to within fifty yards of the tree. It was a long call to expect the leopard family to stay with their kill—slowly we approached the tree.

I realised how clanky and noisy our Toyota diesel engines were and here we were trying to tiptoe forwards! The trick to lessen the noise is to engage low four-wheel drive and adjust the automatic accelerator to slow-run just above idle, then take your foot off all pedals; if the engine is tuned properly—forward movement will be constant and quiet. To stall and then have to restart spells disaster. The sudden high pitched engagement of a diesel Landcruiser starter can startle the most tourist-oriented wildlife let alone a leopard considered to be one of the most timid of cats. Let it not be said they are not dangerous; when cornered or angry, look out; this animal will charge at the speed of a rifle bullet and tear you to pieces, hence the absolute necessity to batten down the hatches and have cameras ready. Hatches were closed and I sensed any further movement forward would spoil the show; they would come down the tree and disappear in a flash.

We were now almost within thirty five yards and could see their forms clearly in the tree—not only were there two, but three—a mother and her two semi-adult cubs; this was a real treat for us; everyone was prepared to stay for as long as it took to get their photograph of the day. Speech was all in whispers and both the vehicles were in the best position for a clear view. The cubs were very hungry and paid little attention but Mother Leopard kept a very alert and watchful eye on us. Kibet was in his element; he wore a big smile—I gave him the thumbs up. Communication would from now on be by sign language only; we both turned off our radio-com. Any sudden loud communication could scuttle this 'find-of-the-day' to pieces. The two cubs were having a tug of war, each pulling at the carcass to get at the meaty part—any moment I expected it would give way and fall to the ground. Mother Leopard was anxiously aware of the developing situation but could not get between the two growling and warring cubs to reposition the carcass in a more secure position. The worst happened—the largest portion fell to the ground; the remaining piece held firmly by the victorious stronger male cub. The smaller cub was distraught. Mother acted in a flash—she came head first down the front of the tree took hold of the fallen carcass and instead of returning it back up the tree, to our surprise, she carried it past our stationary vehicles into the clump of swamp grass close beside us. My passengers were open-mouthed with awe at her beauty.

It all happened so quickly; we could hear her crunching on the bones yet being so close we could not see her. The younger of the two cubs, the female, fearful she would miss out, came down the tree trunk backwards. The intention was to join her mother in the tall grass; her brother meantime was quite content to be left alone in the tree with the prize that he had tugged and pulled at so hard to retain. The young female cub anxious to get to her mother appeared a little concerned at our presence and slunk past wide of our vehicles—we quietly opened the roof hatches. No one had managed to photograph the mother; but most obtained good pictures of the cub coming down the tree in reverse and everyone was well satisfied. The action they hadn't photographed would remain in their mind's eye but we all agreed the mother was a beautiful graceful predator. How could any amorous male leopard not be impressed? Her eyes were a pale shade of green soft and inviting! I felt a little too close and unsafe; Kibet and I agreed to move our vehicles a few yards further away. Would our noisy start up make her charge at us? We took the chance and circled the tall grass but there was not a sign of a sudden or aggressive confrontation. The young male had climbed higher into the underside of the acacia umbrella and was now almost invisible. A re-visit in the cool of the evening might just prove to be worthwhile. An hour and a half had passed; it seemed far less than that, we had been so engrossed! How time flies in such pleasant and exciting circumstances.

I was still pondering the decision the mother leopard had made in not returning her kill back up into the tree. Carrying the carcass into the tall swamp grass would surely attract hyaena, even lions, and without doubt vultures in double quick time. Her hideaway would be a give away. Maybe she would return to the leftovers after feeding her fill, but certainly she could not stay in her present place of sparse cover for long and must find shade.

The morning's game viewing had produced a 'high' and hopefully Leo and his bride were in a sufficient state of rapid fire that would stoke up even the most modest human libidos. Leo's outstanding endurance and unlimited stamina had to be admired. We returned to the mating couple.

Our arrival was greeted with disdainful stares from the courting pair but her need to be mounted 'on immediate request' was first priority—her momentary hot flush signalled the body temperature was ready. Her partner was a fine specimen, matured by years of protecting his genes. The battle scars on his face criss-crossed with the old and the recent—the King's full golden mane, worn like the head regalia of a Maasai warrior, placed him in the front-line of the dating game—a very handsome male indeed. Strong as he is there is always the danger, should a coalition of brothers enter his territory, there would be little this fine specimen could do to prolong his reign. Hc would have to clear out of the area very quickly to survive and hope that his offspring, during the next ninety to one hundred days, would not be slaughtered at birth by the visitors. Interestingly, but sadly, should there be a dethronement within the early period of conception the trauma of losing their King would, in most cases, trigger the female's body mechanism to abort their foetuses. When this occurs Nature will then play her next card within the coming ten days by preparing the mothers for introduction to the new bloodline.

The aborted females will come into oestrus once more. Those that already have young cubs of under three to four months will split from their female companions to avoid the terrible trauma of infanticide and try to safeguard their cubs by seeking out their banished King. He would still be ready to provide the anchor and security for each of the cub's mothers but would require to establish a new territory. The former King will be extra cautious not to voice his presence too loudly—few breakaways survive.

I have come across pockets of small prides; two females with several four month old cubs and a large male in attendance. By studying and reading their body language at close range from the caravan and listening from a distance while staying out with Petal at night I could hear other lions communicating with each other from afar. The split prides would remain totally silent, sharing their King's nervous disposition.

Acceptance of sisters and related other single younger lionesses into their pride appears less hazardous. These young lionesses are quickly recruited and serve their purpose as nannies. The cubs' parents can then hunt with some confidence knowing their offspring will be looked after and for this effort the aunty or nanny who otherwise would have to hunt alone would be permitted to partake in the feast. Humans would understand this as 'paid in kind for services rendered'. This is not so for the female cheetah; she selects her mate and will reject him if there is something that she senses is not quite right; the family bloodline could be too close; this is Nature's way of helping to steer her clear from the sins of inbreeding and a good reason for cheetah females to fight off advances from unwanted males. This is where research should seek to identify who the rejected males are. DNA would tell us whether they are close family. Who is Namibia? Where could he have come from? He is big and powerful and somehow different from our local cheetahs and may have travelled from afar.

At the time of writing only now has Kenya established a wild cheetah research programme. Let us hope those that seek to undertake research into this magnificent beast can provide the answer and put the brakes on its slide towards extinction. They must utilise all the knowledge and progress that science has made in the field of genetics, particularly in recent years.

While still with the mating couple, a wise-crack in our party broke the spell and jokingly announced that we were nothing but a bunch of peeping toms—voyeurism was bad for the heart if not treated in time and would all end up with double vision or something to that effect! This was the signal to head back to camp—I took the hint and we bade farewell to our courting lions. Andrew had laid on a 'pick-and-choose' cold buffet affair; cold meat, sweet potatoes in white sauce, lamb or chicken, salad, fresh oven baked bread rolls, crisp samosas with a choice of vegetables or 'pili pili ho ho' for those who have flame-proof tongues! Delicious chocolate pudding with cream and Swiss roll and custard, baked wild raspberry tart, bread pudding baked in golden syrup—one of my favourites—all cooked in a tin trunk and heated on charcoal embers!

The calorific value having catapulted itself clean off the chart would soon be shed after an evening game-viewing walk, but first an afternoon siesta was uppermost in everyone's mind. It was time to hit the canvas; the lunch had been just perfect. I too should rest but first I must send our two Maasai trackers to recce the walking route. The wildlife was not to be disturbed but the trackers needed to mentally record their whereabouts particularly the large pride of lions and those dangerous single or pairs of bull buffaloes, which make themselves invisible in any type of cover. I will never forget the incident when I was caught unawares.

Buffalo are the most dangerous animals on four legs. Quite recently with tragic results, a group of a dozen tourists from a lodge taking a guided walk with an armed ranger became very unstuck. Two buffaloes appeared out of nowhere and charged the walkers. The ranger leading the group dropped his gun and shinned up the nearest tree. Luckily for the walkers a three-foot deep storm water ditch they happened to be crossing saved their bacon; they threw themselves into it face down and their quick thinking saved them from certain death. One unfortunate lady, the tail-ender, paid the ultimate price. Dawdling along behind, she became detached from the group—that was where the buffalo attack came from. They have the cunning intelligence to allow their quarry to pass and then it's a case of 'mind your back!' Where have I heard that advice before?

There are many unanswered questions about the male cheetah. Is he partly to blame for some or all of the cause of the present breeding dilemma? The mortality of newly born cubs is high—many are stillborn. Could it be that the male sperm is flawed? There are telltale signs that this is so, particularly when sperm is viewed under the microscope—there are many bad swimmers with 'bent rudders'! I discussed this matter with a knowledgeable professor at a Cheetah Research Station in South Africa. There are swimmers and non-swimmers. "Imagine" he said, "you are a sperm participating in a fifteen metre swimming pool, your prize is an egg at the other end. The few that are strong and unflawed will get there first but those with bent rudders will go in circles and die en route. However, there will be those who might just make it. It is they which pass on their imperfections". If this situation can be rectified science could well be on the right track in solving part of the cheetah riddle—there appear to be more bent tails than good ones! Might this be how females can sense the good swimmers from the bad? It certainly is very thought provoking.

Elephants too have a natural trait to survive. Nature has introduced into their pyramid a core of breeding bulls and the bent ones are those that fire blanks. Nature's control mechanism is constantly at work and in the case of the wild cheetah, is it possible that Nature is asking for help? The future of the wild young female cheetah has complications. Having parted company with her mother on attaining adulthood the first signs of oestrus will drive her to wander the fringes of her mother's territorial range in search of a suitable unbent mate   somewhere out there is her father; will she recognise him—a parent she has never met before; how will she identify him? Her father took no further part in her upbringing since his honeymoon with her mother some two years ago. Could the penalty for incest be the continued slide of the species towards extinction?

The existence of Petal in her total wild state displaying her intelligence and understanding of her human foster father made me realise the very privileged position I was in. Our association with each other in the wilds to date had never really been achieved before with a free ranging wild cheetah. George and Joy Adamson's 'Born Free', the lioness of 'Elsa' fame came close to parallel this but Elsa was brought up and reared in a human home then returned to the wild. Pippa, Joy Adamson's cheetah, was a domesticated orphan—so too was her leopard. They were never returned to the wild!

Petal was born free in the wild and grew up as an orphan in the wild. Her instincts carried her through to adulthood. Agreed her survival was assisted in the initial stages by her foster father, for without food and my presence she and her brothers could not have survived in the wilds of Mara. Petal, in due course, will give me the truthful answers of many of the wide range of questions that remain unanswered. There are hundreds of research papers filed away in the archives of those who studied and wrote their Ph.D. theses on the subject of cheetahs. Why is it that so few of their findings are published?

As the days of pregnancy progress Petal may return to her mother's territory to seek out a den there or might she, for safety, choose a spot close to my camp? Petal's search for a safe place will become more frantic as she senses her pregnancy maturing towards her cubs' birthday. Ninety days gestation is a long lonely time for her to fend for herself particularly the exhausting final two weeks. This period takes courage and commitment to complete; her bursts of speed and long runs to capture her prey will cease during this period. She will switch her tactics to seeking out young gazelles or newly born fawns that lie hidden in the grass.

I was looking forward to my return to the Mara—a week would not pass without my thoughts wandering in that direction. I could feel my human instincts of a caring foster father kicking in, anxious for Petal's safety, hoping that her wanderings in search of a place to give birth would not take her into unfamiliar and dangerous territory.

Much as I would like to give myself a break from the exacting pressures of a safari outfitter I too had to consider my camp staff—all of whom had given solid service without complaint over six months at the camp away from their families and friends. They too, needed to go home for at least three months, Kibet included. All had saved their wages and tips and there was much to do to 'make and mend' back in their tribal homes. The rains were due— every available hand is needed to till their small plots of land and plant the seeds of their staple diet—maize and beans. Maintenance of thatched roofs and repairs to their mud huts will keep them busy.

Family bonds become very strong in continued employment. A considerate employer provides the stability in camp and that encourages harmony at camp and in their tribal homes. I encourage letter writing on a regular basis but because there are no post-boxes within thirty miles of the area, passing information by word of mouth via their friends and the 'bush telegraph' assists in maintaining their morale. There are not many land line telephones within easy reach, though the recent advent of instant mobile telephone communication has its advantages and sometimes disadvantages!

CHAPTER 7

GAME VIEWING ON FOOT

A briefing prior to any game-viewing walk is mandatory. The rules are important—never walk in thick bush—always keep a safe distance from the river. If there is forest keep to the visual rules that permit at least sixty yards of uninterrupted line of sight. I do not believe in walking line astern; I prefer two groups with a maximum of four persons in each and two spear wielding Maasai Moran experienced in bush craft; more importantly those who bear the scars of past deeds for this is the signature that guarantees they will not run if we are attacked! I employ two of these Morani braves selected over the years. One owes his life to the first aid I gave him after the incident with the young lioness, which munched on his father's young calf several years back. The other, his brother, had despatched single handedly an enraged female buffalo that had been severely clawed and wounded by a pride of lions.

Kaputei, the Morani, once recounted this incident to me. The buffalo had left a blood trail and he sensed an ambush had been laid for him in the thick bush ahead. It takes courage by any standards to even attempt a 'spear slaying' of a buffalo.

Maasai women and children regularly collect firewood in the area and it was by tribal custom his responsibility as senior Morani in his nearby homestead to attend to the matter. Kaputei knew the female buffalo must have been weakened due to severe loss of blood for he could see this distinctly from the blood trail it had left—a good point in his favour. Secondly, he also carried two spears one short and one long—another two points in his favour, plus a 'simi' (a one-blade double edge razor sharp machete)! One slash across the hind leg would sever the buffalo's hamstring; another in quick succession to the other would render it powerless. He knew that his spear, an effective weapon in combat, must be thrown with accuracy and force to penetrate the buffalo's thick hide. A mature female buffalo has a powerful and muscular neck—an unstoppable hunk of animal likened to an angry bull that would require a toreador's nerve and experience to fell her. If he was to survive he must approach her from the rear. Buffalo are short sighted but their hearing and smell is acute. When her hoof prints and blood trail turned off track he knew his quarry would be standing motionless in the shadows waiting for him. He back-tracked taking a roundabout route and approached her blind spot. It was his agility and speed that took the buffalo by surprise.

I found myself mesmerised picturing the action. His enactment was so real and unpractised I knew it to be the truth. His brother, when called to the site of the dead animal, confirmed this story. The lions fed well that night and for the executioner there was another step up the cultural ladder of warriorship. I had the utmost trust in both men; they too were happy to reciprocate their trust in me. My fire extinguisher was always viewed with suspicion; they asked if it were dropped by accident would it explode like a bomb and we would all perish? I must admit the thought had crossed my mind; pressure filling to capacity over the maximum pounds per square inch permitted would certainly turn it into a lethal killing machine!

On game viewing walks such as we were about to undertake my insurance cover for client injury contained a mandatory clause that I must be armed with a rifle heavy enough in calibre to stop an elephant in its tracks! My Insurer was not impressed and would not listen to my preferred method of defence—my trusty fire extinguisher! I knew it to be much safer and very effective without the disastrous results of having to cope with a wounded and crazed buffalo or elephant—only a very frightened one going in the opposite direction suited me!

I purchased a brand new .458 Winchester rifle that held four rounds in the magazine and one 'up the spout'; this is hunter slang for one bullet in the breech cocked to safe and ready! With the fire extinguisher strapped to my back and the rifle angled across my chest cradled into my left arm leaving my right hand free to operate the extinguisher, I was ready for business. It was very impressive for the clients too; some were hoping to see action. In the unlikely event of the fire extinguisher failing to turn an attack my second option was to shoot during that split second when the surprised animal presented an easy target—I was always ready for the unexpected. The clients were briefed to scatter in all directions—the attacker normally becomes confused and indecisive as to which direction to charge.

I remember an incident where I had to fire several shots into the head of a huge crocodile. By sheer luck whilst on an evening game walk we were observing a rather foolish attempt by a group of riders on horseback attempting to cross the fast running Mara river. One horse missed its footing and fell toppling the rider into the water—the horse and rider panicked; both were floating into deeper water towards a huge crocodile. The beast was basking on the bank some thirty yards down stream and hidden from the rider's view; this was the croc's regular sun-bed and vantage point, overlooking a wildebeest crossing. Here comes his lunch! The croc slipped silently into the water and began to move slowly up-stream. His determination to attack was telegraphed by his increasing speed towards the thrashing pair. I estimated it would take thirty seconds to close the gap. All I could see was the croc's head, my reaction was instantaneous.

I thought no more about where or why, who or what, only shoot first and ask questions later. Luckily my first shot was well placed and unquestionably the fatal shot; the second also found its target despite all the spray and thrashing of the croc's tail. This was a situation where no chances could be taken. The remaining horses and riders crossed with difficulty. The riders were shouting, slipping and sliding, each taking his own track up the bank unaware of the lurking danger. The lucky pair was soaking wet but now safely back on the same side of the bank as when they started. No amount of encouragement would persuade the terrified horse to make another attempt at crossing.

For the shaken horse and rider it was the long way round via a bridge several miles

Looking towards the dead crocodile in the shallows on the opposite side
This photograph was taken minutes after its attempt to attack the horses
whilst crossing upstream.

upstream. With all due respect to the leader, he dismounted and waded back with his horse once more whilst I kept a sharp eye out for any more hungry crocs. I sensed it would be a long time before his horse would ever cross a river again—he was ready for home wherever 'home' was to be that night. Darkness was fast approaching and off they galloped towards the direction of the bridge—with not even a thank you. Their fool-hardiness had gone horribly wrong. It was a close shave—much too close to the red line. They certainly had their money's worth of adventure but I can thing of better ways to die!

I have always pictured how exciting it would be to ride nose to tail with the wildebeest and zebras. Imagine if a predator took up the pursuit? I would run out of underwear in a very short space of time. On second thoughts, my overstretched imagination could easily conjure up something akin to participating in the National Hunt, with all the hounds from hell baying at my heels; this would certainly top my worst nightmare.

I shall stick to walking with cheetahs!

It was necessary for our safety that I brief the group prior to setting off on their escorted game-walk.

First and foremost should evasive action require to be taken—*listen and act immediately* without questioning any emergency instruction that I give—a split second decision will be made on the spot by me. Wear comfortable fitting boots and trousers tucked into socks.

The tables and camp chairs were ready and waiting for our arrival.

Marooned
Our home-made inflatable was a life-saver for crossing flooded roads and rivers.

Adventure Camp

My subsidiary camp situated some eight miles West of the main Out of Africa camp. This catered for eight persons on longer overnight stays. By alternating clients between both tented camps their exposure was increased towards experiencing and sensing the real African adventure. This, together with the freedom of dining out under the stars, listening to the night calls of the predators, and lunch (below) with Petal in the background, was always the highlight of their safari.

Ladies take note! There are hungry ticks out there hanging on the grass stalks all set to hook onto your clothing as you pass by. These pesky vampires have other competitors that also draw blood. The pincers of the black safari ant can be extremely painful when they attach themselves to your privates! Without these simple precautions you will get ants in your pants. Then there is only one option—join the rest and become one of the fastest strippers in the West. Throw all your inhibitions to the wind for you will not be alone The 'siafu' short for safari ants, have an amazing signal that at the given command of 'fire, all bite now', will guarantee to turn most humans including your skirted Maasai bodyguards into gyrating jumping jacks. Your cries for help will go unheeded for everyone else, having stepped onto the same angry line of fizzing siafu, will be dancing a similar jig.

The humiliation comes when a group of cheering tourists by chance stop to witness your amazing dexterity and impromptu strip-tease that your party has unwittingly put on to add to their game viewing pleasure. Your bitten and bruised body will remind you for the next ten days that constant itching is definitely a form of torture. Passers-by too, will give you a wide berth for they will think you have succumbed to the dreaded lurgi!

It's all happened before and is part of the safari scene; a story to be told time and again at dinner with friends and guaranteed to have them in fits of laughter.

Our two Maasai Morani game scouts will by now have reached the end of their out bound trail having recce'd a route for us that would pass through the herds of wildebeest, zebra and giraffe; they would have located elephants and buffalo from a distance and mentally marked their positions.

The Scouts have already communicated with me on their hand held radios. The walkers will leave camp by vehicle and meet up with them in the field. The less mobile visitors will enjoy the short game drive passing by the lion pride and where the leopard and her cubs were last seen. I do not believe in blazing an unchecked walking trail through the bush with clients; it is dangerous and the last thing one needs is a surprise meeting with a dangerous animal at close range.

Those that prefer not to walk will continue with Kibet and keep in touch with us by radio if they come across any interesting situation. Our rendezvous is planned for all to meet at a known high point at sundown, usually 6.30 p.m. or soon thereafter. Unbeknown to the clients there are cool boxes charged with a variety of drinks carried in the vehicle. Sitting on the rocks warmed by the sun and watching the African sun set in the West overlooking the vast Mara plains with a favourite sun-downer, is a memory that never fades.

Our game walk lasts for several hours covering a distance of about four miles, any walking wounded with blisters or heat fatigue are collected by Kibet in his roaming vehicle. The Scouts are in their element, one in front of me and the other bringing up the rear, tracking back along their initial trail. I know instinctively that some of the group are hoping for a 'buzz' of some sort. Without warning an African hare followed by a handsome reedbuck explode out of the bushes a few yards away — I am not the only one who jumps a mile high to the amusement of our Morani guides. They are not impervious to being startled out of their wits either!

A dozen giraffe, a family group, stare directly at us from some fifty yards away; always inquisitive and not frightened by our presence. Zebra and wildebeest keep their distance. That feeling of a thousand pairs of eyes studying your every move can send shivers up your spine. We are now heading towards the high point to view the sunset. Kibet is parked on the next rise and has us in sight. The guides tell me that whilst blazing our trail they had seen the pride of lions in that area walking towards where the female leopard had hidden her kill in the swamp grass. I radioed Kibet for the latest information; "The female leopard and both cubs are back up the tree", he replied "and the lions appear to have eaten the remains of her kill hidden in the grass". His voice had a note of concern for it seemed the pride had parked itself under the tree where all three leopards had concealed themselves high up in the foliage. The lions knew the leopards were there!

A leopard has patience and will out-climb and out-sit any lion that would like to eat it for dinner. Yes, lions can climb trees after a fashion but not this tree. The first fork is twenty feet high; the trunk of the tree has a smooth bark and is not conducive for lions to climb. Mother Leopard had chosen well and she and her cubs were now marooned in the tree. Here was an opportunity to photograph the sunset; the tree with the leopards in it and the lions below all in one frame. Kibet was summoned to pick us up; we parked ourselves at a safe distance to take our pictures through telescopic lenses and enjoy our sun-downers. However, there was a problem—we were not alone.

Several other tour vehicles had arrived at the spot and had moved towards the tree to get close-up pictures. They were a little too close for my liking. I could sense disaster was looming. What if the leopards should panic at the close proximity of all the vehicles and come down the tree? The lions would slaughter the leopards. I voiced my concerns to my clients and the vote was taken not to add to the pressure but to hold back and stay where we were. I had no radio communication with these mini buses; they have a separate frequency to ours. I had an idea; the Maasai trackers would walk the clients to the sun-downer hill; Kibet and I would then drive over to the leopard tree without our tourists—this would give an official stamp to my intrusion. Most of the tour drivers were aware I held an Honorary Warden's ticket. There are some tour drivers that are enticed by the dollar dangled before their eyes encouraging them to move closer without consideration for the animals or other viewers.

Here was the making of a possible showdown. We approached slowly and quietly and reached a point some sixty yards before the tree and stopped. Suddenly all hell was let loose. Mother leopard leaped down on top of one of the vehicles, fell through the open roof-hatch and in her frenzy to extricate herself, clawed a large gentleman on his chest and then crashed through a closed window shattering the glass in making her escape. The lions surprised and bewildered by all the yelling and screaming coming from the tour vehicle scattered in every direction. The large gentleman was protesting loudly. He was about to sue the world, including every wild animal in it! His wife was screaming hysterically at the sight of the blood all over his shirt and was quite sure he was going to die—the situation was fraught with panic.

Our first aid kit contained the necessary requirement to patch him up. I could hardly believe anybody, not even their driver, had not noticed the leopards in the tree. The cubs held their ground throughout the whole drama but now, anxious to join their mother, took courage and came down the tree; once their feet touched the ground it was instant flight. "Wajinga! I shouted (an all-encompassing word for idiots!). I was speechless with anger and so was Kibet. This is the type of rock bottom tour operator the Mara can do without—they had learned a lesson the hard way. There was more pain to come for the hapless individual—clawing from a leopard is almost as bad as a mauling—anti-tetanus, anti-rabies plus an antibiotic would require to be administered in a hurry.

The setting sun was low on the horizon and we had to get back to our meeting point. The sun-downers were contained in our vehicle and the visitors must be getting anxious!

Somewhere in the thick grass was a mother leopard; she too could be injured and bleeding. There was little I or Kibet could do at this stage but we would pass by the spot in the morning and check—meantime we had a story to tell! The walkers, too, had a story to tell us.

Whilst crossing a 'lugga', the bush name for a water course which drains storm water from the surrounding high land and forms pools that serve as watering holes for all manner of wildlife, the sharp-eyed Maasai had spotted a python lying full length by the waterside and from all accounts the lump in its body suggested it had just swallowed a small gazelle or African hare. Large pythons seek out these pools and lie in wait for their dinner.

The party watched her watching them; it was a case of watchers watching yards of the watcher slide into the pool; this was how one of the troop comedians put it. The more the ice-cold gin and tonics and the whisky took effect the longer the snake became!

The Maasai escorts reckoned it was twice as long as their long spears; I guess probably a twelve footer. Everybody wanted to know all the details about the leopard drama they had missed. Kibet relayed the story to the Maasai who fell about with whoops of laughter! My concern was for the leopard; it would be a miracle if she had survived unscathed. A video of the incident would have made a hard-hitting introduction at any tour guide briefing on what not to do on a Mara safari! Pity, I slipped up there. I had my video camera at hand but all intentions of photography went out of my mind when the chaos erupted. If there was to be an enquiry Kibet would certainly stand his ground as a witness on the side of truth.

The soft shades of dusk began to envelop us. The setting sun had disappeared. The crickets chirped the start of their night's business, each male trying to out-do his rival's song to attract a mate. These insects can drive you crazy. If by chance one gets into your tent the high pitched prolonged screech of the male is similar to the sound of tinnitus, a condition telegraphed to the ear when the brain wrongly interprets sound—so the scientists say. I suffer from this high pitched tone often heard in taut railway telegraph wires, it can be most frustrating when listening out for the slightest animal night sound—yet I can hear a pin drop.

Darkness had come and it was time to return to camp; hot showers were awaiting us. The shower water is brought in from a mountain spring some four miles away, by a trailer containing a dozen forty gallon metal drums packed side by side.

A half piece of Alum—a natural mineral block of sulphate of aluminium and potassium contained within a whitish soft stone quarried from nearby—is placed into the drum. The Alum dissolves, then clings to the particles of dirt floating in the water sending the dirt to the bottom of the drum leaving the water clean clear and soft. Galvanised metal containers, for some unknown reason, seem to assist the process. The water is then boiled over a log fire and carried by buckets to the tents where a shower bucket is filled and the right temperature obtained by adding cold water. Your shower bucket is then hauled up by a rope and pulley and all you have to do is turn the tap attached to the shower to the 'on' position. There are precisely three minutes of hot shower water in which to complete your wash and clean up! It is guaranteed there will always be someone who times it wrong and is left standing 'starkers' covered in soap yelling for more water! This signals the moment for a little bit of fun! The recipe is to add a bucket of cold water, call 'ready' and standby for the expletives—they are always worth recording. This is part of the fun and games of being under canvas in the wild.

The campfire stories followed by dinner and wine of your choosing make the evening soon pass. It's been an active and most enjoyable day for everyone; the fresh air has induced a pleasant and satisfying tiredness. Tonight is the last night in camp for the visitors; the group will sleep well though on second thoughts maybe some may not! The size of that python might trigger a nightmare or two!

Plans were set for an early 5.30 a.m. wake-up. A tapping on the tent flap is followed by hot water being poured into the outside wash basin; I announce "Tea and biscuits at the campfire at 06.00 a.m., wheels turning at 6.15 a.m., and it is all go. This is the punishment, folks, that you have all paid for isn't it?" No early morning complaints or headaches are entertained—our visitors just seem to love being organised. The night passed without incident, except a small herd of elephants trumpeted their presence while passing along the camp perimeter. The lions were surprisingly quiet during the night; they probably had second thoughts about staying and moved out after the leopard incident yesterday evening.

My first priority would be to check if Mother Leopard was injured. This could be tricky and would need a careful approach if she was still in the hideout with her cubs. Injured or otherwise the matter would have to be reported to the Maasai ranch owner. Any passing herder with sheep or cattle could be attacked. It would also be wise to warn them personally to give the area a wide berth; this form of co-operation always provided me with another good turn from them. Most herders were always keen to point out locations of the predators including sightings of Petal and her movements, in return for any information on dangerous or wounded animals, particularly buffaloes that we may have seen. Quite often young Maasai herders have been mauled or killed over the years by injured animals wounded by poachers' arrows, hence the need to apply good recce procedures in advance of our game viewing walks.

Kibet and I were now in convoy. I was leading and negotiating a stony outcrop on the track ahead. I just happened to look up and saw the unmistakable crook of the tail of a young leopard skulking across the face of a large boulder—it could only be one of the cubs. Kibet had seen it too and flashed his lights in my direction; the leopard's camouflage was perfect; it was the white of the curved under-tail that had caught my eye. Mother and the second cub must be close by. Sure enough there she was quietly grooming herself with the second cub sound asleep by her side. This was good news indeed; she had moved out of her grass cover some three hundred yards away. Several hyaenas could be seen scurrying around in the long grass where she had first hidden the remains of her kill.

On closer examination with binoculars we could just see signs of blood on the outer side of her chest between her foreleg where a red patch suggested that bleeding had occurred; or could it have come from carrying her kill? Whatever the cause I was relieved she appeared not to be in distress though our presence clearly made her uneasy. Moments later she growled and disappeared over the outcrop followed by her cubs. Once again we had been caught on the hop; not even a camera clicked such was the unexpected surprise. I looked over towards Kibet who raised his hands in a gesture which suggested nothing less than 'darn it'! Land cruiser starter motors are very noisy and sound like nothing on earth in the still of the night or morning; they can be heard for miles on the open plains. A start up close to a timid animal will send it scurrying away; occupants in other vehicles waiting patiently nearby and unable to move forward for a good view become very annoyed and vocal with good reason, particularly at those drivers who leave their engines running because of a busted starter motor are sure candidates for the big end of bush rage.

Is there anybody out there who can design or invent a quiet starter motor? He could make his million overnight. We were lucky, our early sparrow chirp rise and shine gave us an hour's head start on the 'lodgers'. This early morning find had placed us one up on today's leader board. There is always competition between the 'lodgers' and the 'campers' as to who saw what. When asked 'what have you seen' and everybody shouts "Three leopards at 06.30"! "Bloody insomniacs" they reply!

With a sense of relief we left the leopard family in peace and set off towards the group of hyaenas. They are part of nature's clean up squad, dog-like in facial looks with a mouth full of teeth similar to that of the African wild dog. A hyaena's jaw is considered the most powerful of the dog species built to break the bones of most plains game as if matchsticks. Interestingly the hyaena's short back legs provide the pushing power for their non-stop long distance running. Cheetahs will not hunt their prey if there are hyaenas in the vicinity. These menacing prowlers are forever on the lookout for easy pickings and will steal a cheetah's kill without hesitation. A pack can surround a cheetah family and slaughter them in seconds. Lions too have an almost fanatical distaste for hyaenas; given the chance lions will set upon these beasts and destroy them with a vengeance that has to be seen to be believed, leaving the vultures to clean up the carcass. Hyaenas are generally fearful of humans in daylight; most will not stand their ground if approached on foot. Having said this, on seeing packs of half a dozen or more, caution should be exercised particularly at night. They have an excellent sense of smell, sharp hearing, good night vision and have been known to attack and inflict terrible facial wounds on sleeping humans. Always be cautious when sleeping unprotected in the open under the stars.

Elderly Maasai returning to their manyattas after a day's drinking session often fall victim to these scavengers. Drunks have been mauled, disfigured and mutilated whilst lying paralytic along a pathway or a ditch.

I was now able to examine, on foot, the area of swamp grass and could see where the leopard had sought temporary refuge. Evidence of many lion prints indicated the pride had thoroughly investigated the leopard's hideout. The hyaenas had eaten every scrap of the kill leaving no sign of leftovers in the grass.

Kibet followed the scavenging hyaenas across the plains—they led him to a converted den in a dead termite mound; this had once provided an ant bear many months ago with a week's supply of rich proteins. The rake-like claws of this nocturnal anteater had dug several tunnels deep into the core of the mound digging out and devouring the queen ant and all her subjects. The first tenants were wild dogs; they had dug more tunnels as a safe haven in which to give birth to their pups. The wild dog family survived and progressed to adulthood, but within two years all seventeen had died of rabies. The burrow then lay unoccupied for two years. Nature has a way of saying 'off limits' ensuring the virus cycle dies out.

Science should take another close look at this disease that has brought the African wild dog to the edge of extinction in the Mara. This particular pack of wild dogs known as the Aitong pack had been given the name of their territorial breeding range by a monitoring unit during the late 1980's. Their movements and hunting sprees were followed and photographed; including all the gory details of the method of running their prey to exhaustion—usually young wildebeest or Thompson's gazelles. The grisly finale of tearing the live and kicking animal apart has caused many a tourist to scream out aloud in protest. I too have often found myself having to look away from the sickening carnage before me. The chase across the savannah is electrifying. The 'plan' of the hunting dogs' pursuit is well co-ordinated, where the front runner gives way to his second in command; the process then follows down the line and maintains the pressure on their quarry. Each dog has a backup whilst others plan the trigonometry to intercept the fleeing prey. Fox hunting with hounds has an uncanny similarity to the chase; little wonder there is an outcry to have fox hunting outlawed in the UK. Generally, wild dogs will not attack man, but both Petal and I always applied great caution when we spotted them in the wild.

I remember once in the early hours of the morning travelling by road from the town of Nakuru towards Molo; I was flagged down by a young man who it turned out had deserted from the British Army Unit based in Kenya.

Seconds before I stopped I was startled to see a pack of wild dogs by the side of the road, two of which jumped on the bonnet of my open Landrover. They were hungry and very mean adults. Had I accelerated forwards this would have unbalanced them both and toppled them into the cab. Luckily my mind was in the right gear and by reversing quickly the lurch backwards threw them off the bonnet. The deserter realising his near brush with death promptly gave himself up and asked to be handed over to the police. This alarming experience convinced him it would be better to die at the hands of his Sergeant Major than be eaten alive by wild dogs! That incident made me wonder what would have happened to him if I had not stopped and given him a lift. The dogs were in a frenzied state; they could have been waiting in ambush for him as he walked along the road. I handed the shaken 'squaddie' over to the Molo Police Commander who promptly placed him in cells for repatriation back to his army unit—poor fellow his freedom was short lived, desertion or absence without leave is a serious crime in any army; its either a court marshal or the guard house; whichever—he had quite a story to tell.

I have yet to hear of wild dogs attacking humans, but I do remember clearly one other occasion when a group of tourist vehicles had surrounded a pack of a dozen hungry adult wild dogs. The dogs were resting under the shade of a tree out on the open plain. It happened that an overseas wildlife television film crew were in attendance and parked close by waiting patiently for the tourists to depart. I held back some way behind the professionals who were unaware of my presence. The tourists were now preparing to move off.

I noticed that a young ten-year-old Maasai boy had left his flock of sheep and was running towards the tourist vehicles; for no other reason than to beg for chocolate or sweets.

Tourists have the unbelievable habit of handing out the sweeties, pens and pencils, to these youngsters not only along the roads or in the field but when passing by their school playing field whilst the children are out of class. I once watched in horror and humiliation, as sweets were thrown like chaff to the wind; the ensuing free-for-all in the dust brought the headmaster and his angry teachers out in force armed with all manner of missiles including pots and pans which they hurled at the hapless tourists. That incident put paid to uninvited tourist groups to all the schools in the area.

The young Maasai shepherd, seeing his 'tasties' moving off, broke into a sprint and chased after the vehicles. He had not seen the wild dogs—his line of vision had been partially obscured by the departing vehicles. Everything was now beginning to go pear shaped. The boy, I knew, was the simpleton offspring of the local chief. I also noticed the film crew had leapt into action—their cameras at the ready to film all the impending action!

I was not prepared to wait and see whether the dogs would attack the boy or scatter. My instinct told me to drive my vehicle between the boy and the wild dogs which, by now, were standing up showing no signs of retreat; their tails held high, heads down and barking low short sharp gruff warnings of aggression. For a moment the incident along the Molo road many years ago flashed across my mind. I believe it was that encounter which now set my adrenalin flowing; I was not prepared to take any chances; what irritated me more was the film crew were only intent on getting their action pictures be they for better or for worse!

The boy, thinking I was about to provide the sweets, jumped on to the running board of my vehicle. I held firmly on to his loincloth ('shuka') and shouted "suyan" the Maasai word for wild dog. The whites of his eyes rolled into his head and I thought he was about to faint; all he could say was "sweet, sweet," pointing to his mouth. I kept my foot on the accelerator and glancing into the side mirror saw the whole pack was cantering after my vehicle. My clients were shouting "go, go" and go I did! I realised I was heading straight for the chief's herd of shoats (sheep and goats). By now the situation was really going doubly pear shaped; I had visions of the chief frog-marching me out of his area—one, for almost throttling his son and two, for encouraging the 'suyan' towards his pride and joy—a dishevelled bunch of worm-riddled sheep that I was now heading for. The goat herder was still acting like the village idiot when he too noticed the wild dogs cantering alongside us. The pursuers were snapping at his heels. The boy started screaming; all that was needed was for me to hit the largest ant bear hole in the Mara—that would be the last straw; a broken spring or two plus a few passengers with hefty headaches. I veered the Landcruiser away from the sheep. Luck was with me for an old male Thompson's gazelle, resting in the shade of a short acacia bush took flight across the noses of the following dogs. The chase then switched to the gazelle and the gazelle became the hunted—the pursuit was now on. By now the boy shepherd was hysterical and on the verge of apoplexy. With no further interest in the chase, I made for the nearest Maasai manyatta on the hill half a mile away to deposit him, and take on board a sane replacement—a capable Maasai Morani shepherd, spear and all!

Our adventure had not gone unnoticed. The incident had been observed by the whole of the manyatta inhabitants who had witnessed the pandemonium from a distance. For this I was

'Mbwa Mwitu'

This radio-collared female wild hunting dog was a regular visitor to the Mara. I understand the Serengeti Research Institute had plotted her movements for a short while. I was particularly fascinated with the way she always returned with small sub-adult groups of bitches from the Serengeti and brought them to the Aitong and Bardamat Hills in North Mara where they denned and raised several litters that eventually grew to a pack of thirty in number.

pleased and hoped they would convey my deed to the chief. The story did not end there—I was in for another surprise! We passed by the now scattered shoats and dropped off the Morani; he had enjoyed the ride sitting astride the front mud guard hanging on for dear life, his loin cloth flowing in the wind with nothing else but the indicator light housing, to cover up his manhood. He thanked us for the lift and insisted on shaking hands with everybody—his smile seemed never ending it stretched from ear to ear. We all envied his full set of whiter than white teeth; apparently this is all to do with their high calcium blood and milk diet.

I could see with the aid of my binoculars the film crew vehicle on the opposite ridge—this must be where the chase finally ended. We set off in that direction and arrived some fifteen minutes later having negotiated a difficult lugga crossing. The dogs had fed well—not a morsel was left; it was then I was caught completely off guard. The film crew drove their vehicle over to my driving side and let rip a stream of unintelligible abuse. They were upset and accused me of interfering with the ways of nature. I had also wrecked their photographic coup of the century! Their outburst was quite insane—to us this was war; my clients were all World War II veterans itching to start another! Our message was put across in no uncertain terms—that Churchill's Bulldogs still live on to this day! That evening back at camp I was not surprised to find the chief waiting for me. He was happy that I had saved his son from the jaws of the 'suyan' but could he have some money to pay the local 'laibon' (witch doctor) and have the devil 'exorcised' from his boy. I suspected this might be a ruse to help buy a few more jugs of the local potent 'kill me quick' brew for which I knew he had an addiction. To this day I will never know whether those wild dogs were intent on attack, but one thing for certain, I knew I had done the right thing by giving the chief a few hundred shillings protection money. He became a steadfast ally whenever I required support in proving the innocence of Petal and her brothers who, throughout their lives, never to my knowledge killed any shoats. There was always some Maasai willing to put all the blame on Petal's little family—the calf killers. There were also those of my own kind who I knew would like to see my wheels spiked by accusing me of commercialising my association with these wild cheetahs—something I am sure they would like to achieve for their own ends. The chief knew my enemies; they never worked out how their many attempts to discredit me were scuttled and why they suddenly backfired. The Maasai have a built-in cunning and a way of having the last word by dealing the card that destroys unfair play. True to the chiefs words the television crew were asked to leave the area by sunrise the next day—bag baggage, cameras and all!

The transmitter collar, I noticed, had a painted dark green identification spot on one end. Surprisingly her journeys out of the Mara were always alone travelling the full length of the Serengeti ecosystem as far south as Lake Ndutu in the southwestern Serengeti—a round trip journey of some 200 miles.

Eighteen months later rabies and distemper decimated the group in less than three months. A tragic loss that reduced the wild dog population to perilously low numbers within the Mara-Serengeti Ecosystem.

My enquiries regarding Mbwa Mwitu, the name I had given her, fell on deaf ears. Apparently the monitoring researchers at the SRI were regularly replaced by others and for a period of several years no monitoring took place. I believe that their project funding had run dry. Pity: I would have liked to have knows which pack in the Serengeti or wherever she had originated, and from which group the young females came. I suspect that the young adults, younger than she, were picked up by her from fragmented small groups within agricultural lands bordering the protected areas.

The identikit card index held by the SRI should be able to match up Mbwa Mwitu's markings with her trail and wanderings (circa 1988).

These wild dogs were the start and the end of the Aitong pack; little did I know that in the months ahead most would die. Now some two years later their dens, spring-cleaned by time, had been occupied by a pack of hyaenas and their families. Hyaenas too are susceptible to rabies and distemper. Now the den is occupied once again it will be interesting to see whether this hyaena family will progress with a clean sheet. One of the hyaena mothers had disappeared down into the tunnel leaving another at the entrance to act as guard. This behaviour, plus obvious signs of suckling impressions around her teats, suggested they had puppies down below, probably still too young to venture out of the burrow. Kibet had now set off in the direction of the cattle herd—I knew he was keen to pick up any clues and obtain firsthand information that might suggest that Petal had returned from her honeymoon on the mountain.

I too was keen to investigate—it would be a fitting end to a successful safari; my spirits were up and expectations high. Kibet radioed back that the young herders had seen a lone cheetah late the previous evening sitting on top of a termite mound in the area where they were now grazing their cattle. This could be Petal or Astra I thought, maybe even Namibia, my instincts told me it might be Petal as three days had passed since she went to the mountains with Namibia in tow. Our mid-morning coffee break did not pass without this thought being discussed; time was flying and I had organised for a bush breakfast on Euphorbia Hill. I could see the camper van was in position, a white tablecloth laid and Andrew in charge. The better plan would be to break off the search for the cheetah, have our breakfast, then return to comb the area where the herder had seen the cat at last light yesterday.

Breakfast was perfect, followed by a short walk-about and stretch-exercises for those with aching limbs and numb bums. The safari seats in the vehicle are comfortable but I always recommend carrying a sit-upon air ring; those that suffer from backache find this useful piece of air filled comfort absolutely essential for safari travel.

Many an all-terrain safari driver succumbs in the end to Landcruiser crick neck and stiff back, caused by continued compression to the base of the spine. Who wants a bent chassis at the wheel? Nobody will love you for that image; so it's very important to treat the body shock absorbers with care. We were tempted to take some extra time to laze around but that old enemy waits for no one. Andrew was agitating to pack up and get back to camp to prepare early lunch. The next couple of days for the camp crew would be pressurised into packing away all the camp gear in three forest-green coloured steel containers. I could sense an air of excitement amongst the crew akin to the end of a boarding school year and Christmas to look forward to.

I remember my school days—they were happy and carefree, memories of growing up healthy in mind and body; my early years to puberty were charged by the adrenalin of my progress in sport and an acceptable level of academics that any outdoor oriented boy could wish for. These years were exciting for me though my parents sometimes wondered what direction their youngest was heading. I am one that believes that our decisions, successes, failures and our health, wealth and happiness in life are planned in advance along that path called 'destiny'. It is as if by some strong continuous power a direction for each and every one of us on this planet has been set and timed for a specific period. We each have a purpose in life and when that distance is through and the tasks set for us are complete the spirit of your life will finally rest in the creation you have made. This is my belief—I am at peace with it.

It is now time to get the wheels in motion and head towards the 'Tiri Tiri' a name given by the lodge tour drivers for the proliferation of the 'acacia lakai'. The Maasai call it the Oltepessi tree—the wood is red, very hard and durable. This is the area where I often look for Petal; it overlooks the camp and was once contract ploughed by a short sighted buccaneering young Kenyan white who had little idea that without fencing and an army of carers to chase off the wildlife, the expected biannual crop of maize would not see the light of day beyond a few inches of sprouting. This five hundred-acre experiment was abandoned and never harrowed after the first plough – it now tests the best of shock absorbers, springs, backbone and resolve. Few tour drivers would attempt this ordeal in their vehicles. I warned my passengers to brace themselves for the turbulence ahead. My plan was to drive along the length of the furrows in low range four-wheel drive; set the auto accelerator to slow running and crawl along like the tractor and plough responsible for this mess in the first place.

Kibet had wisely chickened out preferring to follow his instincts around the perimeter to check out the wooded luggas. I saw him stop and get out of his vehicle to examine a spot on the ground where some vultures had been. This was encouraging and would suggest that the vultures had been feeding off a carcass. I called him on the radio asking for news of his find. He was certain it was the remains of a cheetah kill within the past three hours. Kibet believed a Thompson's gazelle fawn had fallen prey to a predator whilst we were at breakfast on the hill. Now it was a question of searching the area. A cheetah will not travel too far after a meal, maybe a kilometre not more, and then flop down under a tree or head for the nearest water. I briefed my passengers that we would stop every two hundred yards so each would cover a quarter of the 360-degree sweep with their binoculars. In this way a thorough examination of the landscape around us would be examined—everyone had a job to do—find that cheetah! Try standing up through the twin viewing hatches or even climbing on top of the roof for a better view. With all the movement in the back I found it impossible to get a steady fix and decided to step out of the vehicle and bend over the bonnet using my elbows as a tripod. We were busy asking each other "do you see anything"? Each distant tuft of grass or stump became an object for double-checking. Not one of us saw the cheetah approach the vehicle from the side. I had my back to her—the first thing I knew was all four feet landing on the bonnet beside me—it was Petal! I was taken by surprise and looked up to see those standing up in the back of the vehicle grinning with pleasurable shock!

This was not the first time Petal had done the exact same thing to me catching me unawares. She had emerged from an area of tufted swamp grass similar to that which the leopard mother had hidden herself in the other day.

Kibet was already making his way towards us; his group had seen the whole drama unfold and were now in fits of laughter. Petal too had that 'gotcha this time' look on her face; her message was so clear as if to say 'I'm back'—and promptly rested her front half onto the Landcruiser cab roof supported by her hind legs on the bonnet. The group slowly regained their composure and were standing up with their heads and shoulders through the hatch. I could hardly contain myself from laughing out loud at Petal's cheeky display. She appeared delighted to meet them and they, still frozen in disbelief, remembered not to smile. The show of teeth to any wild animal telegraphs aggression and with direct eye to eye contact could provoke an attack. My clients behaved remarkably well—most people would have freaked out. They had listened and clearly understood my safari introduction and briefing and reacted accordingly.

For my clients this was the highlight of their safari. Leopards and cheetahs to the uninitiated look alike and the story of the previous day where the mother leopard had clawed her way to freedom was still very fresh in their minds. Now this close encounter face to face with a wild spotted cat that came to greet them would remain a memory for their lifetime. I was delighted but my mind was racing ahead. Where was Namibia? Had Petal and he parted amicably? Was their honeymoon over? Petal's body language and demeanour seemed calm—this was a good sign. It would be her first mating and possibly her first serious oestrus. The chances of not conceiving at first copulation would be high. There was nothing I could do except hope, pray and count each day—all ninety of them. I would miss the early subtle signs of confirmation that she was pregnant. My journey to Australia might have to be cut short.

My twenty-five year old daughter had married for the sake of security in the mistaken belief that a ready-made home, car and all the trappings of life without her own children would make for a happy marriage!

Minutes before I walked down the aisle with her on my arm her mother divulged her secret to me not to expect any grandchildren from the marriage. Little did I realise that destiny had already planned ahead to cut short her life.

At the altar a pain and hurt surged through me. I had an overwhelming desire to voice my objection, as a father, when the Christian clergyman asked the congregation if anybody knew of any reason why those now before him should not be joined in matrimony as husband and wife. Was it my business to disclose the secret? I would have to live with the pain that any father must bear when he knows full well, with the passage of time, without her very own children to love, could tear her marriage apart. That tremendous pull towards the creation of a life within your own body as one of your partnership's making cannot be underestimated. I too have been there; by a similar parallel a man who is faced with going to war in the knowledge he may not return to see his protégé strengthens the overwhelming desire to leave behind his genes as a mark of having been on this planet. My marriage bore a son and two daughters; I was lucky to live to see all of them mature into respected adults blessed with good looks and the will to succeed in life. My son and youngest daughter brought up their offspring in the Christian tradition.

Africa was not to be their chosen home. I could not see any real future for a second Kenyan born generation in a country that, after many years of independence and self government, continued to struggle with the principles of human rights, fair play and the rule of law. England and the British way of life seemed a better bet for my children's future. My roots in Kenya were too deep to be uprooted—I elected to stay in Africa.

As predicted, my middle daughter's marriage began to fail. Her past interests in her single life prior to her marriage were clear to me. She was biology oriented and possessed my genetic empathy with animals. I had inwardly hoped she might choose to get away from the humdrum life of a UK based laboratory technician and settle for a wildlife hands-on practical approach that would provide in a very short time a scientific research platform to work from.

Petal and her future family was the ideal opportunity to fulfil my daughter's full potential but I had not envisaged her considering bringing along another piece of trial baggage from the merry go round of suitors who preyed on the rebound of failed relationships. I had a sneaking suspicion that my offer for her to join me on her own was being misconstrued by others as a ploy by her father to steer her in another direction. The affairs of the heart of one's children, I know, are best avoided—any mature advice is guaranteed to fall on deaf ears. I could only wait and hope that common sense would prevail but as time went on my hopes began to fade. Marriage was on the chart once again for my daughter—for better or for worse! Not like the first time, this time there was a chance that most parents wished for—maybe a third set of grandchildren?

I had strong inner feelings that fate was in the process of finalising her destiny. I was right; her path and given distance to run in life was short-lived when ovarian cancer was diagnosed in Australia shortly after her second marriage. This was a bolt from the blue that blew everything apart for all of us.

Australia was to be their new home, with a healthier environment in which to raise a family—this was not to be. Fate dealt her a cruel hand in both her marriages. In hindsight had I objected at the first church altar, might this have triggered a pointer to an earlier realisation by her confused UK specialists that something was wrong in the reproduction line? That deep sadness at the loss of a very special daughter for any father and particularly for me—refuses to go away. She took with her a part of my make-up in her passing.

There was now nobody who would be capable of handling the situation whilst I was away. Petal would not relate to just anyone. My young married female assistant was about to follow her husband to other pastures overseas to start her family. Her introduction to Petal had taken time; I saw a bond forming between the pair though she had much to learn. Jamie had the right credentials, patience, a fertile brain and a feeling for wildlife. She was capable of tackling most situations and was not frightened to do anything, even to driving the camper vehicle at night alone in the bush looking for me in a thunderstorm! This experience would tax even the hardiest of the male species. Jamie made her decision; it could not have been easy. I was very sad to say farewell to her and break the bonds of mutual understanding between us. I was now in a quandary; I had no-one to follow in my footsteps or stand in for me to cover my final visit to Australia to say farewell to my ageing father. I would have to consider closing the camp for the period I would be away, and send the staff on a well-earned rest. I made the decision to close camp in the coming days.

Petal was now well on her way to becoming famous. I was destined to be Petal's only carer for the next fifteen years! Whatever may happen I am determined to see her live out her natural lifetime. I had many offers of assistance, mainly from the less mature and younger generation seeking the adventure and excitement that a carer of a wild animal, especially a cat, would provide. This was despite the fact that there was little remuneration, sponsorship or insurance on offer. Most were willing to give up their overseas jobs but many credentials were required: work permit, subsistence, living rough, high risk of malaria, language and a complete

Getting to know Sprite
Jamie had the right credentials, patience, a fertile brain and above all a feeling for wildlife.

understanding of the wildlife dangers around them, and the need to possess a sixth sense to tune in to the mind of a wild animal. Only one person came near to any of these qualifications, and we became friends. His name was Jonathan Scott, later to become a renowned artist, wildlife photographer and presenter. Jonathan is the author of many illustrated books on the subject of the wild animals of the Mara.

Jonathan arrived in Kenya with a degree in Zoology. The Mara became his love and from the word go I could see this young man had talents of which he was unaware. He possessed a calm and pleasant nature, always willing to listen to his mentor, never a harsh word said about anyone, intelligent and good looking—it seemed little could phase him but Jonathan was also not to be Heather's or Jamie's replacement. I knew his talents would take him to the forefront as a world class wildlife presenter. In the meantime it was a pleasure to have his contribution to the team, albeit only for a short period. We gave lectures on wildlife to many of the American institutions, the Smithsonian for one. We visited lodges and presented slide shows. On one amusing occasion, whilst I was labouring through with the difficult subject of 'insectivores' to a rather heavy audience whose questions were somewhat bizarre, I remember one question was along the lines of, "Why don't elephants eat meat." Somewhat taken aback and with tongue in my cheek, I turned to Jonathan and asked him why was this so, only to

Scott's Doodle

To this day I am the proud possessor of this doodle.

find his concentration on my subject had lapsed whilst he doodled a pencil drawing of a cheetah on his briefing notes. His face was totally blank and the only words he could blurt out to cover his temporary lapse of communication were "Because they eat grass". This was my cue for him to take over and launch into the 'whose-who' of grazers. We had a good laugh. To this day I am still the proud possessor of this doodle. In my opinion the best drawing he has ever produced.

A world-renowned conservationist wrote a preface on one of his books, 'The Painted Wolves' (Wild dogs of the Serengeti Mara). This was one of Jonathan Scott's literary and artistic masterpieces.

Sir David Attenborough wrote these words; "Jonathan Scott understands the animals he draws and photographs so well that it is as though he has entered their minds and can see the world as they do. Only by doing that; plus endless patience and inexhaustible energy is it possible to produce a full and intimate record of an animal's life".

Jonathan autographed this message to me on the 23rd of May 1991. In the same book he wrote, "Dave there are lots of happy memories amongst these pages of times together in the Mara, I am waiting for your book on the Cheetahs".

Now, some twelve years later, my promise to my daughter is about to be fulfilled. This is my book—an intimate record of the life of an incredible wild animal and her offspring – at last in print.

An hour and more had passed; Petal's cheeky introduction had transfixed us all. She had paid her respects personally to the tourists and was now resting in the shade of a nearby tree, alert to the wildlife around her. I had chirped gently as an acknowledgement of my pleasure at her presence; the compliment was returned and I took this as the sign for me to join her under the tree. I walked quietly and slowly over to her, sat down and was welcomed with a loud deep and contented purr. My mind was racing ahead again, how could I leave her now, she had come a long way. Petal rolled onto her back, paws in the air, wriggling gently using the rough ground and grass as a scratching pad. I was tempted to help scratch her back but my principles of minimum touch with her kept the dangerous gap of encouraging domesticity apart. All I wanted was for her to trust in me and for me to display my trust in her by standing on the boundary of her wildness to protect her and her future offspring. I felt my sixth sense telling me Petal would soon be a mother. Yes, I had unlocked her mind and could feel and see her world as she does. I stood up and walked back to the vehicle. I always carried her aluminium 'karai' and clean water in a plastic five litre can in the vehicle. Petal was hyperventilating in an effort to retain her body fluids—it was midday and hot—the nearest water was almost three miles away. I returned with the can and 'karai'. Petal was looking at me expectantly and no sooner was the water in the 'karai' than she began to lap, often looking up to take stock of the situation around her and purring loudly. I've often likened this sound to that of a lawnmower with a dirty carburettor, sputtering and choking. Having fed earlier and now quenched her thirst, the chances were she would rest for most of the day by taking cat-naps. I would then move away; allowing Kibet and I to take our now thirsty, hungry and excited clients back to camp for an early lunch and prepare them for their afternoon flight back to Nairobi.

My plan was to see everybody off safely, return with the camper and spend my last night with Petal, whilst the crew broke camp. The camp crew would be free to work at their pace; I had food and all the necessities in the caravan to cope on my own. Petal would probably decide to jump on the bonnet, stretch out and fall sound asleep, being off the ground and knowing that most predators tonight may prefer to steer away from the odours of diesel, humans, chicken and curry pilau, my favourite dish!

Lunch was almost ready and waiting at camp when we arrived. Time was running short and packing bags ready for the flight would be best done first. Andrew had set up a delicious salad and cold meat buffet, rather than an all sit down affair at the table—plates on knees suited most. I am a serial sweet tooth, custard and cream, with honey and sponge cakes; I could eat it all day!

It was now time for everyone to say their fond farewells to the camp crew. Last minute photos are a must of the kitchen magician, Andrew, bedecked in his white apron and tall chef's hat. We left the tip box filled to overflowing and set off for the landing strip. Everyone waved goodbye to the crew who had mustered themselves in the vehicle park to say their goodbyes. Most of the clients, if not all, would have stayed longer. However, duty called for them to be back in Nairobi, rested and relaxed, ready for their eight-hour duty flight the next morning back to Switzerland, their home base.

The Dakota scheduled flight on the Mara route is secretly referred to as the vomit comet, a name aptly chosen for the usually bumpy afternoon journey back from the Mara to Nairobi Wilson Airport. Most airline crews are used to turbulence, but for some passengers their disembarkation is a relief at destination. Many complain their stomachs have been left somewhere over the Mara! Much of my feeling of airsickness was in my mind. I have little experience as a sailor, but as a boy I would become ill before boarding any aeroplane. Yet in later years it became one of my passions to fly. I was never too happy about heights, so one day an old wrinkly pilot took me for a flight and sat me next to him upfront. I must have been about ten years old. He gave me two words of advice. "Son, if you feel queasy in straight and level flight, fix your eyes on a cloud and don't take your eyes off it. Number two, if we bank steeply look at the ground directly below and if you have to be sick, make sure it's not over me otherwise I will throw you out of the door." I did as I was told and never had a problem since, except when flying in the continued murk of thick cloud, or thick smoke haze hour after hour. Then I still feel queasy—I get the feeling that my inner ear and my backside are having an argument as to which way is 'up'.

The DC.3 landed; the engine popping and spluttering as all DC.3's do when the throttle is pulled fully back to idle on taxiing. To me this is a comforting sound that all cylinders are firing correctly, to others not accustomed to these backfires they believe the bird is about to take its last breath and collapse. When full throttle is selected for takeoff the sound of the engine develops into a solid and confident roar of power; just to listen to it is very comforting to any white-knuckle flier. I was sad to see such a happy band depart; we had experienced wonderful sights and feelings of togetherness on this safari and shared the closeness and the friendliness of Petal. Everyone promised to come back to see her babies; we all shared that same hope!

My drive back to camp from the airstrip took a short cut from the airstrip across the plains to pick up the camper-van and clear out my belongings. On arrival at camp I was not surprised to see the progress they had made. By morning I knew every tent, toilet, dining tent and kitchen tent would already have been taken down and stacked tidily in the lockup containers. The Maasai landlord was at camp waiting to receive his rent for the next quarter, he was always paid in advance whether the camp site was occupied or not. This is the campsite land-rent, which he seldom shared with his brother. A few years ago his feisty brother trebled the rent overnight without warning. I objected and moved out to another landlord's campsite, hoping the former landlord would relent knowing the rent increase was a complete try-on. The Maasai have a habit of doing business this way—they are the inventors of gazumping! Nothing was said about my vacating. Forty-eight hours passed and then, in the middle of the night, a mysterious grass fire broke out. The fire started about three hundred yards up wind of the new camp; luckily the camp was empty of clients except for seven staff. I had taken on a young, white, twenty-one year old Kenyan assistant to set up the new camp. The camp was sited among leleshwa bushes and trees and the perimeter surrounded by long dry grass. The crew had set about cutting the grass with 'slashers', (a metal strip shaped like a hockey stick sharpened to razor sharpness on both sides of the curved blade end). This enables an effortless swing back and forth and soon makes short work of cutting down thick clumps of grass both inside and outside the campsite. Short grass keeps away creepy crawlies, particularly snakes and encourages the non-dangerous wildlife to graze in camp at night on the sprouting green shoots after rain.

The fire raged all night around the perimeter of the camp and for almost the whole of the next day, but not one item of camp equipment, fuel or vehicles caught fire. It was impossible to try and extinguish the blaze. The wind direction then changed and the fire took off towards the homestead of the perpetrators—razing theirs to the ground! Justice was seen to be done.

The underhand attempt at scuttling my business had backfired on the brother! It soon became apparent that the mischief-makers, most of whom were known Maasai drunkards, had been bribed to do the job by one of my competitors. I had a feeling I knew who the instigator of the bribe was.

For this reason I prefer to employ staff from up country. Eighty percent of their monthly wage is sent back to the family for their subsistence and education each month. The system works well and the staff appreciate this method of saving. Many have now purchased an acre or two of land. To an African this is one of life's most important achievements. Add to this another half a dozen children! To have many children (boys preferred) is investing in old age. When the children become adult they take over as the breadwinners for the family.

Tribal culture dictates they are responsible for the care of their parents when old age or illness renders their father or mother incapable of earning a wage. Daughters are valuable too. Culture also dictates a bride price must be paid in kind, usually sheep, goats or cattle, even chickens are acceptable to the parents of the bride. Land is considered a worthy and precious asset, more so than money. To own land is a first priority among the African tribes.

The foundation weakens when the family does not own land; this leads to slum dwelling, congestion, disease, poor sanitation, squalor and more poverty follows. The family structure breaks up and the children head for the streets to seek a crumb by whatever means necessary, crime soars and security deteriorates. This is Africa and much of it will remain this way for centuries to come. At present the population of Central and South Africa is still increasing, despite the scourge of aids, malaria and malnutrition. The quest for land and its equal distribution amongst the indigenous population has become a matter of concern between the have's and the have not's. The next twenty years of this century will see land grabbing, corruption, the destruction of prime forests and the slaughter of wildlife as a major problem for these Republics.

I must find Petal before sunset. She may have moved away from her last position or have been disturbed by a predator and Maasai cattle. On previous occasions, I have returned to her last place of rest only to find darkness had set in and so missed out on her company for that evening. I cherish the times we are together alone, enjoying the sunset in each other's presence. These are magic moments for me; great for my morale and the perfect therapy to unwind from the stresses of providing and giving value for money to my clients. If it were not for their support, I could not possibly afford to visit the Mara on a regular weekly basis.

I was expecting to see her head pop up on hearing the distant sound of my approaching vehicle. On arrival at the tree I could see the impression of her body on the flattened grass where she had lain. I got out of the vehicle and examined the blades of grass. The grass indicated her departure was within the last half-hour. Where to and in which direction did you go Petal? I asked myself. Now, on my own without Kibet, my other pair of eyes, I could easily find myself spending the night alone. Petal would not return to her kill. Cheetahs, once having left the remains of their meal to the aerial scavengers, do not usually return to their kill or pass close by; they normally give the area a wide berth. I decided to head south towards camp, my supposition being that when I left her she would have seen my vehicle heading in that direction. My intuition was rewarded after some ten minutes of driving; there she was sitting down on her haunches, nonchalantly looking into space portraying, as all adult cheetahs do, an aloofness that imparts a feeling of profound superiority over the human race! There was an anthill close by and knowing her liking for resting and sitting atop these mini hills, I drove over to this spot, got out and sat on the mound; first checking that the disused air vents did not contain any surprises like a snake or two! I have often noticed Petal paying particular attention to this, as I do, for my personal safety. It can be embarrassing if a fanged occupant objects to you cutting off the escape route—one could get severely bitten!

I remember once placing my hat over a vent hole. I laughed out loud as a child would do to see my battered kofia, (a Swahili word for hat), sprinting off into the sticks on its own accord. Four little feet could be seen propelling it along; the feet belonged to a lone banded mongoose left behind whilst checking out the underground channels for a tasty meal—a lizard or a snake. The petrified animal decided to make a break for it. Petal was surprised as I at this mobile piece of headgear making a quick getaway. I then retrieved my hat and placed it back on the hole once more. Petal was not sure of this new type of animal and viewed the hat with great suspicion from a safe distance before coming over to check it out. Curiosity killed the cat, now satisfied it was a harmless phenomenon she relaxed and lay down beside me.

The moment had been timed perfectly; the sunset was turning the clouds in the sky a bright yellow. The picture this evening was somehow different from the normal; the sun had dipped down beyond the horizon giving off a kaleidoscope of changing colours. The sun's warmth had cooled and it was becoming a little chilly. Stupidly, I had left my camera in the camper; other matters of planning and thought had distracted me. I remained on the anthill with Petal who seemed in a trance in her usual animal way. We were both in tune, admiring our sun and our sky painting this incredible picture for us as its curtain ushered in the nightfall ready for the animal world to rest and sleep under her blanket of stars.

Under a clouded sky the African night can suddenly turn very cold. I could hear in the distance the Maasai singing their impromptu jump-up dance in vocal harmony; they seldom venture too far from their manyattas at night. Their voices and singing carry great distances on the night air—this really is Africa. It is so satisfying to listen to the combined human and wildlife orchestration; the beautiful night sounds of the Mara, these are the sounds that penetrate deep into the soul. I hear the voice of my mentor saying to me "the call of the wilds will never leave you now David, you are hooked!" I was beginning to shiver.

The mosquitoes were also telling me it was 7.00 p.m. Now it was their turn to feed on me! Petal was not bothered by these biting insects, in fact I had a suspicion they targeted me as the juicier of the two. I moved towards the caravan – Petal, not wanting to be left alone— followed. This was good news; it signalled her intention to stay the night. Nyundu, the mechanic, had fitted an anti-slip rubber mat fixed with glue to the bonnet. This mat had several uses. I was always concerned that the shiny polished surface of the bonnet would cause Petal to slip and fall, breaking a leg or dislocating a shoulder or hip joint. That could be an accident from which she would not recover. It was also a handy non-slip flat surface to place the necessary cups and thermos for a 'stand up' tea break for me. Prior to this mat being fitted my tea break was often ruined.

My spotted companion, with typical cat-like agility and precision, leapt straight onto the bonnet and in the next bound, onto the top of the caravan. I had not seen her do this before, it was quite a departure from the normal. She stretched then flopped down, yawned, and went to sleep almost in one movement. "Make yourself at home, be my guest" I muttered! My opening and closing of cupboards and general shuffling around below did not seem to disturb her unduly. My dinner tonight was chicken pilau, several small boiled potatoes, carrots, a little broccoli and some green peas made up a tasty dinner served with a glass of Tusker, a pleasant popular brand of Kenya beer.

Petal should sleep well tonight on her high-rise apartment some ten feet above ground, safely out of reach of any marauding predators which otherwise could easily creep up on her when asleep on the ground. Wild animals seldom sleep the sleep of the deep, most catnap; but tonight if all went according to plan, with no disturbance, she would have a well-earned rest. Cheetahs do not sleep in or climb trees as leopards do; though low over-hanging branches do provide cheetahs with a platform to see over a distance when the plains grass is long. Petal's high perch was ideal and out of harm's way—my presence too would make her feel secure.

The night sky was a shimmering mass of stars twinkling like fireflies. The occasional gust of wind indicated unstable air currents were forming, suggesting rain before morning. I slept heavily for most of the night and awakened to spots of heavy rain on the caravan tin roof. How would Petal react? I could hear distant sounds of thunder in the hills—more heavy rain was heading our way. Cheetahs sleep out in the clear avoiding flat ground where puddles form during heavy rain. They prefer to seek out sloping ground. I could hear her stirring from her indented flat roof surface; this would only serve to form a puddle if it rained. There was a patter of feet and the unmistakable 'boing-g' as her body weight landed on the bonnet in the usual cat-like four-point landing. For the next two hours, into the early dawn, the heavens opened and soon the plains were awash with floodwater. This was the first heavy rain in Mara for several months. My concern also was for the tentage and the staff back at camp. Hopefully, they would have managed to take down, fold and store all the canvas tents. Rain is a camp fitter's nightmare and crews must not be caught in the middle of dismantling camp in a thunderstorm! The canvas must never be packed away wet; mildew will form overnight and then the rot quickly sets in. The only cure is to lay the canvas out to sun-dry and that could take several days or more provided the sun shines and there is no more rain! Meantime, if the rain continues and there is no sun, watching tentage dry is like watching paint dry—all forms of planning are scuttled!

I may as well put the kettle on and herald the wet dawn in with a cup of tea. It is still raining hard and my thoughts turn to that hell road back to Nairobi. The heavily laden juggernauts, carrying grain from the encroaching wheat farms, slither and slide and their huge wheels carve up the road for long stretches making it impossible to traverse any distance even by four-wheel drive. The only alternative is to take to the bush. Sometimes these monsters are stuck solid for days necessitating tractors and earth moving crawlers to pull them out.

Tomorrow's five hour drive back to Nairobi over a pot-holed, unpaved road always tests man, machine, shock-absorbers and springs. The roadside bush mechanics do a roaring trade, quick to double their charge knowing there is still another eighty kilometres to the next garage!

I have heard the good news that the Chinese have won the next contract to build a tarmac road that will pass to the north of the Aitong hills. This will be a blessing for, at present, most tourists have taken to travelling by air to the Mara. Frankly, I don't blame them—it's safer.

Despite this hell-road some clients preferred to travel by road just to experience the adventure. Many clients come back time and again and never seem to tire of this journey. Word of mouth was my only advertising media and most will agree there is no better way to promote a product. Not once was I or my clients ever bored; there is always something exciting happening, even punctures and wheel changing in the bush was acceptable! A safari was not considered a safari without one; a mechanical breakdown, however, was frowned upon. It was embarrassing for the outfitter and very unsettling for the passengers. If one's mechanical skills saved the day then you were forgiven and client confidence was re-established in you; it was therefore imperative that preventive maintenance became a daily routine.

My safari drivers were able to cope with most of the minor common mechanical 'hiccups' in the field, but the real Mr. Fix it—self taught to fix anything and everything from a major engine failure to broken springs and drive shafts—was back at camp. If disaster struck in the field 'Nyundu' (pronounced Nyun-dooo, Swahili for hammer) would be brought to the scene of the breakdown. He would work late into the night. Tea laced with a tot of whisky at not too frequent intervals ensured that the heap of engine parts that lay scattered on the ground would eventually be refitted from whence they came. I never ceased to be amazed when every nut, bolt, bearing and cog found its rightful place and at the press of the starter the engine roared into life; never a cough or splutter! This amazing miracle man made anything work— his overalls covered in grease, oil and grime—had not seen a washtub in their lifetime. This is the true stamp of a bush mechanic. His overalls would remain that way just for 'prestige purposes'. We had one problem—many others who broke down sent their 'runners' to us for help. Our camp was known as Drummond's Garage. Nyundu's skills were always in demand!

My attention is diverted back to the job in hand; the kettle is whistling merrily reminding me I had promised myself a cup of tea. The rain had stopped and the heat from the gas stove has warmed up the area inside the caravan providing an opportunity to dress in comfort. I was particularly interested to see in which direction Petal may have gone, I could also hear rushing water; the luggas (water-courses) were in flood taking much of the storm water off the plains. Luggas become death traps for newly born cheetah cubs; their lives are constantly in danger from flooding. More good reason for me to be back in harness ready and at hand for Petal's first litter, to ensure her choice of den is safe from these hazards. Often inexperienced cheetah mothers that give birth to first litters are insufficiently streetwise in their choice of den and soon fall foul of the elements. A cheetah, having lost her litter, will come into season within two months and once again the ninety-day pregnancy begins. Too many of these natural disasters drain the mother of her strength and vitality in continually having to nurture new offspring.

I recall a cheetah mother giving birth to nine cubs. I still prefer to call them kittens but science says no, so be it, they will be called cubs. As expected the litter of nine was too much for her to cope with. Some were abandoned, others lost to feathered and four legged predators until there were none. The trauma of carrying and producing this rat pack delayed her coming into season for almost four months.

The wildlife park authority could have stepped in here and lessened the burden by taking out the runts, which were plain to see, then fostered them in the wild as was done with Petal and her brothers. With commitment and care, several little cubs may have lived to adulthood and established another platform for behavioural and scientific study right on Nairobi's doorstep.

Unfortunately, my efforts to even suggest this trial were vetoed by a group of short-sighted conservationists who believe nature must take its course. My argument to this is that man's greed is party to the decline in the cheetah population by intruding upon their rangelands and disturbing their breeding grounds. Yet here was man, the professed conservationist, turning a blind eye to the predicament before them and ignoring a simple remedy to a situation that was calling out for help. We see this derailed thinking in our everyday life and find it intolerably frustrating.

Now fully dressed, gum boots and all and with tea mug in hand, I stepped outside the caravan swinging down from the rear door handrail. To my amazement there was Petal curled up under the vehicle. Smart lady, she had chosen the driest place in town! It was still cold outside; the early morning chill after rain always encourages a short walkabout and stretch and this kick started my mind into accepting today was departure day. Petal seemed not too interested in my exercising antics, but kept a watchful eye on the bouncing ball, the size of a tennis ball, that I always carried. I am sure she was expecting it to grow feet and run off!

This ball is an amusing play thing for the young Maasai goat herders. When thrown high into the air above one's head and its subsequent return to earth, the first and second bounce would return it back to the same height that was achieved in the initial upwards throw. Surprisingly, the young Maasai had difficulty in co-ordinating a clean catch. I was amazed at their lack of hand-eye co-ordination, yet their spear throwing and dance timing was well above the norm of the average modern day disco dancer. I had plans for this ball in the months to come. I was interested to see how Petal's cubs would react to it when the time came for them to progress into the natural state of 'catch as catch can'. Domestic kittens and puppies all go through this amusing, wide-eyed, excited make-believe phase of chasing after an imaginary prey. Petal was always mature and regal in her poise and manner and so often gave me that look of pure disdain at my attempts to attract her attention to play ball with me.

I called camp on the radio-com requesting a progress up-date on the dismantling. To my relief all was dry and tidily packed away, they had worked non-stop until two in the morning. The vehicles were loaded, ready and waiting to roll. Andrew was now preparing their breakfast and picnic lunch.

It was necessary to attend camp inspection, a discipline that is important to ensure that no rubbish, plastic or other offending litter, should be left behind within the camp perimeter. Baboons can make short work of an uncovered rubbish pit; if this is neglected, within days your rubbish will be found spread beyond the compounds of your camp and the Maasai Mara. The local council authority for this type of mindless carelessness imposes a heavy fine.

The moment had come for me to say goodbye to Petal. I walked to within several feet of her, sat down and said my farewells. For a fleeting second or two our eyes met. Her golden eyes seemed to speak to me. Petal sensed I must leave her—was there a look of sadness in her eyes? It was easy to convince myself there was. I promised her I would return as soon as possible. I stood, then turned slowly and walked to the vehicle. The tears were blurring my vision and I wanted to remain with that last picture of her sitting on her haunches looking straight into my eyes. The camp was spotless, the only evidence left behind would be human footprints, and they too would soon vanish with the next downpour of rain.

We were now a convoy of three all-terrain Landcruisers. Our first task was to trail-blaze a track through the mountain range, hugging the rocky slopes, avoiding the dangerous black cotton soil patches that would cling like glue to our spinning wheels, sucking the vehicles deeper into the quagmire-like quick sand. If the road was passable we should be seeing others approaching inbound within the next hour from the other side of the mountain pass. My other concern was the drift that cut across the road. This, when filled with storm water overflow from the hills, could be dangerous, bringing with it boulders and uprooted trees to block our route.

I was confident we had all the necessary equipment, including high lift jacks and strong nylon tow ropes. These ropes, some thirty to forty feet in length, provide sufficient elasticity to allow the pulling or towing vehicle some movement and gradual dead-weight pull, rather than a steel wire cable that will not stretch and is guaranteed to burn your clutch or break your drive-shaft when power is applied.

From the look of the large storm water ruts, the Aitong hills had received a good three to four inches of rain during the night, much of which had passed through our intended track on its way to the Mara River some four miles to the north of us.

A large herd of elephants had traversed our intended path minutes before our arrival. Their steaming droppings provided us with a sure-footed guide that paved a less slippery pathway ahead. Our progress was slow but sure, I was in no hurry to join the elephants and estimated the herd to be at least fifty in number. Various dung piles suggested a mixture of young, medium and mature adults. For the moment they were heading in the right direction— that was good enough for me to follow.

Our progress for the next half-hour was encouraging, but the elephant track began to veer up the steep hill and not in the direction I wished to proceed. The going was becoming difficult. Without our pachyderms to guide us I had to carefully plan the next route.

The elephants' plan was obvious, the higher they went the easier it would be for them to cross the 'donga', (the starting point of the downward tributary). Now the surrounding vegetation was beginning to thicken and the elephants had chosen to adopt single file, making the trail too narrow for us to follow. We stopped and tied our vehicles bumper to bumper allowing some ten feet of slack on the rope between them. We could hear the elephants nearby but out of sight. Andrew, in particular, was showing his usual nervousness and was story-telling to the others his version of us being flattened and trampled to death. He was also bemoaning the fact that his hard earned savings would be scattered around the hillside convincing some drunk, honey-hunter Maasai into believing money does grow on trees.

We now had no alternative but to blaze our own trail and head back down the slope towards the river crossing, hence the need to hold the vehicles together providing the convoy with ample engine brake power from three 4 x 4 drive in low range. After negotiating several slippery rocky outcrops, we arrived at the crossing point. A slow flowing expanse of water, some fifty yards wide, convinced me this was the end of the line for the day. With some six hours of daylight left the only thing to do was to build a small fire and cool our heels. Kibet, in his usual boy scout way, cut a stake and hammered it into the ground as a point of reference—this would indicate the rise or fall of the water level—it would also give us the measure of waiting time until we could cross, assuming no more rain was falling in the hills.

The stake became the constant focus point for our attention over the next hour. Andrew opened his betting shop and each crew member laid a ten-shilling wager as to how long the water would take to subside and permit us to cross. The water level was receding about an inch every ten minutes with another six feet to go before we could consider an attempt. All the vehicle engines were diesel fuel operated therefore water entering the engine compartment would not cause a problem for us. The drift had a long concave concrete base and hopefully no big holes to disappear into.

No tourist vehicles had arrived on the opposite bank—this suggested trouble ahead. The regular air service to the lodges in the Mara should be passing over us within the next ten minutes. I would try and communicate with the pilot on the radio. Hopefully, he might be in a position to give his bird's eye view of what lies ahead. VHF radio contact is line-of-sight and so the aircraft would need to be almost overhead for contact. We were in the Aitong Valley – an amphitheatre of high hillsides surrounding us. The camp staff were busy chattering to each other when Kibet pointed skywards—he already knew what my intentions were.

Most of the regular pilots are conversant with my call sign 'X-Ray Mobile'. As the aircraft passed overhead I called "Any inbound aircraft to the Mara – can you provide a road condition report on the Aitong/Narok sector for me please?" The reply came instantly. "Dave, I hear you loud and clear, the road is like a river—suggest you paddle; there is no movement of vehicles and those that are on the road are totally bogged down." "Thanks" I replied. "You'll need your webbed feet today, quack, quack" was the pilot's cheeky reply. Such was the good-humoured banter that always passed between us.

This was not good news. If there are tourist vehicles bogged down, they will be in for a push and shove day and possibly a night without food. Most tour drivers carry a cool box with soft drinks but not much else except a blanket or two for use as dust covers for the occupants' baggage. It could be an uncomfortable and cold night for those stuck in the mud and unable to move.

Once the cross flow of water receded and with daylight still on our side, we would cross over and push ahead. The crew was used to bedding anywhere en route in the vehicles—they all carried their emergency rations and blankets. I had the caravan with cooking facilities and Andrew would cook the dinner—African style posho (a maize meal porridge), gravy, sukuma wiki (a wild cabbage leaf that can be plucked from the roadside), topped with baked beans in tomato sauce (the tinned type).

African beans are banned in my book and must be avoided by all staff at all times. I am sure NASA could find a better use for them as a substitute form of human propulsion to the moon!

Kibet was the first to stake his reputation on the crossing time. "Two hours from now" he said, "would make it one o'clock." The rest of the crew claimed their times in quick succession; two o'clock, three o'clock, with Andrew following up the rear. "This time tomorrow", he said. Now it was my turn—the 'boss' has the last say; it was agreed my donation to the kitty stakes would not be less than 100 shillings (about five pounds in English sterling pounds). It was a no win situation for me, my position as chief chicken necessitated I should only be the banker entrusted with the security and final pay out of the bet.

In Africa, most Africans living in the bush walk everywhere. Soon our group began to swell with new arrivals from nearby manyattas. Maasai in general are tall people, unafraid of water, though few can swim. When sufficient numbers arrived it was clear their plan would be to strip off their red shukas (a wrap around material hung from the shoulder), wrap it around their heads. Then, with spear in one hand to measure the depth ahead and the other holding the next man, they would make an attempt to cross naked. This manoeuvre would provide me with an indication of the present depth of water. In return I would be expected to ferry the women and the elderly when our turn came to cross over in the vehicles.

The moment of truth arrived—the leader was chosen—he was a beanpole of a man almost six foot, five inches tall, the type that is often seen loping across the plains. Their lithe, articulate bodies appear to float on air, one moment here, then suddenly out of sight. No wonder they are known as the best long distance runners in the world. Nature has adapted their bodies to leg it over the plains. Western man invented the wheel and now no longer requires the long distance mode of two-legged transport. Few Maasai, if any, suffer from blood pressure or heart attacks, not yet anyway, but soon it will happen—many are becoming wealthy and westernised—some already battling with their bulges.

Our chosen one, unanimously agreed by all those present, was now fired up and ready to prove his courage. The question of stripping naked in front of his audience never entered his mind; he was totally focused on the task ahead. The flow was gentle with insufficient force to pose any threat of losing his footing or being washed away down stream—my concern was the depth. Our trailblazer was halfway across and had reached the point of no return—to return now would be unthinkable. Red lights were flashing inside my head! The water was halfway up his chest and there was still another thirty yards to go. Sporadic shouts of nervous encouragement from the bystanders echoed across the water. I had to admit to myself that the whole exercise was now fraught with danger and really quite pointless. Was the risk worth it?

Not in my opinion. I was not the instigator so my conscience was clear. No sooner said, the chorus of cheering turned to shouts of frantic warning – a massive tree had been uprooted upstream and was bearing down river directly towards him—the water was still at his chest level.

I leapt out of the vehicle and yelled at the now frenzied group to stop shouting. Our hero was unaware of the approaching danger and had mistaken their shouts for encouragement. I had inherited a good pair of lungs. I shouted the word 'hatari' in Swahili, this is instantly recognised as 'look out – danger!' He had only seconds left to react before the tree engulfed him. To my surprise he had the presence of mind to plunge his spear into the tree trunk and take hold of a passing branch. The danger was not over. The women were 'ululating and woi-ing' (the African high pitched vocal method of sounding alarm bells to all and sundry)—this call summons urgent additional help. Sooner or later the tree branches would strike bottom and anchor the tree somewhere downstream.

Kibet and I hurriedly took hold of several lengths of standby nylon towrope and armed with a machete and my fire extinguisher, we ran after the crowd, which was following the progress of the tree down stream. Finally the tree ground to a halt. Frantic calls for help could be heard coming from our marooned brave. He claimed he had unwanted company in the form of several large snakes; they too had sought refuge in the branches and were too close to him for comfort. His voice went into high gear as he shouted "nyoka, ni mamba" (one of Africa's deadliest snakes, if bitten there is no cure). The Maasai women were the first to offer assistance in forming a line to hold one end of the rope as both Kibet and I took it in turns to throw the lasso in true wild-west fashion, hoping it would catch on some protruding branch. After several attempts we realised the tree was too far out in mid-stream and our lasso efforts to hook on were falling yards short of the target. We required a longer, thinner, lighter rope with a modified plumb weight on the end.

Maasai women never travel without sisal string—a handy tough local tie-anything woven cord. A cloth bag and a pebble the size of a tennis ball were soon produced. The slingshot was prepared—we were now in business. The demented Maasai on the tree was shouting much louder for us to hurry up—he was quite sure the snakes would attack him. It is a known fact that most snakes can swim and unless disturbed will seldom attack, but the black or green mamba and spitting cobra have a reputation for launching an attack at the slightest sign of any aggression towards them—as Petal and I know only too well!

Our first sling shot was on target, just within his grasp; the sisal rope was pulled in and attached to the nylon rope and then tied solidly to the tree trunk. Some fifty or more Maasai, old and young, had now answered the emergency call. I'm always amazed how Africans just seem to appear from nowhere. With fifty pairs of hands and a combined 'heave ho' the tree came alongside. The snakes quickly abandoned the tree—scattering the watching crowd in all directions.

Our brave had become an instant hero for the day, despite out-distancing the rest of us to higher and safer ground. I sympathised with him in his hurried parting from the reptilian Noah's Ark. My experiences with snakes were still very fresh in my mind. An hour had passed since his first attempt at crossing by foot; undaunted, he was prepared to try again. The level of the water had, in the meantime, subsided sufficiently to make the crossing by vehicle. It was my turn to trail-blaze and lead the threesome with all three vehicles roped to each other with the last vehicle trailing some fifty feet of nylon rope for the waders to hold onto. 'Nyundu', the mechanic, won the bet. We entered the water at one hour and forty-five minutes from 'stake down'!

Attempting to drive through a fast or slow running river requires a cool head, as there is a real danger of succumbing to a form of vertigo. To overcome this the eye must not wander off a fixed point on the opposite bank. If you transfer your driving line onto the flowing surface of the water your brain will signal that a correction is required, and without knowing, your instinctive reaction will be to steer with the flow. Fear will compound the error and other senses will convince your mind that the front end of your vehicle has lost contact with the ground and is floating. You realise, too late, that the trap of your own making has ensnared you—the die has been cast and now disaster looms.

Prior to attempting any river crossing my checklist takes the following form; engage low four-wheel-drive gear; (diesel engines are impervious to water), ensure the air intake is above cab level, attach a floating plastic tube to the exhaust outlet and arrange for a few extra people to sit on the front bumper, holding onto the cow catcher to add weight up front—you are then ready to go. Engage brain and enter the water slowly gauging the depth as you move forward with the front wheels. Should the flow of water begin to rise above the top of the wheel, it's time to back off—never switch off the engine!

We were ready to move—our hero perched himself on the front bumper using his spear as a depth plumb whilst others clambered on board. Anyone observing this overload would have agreed we resembled the last bus to Istanbul. We made the crossing without mishap though having reached the other side there was no way the vehicles could proceed. We were dangerously over-loaded—it had to be everybody off—with no exceptions. The last thing I wanted was broken springs—a nightmare to refit in muddy conditions. The road to Narok was a quagmire with bogged down vehicles—only a heavy tractor or bulldozer could shift them. Today would be a profitable day and night for the drivers and headmen of the local road contractor. Tourist vehicles en route to the Mara always received immediate attention—the almighty Dollar begets priority!

Our day became long, slow and tedious. Much of our progress was with vehicles tied together and mostly off-road, circumventing the push-pull, tourist shove brigade! Finally we arrived at Narok, tired and weary. The fifty kilometres of this hell run had taken us almost five hours. The rest of the one hundred kilometres was tarmac, though care and concentration was still needed to avoid some of the largest potholes I have ever seen. On arrival at base in Nairobi the crew summoned up their hidden energy and were keen to off-load and store the valuables in lock-up. Surprisingly most were ready to take the long distance night bus to their homes. The safari was not over for them; they still had another six hours of coach travel through the night to far-flung places like Kisumu on the shores of Lake Victoria and beyond, where most had their ancestral homes.

The landscape there is beautiful, coloured in deep green by banana and maize plantations. Maize, bananas, beans and fish from the lake form the base of their staple diet. Sugar cane is plentiful and sold in short lengths of twelve to eighteen inches. The stick is then chewed to extract its sweet watery liquid before spitting out the pith. Driving behind a bus or coach has its hazards—the rough fibres can destroy a set of windscreen wipers in minutes. Their women folk are tall and slim with shapely bodies covered by colourful kangas, (a wrap around cotton garment). Amazingly they carry everything balanced on their heads and most have poise and elegance with friendly faces, always ready to return a smile and a wave. How they do all of this and control their balancing act is an art in itself.

I remember my mother trying to teach my sister, at the early age of ten, how to walk elegantly and attain poise by placing an encyclopaedia on her head. Watching her ensuing gyrations never failed to reduce me to uncontrolled laughter. My sister had one problem—her low centre of gravity! The Giriama tribe that lives on the Kenya Coast takes great pride in their big-end 'wobble'—they too have perfected an intriguing balancing act.

I too had a problem in my early youth. I was showing signs of becoming pigeon-toed; my duck-like shuffle was very noticeable when I wore shoes. From the day I could walk, shoes were not part of my upbringing. My introduction was blisteringly painful; each time I was caught not wearing shoes, I received a severe tanning. Many trips were made to the shoemaker, an old bearded Indian named Pitamber Khoda. He worked in an open alleyway in downtown Nairobi. Pitamber was synonymous with made-to-measure shoes—my pigeon feet were finally mastered and moulded into shape. Sixty years later, his family name and business still exist today but not on the sidewalk. Before he passed away he purchased the whole two-story building where he once sat outside on the street.

The time had come for me to reassemble my thoughts and refocus on finalising my overseas travel plans. My planned sea cruise from Cape Town to Australia fired up memories of my childhood days. I was no seafarer; the slightest rocking movement always sent me 'honking' towards the ship's side. My father was employed by the Kenya/Uganda Railways, laying and maintaining railroad tracks through the Kenyan hinterland. He told the stories about the man-eating lions that terrified and killed many railroad workers – the lions almost brought the railroad project to a halt.

The gruesome true story was vividly brought back to me in a personalised tour of the coach where the 'Man-eating Lions of Tsavo' entered and took hold of a foreman from the top bunk and then crashed through the window, taking the screaming human into the night. His remains, when found, bore stark evidence that the ghost of the darkness had fed well.

The British Colonial Government offered a generous home leave package to their overseas servants, which included a return sea voyage for the employee and his family. The passenger liners regularly plied back and forth to the U. K. via the Suez Canal from Mombasa, Kenya's main port where, in later years, I was to become the Security Chief.

Children of all ages had the run of the lower deck and the children's entertainment area— the oldies had the spacious upper decks to relax on in peace, making new friends and chatting with old friends. By the end of the voyage most of the passengers had come to know each other. They were all individuals to a man; most became part of the Railways backbone that made the wheels of progress turn for Kenya's flourishing agricultural and cattle-farming community.

Father was a workaholic and took his home leave vacations once every decade. Staying with overseas relations was fun for us and his generosity towards his Scottish bloodline was always appreciated.

Much of his accumulated leave that ran into many months was spent on the cattle ranch in Kenya, giving my mother lots of advice on how to run it! Father was another habitual controller—a gene that has been passed down the family bloodline for centuries.

Bwana 'Nyum nyum' as he was nicknamed by his farm workers, had the strength of an ox and could put his hand to any task. If there was a mountain to be moved, he was always the man called upon to do it!

When the enormous one hundred and fifty-ton Garrett steam engines and passenger coaches derailed at line wash-aways along the Nairobi to Mombasa railroad, it wasn't the Chief Engineer who was called to sort out the mess and the bent rails. The call went out "Get Drummond!" Drummond would arrive with his engineering train, the ten LSB's (low sided bogies) full to overflowing with quarry ballast, sandbags and new rails, together with his work force of some three hundred workers sitting atop. The detour around the wreckage would soon be put in place—even if it took the whole night in conditions that no one in their right mind would venture out. The 'mountain' was moved, come hell or high water!

CHAPTER 8
MARCO POLO

MY planned cruise was not entirely supported by a bank loan. I was invited to 'sing for my supper' by providing lectures with backup video footage of my years with the Queen of the Mara cheetahs. I was anxious that nothing should go wrong with the slide and video presentation – but I had not planned for the ship's projector to be out of date. Disaster was avoided. My investment in a state-of-the art camcorder, prior to boarding the ship in South Africa, saved my day.

The ship's auditorium was filled to capacity and from there on, each time I travelled by sea on the Orient Lines' Marco Polo, I was invited to speak as a wildlife guest lecturer on her Africa cruises. Petal shot to fame overnight both on land and at sea; she became a great ambassador for Kenya's tourism.

Everything was set ready for go – air ticket, cruise tickets, visas and those fearful jabs that always brought the sweat to my brow – I hate having injections!

I had one more safari to make. It was a business visit to a Maasai friend of mine who wished to sell a small portion of his land adjoining the Nairobi National Park. I had always dreamed of owning a wildlife sanctuary. This could be my ideal opportunity. I had two days in hand before my four-hour flight to join the ship in Cape Town. My trusted four wheel drive 'Mzee Kobe', the Kiswahili name for old tortoise (my home on my back), would be the ideal form of transportation to visit him and be independent without having to participate in the usual Maasai traditional food and overnight welcome – any excuse for an all-night party on the local 'blow your mind' brew is not my idea of fun.

Large cumulonimbus clouds were 'towering' – a sure sign that heavy rain was due, no sooner spoken than the distant sounds of thunder suggested I must be on my way. Black cotton soil turns to a black mass of solid 'stick in the mud' once it has absorbed water roads get waterlogged in minutes, one can spend days in the sticks bogged down waiting for the sun to dry out the land.

I was very impressed with the acreage of land on offer. It was well positioned, sloping to a river frontage bordering the Nairobi Park boundary. It was perfect – I closed the deal there and then, the title deeds appeared in order – my solicitor would do the rest.

Darkness was now setting in – tomorrow morning I fly.

I must get back to Nairobi, it had rained intermittently most of the day but now it was bucketing down. I knew I had three deep gullies to pass through and flash floods would appear without warning, the black cotton soil by now was almost soaked to saturation. The undulating land was directing the storm water across the surface of the plains into the gullies. Gully number one was filling quickly; I passed through it with no problems; number two was still some distance away and the road, furrowed by the rains of previous months, had become a torrent; the night was pitch black save for the fork and sheet lightening that lit up a landscape that resembled a skating-rink. I had that horrible gut feeling that problems lay ahead. I would be lucky to make the safety of the tarmac still some five kilometres away. My mind was racing – should I head for the high ground and wait out the storm – or press on. I could feel my four-wheel, low-gear drive labouring and the 4.5 litre engine straining against the clawing mud that was sticking like glue to all four wheels. My trusted sixth sense told me 'Head for high ground, David and stop'—but the gremlins too were hard at work – 'Press on, press on' they said. I began to analyse the risk. Should I stop? What if the heavy rain continued? It would take the rest of the night and most of the next morning for the road and gullies to become passable.

My flight was scheduled to leave Nairobi at 10.30 a.m. the following morning. Visions of missing my flight and the ship's evening sailing from Cape Town the same day, made me realise my plans were about to become unstuck. I pressed on, gully number two was a raging torrent but the depth was a little under three feet and the road across it passable. Onwards to the next hurdle – the number three crossing had a concrete drift!

The going was touch and go but this Toyota Landcruiser was tough; it had never let me down. As I approached the drift my searchlight picked up the silvery glow of high, fast flowing water. There was no way I could cross; it would be suicidal to even try. Now it was time to stop for the night. I climbed into the camper and cooked myself dinner, it was still raining heavily with little sign of easing.

All the signs were pointing to a wakeful night but I was thankful for the home comforts.

Mobile phones were still on the drawing board. What a revolution it is now in communications. This hand-held, 'can't do without' press button object has revolutionised our everyday life, even in the third world how did we manage without it before? Smoke signals come to mind!

The sound of constant rain on the tin roof has always, since I can remember, been the best sleeping pill that the good Lord ever dispensed to me. I awoke still fully clothed. It was 4 a.m. The rain had eased but the crossing had been transformed into a flowing mass of water fifty yards wide moving purposefully and silently on its way to the sea off the coastal resort of Malindi some three hundred miles away.

My world was collapsing around me – the next port of call for the ship was Penang, a few days out from my disembarkation point of Darwin. The cruise would be over and so would any future offers with Marco Polo as a guest lecturer. Heavy cancellation fees from all quarters would come pouring in on me. I would need to prove to my insurers that I was still alive and my only excuse was I had been marooned in the Bush. Would the small print cover that, I thought not. An act of God? Yes, that would be their loophole and it would see me footing the bill! The whole exercise was now looking exceedingly costly. This travel insurance game is a complete lottery! The world of to-day is a zoo. What would my bank manager think? To get my loan I almost had to prove to him that I didn't need it to get it. I realised I was in panic mode looking for excuses to put the blame for my present predicament elsewhere. The bottom line was, no other person was to blame but myself. Such were my thoughts. Daybreak came slowly.

The rain had stopped, back home my faithful house servant of 30 years standing would be worried out of his mind; I had told him I would be back before dark the previous evening, that by now was yesterday. He would have painstakingly washed and ironed all my travel clothes, had dinner and breakfast waiting, for an 8.30 a.m. taxi pickup to the airport. He too would be having panic symptoms. All my camp crew had left for their distant homes, he was alone and the master of the house was missing, with no one to turn to except the police. To lodge a missing persons' claim was out of the question, the report would take all day to write, such was the efficiency of the 'boys in blue'. Some days you are the 'dog', some days you are the 'lamp-post', today I am definitely the 'lamp-post'. Mobile phones had not yet come to Africa and my VHF radio was not in 'the line of sight' of my home aerial.

It is now 9.30 a.m. The realisation of a missed flight and my ship sailing into the sunset was just beginning to dawn on me. My breakfast was quick and short, cornflakes and a slice of buttered bread plus an overly hard-boiled egg. Within the hour the nightmare of my dreams, and the airline that had Africanised me, would pass directly overhead minus its 'no show' passenger. The overnight rain had absorbed the dust and returned it to earth, visibility was crystal clear and I could see the International Airport fifteen kilometers away from my vantage point; all I could do was to sit and watch my flight take off and give vent to my frustrations by waving madly as the Airbus passed directly over me. I found myself frantically jumping up and down in some kind of lunatic gesture calling out a string of Kiswahili profanities that suggested the devil himself had taken over my senses.

I walked dejectedly down to the water's edge, could it be that the flood was receding? I pushed a stick into the soft ground as a marker as Kibet had done on previous occasions when we arrived at a flooded river; minutes later I returned to the spot. Yes, the water level was down several inches – the signs were there.

An old wizened Maasai appeared from nowhere and joined me at the water's edge. I asked him how long did he think it would take to navigate a crossing – he knew the river well. He looked into the sky and pointed to the heavens directly above, that meant the sun would be at its zenith, midday on the Equator. He had experienced this very situation many times and was prepared to sit and wait. I admired his patience. He had business to attend to in Athi River Town, but time was of no consequence to him.

The Maasai seldom suffer heart attacks or strokes for there is little stress except during times of drought. Make sure you avoid ruffling their feathers during this time. Many despair and become intolerant and very angry at the sight of their cattle dying.

I could not remember whether any other airlines flew to South Africa. Those that did over flew Nairobi on the long haul direct from their European home bases. The advent of the long range Boeing 747 had arrived. This mighty bird when heavily laden appears to fly so slowly after take-off that its' climb seems to confound the laws of gravity and flight.

Once out of here I planned to call in at the airport on my way and check whether Lady Luck was to turn in my favour. The old Maasai was staring at the water level and gently nodding his head; this wise old man's prediction, at the hour of zenith, was spot on. For his efforts I offered him a lift to town.

I arrived at the airport. Yes, there was a South African Airways flight leaving at 4.00 p.m., arriving Cape Town an hour before the ship's departure. For me suddenly the world was now a better place to live in. All haste now to collect my belongings – once again I was chasing my enemy 'time'. When I arrived back at home there was relief and smiles all around – my taxi was still waiting. I prayed there would be no delays to my departure time out of Nairobi, and all that was required now was a delay in the ship's departure. The latter was most unlikely, the former very possible.

To hell with speed limits! I will pay the taxi driver's fine – minutes later I realised I had unleashed a maniac behind the wheel – Kenyans are not renowned for keeping to speed limits at any time. Most taxis are privately owned and very second-hand. The owner lives off his day's takings and maintenance is left to God, often advertised on windscreens plastered with stickers like 'In God we Trust', another 'Chariot of the Road' and 'Mind Blaster', the 'Rocket' and other appropriate adverts adorn their windscreens and sometimes the bodywork of these 'killing machines'. My 'Chariot of Fire', on reaching forty miles per hour shuddered and juddered out of balance. Instead of easing up on the speed, as any sane minded person would do, his foot went to the floorboards; with eyes now transfixed on his speedometer, he urged his chariot to greater speed. At seventy miles per hour the juddering stopped. "Ah" he said excitedly, "we've broken the sound barrier!" Somehow we made it unscathed to the airport, the cops and God were both on my side – at last lady luck had not abandoned me.

The flight was on schedule, no snags, and soon I was looking down on the exact spot where I had looked up some hours before, this time I was not the 'no show' passenger. These happenings seemed quite surreal, was I having a bad dream? The raging torrent was no longer, but for sure I was on my way.

"Fly bird fly, find a jet stream flowing south and go for it". I was talking aloud to myself.

What a relief it was to walk up the ship's gangplank with only half an hour to spare and to be shown to my cabin. I collapsed exhausted and missed the famous Cape Town dockside farewells. I awoke to a gentle rolling motion, the ship by now was well out to sea, dinner time had come and gone, all I wanted was a strong drink that would serve as a fitting nightcap for me. It had been a stressful day. I took the lift to the top deck and watched the lights of Cape Town fade into the distance. All the night stars were out in force, it was a perfect evening in the company of young and old.

That very first meeting formed into a friendly group for the rest of the voyage. We enjoyed each other's company at dinner time and participated as a group in all the fun and games of onboard entertainment. The floor shows were fabulous, the ventriloquist most amusing, the magician and illusionist had us in fits of laughter and totally bamboozled; the juggler was a master of his art – jokes galore flowed, clever amusing and suitably presented for all ages. The beauty about a sea cruise is that every day at sea, if one so wishes, can be fitted in with activities of one sort or another—bingo sessions, bridge, deck games for the agile, singles only get-togethers, no unruly or noisy children, they have their own play-deck area.

Guest lecturers, all experts in their field, take turns in providing interesting topics. The story of the video presentation 'Petal Queen of the Maasai Cheetahs' was an outstanding success. My allocated sixty minutes was extended for another half-hour, by popular request. My next lecture, four days later, was built around a slide show called 'Kenya, Land of Many Faces'. This proved popular particularly the video coverage of a Maasai ceremony where young men prepared themselves for their warriorship.

The arrival of puberty is an important milestone in the life of any human. For the Maasai marriage comes at a later date, but in the meantime life is for living dangerously, exploring the mysteries of the fire in the flush of youth. The Maasai warriors feuding exploits against their cattle rustling neighbours and vice versa gives rise to a fearsome courage in the face of adversity; each warrior will, in a short time, find his pecking order within his clan according to the courage and youthful daring shown without fear. Their acts of lion killing are fast fading. Sadly, civilisation is beckoning to them. If I had my way and the power that controls man's destiny, I would leave them to be happy, carefree people untouched by the harsh world of civilisation. I envy their way of life, living in peace with their cattle and the wild animals. Nature has brought me close to the edge of their civilisation. I had looked in and was welcomed and I found myself walking in the wilds with Petal. It was for me the most fulfilling period of my life. I am a firm believer that our lives are inextricably bound to the higher order of our natural world; if we destroy it, we too will face extinction.

'Kenya, Land of Many Faces' proved to be a popular subject at my lectures. Each face has a character of its own moulded to its tribal ancestors. Though they may be black and dark-skinned, the trained eye of a Caucasian born in Kenya, who has lived amongst them for many years, can tell at once which tribal district they are from. Visitors from abroad are always surprised when these differences are pointed out to them. The same applies in reverse. The Maasai are convinced we Caucasians are all related—to them we look so alike.

Now that my lecture duties were complete I was able to relax and enjoy the rest of my cruise. The weather was perfect and the sea as calm as a pond. My thoughts now turned to Australia. I had spoken by ship to shore radio with my father—seldom did he ever show any emotion towards me, a man moulded into steel in his early years of sweat and toil and laying the railroad; he was a cattle rancher at heart, a man with incredible energy and foresight. He expected no less from his youngest son. I could just detect the slightest indication of excitement in his voice at my coming. Many years had passed since we last met. I hoped to spend some quality time with him. In my early years he never permitted me to get too close to understanding his ways; but now in his 'evening' years he had mellowed and opened the steel doors for me. He knew full well that my loyalties leaned more towards my late mother.

Several months later I received a letter from the Public Relations Coordinator of Orient Lines expressing appreciation of the effort I had put into the lectures. It read, in part, 'Your lectures on the Marco Polo Africa Egypt Cruise in November 1998 covered a wide range of captivating subjects, wildlife in particular. Your video presentation is unique and rightly several standing ovations were accorded to you; a mark of respect and difficult to attain particularly when lecturing to a cross-section of many seasoned professionals from all walks of life. You made your mark as a true professional with an appealing sense of humour. We hope that Orient Lines can offer you further cruise and destination enhancement lectures in the future.' Another window of opportunity had opened up for me.

The port of Penang was less than twelve hours away. The ship would refuel and revittal and then we would be on our way to Darwin where I planned to disembark and fly to Perth, one of Australia's beautiful cities, to stay a few days with my father and then take the long haul flight to London to visit Heather, my daughter. Heather had been flown to London for specialized treatment.

The telephone rang in my cabin, it was early afternoon and I was about to take an afternoon nap. The voice at the end of the phone was my son; my daughter had been rushed to hospital. For years she had suffered stomach pains and the cause had not been pinpointed until too late. The situation was desperate and life threatening. I must hurry and come immediately. In those few seconds all my travel plans were shattered to smithereens. I never did get to see my father.

My mind went into overdrive. The ship's administration were well trained to handle situations just like this and by the time we arrived in Penang, my disembarkation papers were ready, my flight was already booked out of Kuala Lumpur and I was on my way to London.

Fifteen sleepless flying hours later I arrived at London Heathrow Airport, my son was there to meet me. My sixth sense warned me to expect the worst. The words 'You are too late Dad', required no further explanation; my mind went into a stunned and deep shock; my body safety mechanism clicked in and the steel shutter came crashing down.

I pondered and reflected how it is that some wild animals feel and show little grief – but elephants grieve for years, domestic dogs, especially so if they lose their human friend. Humans grieve deeply at the loss of their loved ones and their pets until they are replaced, but what is it about the cheetah, the lion and the leopard. The sorrow is transformed within hours of losing their litter. It can only be their body mechanism that triggers the switch to procreate almost within days. Yet a cheetah or an animal can bridge that gap and sense the sorrow in humans. Animals have a very special therapeutic way, especially with children who are suffering in sickness. Also there are humans with special powers of healing for animals – take the Horse Whisperers of this world. We still have so much to investigate. There are no adequate words to explain the pain that a father feels at the loss of his child so early in life. The grieving never seems to go away, that ache somewhere deep within my soul is always there to remind me that a very special part of me was taken away from me before its time.

The funeral and reception was a very sad occasion with many of her tearful friends offering their deep condolences. All I desperately wanted now was to be alone in my sadness. How I wished I could be with Petal, she could sense my moods and would often edge closer to me when my spirits were down, silently understanding my inner turmoil. Even my own feral cat could sense my moods and my sorrows. Their company has always had a calming effect on me.

The call to return to the wilds of Africa grew stronger each day. It was pointless hanging about in England any longer; the thought of the long haul back to Australia once again had lost its pull. I urgently required a different type of therapy. Was there anyone out there who could replace either my daughter or Jamie? Such a person would be difficult, if not impossible to find. That person would have to possess all the ingredients, the list was as long as my arm, but above all, they will need to possess the chemistry that would permit acceptance by Petal.

I arrived back in Kenya to a warm welcome from Kibeso, my loyal and trusted servant. For the period I was away he took on all the responsibility of house security and care day and night. He refused to sleep in the quarters provided for him and took to sleeping on a mattress on the floor in the main house, near the telephone. Throughout all the many years he worked for me, he never gave me any reason to doubt his absolute integrity. When it came to retirement, his old age required that he should live close to a main hospital and he was happy to spend his days with me until the end, occupying his double room, with all the comfort and facilities at hand. Kibeso was part of 'family', he shared my sorrow at the loss of my daughter – in his own Kiswahili words he said, 'Tuta endelea, kila kitu iko kwa mikono ya mungu' translated into Swahili—'Life goes on, everything is in the hands of God.' Kibeso was indeed a true Christian.

I made arrangements to go on safari to the Mara and prepared Suntrekker – for how long was to be in the lap of the gods; circumstances would decide. First I must find Petal, hoping that nothing untoward had befallen her – life in the wild for any expectant mother is dangerous; she lives by the day as dictated by Nature's court.

The road to the Mara was still pot-holed and rutted from the heavy rains. The local Maasai Council's grader had broken down again and lay in pieces at the side of the road. Someone had pocketed the funds and the till was now empty. Millions of shillings are earned from Tourist Park fees; one can see the physical well-being of the councillors expanding by the day. The whole set-up is corruption personified.

The one hundred and sixty-kilometre journey had taken longer than expected; it was almost six hours ago since I left Nairobi. The rains had come to an end and the road was bone dry all the way with some untarred sections a foot deep in fine dust. Any speeds in excess of ten miles per hour had the tendency to suck up the dust into the cab and engine compartment, choking up the engine air filter system and me!

As I write my mind reflects on the impending war against Iraq. I can imagine the choking sandstorms, where the desert sand clogs up everything, Sand in your food, sand in your eyes, sand up your nose and in your ears, in your clothes and permeating into the machinery and air-conditioning. No matter what you do to keep it out it never fails to find a way in. Sand, day in and day out, the dust begins to play on your mind. Elsewhere all is forgiven after a shower of rain, but this seldom happens in the desert.

Many a young serviceman will crack; the psychological manifestations of desert warfare are many. Gulf War Syndrome must be investigated – it is not a myth or a figment of imagination. There will be many soldiers who will develop unusual stress symptoms because of the harsh terrain. After three to four months in a desert anywhere else, no matter how bad, is paradise. The mind and the body screams, 'Get me out of here quick!'

Darkness had fallen – the sun had set directly ahead of me in a red fireball of glory. Now I was negotiating through thick bush and open glades, on some occasions taking the 'off road' route I had blazed six weeks ago where others had later followed in our tracks. My spotlight picks out a herd of elephants heading downhill towards the river below, some impala and several bushbucks scamper across the road in front of the vehicle headlights; I pass a herd of buffalo resting quietly in the open glades, chewing their cud. The night air is cool. Suddenly there is a large herd of giraffe, almost a hundred of them standing in the road; they are dazzled by my lights. I stop and switch off my headlights to avoid panicking the herd and making them charge into the bush. Stumbling around on uneven ground in the dark can break legs. I had never seen so many together in one large herd.

There are certain times in the year when elephants, giraffe and buffalo, apart from migrating wildebeest, all congregate. It is nature's call for their Annual General Meeting of their species; no doubt the years' accounts of their numbers are examined and the imbalance attended to by Nature's way. I thought of my tax accountant and hoped he too was doing his bit for me with the Inland Revenue.

I am one of the frustrated to whom the taxman owes money, but he never seems to reply to my constant requests for refunds! What's new?

The giraffe were content to amble along the road ahead of me, taking their time. Not many budding PhD's have studied giraffe behaviour and population dynamics, but interestingly during the night, giraffe can be found in the woodland areas where they group together for the security of their young against predators. In the morning hours, as midday approaches they move to the open ground and spread out. Giraffe have the advantage of excellent height and good eyesight; at night their hearing is acute but night vision is poor.

As evening approaches, once again they head for the woodland but seldom take the same path. Nature has taught them how to conserve the remaining leaves and permit the bush to recover from that morning's browsing.

Science has discovered that the acacia tree has an effective 'don't browse me today' mechanism which produces phenol, a form of carbolic acid. The acacia leaves absorb and hold a high proportion of this unpalatable liquid and several or more days later allows the phenol level to drop; this permits the giraffe to browse the tree once more. Science is also exploring the various grasses that produce a form of arsenic when attacked by the scourge of army worms; grazing wildlife will circuit around these inch long caterpillars that swarm over and decimate large areas of green grassland like locusts. The army worm triggers certain grasses to become highly toxic and inedible. This is Nature's way of protecting her environment.

My thoughts turned to where to stop and rest up for the night. I had no idea where Petal might be. Sometimes, I would meet tour drivers heading out of North Mara; recognising my camper they would stop and give me information on what they had seen. The drivers were always keen to introduce me to their passengers as 'The Man that Walks with the Cheetahs'.

They too had spent precious minutes with Petal – she had jumped on their vehicle bonnet and frightened the life out of them – but more importantly she had let her feelings be known by marking their windscreen; her way of claiming another territorial post box. I always had great fun in telling those that had experienced her habit that because they had been noisy, inconsiderate tourists, that this was Petal's way of saying what she thought of them.

German and Japanese tourists saw the funny side and always burst into peals of laughter. In contrast the Americans and the Brits. were less pleased when she decided to dump her calling card on them in the presence of the other onlookers; some of their unprintable comments were colourful in the extreme. One particular wag, I remember, was quite vocal, "Very strange! Why does everyone want to shit on us?"

I parked for the night on Euphorbia Hill that overlooks the rolling plains to the west; this is the heart of Petal's territory. I was tired and muscle weary, driving a Land- cruiser without power steering for days and hours on end builds strong arms and broad shoulders.

The night was uneventful, I could hear distant lion calls, hyaena whooping down in the valley, they must have made a kill, the odd jackal calling his mates suggested they were standing by to participate on the crumbs from the hyaena's table. Seldom does the hyaena ever leave any scraps – mostly the tell-tale blood stained grass where their unfortunate quarry paid the ultimate price by falling victim to this ugly scavenger of the night.

The first signs of dawn were beginning to creep over the Aitong Hills, I was alert and awake. Petal was always a late starter, preferring to lie curled up to await the warmth of the sun to dry off the night's frost. The dewy droplets on the blades of grass are icy cold and uncomfortable when walked through. This can be very chilling, to the point of frostbite for padded paws open to the elements.

With time in hand for an early breakfast, I set up the portable table-top, screwed on the legs, positioned the lightweight canvas camp chair and settled down to a hearty bush breakfast of fruit juice, cereal, sausage, fried egg and bacon, toast, marmalade and a good cup of Kenya tea! My mobile camper-van was kitted out with all the essentials; freezer, gas cooker, water pump and electric lights supplied by a 12-volt heavy duty battery. Luxury living in paradise and not a soul in sight except animals for as far as the eye could see!

Using my rugged and battered binoculars, I could see hyaena packs heading home to their burrows with sagging bellies, a sure sign they had all fed well during the night. A pride of two female lions and three small cubs in attendance were strolling slowly towards a 'Kichaka' a small outcrop of thick leleshwa bush that would provide cover and shade for them during the heat of the day. This would be their resting place until the cool of the evening.

Several days may pass before their next meal, but in the meantime, under cover of darkness they would travel in search of water normally found in the storm-water courses known in Kenya Safari speak as 'luggas'. Here they would quench their thirst and probably stay around – why go for dinner when it will come to you?

Lions are not the most energetic animals in times of plenty but when the rains fail the wildlife will move away in search of greener pastures. Many lions will follow the herds, leaving behind those with young to hunt within their territory. Prey becomes scarce and the resident Maasai cattle are then targeted by the lions. These pastoralists will not tolerate lions munching on their cows, night or day and I have witnessed terrible, terrible killings; there is no mercy shown. Cubs and all, no matter how young, die under their spears.

I was in no hurry to move away from my vantage point on this hill; not only would there be a source of shade for me, but the crown of the hill had a forest of thick leleshwa. Often Petal's brothers would lie up for days in this three-acre patch. Spring water was close by. Not far away was an almost impenetrable close knit low veldt, short thorny acacia bushes. The only wildlife that seemed impervious to their thorns were giraffe, they were able to step carefully around and over their spiky foliage whilst browsing

Once again nature's defence mechanism has been brilliantly incorporated into the whistling thorn shrub, easily recognisable by the swollen black glands at the base of the largest spines. These black balls are hollow and inhabited by ferocious black ants and when disturbed – look out! Their sting is worse than the safari ants. Giraffe are very careful not to disturb them. At night when the breeze blows across the plains, the pinhead holes made by the ants produce a gentle, pleasurable whistle, hence the name 'whistling thorns'.

Interestingly, the biochemical reaction in the bush is linked to its survival and has evolved over many generations. Man's science must continue to study nature's ways and the interaction between the wildlife, the trees and grasses in the Savannahs.

When triggered, the high tannin content becomes highly toxic and browsers will avoid these bushes which also emit ethylene into the air. The browsers' acute sense of smell picks up the warning signs given off by the acacias, "Keep off" it warns, "Come back some other day".

The boys have little fear of being disturbed here. There is only one problem, the shrubs provide little shade during the heat of the day – but at night this hideaway has its safety advantages. Their enemies avoid these thorn-covered areas during the night time.

Several tour vehicles are heading my way. I may not know where the cheetahs are but I do know where there are two lions and three little cubs that they have just driven past unnoticed and now it is bartering time for me. Any information on their yesterday's or this early morning sightings of cheetah, will give me an idea if I am close to Petal or better still, Petal's last seen area. Sometimes they don't believe me when I say I don't know where she is. Their suspicions are bolstered by the fact that she was seen in the area where I am now parked, when passing by forty-eight hours ago. Naturally, I am pleased to hear their news and for them to hear about the lions and their cubs.

I engage in a friendly chat with their American tourists. They too have come out with breakfast picnic boxes. I offer them tea and coffee, toast and marmalade and a portable loo which I had already placed in the nearby bushes with some home comforts, a canvas wash-basin, soap and hand towel and there is relief all round. I am in no hurry; they are in no hurry. Most Americans on safari come dressed to resemble Hemingway himself; this does not bother me. Everybody wants to take a photo. I avoid this group type, stand-up and smile poses and suggest the natural take. No false, monkey-type presentations or 'Look it's me' stances. Everyone is relaxed and has a story to tell, their drivers happily wander off a little distance, glad for the break and the chance to stop for a while away from the pressures of having to produce.

I had already passed on the whereabouts of the lions to their drivers in our bush language way. Each kichaka, or area, has a name. 'Kifuko Mbaya' – Bad Crossing, 'Pembe Ya Ndofu' – Elephant Tusk, a place where a lone elephant tusk was found abandoned by poachers and the skeleton spread around by the passing elephant herds, paying solemn tribute There are rules of communication when vehicles meet up. Never point to a place, it is bad manners. Never let on to their clients the information you have passed to their driver; that is contrary to the book of unwritten ethics. Playing this game with the tour drivers makes for a reliable and friendly exchange of good information. Never exaggerate; it is so easy to fall into the trap of arrogant one-up-man ship.

Petal, I sensed was not too far away; she could well be resting up in the thick leleshwa on my very doorstep. What if she should appear this moment, I would be branded a liar by the drivers, never to be trusted again. It was time to break up the coffee party and get the tourists on their way. I must take a good look around, but in the opposite direction. We bade our farewells and exchanged addresses. They were all keen to hear continuing good news about Petal and her cubs to be.

I had received no solid information or direction in seeking out Petal, but I was encouraged to hear that she had been seen in this very area. It was now a matter of visiting her nearby haunts and studying the reactions and body language of the wildlife, particularly the Thompson's gazelle and the impalas, noting the make-up of the herd. Those with young would attract her attention. Petal would not be looking for a large meal.

Pregnant female cheetahs on their own are selective and will seek out fawns; this is not an easy task. I have often watched Petal study a herd of Thompson's gazelles from a distance. Her eyes focus on any mother that wanders away from the herd – a sure sign that the mother has a baby hidden in the grass and it is now feeding time. Petal does not act immediately but continues to watch intently, marking the position in her mind. After the feed is over the babe returns to its hideaway and the mother moves back towards the herd and continues to graze, ever watchful with attentive glances in the direction of where her baby lies.

Petal's hunger now triggers the urge to get up and go, and without trying to conceal her approach she confidently walks towards where she believes her 'snack' awaits her. The distance is well over a hundred yards. Her direction finder is locked in, but her mileometer is a little short. She seems to have trouble in gauging the distance. Now the criss-cross search starts. The fawn gives off no odour and lies flat and absolutely still. Her mother sees the cheetah approaching and snorts a danger warning. The fawn is seen to flatten out even more; the herd now moves, en masse, towards the cheetah to distract her. The gazelles are milling around, the scene becomes frenzied – the cheetah becomes a little confused, her direction finding goes off track, and the operation is then abandoned.

The fawn continues to lie absolutely doggo—I have often laughed at Petal's annoyance, flicking her tail and with a look of disbelief which says one thing, 'I've been fooled'.

Most of the animals seemed calm, nothing exciting happening. It is now well past mid-day and an oppressive heat is building up. There are cumulus clouds over Lake Victoria in the West, the temperature is rising and the heat haze begins to form horizontal wavering mirages.

Many animals are heading for the shade. I hardly think a pregnant Petal will hunt under these conditions, though cheetahs are known to hunt when tourists have retired to their lodges for lunch; the reason being that they are free to hunt without having their attempts to stalk disrupted by vehicles following them and moving in close to observe the kill. I decide to return to Euphorbia Hill, my established observation post.

For the first time since I left Petal in the Mara seven weeks ago, I was now able to slow down and think without the distractions and daily pressures that are always part of living. The Maasai Mara, the wild open spaces and the wildlife have a calming effect on me; sometimes I just sit – sometimes 'I just sits and thinks'. My mother often used that phrase when she caught me gazing out of the window when I should have been concentrating on my homework. My end of term school reports always contained the comment by the Headmaster, "Can do much better when he concentrates".

I always had a wandering mind; much of it concentrated on the outdoors. I lived for the action; school routine bored me stiff. Latin and French were subjects that I believed were for the birds not me. I preferred to stick to English and the Arts. History and Geography had their moments of wisdom. Maths was all right, though Algebra and Trigonometry were, I am sure, designed by a cranky psychiatrist. I had great trouble understanding this subject, but with perseverance Trig. became a fascinating challenge and Algebra consigned to the dustbin! Chemistry was good fun though my tutor never left my side when I was in the laboratory – he sensed my efforts to experiment with anything that would produce a bang and ending in disaster. He firmly believed that my concoctions were designed with an end result in mind that threatened to blow his laboratory to smithereens and the school with it.

Little did he suspect that in later life my interests in explosives would not go unnoticed by my military training instructor who recommended a posting for an intensive crash course with the bomb squad.

My knowledge gained there was instrumental in being selected as Chief Security Officer for a group of airlines that passed through Nairobi International Airport. Later I was posted to Aden during the problems there. My specific task was to ensure the flight safety of those commercial aircraft carrying British troops out of Aden to Mombasa. My efforts were successful, several attempts were foiled and explosives diffused. The freedom fighters for the liberation of South Yemen did not appreciate the British presence. I had to be one hundred per cent certain that our flight would arrive at its destination in one piece. I always travelled on board with my team. This provided the necessary confidence, the bottom-line being if I flew, they would fly with me.

Having returned to Observation Hill and admired the view while sitting on my strategically hidden throne, it was time for a snack. Time, as usual, had passed quickly and soon the cool of the late afternoon set in. The floating mirage had disappeared providing a settled and undisturbed view across the plains in every direction.

Now it was time to sit and observe the body language of the sentinels of the plains. The topi, the giraffe and impalas would soon tell me if predators were around. Several tourist vehicles stopped by, their drivers passing on information on what they had seen. Everything except cheetahs – you guessed it! Cattle herders too had nothing to report; information on cheetahs seemed to be as scarce as chicken's teeth.

If this situation continued to draw a blank I would need to move my position towards the West and check with the drivers from that area and Buffalo Camp. They ranged further and stayed out most of the day. I would make that decision in the morning. The setting sun was providing its usual stunning performance; no two sunsets ever seem to be the same. Somewhere out there my Queen would be watching without me.

My mind was wandering in and out of conscious thought, excited by the thought of our meeting soon. I was fervently hoping that her first honeymoon with Namibia had been successful and that she was now pregnant. If my calculations were correct I must definitely be present in the Mara. Ninety days is the usual gestation period for a cheetah and now there were only three weeks to go. Those weeks would pass very slowly for me.

It was now 7 p.m. and the mosquitoes were beginning to bite. This is a malaria area. I have always been very conscious of this debilitating disease, particularly so the dreaded falciparium. This disease can kill humans quickly. It is a stubborn disease that defies most prophylaxis. Immediate hospitalisation is necessary.

Throughout my lifetime I have avoided the very many recommended prophylaxis pushed out by the Medics and the Pharmacies. I insist on mosquito nets, netting around tented windows and doors, repellents, long trousers, long sleeves, preferably dipped in repellent. The camper windows and doors are well equipped and each is fitted with a mosquito proof awning. So far I had been lucky.

I never get bored listening to the sounds of the African night – piecing together in my mind's eye the blind man's picture of the animal calls and their movements; I hear the Maasai singing and their laughter drifting in on the wind. My sense of smell is acute; that unmistakable smell of 'manyatta' I can do without, it is a mixture of everything—cattle, goats, smoke, humans and something from which I prefer to get up-wind.

My dinner was bubbling noisily on the gas cooker, a mixture of rice, peas, potatoes, onions, carrots, broccoli and mince, all in one pot. My special goulash as I called it. Cube veggie soup, as a starter, in a mug. Earlier the sundown was celebrated with crisps, cashew nuts and a Tusker beer. What more could one wish for? I wondered what the rich were doing tonight – not much I guess, certainly nothing as interesting as this.

I can hear the grunt of a single lion close by heading down towards the spring; my night vision binoculars are invaluable at times like this and are always placed near at hand. The stars are out and sparkling, the moon is not due to rise for another hour. Close by there is an animal track that passes in front of my netted verandah, some twenty yards away. The chances are that lions may use this path. Sure enough, within minutes, a lone adult lioness walks purposefully down the path totally ignoring the sounds and smells of my goulash bubbling away in the camper.

The wind was towards me; maybe she is concentrating more on quenching her thirst than laying an ambush at the spring's edge. Who could blame her – dinner was uppermost in both our minds; if she attempts to kill, the chances are I will hear the commotion.

The spring was situated a little over fifty meters away. Lions do not have very good night vision compared say to the leopard, or my night vision binoculars which have the added advantage of reflecting the starlight into its prism lenses. The pencil batteries provide the electric current that dissipates the molecules of invisible light forward. The naked eye cannot pick this out except when transformed within the binoculars as a green haze. When the moon appears visual acuity is enhanced even more; good forward visibility can reach to almost three hundred meters with these night vision binoculars, but when in constant use care must be taken. The human eye starts to object after long periods of use, in excess of twenty minutes, will cause headaches that last for days, followed by migraine and peripheral vision flutter.

I could hear the muddied area around the spring being trampled by many hooves, which indicated that some zebra and wildebeest were having a drink. The zebra stallions high-pitched neighing was calling his herd together; probably he had sensed danger nearby. Distant whoops of a hyaena pack coming from the direction of the Maasai 'manyattas' suggested that a diseased cow had been put out for the scavengers to attend to.

I was tired and must get some sleep but it was necessary to pay nature a final call before 'lights out'. That feeling of drifting in and out of sleep, pushing aside the uncomfortable necessity of paying a toilet visit is a definite prerequisite for a bad night. I usually end up giving myself a strong reprimand in the morning, for not going. Whilst sitting comfortably on the box, keeping my ear well tuned to the surrounding darkness the bushes always seemed to move. It is funny how that illusion sends a chill up one's spine! Having a buffalo charge you whilst you are on the potty is not, to my mind, a way to experience an adrenaline rush but a cure for constipation.

I had stepped back into the camper when all hell was suddenly let loose. Stampeding zebra and wildebeest were fleeing in all directions from the spring area, a group of zebra, in full flight, passed close by the camper. The lioness had pounced and by the sound of the bleating it seemed as though she had successfully caught a young wildebeest calf. If Petal was anywhere near I was sure she would decide to keep well away. There was little I could do about anything so I decided to turn in for the night and leave the lioness to her meal. I would visit the drama in the morning. I slipped into my sleeping bag, dressed only in my underwear and fell sound asleep. The camper door was locked and the sliding window open to allow the sounds of the night and the fresh air to pass through. The mosquito net attached to the open window was fixed firmly with Velcro; no bugs or pestiferous mosquitoes could enter. These wretched insects could find and pass through the smallest of holes

At around 5.00 a.m. my sleep pattern changes to a semi-wakeful state, not quite with it, but ready to snap into wakefulness at an instant. Many years of guerrilla training and living in the forests had taught my brain to react instantly.

I subconsciously heard a heavy thump followed by a horrible screech of claws on tin, exactly the same sound as chalk makes when it breaks on the blackboard. My teeth stood on edge. In a split second I was wide-awake. Could it be Petal on the bonnet? I looked out through the window – nothing there. What could it have been? Then came another thump, this time sufficiently heavy to make me realise it came from the camper roof. I quickly slipped out of my sleeping bag and gently opened the back door and looked up. The silhouette against the dawn sky was the sitting outline of a cheetah. Unmistakably Petal!

In my excitement I stepped out into the cold dawn in nothing but my underpants and quickly realised this 'lady' had never seen me dressed in that state before. Wrong man! No wonder she did a double take – it was my voice calling her name that stopped her short from leaping off the roof in panic. I moved quickly back into the camper and dressed into my everyday standard khaki safari outfit.

Petal always recognised this dress even from a distance. Once dressed I left the camper again and walked towards a nearby tree. I remembered I had completely overlooked to carry out my defuelling stop when I had first arrived. Petal, I believe, had laid up in the leleshwa bushes nearby; either that or she had spotted the camper outline from far off. Whichever, she was now with me, stretched out on the top of the camper-van with her tail hanging over the side. I have often played tail-tag with her in situations like this, but she seemed tired and had lain full length in a sleeping pose. I let her be and toyed with the idea of taking myself and my trusty fire extinguisher for a short walk down to the spring; but then I thought better of that. What if things went wrong? I hoped the lioness had already spotted my visit to the tree and having fed would not venture back the same way that she had come to the spring. I suspected she might have hidden very young cubs in the lugga some five hundred yards away from this hill. I would need to see her in daylight at close range to confirm this possibility.

Now wide-awake I may as well start my breakfast fry-up. Bacon and eggs, sausage and baked beans on toast, some fruit and cereal, the thought made me hungry. Petal never seemed to bother about the cooking smells though sometimes she had a sneezing spell when I cooked onions. Any form of body spray, including mosquito spray or repellent was a 'no-no' and totally banned in her presence.

Now I had a problem, I would need to think what story I would give to the two tour drivers who were bound to visit me. There would be no 'bush toilet stop' for them or those in urgent need. (Not everyone likes to wander off with toilet roll and spade). They might just run into the lioness with her kill if she was still at the spring. Today was red flag day. Keep away; come back later when the flag is yellow. Petal would be my companion and enjoying my security as long as she wished. If she moved away, I would follow her and go wherever she pleased. Without Kibet or Jamie to assist with driving, a 'walk on the wild side' with Petal would not be easy.

Usually when Petal decided to move she appeared to lock into one direction and from there on, in a straight line. I could take short walks with her, but when darkness came I would need to walk back to the camper-van. In the meantime I could lose her. I made certain that I judged these sorties out from the camper-van carefully, sometimes driving well ahead of her and then walking back towards her. This seemed to meet with her approval; she would lead me and then flop down on arrival at the camper-van. A drink of water from her 'karai' was always welcome. This important service was appreciated particularly after one of her long hot walk-abouts. Later on, availability of instant water on request was to prove invaluable; there was no need for her to seek out water in my company during the very dry spell. Some researchers claim cheetahs seldom crave for water and satisfy their thirst from the blood of their kill – I would agree to disagree in part but not in whole, particularly so if there are suckling cubs, when water is very important. The cheetah territorial areas in Mara are never too far from water. Petal would never drink tap water that had been treated. I always siphoned and stored pure water for both of us by laying down plastic sheeting on my lawn in Nairobi but later abandoned this idea when I discovered that the water tested positive for heavy contamination from industrial airborne pollution. The Mara rain collection was safe, pure and distilled serving three masters, myself, Petal and my camper vehicle and batteries. The Nairobi tap water was heavily chlorinated; yet she would happily drink from the muddiest of pools.

The rising sun had now appeared over the Aitong Hills, soon the heat would become intense and force Petal to come down from the top of the camper-van and seek the shade of a tree. I enjoyed my breakfast, washed up the dishes and generally tidied up. I shaved and brushed my tusks, folded the mosquito awning and made ready to move if necessary, should Petal decided she was going to go on a long walking safari. I must remember to retrieve the toilet – a very handy piece of necessary equipment, simple, hygienic and comfortable for me. I dislike squatting!

I positioned myself near the front mudguard and waited; as predicted Petal came down onto the bonnet. Her movement was calculated and careful. I was overjoyed; there was the tell-tale bulge; I spoke to her in a gentle tone of voice. Maybe I said "Hello Petal, you are going to be a mother." It was something on those lines I am sure. She sniffed at my arm and shirt; I so wanted to touch her but remembered I had disciplined myself not to do so unless the first approach came from her. Petal would sometimes, when lying down close to me, put out her paw and I would return the compliment by placing my hand on her paw and she would then pat a short pat-a-pat upon my outstretched hand; similar to a house cat when it wants to play.

An occasional tail tug would provoke a playful swipe. To this day I bear a three-inch scar from one of her enthusiastic swipes across my right arm. It drew blood and required a little first aid. Hydrogen peroxide and a plaster cover for a few days encouraged quick healing. This incident made me check that my last anti-tetanus was still valid; an important, often forgotten and very necessary precaution when in the bush.

Petal was content to sit on her haunches for a while, taking in the distant and uninterrupted view around her. I had placed the water 'karai' on the ground in front of the vehicle; it soon caught her eye. I marvelled at the length of her long and slender body as she dismounted off the bonnet and realised that if she stood on her hind legs with her paws on my shoulders, she would be a foot taller than I, at least seven feet and more.

My mood was on a high today, the world was a wonderful place. Petal was now tanking up, a sure sign that we were about to embark on a long distance safari. Her plan fitted well, by late afternoon the daytime trek would tire her and she would hunker down with me by the camper or, most likely, spend the time on top. I much preferred her to sleep upstairs. This gave her added security and also should she decide to move I would at least be able to follow her by foot or vehicle, dependent upon terrain, using my night vision binoculars when the moon was up.

Petal set off in a westerly direction avoiding the odd patch of leleshwa bush and keeping mostly to open grassland; a few Thompson's gazelle were dotted about grazing near a small herd of impala; maybe she had spotted them whilst on the camper top. I was content to give her a long hundred-yard lead; this would avoid her being spotted by a tour driver who might be watching me from a distance. I felt it right that she should be left undisturbed without a bunch of tourist vehicles following her. Petal was on the move – with a purpose in her mind – there was no dilly-dallying or sniffing here and there hoping for a startled African hare to bolt out from the undergrowth.

Approximately five kilometers away there was an area of musewa acacia spread over a large rocky area. Once reached it would be impossible to follow her by vehicle. I would have to make a half-moon circle bypassing her and position my camper well in front, stopping before the rocky outcrop. I continued and made several stops, looking back to check that she had not changed her course. I knew the area well. There used to be a vehicle track through this rocky area; Petal would most likely follow that route if it were her intention to pass through. We had often walked in this area inhabited by elephants and buffalo and the odd tsetse fly that had a bite like a hornet. If there were buffalo around, so would be the tsetses. They are inseparable companions.

Tsetse flies are drawn to the smell of buffalo urine – flytraps are set up but I have yet to discover where the trappers get the urine. Interestingly, the tsetse appeared to be attracted to the colour of blue. I always advised my clients not to wear blue shirts when we were traversing that area, for that specific reason, as the colour blue seems to attract every tsetse fly in the area. However, I believe the urine side of it is a scientific concoction obtained from cattle. The International Livestock Organisation in Kenya has long experimented to find a cure for Trypanisomiasis, a deadly tsetse disease that kills cattle and humans. Slow progress and lots of international funding makes this a lucrative lifetime research for some scientists.

Having reached the rocky outcrop, I parked under a heavily foliaged fig tree often used by a large territorial leopard. He was a fine specimen, cunning and cautious. Petal and I had seen him before. I also knew of two adult females within his territory. He had sired all of their cubs; sadly like the cheetahs, their cubs are often predated upon by hyaenas and lions and few survive.

The BBC Big Cat Diary, often shown on wildlife television, has followed the progress of these leopards for many years. The filming of their haunts brings into graphic detail their daily fight for survival. Like the buffalo, I have great respect for the leopard. Look out! When cornered their reactions are as quick as lightening. I have had a few terrifying brushes in my time; thank goodness they were behind wire. In my other face to face contacts they have moved swiftly out of my way, growling and warning, "Don't mess with me." On every occasion to date, each of my three contacts in the bush have been when doubling back on my tracks to the camper after leaving Petal – maybe either I or both of us were being followed!

I made sure there was nothing in the tree above me, remembering the incident of the tourist vehicle that parked under a tree when a leopard, unseen to all, panicked and came down through the viewing hatch, clawed a German tourist and then crashed through the vehicle window. I took the opportunity to examine the tree trunk closely for recent claw marks. Yes, the tell-tale signs were there, maybe a couple of days old. I felt guilty that I was infringing on his territory. Petal would also be interested to check out this tree; more importantly to make a mental note not to establish her den within several kilometers or more of it. I do believe that she plots and marks, in her mind's eye, the leopard's territory by checking out these trees for their smell; similarly other urine markings left by male cheetahs and indeed other female cheetahs who have over-flagged these trees in search of a mate. Petal, on the approach to these post boxes, never fails to look upwards into the high foliage. When satisfied that there is no danger she approaches cautiously, sniffing around the base of the tree and then up the tree trunk where a wealth of information is obtained. It is like reading the morning's newspaper. Both male and any female cheetahs coming into oestrus and looking for a mate will have left their skat. The under-belly brush against the trunk left by a leopard, while hoisting its kill, will let her know when, where and who is active in the area. The jigsaw pattern begins to emerge and so the process is repeated until she has circumvented the outer circle of her twenty-five square mile territory.

I had guessed right, Petal was now heading towards me. She had made steady progress since she left me four hours ago; no attempts had been made to hunt and her mission today was to reconnoitre her territory. Having checked out this tree it would be interesting to see what her plans would be and in which direction she would choose to go, if at all. It was now mid-afternoon. My guess would be that she might seek shade and rest up for the remainder of the day but move away from this particular tree that could attract dangers and unwanted surprises for her. There might be a possibility that she will hunt before dusk or during her travels the next day. I moved some fifty yards away to give her unfettered access to her post box and to carefully study her actions; it was as I had predicted. I was totally taken aback as she marked the tree. I gave this behaviour a lot of thought and then realised, of course, it was simple; she was leaving her message to her subjects. I guess the message of the unmistakable perfume said something like: 'This is your Queen and I am pregnant.'

My thoughts turned to Namibia; I wondered where he was. Few tour drivers knew him; others referred to him as 'Duma kubwa sana' (The very big cheetah). No information had come my way and nothing either about Astra. It seemed to be not beyond the bounds of probability that Namibia had mated Astra as well, remembering that Astra was in the vicinity during Petal's honeymoon—then again it was perhaps more likely to be Hackles. Whichever, I was looking forward to a crop of baby cheetahs in the next month!

Petal had given the tree a thorough inspection and without resting set off on a northerly heading. This I had not anticipated; the direction would lead towards the Mara River, a distance of some three kilometres where tall acacia and riverine acacia trees were prevalent, and so were the tourists. Many could be seen buzzing around in their microbuses having come from the nearby Buffalo Camp and Mara River Camp, and an area heavily populated by Maasai cattle and manyattas. I felt a little uneasy, but it was not for me to interfere. I had no say in the matter; I would follow and not make any decisions for her but just concentrate on trying to guess or predict where she would go next. I was beginning to get quite expert at predicting her movements and was happy to feel that she never wanted to give me the slip.

By nightfall Petal had checked out her other three post boxes but had not marked them. This had been an extraordinarily long safari for her all in one day; she had not even taken on any more water. Maybe, if I offered some to her in her 'karai', she might decide to stop overnight. The idea worked. I parked in an open secluded area on a hillock surrounded by football size igneous rocks. I often thought these scattered outcrops could have come from meteorite strikes hundreds of years ago. There must be some other scientific reason which geologists have yet to publish. This area is part of a caldera which had imploded on itself. The escarpment which surrounds the Northern Mara suggests this is the outer part of the Great Rift Valley Divide and the rocks are from debris hurled far and high by volcanic explosions. This sounds more like the truth to me.

Petal was tired and I think grateful for my company – she at first settled down amongst the rocks – but as the evening sun set she chose to park herself on the camper roof. This was becoming quite a habit. I was there to be of service to her: Petal seemed not to be disturbed by my movements in and out of the camper when setting up the mosquito proofing verandah etc., and other comforts of home, a chair, camp table and, of course, the 'forget-me-not' toilet.

The fluorescent light from inside the camper provided a pleasant glow into the sitting room extension. By drawing the thick camper curtain I could block out unnecessary light that would advertise our presence.

'Nosy-Parker' hyaenas seemed to like taking chunks of rubber out of the vehicle tyres. I once had my aircraft tyres chewed almost to shreds in the Ngorongoro crater in Tanzania. I had landed in the crater on an old Land Rover vehicle track. I left the aircraft overnight and the next morning when I arrived, with extra fuel to top up, to my horror both tyres looked somewhat moth-eaten and the rubberised leading edge of my aircraft had several puncture holes. The hyaenas had taken a liking to all things rubber during the night. It took me much of the following day to locate another tyre; I always carried a spare, but never two. One has to expect all manner of surprises. This is bush flying at its best.

The holes in the leading edge of the starboard wing were patched over with duck-tape. Removing the outer safety rings of the wheel with a ratchet spanner was straightforward; to lift the wheel off the ground meant lifting the one side of the aircraft; it is amazing how heavy they are and yet they fly. A Tanzanian jack,—a ratchety type of jack which is hand operated, borrowed from a Land Rover—is the type with a wind-up crank handle as opposed to a high-lift jack. This soon had the wheel off the ground and the job was done. The tyres had several deep chunks of rubber missing exposing the inner tubes. No pilot in his right mind would risk a blowout, either on take-off or landing. Normally, this operation of wheel changing would require a qualified aircraft engineer to carry out the repair and to fly one in to do the job would cost a small fortune. It was my own personal aircraft. I had no passengers; it was my skin and insurance at stake. One has to be a bush mechanic, a jack of all trades, and rules are made to be bent just a little, some of the time. Life in the bush is full of risks; it is how you decide to tackle them that matters.

Happy hour had passed, watching the sun go down. Petal had witnessed it too from her vantage point on the roof whilst I stood on the bonnet. Our heads were the same level, only a foot or so distant from each other, each with our own thoughts. How I wished I could tune into her mind. I was picturing the day's events and analysing her body language as she checked out the various trees on her route here. There was no doubt about it that there was a method and a mission in her mind; it would all come to light as our safari progressed, but it was fun all the same, second-guessing and mapping out what I thought would be her route the next day.

After a light dinner, I dozed off in my camper chair. It was a sort of catnap, half my brain tuned into the world around me and the other half in limbo. The sounds of the night never bore me. The continuous chirping of the crickets; they were my night guards and as long as they continued to chirp their mating choruses, I knew that nothing dangerous was lurking or creeping up on me. The human brain is like a computer. I am lucky to be able to slip into a shallow sleep mode and then, at a moment's notice, click into immediate awareness.

I retired to bed at about midnight; Petal stirred several times to change her position. I was happy that she felt safe on her high perch and confident that both our intentions were to stop the night and rest. My regular 3.00 a.m. defuelling sessions, standing at the back door, must have triggered her system to react in the same way. She quietly and nimbly maneuvered herself down onto the bonnet and then, in her ladylike manner, proceeded to do 'the full Monty', calling card and all. My vehicle had become a moveable post box once again. I was relieved when she returned once more upstairs. Petal was becoming house trained, well almost!

The 5.00 a.m. twittering of the weaver-birds in their nests heralds the coming of the dawn. It is still dark outside but without fail the first shards of the dawn light triggers a song from a single bird. This is the wake-up call from the night sentry, then another starts and soon the dawn chorus is in full swing. The impala are resting quietly at a distance. They begin to stir; soon they too will stand and stretch. The Mara is waking to a new day. I can hear the distant grunt of the hippos, a single lion roaring in the distance announcing its resting place to others of its kind. The predators are going home to sleep. A zebra stallion calls his harem to follow him to better pastures; the dawn has brought the clear light of day and the air is cool and fresh after the night's re-oxygenation. The tall acacia is in bloom and the honey bees are already at work. Anyone suffering from asthma would be hard pressed to stay around here for any time. The pollen count must be exceedingly high.

Making sure I was ready for Petal's departure, I quietly took the awning down and packed away the chair and table. The toilet would have to wait until after the 8 o'clock feeling. I wondered what the world outside was doing today. The Gulf war had come to an end, I thought prematurely. The politics of this world of ours never seems to finish their business and this war was surely another example of unfinished business. It will return to haunt the Western world for many years to come. I tuned into the BBC World news, placing the radio earplug into my ear. Radios are not permitted when I am on safari with clients but I was bending the rules just a little and not disturbing anyone. Occasionally I allowed myself to listen into another world that has so many problems.

Being among the wild animals has taught me patience; I can sit for hours watching, waiting and listening without becoming restless or bored. It was 8 o'clock in the morning and Petal had not stirred. 'Madam' was in no hurry today! I retrieved the fold-up camp chair from the camper and placed it a few yards in front of the vehicle. From this point I could see her waking movements. My presence nearby would also reassure her that I was on guard. The impala, with their young of various ages, seemed undisturbed at my presence. They were grazing some one hundred yards away, among the acacia; little did they know that a spotted predator, their most feared enemy, was close by. Impala have excellent eyesight. The alpha male, in charge of the harem, forever alert, was regularly calling out his dominance to other male contenders. Occasionally, he would snort a false warning believing he had seen a furtive movement. He would stand stiffly, head raised, looking in the direction of his imagined predator. Some of the females would stop grazing and look over towards him; others would close ranks with heads raised high, taking up his stance. When the female starts snorting usually it is the real thing and danger is lurking in the bushes.

Petal was stirring and becoming conscious of the world around her. I sensed impala steak might be on her menu this morning! True enough, she quietly negotiated her way down from the camper top with a quick look of recognition in my direction. Her body language was speaking volumes; she was using the vehicle as a cover to scan the open area that lay between her and the woodland. The grass was short. Cleverly she slunk away in the opposite direction lining up the camper as a blocking feature from the impala and his harem. It was amazing how much distance she was covering in those few low crouches, floating away as if in fear of something. Had she had a bad dream? No, these were her tactics.

In the distance I could see clouds of dust and my worst fears were confirmed. A fleet of six white minibuses were travelling abreast, some two kilometers away, heading in our direction; I was sure they had not seen Petal or me. It was time to move quickly, I made for the forest where there was an old vehicle track that would lead me to cover from where I could be out of sight and watch Petal's progress. I did not want to draw the tour vehicles towards me. If they saw me they would stop their searching knowing a cheetah or cheetahs might be in the vicinity and head directly towards me. Petal's attempt to hunt would then be thwarted. They would encircle her and she would then have no other option but to flop down and abandon her hunt until the tourists had taken their pictures. Should Petal show any signs of hunting, they would hang around for hours hoping to see her make a kill. It was now up to Petal to move quickly or lie low. I watched with my binoculars, scouring the area where I had last seen her but my vision was partly obscured by tree trunks and long grass. I could just see her moving from left to right circling back to where I was in the forest. The impala had now moved further along the edge, distancing themselves from me.

The vehicles were now only several hundred yards away, the drivers had spotted the impala and veered off towards them. Their manoeuvre would give Petal a little time to make cover. I decided to stay where I was. The presence of the two vehicles had unwittingly turned the impala back to the original area where they had come from. The tourists were keen to photograph the 'bambies' and the situation looked promising. Petal had now disappeared from view, I had lost sight of her but sensed that she would not be far away and was probably making her way through the thick bush towards where the impala herd had been. The scene was looking even more promising for Petal than I had expected. The tour buses would soon move to search new pastures and leave us alone. I could hear the tourists chattering in Japanese; it is amazing how some of the African tour drivers can speak that language fluently, including Italian and French.

Their English too is almost perfect. Kenya and its peoples have so much potential but sadly the poverty of the majority is a fertile breeding ground for crime and bad overseas publicity follows. The big cities of Kenya have become prime targets for crime.

Those of us lucky to be in the bush are much safer amongst the wildlife.

My wandering thoughts are suddenly shattered; impala are breaking loose all around, snorting and leaping through the acacia trees. The place has erupted into bedlam. I hear the tourists shouting and the startled drivers have hit their starter buttons simultaneously. Petal has struck somewhere ahead of me. I move slowly out of my hiding place into the open and my cover is blown. The drivers are all surprised to see me appearing from nowhere. Yes, Petal has caught a three-week-old impala fawn and has it firmly gripped by the throat. Petal holds on for a moment making sure her prey has no surprises in store. I have seen inexperienced young cheetahs lose their kill by letting go of their hold too early; none so surprised as they who see their quarry get up and escape into the undergrowth. Everyone is excited; the tour drivers even more so, big grins showing big white teeth confirm they share their clients' mood. The tips will flow today and there will be drinks all round when they get back to the Lodge.

Petal is nervous and threatened by the close encirclement of the vans and decides to pick up her kill and, to my embarrassment, brings it over to my vehicle and promptly drags it underneath the chassis, setting about her breakfast with a vengeance. Once again I am on guard duty and we both become the most photographed objects of the day. The drivers acknowledge my presence and ask whether the cheetah is the famous 'Queen', a name that is revered by most of the tourists that visit the Northern Mara.

Without doubt, Petal has become 'Queen of the Mara'. The campfire stories are beginning to circulate like the flu. An hour has passed since Petal's sudden and spectacular appearance. The moment had surprised the tourists and fired up their adrenalin; some managed to film the whole sequence on their videos. This was an exciting start to their ten-day adventure in the African wilds.

CHAPTER 9
KENYA'S WILDLIFE WONDERLAND

THE Queen had fed, her choice fitted her appetite and there was no wastage. Single cheetahs, females in particular, will select the size of their prey to satisfy their hunger, taking into account that sometimes it is necessary to have a quick snack and maintain a low profile in areas where other predators are operating, particularly hyaenas. Cheetahs will, in most cases, search elsewhere if there are hyaenas in the vicinity.

There are seasons for giving birth in the Maasai Mara; these are well depicted in a poem penned by my very supportive and poetic mother-in-law. It reads:

> *Thirty days hath September, April, June and November,*
> *All are beautiful to remember in the fairest land on earth.*
> *Milling herds are giving birth,*
> *Mountain slope and boundless plain are starred with flowers after rain,*
> *And where man's foot has never trod,*
> *Lions still seek their meat from God.*
> *The other months have thirty-one, save February alone,*
> *October Spring has lately come,*
> *December Spring has hardly gone,*
> *January and February are Summer yet.*
> *March is warm and should be wet,*
> *July and August scarcely cold,*
> *But then the Kenya year grows old.*
> *Come and see on every hand*
> *Kenya's wildlife wonderland.*

The Japanese tourists waved their dignified goodbyes. So many pictures had been taken. I picked up a handful of empty Fuji film cartons, carelessly thrown overboard. This can be quite annoying, litter all over the place.

Petal was hyperventilating. Although the vehicle was in the shade the limited space on the underside can be claustrophobic and hot for any animal that stands a good three feet high on all four legs. Petal chose to move to a single shady tree some three hundred yards away on the forest edge, a precaution she always took against surprise attacks from scavenging hyaenas or other dangerous predators drawn to the spot by the smell of the carcass. The contents of the intestines are sometimes inadvertently punctured and the hot rising air carries the pungent tell-tale sign of death high into the atmosphere; high flying vultures will soon home in and spiral down to clean up the scraps. I have often watched fascinated how soon these feathered scavengers arrive on the scene. Within minutes they are joined by a hyaena or two that have zeroed in on the descending flight line of the aerial clean-up squad. Hungry lone male lions and lionesses are also adept at spotting these signs in the sky, arriving huffing and puffing sometimes too late, only to find the spoils had gone. I can relate to that 'lost out' feeling only too well as a child when the last cone of my favourite ice cream was sold to the person in front of me and the 'Sold Out' signs went up.

A few vultures have appeared on the horizon, their undercarriages outstretched in preparation for a spot-on landing. I envy their maneuverability in flight; each outstretched wing perfectly angled to slow their approach, each tail feather and wing tip feathers twitching and adjusting to effect a controlled into wind landing. Marabou storks known as the feathered undertakers of the plains are considered the masters of glide, second only to the albatross that roam the oceans of the world held aloft by floating on a cushion of air just a few feet above the waves. How do they sleep, I wonder?

I drove near to where Petal was and hid the camper in the acacia forest knowing that a drink would be appreciated. I carried the 'karai' and a two litre plastic can of water over to her. These are the thoughtful things that continued to cement our relationship; sometimes I assisted her in carrying her kill to a shady spot – it can be an exhausting business for a mother-to-be. The water was most welcome. My trusted wildlife vet had suggested I put a tasteless tablet or three of soluble calcium in the can, particularly to assist in the making of strong bones for her and the babes she was carrying.

Rickets in young newly born cheetahs is not uncommon, seen often as an outward buckling of the front paws. There appears to be a deficiency in the Mara black cotton soil. This is surprising when so many animal skeletons are scattered about and gradually break down to powder over time seeping the calcium deposit into the soil.

Much of the top soil in the Mara is washed away off the plains by flood water and finally carried by the Mara River to the silt flats of Lake Victoria, where the calcium content of the soil is found to be extremely high. The human plant food chain is boosted by the calcium breakdown of the bones of thousands of wildebeest that drown up-stream each year on their migration crossings to and from the Serengeti plains. The Luo tribe that live by the shore of Lake Victoria are sturdy, tall and well-built men and women. Their strong white teeth can remove most bottle tops with ease! No shortage of calcium here!

Petal was comfortable with my presence; I sat down within a few feet of her supporting my back against a tree. She was content to stretch out and close her eyes and within a short while, fell into a deep sleep, trusting that I would safeguard her while she slept. I was happy to oblige. Soon I was forced to shift my position, pins and needles plus a numb bum had set in. My new positioning movements did not awaken her, another good sign that she was confident in my presence. I was happy that this beautiful wild cat had placed her full trust in me.

I realised my 'on guard' duties could last for several hours. Soon that '8 o'clock feeling' that was already several hours late, would force me to leave her unattended and vulnerable. I must, for her safety, wake her up. She might understand my departure from her towards the caravan had a purpose. I collected the 'karai' and water can and chirped my cheetah call. Petal stirred realising I required her attention; her first reaction was to look around for the reason. The bush telegraph, Japanese style will have been active and broadcast their experience to others of their tribe; soon this place would be crawling with mini-buses. It was time to move out of here. Two hours had passed and I required a complete 8 o'clock 'bush stop'!

Petal had not gorged herself as some cheetahs do. Did I detect a larger than usual bump; she appeared to be a little more distended than yesterday! Or was it that gremlin playing tricks with my eyesight again? I wondered how many babies were in there. Soon I must start thinking up names for them. Maybe four, I thought, but as a first timer I think, three. Imagine nine! I had heard that figure had been achieved by a cheetah in Nairobi Park recently, an impossibly large family to care for.

Petal had now taken up walking in an easterly direction; her territorial circle was beginning to take form, once again heading to check out prominent single trees. I was hoping that some result would come of to-day's trek. Maybe the cheetah 'newspaper' might give her some information as to who of interest was in her domain; possibly Namibia or Astra, her brothers, or others of her ilk, passing through.

I decided to take the twisting track that ran through the acacia forest by heading eastwards along the river. I was confident I could locate Petal any time by visiting the various prominent trees out on the plains. I came across a herd of giraffe browsing on the short acacia tops. They appeared not to be accompanied by their young – too dangerous for them to be in these thickets – their babes would be out in the open with an adult or two in charge of the nursery. As I progressed along the track my eyes, accustomed to looking deeper into the thickets, were attracted to several silver reflections in the undergrowth. I stopped; my sixth sense was telling me something was wrong. I felt decidedly uncomfortable, that unmistakable smell of rotting rubbish filled the air.

Looking through the binoculars I focused on the area where I had seen the glints of metal; were they discarded Coke cans? I approached on foot and was shocked and sickened at what I saw. Rubbish, plastic, beer cans, a goulash of dumped swill, the area was littered with garbage for some fifty metres around. A nearby tourist lodge decided to get rid of its rubbish and this was their dump. How could this be? Here was a flagrant breach of the rules of lodge or camp garbage disposal. I took some photographs; these would grace the desk of the Director of Wildlife and the Tour Operators Association. The matter required an immediate and full investigation. The evidence was plain; the offending lodge was well advertised on their discarded picnic boxes. This was now a matter for prosecution.

I returned to my vehicle disturbed and upset. It took me a full five minutes for my adrenalin to settle. The Maasai landowners would not be pleased to hear about this mess. I would make a point of getting a message to their Chief that their land was being polluted indiscriminately.

My thoughts had been temporarily distracted. It was time to return to Petal and observe her movements from a distance, there would be some clues that might make sense to me in her walk-about. Petal had covered some distance, almost two and a half kilometers from where I had first left her. The fig tree that she was now cautiously approaching was large and thickly foliated. I noticed she carried out her normal careful approach procedures but this time she circled the base some twenty metres out, sniffing on the ground and looking up into the tree. Her body language was visibly unhappy and her movements very wary. This tree was hiding or had been visited by a leopard. If it were baboons I would have heard their warning barks by now. Petal must have come across the fresh smells of an aggressive predator, one of the cats, and decided to bolt.

A cheetah, even at a canter, covers distances as if it were flying, and Petal was doing just that—'gapping it'—the safari slang for putting as much distance as possible between that tree and herself. My mind was temporarily thrown into confusion. Should I follow her, or investigate the tree. Within seconds, Petal was already out of sight, her camouflage made her invisible in the surrounding grassland.

I chose to stay where I was and watch carefully, checking out the surrounding area through binoculars. Not a single impala or Thompson's gazelle was to be seen; a lone wildebeest, left behind by the long departed migration, and some young playful pigmy mongoose could be seen darting in and out of several holes in an abandoned anthill, plundered by an ant bear some while ago. Nothing else stirred.

The adult troop of mongoose, tired of their children's playfulness, were sunning themselves on an outcrop of rock close by, ever watchful and taking turns, searching skywards; the danger zone from where their predators hover and strike. It is interesting that the banded mongoose can look directly into the sun. They appear to have some form of protection that prevents their eyes from being dazzled by the sun.

The Marshal eagles are strong and agile enough to swiftly swoop, attack and pick up a two to three month old cheetah cub in its talons. These little mongooses, not much bigger than a cane rat, are as quick as lightening and at the sound of their parents' warning their reactions are instantaneous. They dive as one directly into the ant holes and then, minutes later, cautiously appear at the entrance of their den, twittering excitedly, hesitating to come out into the open. They know that pesky eagle is watching and possibly waiting to pounce on them from the nearby fig tree.

All signs of Petal's rapid departure suggested a leopard might be in the tree. The beast may however be sound asleep and totally unaware of her or my visit. I moved in for a closer look and maneuvered the Landcruiser some fifty feet short of the tree trunk where I could look up into the thick foliage. I could not see the tell-tale sign of a tail hanging down. This is usually a dead give-away when looking for leopards in trees. Many over eager safari guides, including myself, have hung their heads in shame when announcing "Look there is a leopard in that tree." to the expectant tourists only to find the 'tail' is a vine dangling down and swaying in the breeze.

Despite searching each branch with meticulous care, I could not focus on anything that resembled a leopard. Then I saw a flicker, was it a leaf blowing in the wind? Sure enough there, looking directly at me were two greenish eyes of a leopard, it was impossible to make out the rest of the face and body, the animal being so well camouflaged. On eye contact the leopard gave me an aggressive hiss and snarl displaying four fearsome fangs that sent shivers up my spine.

Petal would have had no chance if she were caught unawares by this beast. Life hangs by a thread each day and these risks have to be faced. The odds of any cheetah living out its full life span of fifteen years are a gamble. This incident made me more determined than ever to help and provide Petal with her security, so important for the survival of this project. I did not want to get entangled with official scientific approval that would require the submission of reams of paperwork that draws unnecessary criticism of an unqualified individual who is analysing his own 'hands-on' experiences that do not follow the laid down lines of scientific procedure.

Take African traditional medicines for example. These discoveries have not passed through any scientific procedure but evolved through nature's wild process before modern boffins were ever invented. The tried and tested bark of a certain acacia tree, when boiled and the juice extracted, is a certain cure for malaria. Modern laboratory tests show a high quinine content. The chewing of the stems of the Miraa plant provides an effective amphetamine. It alleviates tiredness and although addictive, it has other values such as firing up a failing libido for man. How were these discoveries first made? Not through science as we know it today but through trial and error of the bushman's 'hands-on' study of nature.

According to the Maasai it was the elephant that brought their attention to bark stripping, as elephants do this by stripping and chewing the bark and extracting the juice. The juice it is claimed clears the liver of unwanted parasites ingested by drinking infected water. Bilharzia (Schistosomiasis) destroys the liver. Modern science is now investigating these claims; some will hold water, others not. The western world has so much to learn from traditional herbal medicine. The medicine trees and bushes still have many hidden cures for man and wildlife. The traditional Medicine Man and his concoctions have some merit.

My enemy, time, had passed unnoticed. Where had Petal gone? She had good reason to put as many miles between her and this tree, not only that but she would have made a mental note of the predators territorial base. This was not the place to seek a den in the leopard gorge area.

I set off in the general direction Petal had taken. Her initial track, I remember, had taken her through outcrops of rocks strewn around like pebbles on a beach. Not easy territory to try to negotiate through in the Landcruiser. Springs and shock-absorbers protested as each wheel passed over this bone-jarring, back-breaking terrain that seemed to stretch before me forever. I was forced to change direction; the bouncing and bruising was making me feel quite sick.

I knew Petal had not purposefully given me the slip. She had acted in self- preservation, though at times I recognised that mysterious and skittish behaviour was leading up to a 'find me if you can' act. But, yes, the last few days had purpose in her movement. No body language was being exhibited by any of the wildlife though I took notice of two crested cranes, flying several kilometers away, that suddenly transformed their horizontal flight into a vertical climb-out, legs and heads outstretched, this is usually an indicator of a surprise sighting of a predator along their ground track. That might be Petal, if so her direction was in the middle of a very heavy larva rock-strewn area.

I made a mental note of the compass bearing and surrounding terrain. It was not going to be easy and would be impossible to drive through 'as the crow flies'. A detour of several kilometers back-tracking and a good half-hour roundabout drive would finally get me there.

It was 5.00 p.m. Some zebras, not blessed with eye-shades, had turned their backsides towards the sun. The same principle applies at sun-up; they turn their backsides towards the sun once more. I was, therefore, approaching them from the rear. The African light, at this time of day, has a clear cut sharpness and in my opinion is the best time for photography, but most plains game are showing you their rear-ends!

The scene in front of me was dazzling. The criss-cross of so many black and white stripes going every-which-way, had to be caught on film. I stopped to take a picture.

Was I seeing things? A log some six feet long and a good six inches in diameter was moving along the ground attached to a length of fencing wire. I focused the binoculars on it and followed the wire along its length for some fifty feet to the neck of a zebra stallion. This animal was in great pain; his head hung low in total dejection. The wire had dug deep into his muscular neck. This proud zebra's days were numbered—unable to move quickly he found himself at the tail end of the herd – an easy meal for any predator. The open wound was still bleeding. I felt sickened at the sight and angry that the bureaucracy did not permit me to carry a dart gun. The firearms law in the country is very strict and to possess a dart gun one had to be a qualified wildlife vet but the nearest vet was a hundred miles away. I promised myself that I must get Petal's doctor to put me through the complete course that required one to know and judge body weight and calculate correctly the quantity of anaesthetic required, and much more, of course. For the moment, I felt totally helpless. I just could not leave this suffering animal to die in this way.

I must think of some way to solve this problem. I scoured the area with my binoculars; not a vehicle in sight. Murphy's law was at work to-day. When I wanted someone to be around, everybody and his aunt was out of sight and the opposite when I wanted to be alone—I was always inundated with tourist vehicles. The nearest lodge was five miles away and my radio frequency was only ground to air. Somehow I would have to manage by myself. The scheme I came up with in my mind was crazy but something about it was practical. Yes, I've got it! Necessity being the mother of invention, I drove over to the log. I placed both front wheels on the wire, cut the wire with sufficient lead to attach the wire to my electric winch on the front of the vehicle, engaged the winch gear into reverse. I moved forward with the vehicle in gear as it wound itself onto the drive shaft and in this way moved forward slowly so as not to drag the zebra to me, but to gently take up the wire slack and let the winch do the work. In this manner, I could drive the vehicle right up to the animal and touch it with my bumper that would protect me from any flailing hooves or zebra bite, which is worse than that of a horse. I would then be able to get out, climb on the bonnet and snip the wire with the cutting edge of my pliers. It seemed impossible, but there was no other option and I had to try.

I always carried a large bottle of Pickric disinfectant in my first aid box. It was my mother's cure for all manner of cuts and grazes on the farm for the farm labourers and the cattle. This yellow liquid stained but thoroughly disinfected everything it touched. The local Maasai swore by this cure. Their elderly suffer terribly from leg ulcers brought on by a diet deficient in minerals. I was the local daktari (doctor) and carried and dispensed this cure for all ills. My healing Pickric had become famous.

To my surprise the stallion never moved, he was totally exhausted and the fight had gone out of him but I still had to be very careful. Zebras can bite like any horse will, with jaws that clamp onto your wrist or arm and there is no letting go. I emptied the dish washer soap bottle, tightened the trigger-press adjustable squirt to allow a quick spray to penetrate the deep wound encircling his neck. I could see the wire was embedded into his flesh by an inch and more. The wound was recent, maybe twenty-four hours or less. This was a poacher's wire snare without doubt and the 'fence post' was a thick dead branch broken from a fallen tree which had been used as an anchor for the wire snare.

In the stallion's panic and ensuing tug of war when trying to release itself, the noose had tightened to almost throttling point. This brave zebra was shivering uncontrollably. His pitiful neighs for help brought his harem to witness what I am sure they thought was to be the slaughter of their leader by this green four-wheeled predator. I sprayed the wound and to my surprise he never flinched. The yellow Pickric, unlike iodine, does not sting. The two-inch yellow band that now encircled his neck would stand out well as a future marker for me.

Now came the difficult part, to snip the wire on the hoop and gently remove it from the wound. I realised my patient was in deep shock. He just stood there shivering and shaking, his head bowed in surrender. I gave a little tug with the pliers and the noose fell away. The job was done!

I became aware of a tourist van parked some thirty yards away. My concentration had been so focussed with the job in hand that I had not noticed the van's arrival. Guess what! They were all Japanese and had witnessed the whole drama. Addresses were exchanged and promises were made to send me their pictures. I felt good and 'Zebee' looked so relieved. I reversed slowly backwards and joined up with the Japanese. Some fifteen female zebra admirers became curious and approached their stallion. They began sniffing around his neck and ears, mystified by the smell and the yellow band. Now, fortified by their presence and free from his bonds, he trotted away, head held high, proud once more to be among his harem. The courage of 'Deed-a-day Danny' had been tested today, but I was happy that my harebrained idea had worked so perfectly.

Daylight was running short and I still had some way to go, almost two hours had passed unnoticed. Petal must have moved on. Was it her that the cranes were making such a song and dance about? I was anxious to locate her before dark, as, should I fail, it would be a lonely night for both of us. The zebra-snaring incident troubled me deeply; there was now no doubt that poachers were active in the area. Several tour drivers had seen impala and giraffe with nooses around their necks and an eland was also observed recently, trailing a wire noose attached to it's hock.

Officials employed by the County Council showed little interest when such matters were drawn to their attention. I knew my intended report would fall on deaf ears and considered it would be best dealt with through the Kenya Wildlife Service and the Tourist Security Department (of which I was its honorary representative), and the local police. I sensed the Rangers were reluctant to take action. Somebody in authority was getting a back-hander to turn a blind eye in that direction. I was almost certain that I knew who it was and had suspicions we would soon meet face to face. Meantime, I must make certain of my facts for if my accusations were not water-tight I could find myself banned forever from the Mara. The gentleman in question held considerable sway in Kenya's political circles so I must tread very carefully or my personal safety could be in jeopardy.

Darkness had settled in and it would be unwise to be driving around the North Mara at night searching with headlights and searchlight. I could find myself surrounded, shot at, killed or arrested for whatever would hit the headlines. In Africa corrupt authority has a way of making life very difficult for those that rock the boat!

I donned my night vision binoculars, switched off all forms of vehicle lighting, reminding myself not to touch the brake pedal, (the glow of the red rear brake lights can be seen for miles at night). The wildlife would not suffer the pain of being blinded and stupefied by bright headlights.

I was looking forward to intruding on the nightlife and activities of those predators which know by instinct that humans, like most herbivores, without light are virtually blind at night. The leopard in particular springs to mind immediately. Lions have reasonably good night vision, but for the cheetah there has to be a moon. However, Petal and I have a secret. We can see in almost pitch black conditions but I have to provide the equipment, a strong five or six cell torch with a large reflector and the right density of red photographic dark-room film cut neatly and placed into the glass. Petal walks ahead of me, I can see clearly with my night-vision binoculars and she follows the beam of my homemade, hand-held torch. By some make-up in her eye lenses she appears capable and confident to slowly stalk to within striking distance of any selected quarry. A short sprint of some fifteen to twenty yards and dinner is served. One problem that neither of us has yet mastered is the shock that we both receive when a startled guinea fowl or francolin suddenly leaps up into the air with a loud screech, flapping its wings in our faces. Our nerves are shattered whilst the surrounding wildlife takes off in complete pandemonium. The intended surprise approach on our quarry is instantly scuppered.

These situations can become very dangerous particularly when zebra or wildebeest are panicked. There is every likelihood that we could be knocked for six and trampled upon by flailing hooves. I always carry my trusty fire extinguisher on these night escapades, but here again caution has to be exercised. Should I have to open fire, I know Petal will panic and bolt blindly into the darkness – not good! Aggressive lions, leopards, elephants, snakes and buffalo are reasons to activate the squirt. I sometimes head for the nearest ditch or large anthill. Waving my homemade, hand-held infrared gismo has no effect on the charging herbivores. They seem not to see the glow. I think they do not see it as a reddish glow as we humans do and yet Petal's predator eyes seem to do so. Science tells me it is all to do with colour segregation within the retina, a form of colour blindness where certain animals only see certain colours. I often wonder how these scientific conclusions are reached.

My progress is slow as I need to concentrate on the way ahead. Distant lights through my vision goggles are seen as a static green flare. Zebra and wildebeest and many impala were crisscrossing in front of my vehicle, some unsure of this lumbering hulk that appeared from nowhere. They are in control – no bright lights to blind them – I marvel at the way they choose their path through the surrounding bush without stumbling. There is a difference, my sight is eerily mechanical and clumsy, theirs is instinctively natural.

My plan is to locate and stay the night a little beyond where I saw the cranes performing their aerial dance. If Petal were still heading east as darkness sets in, then I would be required to make a slight adjustment in that direction. It was going to be a shot in the dark; the rest would be left for her to show up on one of her 'turn-upmanship' appearances. Petal had done this several times before to me; maybe tonight would be different. It was now pitch black with thick cloud cover and my night vision binoculars were struggling to find enough starlight to be of any use. I arrived at the rocky outcrop similar to what I had earlier pictured in my mind's eye. I switched off the engine and sat for a moment. Eyestrain was telling me to ease up; I could sense the first inkling of an approaching headache that can trigger a migraine. The makers of these binoculars recommend that not more than twenty-minute stretches of constant viewing is advisable.

The night air was cool, a gentle breeze blowing through the cab. I sat with my head supported on the headrest; a cat-nap would cure the dull ache behind my eyes. Awaking from these half-hour switch offs, my body batteries kick-in and energy flows back once more for an hour or so.

I must have been snoring as sometimes I do when I fall asleep sitting up. I was awakened to the 'kaawow, kaawow', the unmistakable call of the crested cranes. They were objecting to my presence and kept on repeating their call; they were close. My night navigation by compass was spot on—if Petal was within half a mile she would have heard their call. I had some feathered night-guard company tonight so I decided to stay.

The cranes had roosted on top of a flat acacia Tortilis tree. These trees offer a resting place for many of the small predator cat family who find it easy to climb on to the low thick branches. The feathered carrion eaters also prefer the security that these trees offer them. The flat top is almost impenetrable from beneath, even the nocturnal genet cat, which predates on smaller birds like the quelea and weaver, has great difficulty in making its way onto the top-most flat. It was time to shut down for the night. I cooked a light dinner, washed up, put the toilet outside the back door and turned in. Tonight was pyjama night and clean sheets on the top bunk with the front flap window open. I, too, had a clean and comfortable perch to relax and think about the day's happenings. I was pleased that my extraordinary harebrained idea had saved a beautiful and proud zebra stallion from a slow and painful death. Damn those poachers! That is looting by another name. Poverty in Africa is the ingredient for corruption and destruction; will it ever stop?

It was 3.00 a.m. when I awoke; my bladder had signalled it was defuelling time. I lay awake arguing with my inner self whether to get up and go. I was as snug as a bug in a rug, trying to convince myself with unreasonable excuses as to why I shouldn't get up and go! The Arctic conditions outside, a lion or a leopard waiting at my back door and spitting cobras were all alive and present in my imagination. What a waste of good sleeping time I thought. My inner discipline was urging me to get up.

Suddenly my dozing state was rudely shattered by a heavy thump on the bonnet. I have never believed in levitation, but at that split second I proved to myself that it was no illusion. Adrenalin, fright or sheer muscle reaction made the length of my body rise off the mattress. It was the dark outline of a large cat – that put the cat amongst my pigeons! Somewhere, in my stupor I knew it must be Petal but my childish thoughts of imaginary dangers lurking outside in wait for me had not entirely subsided. My moment of truth had arrived and all I could blurt out aloud was 'Jeez, Petal, couldn't you have knocked? You almost scared the water-works out of me'. I had forgotten I was on the top bunk; I banged my head soundly on the ceiling as I sat up. What next? This was turning out to be a painful wake-up call. My feathered friends in the tree were also objecting to being rudely awakened by thumps and bangs at the deep-sleep hour of 3.00 a.m. Concerted chaos then broke loose. Out of unison 'kaawow, kaawow, kaawow', flapping wings and general confusion erupted out from the acacia flats.

Petal stood her ground wondering, I am sure, what the heck all the fuss was about. Did I imagine a wry smile on that spotted face of hers? All forms of any bladder control had vanished. It was a hurried and unsteady climb-down from my bunk, missing my footing on the step and landing flat on the floor. 'Kaapow' – this joke had gone far enough! In a matter of a few moments I had pumped enough adrenalin in my body to precipitate a major heart attack! Madam had now decided she would spend the rest of the night on her favourite roof-top. I never cease to be amazed how she seeks me out, though I am happy that she likes my companionship. Now defuelled, I return to my comfortable bunk, but not before a quick brew up on the gas stove. A cup of tea would help calm my shattered nerves. Order and quiet had returned. Whilst nursing my bruises, I fell sound asleep. It was a short night.

Soon the dawn chorus wakened me. I lay looking out of the bunk window taking in the view and surveying the vista around me. The cranes were still in the acacia tree, their shapes outlined against the sky, crouched side by side as in sleep, their heads held across their chests. Interesting, I thought they don't tuck their heads under their wings like chickens. I chuckled to myself – maybe they do it this way to avoid spoiling their colourful hairdo. These stately birds, some thirty-eight inches tall, have a bright yellow crest with a blood red necktie and a whiter than white cheek patch. Their forehead sports a black topknot of stiff feathers. To witness their courtship dance is a sight to behold, strutting proudly with heads held high, circling each other with quickening steps and wings at half stretch, then leaping high into the air, their legs dangling gracefully below them, followed by deep bowings towards each other. These graceful antics are fascinating to watch.

I remember once walking and talking with a Maasai herdsman. We stood together and watched a crowned crane couple display. He could hardly contain his enthusiasm and wanted to dance in rhythm with them, excitedly explaining to me that one of the Maasai traditional dances is that depicting the crowned crane. The headdress, the stiff legged leap into the air, the bowing and strutting and the whoop; I had often wondered how the format for this graceful Maasai dance originated. I learned something new that day.

It was cold outside; the dew on the grass sparkled like diamonds. There had been a grass fire and the dry and not unpleasant odour of burnt stalks was still present suggesting the fire had passed through several weeks ago. Rain had fallen once since and the first flush of grass shoots painted the scenery a lush green, beckoning the wild herds and Maasai cattle to the table of plenty. The clouds were building again over the Aitong Hills, a sign of changing weather.

The next few days would become hot and muggy. When it rains in Mara it buckets down, the dust is washed from the air and the many catchment areas and luggas are replenished with pools of water. After rain, an air of relief permeates across the open plains, the Maasai smile and wave, every living thing is happy. Nature has presented all of her subjects with a welcome carpet of white flowers; they flower to-day, are there tomorrow and disappear the next.

Petal, like my neighbours, the crested cranes, seemed in no hurry to leave their comfortable perches, though I suspect the cranes will have something to say soon when they see the spotted predator resting on my roof. Petal was about to get a noisy wake-up call.

Getting up in the morning has never been a problem for me in the bush. Daylight has come and there is so much activity out there that I must not miss. I find great delight in sitting and watching Nature's bugs, bees and birds going about their business. In the distance, smoke filters through the roofs of the squat mud houses of the Maasai homestead. The inhabitants of the manyatta are awake. Several men are maneuvering through their cattle corral in search of a cow for blood letting. Blood and milk for breakfast – no thank you, not my cup of tea!

The Maasai seldom let their cattle out to graze before 8.00 a.m. for fear of bloat. Grazing on the green, wet grass is a killer. I have seen the disastrous results when their surrounding cattle enclosure has been breached at night, unknown to the sleeping inhabitants of the manyatta, and many of their herd can be seen lying prostrate on the ground, with bloated stomachs, their hind legs kicking as if in the last throes of death. Fermenting grass builds up gas and the pressure becomes too great on their lungs and heart. Death comes quickly unless treated. A douche of liquid paraffin is slow acting and is the sure and best cure for the less severe cases, but the more instant and effective relief comes with a practiced hand and eye— puncturing the stomach with a pencil sharp, quarter inch hollow stick called a 'trochar'- an instrument that every seasoned Maasai cattle farmer knows he must never be without. I tried it once, never again! The five-finger-outstretched palm measured at forty-five degrees from a cow's hip marks the spot to puncture. I plunged the stick into the suffering beast, much to the amusement of my Maasai tutor; he conveniently forgot to tell me to place my thumb over the exit end of the tube. Seconds later, I was sprayed from head to foot in a green, foul-smelling liquid. I was truly christened, Maasai style, in their age-old art of 'toboa'.

What's for breakfast today? Fruit, a tasty grapefruit twice the size of a tennis ball, porridge today, why not? A boiled egg, toast and marmalade and, of course, a cup of tea, English style. Kenya tea is a must; it just has that difference, an acquired taste I suppose. I have been brought up on the taste. Breakfast now done and dusted, it was almost 9.00 a.m. and my feathered guests were still taking their time. The two crested cranes were making gurgling sounds at each other, possibly a mating pair. Ground nesters? Odd, I thought, when most birds of their size prefer to make their nests in the safety of tall acacias. Crown cranes prefer the swamps and usually make their nests in amongst the reeds, close to water. The survival rate amongst their growing young is very low. Their enemy, the monitor lizard, consumes their eggs and marauding jackals kill their young. Seldom does the female lay more than two eggs in her nest and it is rare to see two chicks survive to adulthood.

The two cranes were intrigued by Petal's presence on top of the caravan. After taking off from their perch, they flew about the caravan, sometimes hovering directly overhead, their kaawow-kaawow calls were deafening. Petal moved quickly and sought refuge under the caravan. For a few moments both cranes landed on top, peering over the side to see where their adversary had disappeared to. Both were somewhat startled to find themselves looking into the face of a human being! I had stuck my head out of the window and looked upwards. What beautiful blue eyes they had. Was this not unusual, I asked myself? Don't males have a different coloured eye to their females in this clan? But on referring to the bird bible, I found it is the stork family that do. The Saddle-bill stork, for example—'male: blood red eyes. Female: bright yellow eyes.' Fascinating, I thought. I have learnt something new today. Everyday, I learn something—there is no time in Nature's paradise to be bored.

The surprised cranes then took off gracefully, flying away in tandem. They flew straight and low, wings flapping in unison, over the open grassland to alight almost a mile and a half away. They had joined another couple. How did they know their friends were there?

Sensing the coast was clear; Petal came out from underneath the vehicle and proceeded over to the acacia tree. Something on the bark held her interest and after looking around she made tracks eastwards, back towards the Aitong Hills where we had started our journey several days previously. By sundown we would be there. What will have been the purpose of her journey? I thought. Just checking out her territory and reading the morning newspaper as to whom and what was where? Soon she must start searching for a safe haven for her den.

Tomorrow I must return to Nairobi to prepare for the coming tourist season. My crew would be heading back to their Nairobi base in a fortnight's time and Petal's energy appeared to be lacking. She meandered here and there; purpose had gone out of her stride. When an African hare bolted from an outcrop of tufted sour grass, I was surprised she took no interest. This inedible grass grows tall and thick in shallow, disused buffalo wallows and provides effective, secure daytime cover for leopard, cheetah and warthog. Its razor sharp blades can cut deep into soft human flesh if walked through at the wrong angle.

Petal often gave me many surprises when she appeared unannounced from these wallows.

One early morning, I had stopped by chance close by one, having searched for her for over an hour. I had placed a thermos of tea and picnic breakfast box on the bonnet, and then supported myself by leaning over the mudguard, facing the opposite direction and scouring the plains with my binoculars. Petal must have been lying up during the night in this wallow. She crept quietly up from behind and leapt, passing over my left shoulder and landed neatly onto the bonnet. She sat down on her haunches, looking intently in the direction, in which I had been searching, and then looking at me as if to say, 'What's so interesting out there?' I was startled and speechless; my heart was pumping ten to the dozen. All I could do was raise a stutter of choice, unintelligible words that no self-respecting lady would wish to hear. Did I detect that glint of mischief in her eye once again? In seconds she was on her way, as if to say, 'Time for walkies!' Unfortunately, I was alone. This would have been an ideal opportunity to walk with her in the cool of the morning.

It was essential to have a second driver to accompany me in the future, capable of taking video and still photographs. There are few people, it would seem, who can do all three and be footloose and fancy free, without charging the earth to do so. Maybe my thinking that they should be paying me for the experience was selfish! Kibet was away on a well-earned two months leave. I couldn't quite figure out Petal's lethargy, maybe she was beginning to feel the strain of her pregnancy with three weeks still to giving birth. Much as I would like to spend these days with her, other priorities at the Nairobi office were piling up.

By now my solicitors should have completed the arduous paper work in transferring the property purchased from my Maasai friend, into my name. It was to be called 'Sanctuary Place'. Here I would design and build my final dream house among the wildlife. The view and its position overlooking the Nairobi National Park were perfect. My days in retirement would be spent in planning and building, with my own crew, just the way I wanted it to be, without being over regulated. The lions, the leopards, the cheetahs and every conceivable type of wildlife, except elephants, would be living free on my doorstep. I craved for the African night sounds in this sanctuary of peace.

It would not be possible to translocate Petal from her kingdom in the Mara that is her privileged and wild domain. I knew in my heart of hearts I could never find another Queen – she was an extraordinary wild animal, intelligent, undemanding, trusting and loyal to one human, and giving other impersonators a wide berth.

It was now mid-day. Petal had sought the shade of a tree. I have noticed when I move in close to her, by my vehicle or on foot, that she sleeps for longer periods without constantly looking around.

It is my turn now to be alert and on watch, part of our unwritten agreement. I am pleased she has this confidence in me. Occasionally she wakens and looks directly at me to check whether I am fully awake. When she does this, I exaggerate my head turning to show that I am on the ball; satisfied that I am, she returns to sleeping deeply. I try not to fidget and pay the usual price by enduring a painful numb bum plus a heavy dose of pins and needles in my legs. The time comes when I must move and walk about. In one's younger years, these nuisance conditions are not so prevalent. There is much being said about deep vein thrombosis these days, so I apply the recommended in-flight gymnastics.

This afternoon is stiflingly hot. The humidity is rising and the Mara desperately needs more rain. The wind is kicking up the dust in the distance, interspersed with many whirlwinds.

A herd of Thompson's gazelles are all running in one direction. It looks like a Maasai herder's domestic dog is chasing them. There is little hope that the dog will catch one, the gazelles are much too fleet of foot. Some of the gazelles are stomping, in a stiff-legged, bouncing, head-held-high attitude. This is usually their body language sign to others that a predator or predators is on the chase. I reach for my binoculars and focus on the scene. There is no sign of Maasai cattle or herders. On taking a steady stand by placing my elbows on my knees and sitting on the ground, I found myself exclaiming 'my God, it's not a Maasai dog, it's a pack of wild dogs on the chase, heading on a crossing angle almost towards us!'

This is bad news for me and very dangerous for Petal. My instant departure to the caravan awakens Petal with a start. I return with the red fire extinguisher. Petal has got the message that there is danger about, and is alert, looking around anxiously. The wild dogs are still distant, some three to four hundred yards away. The pack has split into two sections of about six per group. Now it seems there is chaos and the dogs are running in all directions, so are the gazelles. There is mayhem out there. Petal recognises the extinguisher and knows there is trouble brewing. There is no way she could out-run them if they see her and decide to attack. At present she is safe whilst they are busy running down their prey to exhaustion.

Petal, for a moment, looks indecisive. What best to do? She has adopted a 'slink away' posture. If she stays with me, I am in for a battle royal, but I cannot expect her to stick around. These wild dogs are silent killers and have no fear of taking on single lions or hyaenas. Leopards too, have great respect for them, but know they have the advantage of being able to climb swiftly up trees. Petal has no climbing claws and has to make do with her speed, but can only manage that for a comparatively short two to three hundred yards. Wild dogs are long distance runners; there is nothing they cannot run to earth.

I find my heart racing; I do believe I am scared, more for Petal than myself. Seldom do I reach for my rifle, but on this occasion, it appears that I must do so. I hurry back to the caravan some ten yards away but Petal, surprisingly, follows me. For a split second I thought she was considering taking refuge inside the caravan – the door was wide open. That's good thinking Petal, I thought. It would be a first, certainly the best place, but she would feel trapped, I am sure. Underneath would be no good either – they could get at her easily. Quickly, she made her way to the front of the vehicle and leapt onto the bonnet and up onto the roof, flattening her body almost to a pancake and out of sight. My place would be on the bonnet to protect her, armed to the teeth with a choice of fearsome weapons. Gazelles were being pulled down like nine pins, three, maybe four. There seemed to be even more dogs now. I counted sixteen in total.

The dogs had downed their quarries and were now engaged in a frenzied tug of war, ripping their kills to shreds and gulping down chunks of flesh; a sight not for the squeamish. But, would four gazelles be sufficient to satisfy sixteen hungry wild dogs? Those at the bottom of the pecking order might not be satisfied with the crumbs and start looking around for more in our direction! Petal had to make that decision. She was looking, crouching nervously from the roof. One by one the dogs began to leave at a trot, the way they had come. That suggested they were returning to their den. They must have pups somewhere hidden in a disused, underground burrow. Wild dogs have the incredible ability to regurgitate their food on arrival back at their den, always to a frenzied puppy welcome.

I watched intently through the binoculars until they disappeared out of sight, into a forested area. I had heard from some local Maasai that their dens had been seen on top of the Aitong Hill, a distance of some five to six miles from where we were. That is a long way, but not an impossible distance to cover; their den must surely be closer than that. These dogs might be some of the Aitong pack that had decided to move into an area of plenty. Petal and her kind must keep well clear of them.

Rabies could wipe out all the cheetahs, particularly those that were not so fortunate as to have a two-legged guardian angel. Cattle and goat herders reported finding wild dog carcasses, a sure sign of rabies or distemper, the curse of the wilds. Bat-eared foxes, jackal, and domestic Maasai dogs can easily contract the disease. It is a terrifying contagious, unsightly sickness that will decimate the wild and domestic canines of Aitong, once the virus takes hold. The virus can lie dormant in a burrow for up to a year and more.

I could see some of the wild dogs busy mopping up the leftovers, others flopping down and rolling on their backs, punching the air with their feet, using the rough ground as a scratch pad; a sign that the dreaded canine disease was taking hold.

Petal had every reason to look unhappy. I too, would have to make a full report to the wildlife veterinary authorities in Nairobi, for them to urgently take control and vaccinate every canine in sight; a major task for the already cash-strapped organisation. The happenings in the past twenty-four hours gave me much to be concerned about. Poaching, now rabies and possibly distemper – what next? If this disease found its way into the cheetahs, it would be a total disaster. I too, must take precautions and have the anti-rabies booster jab. Not a pleasant thought, but very necessary in view of the exposure I am operating under. Petal has only scratched me once; it was an unsolicited love stroke on my arm that drew blood. It would be foolish of me not to heed this warning.

My concern now was what Petal's next move would be. She was obviously agitated and waiting for all the dogs to be on their way back to wherever.

Private radio or telephone communications, with officialdom in Nairobi, from the Mara bush is presently nonexistent but progress is underway in completing mobile phone communications countrywide. The pylons for mobile phone transmission have yet to reach the Mara. I have been toying with the idea of purchasing a satellite phone. The camp, when in operation, has a VHF to my Nairobi base, but at the moment its currently packed away. My hand held radio communications can raise one or two lodges on the game reserve perimeter, in an emergency, but otherwise it is smoke-signals for me to-day.

Some of the wild dogs, the tail-enders, were in a playful mood, behaving like schoolchildren walking their way home. Finally, they were now out of sight. Petal then made her move, keeping to the bushes and using the gullies as added cover, she headed north once again, down towards the river and the acacia forest. This area would provide more cover for her. I let her use her intuition and held back for several hundred yards, keeping her in sight with the binoculars. I could see that her plan was to put as much distance between the dogs and herself as possible, and then head eastwards towards the hills. She would be safe there overlooking the plains below. Her nimbleness on the steep slopes among the large boulders would deter most predators from contemplating or even considering hunting her, though mountain slopes are favoured leopard country, the risk of being cornered by a pack of wild dogs was far less. If this was to be her plan, it would give me the break to head for Nairobi. I would have to be patient – Petal had tested my patience often – I envy predators allied to the cat family, they possess such extraordinary patience. Humans with short fuses and high blood pressure will find difficulty in handling this type of stress!

Petal had purpose in her stride, she was 'gapping it', a phrase often used by hunters describing their failed courage in the face of a charging wild animal, in other words, they are getting the hell out of there! Petal's body language was all too clear, 'I am out of here'. Making a beeline for the river was her only option, then following a tourist vehicle track up-stream alongside the riverbank. This would bring her on course for the hills. It was not too difficult to follow her paw marks along the soft sandy soil, which had been carried, into the tracks by the last rainstorm. I continued to follow at a distance, much of the time she was out of sight but as long as I could continue to see her pugmarks, the situation was under control.

Petal was walking along the track making it an uncomplicated tracking exercise for me – a good half-hour had passed. Impala, grazing on the road side verge scattered into the bush, and the hippos wallowing in the river made their thunderous grunts as they became aware of our presence. Judging from the intervals between grunts, I estimated Petal was about a hundred yards ahead of me, and then suddenly the trail ran dry. The prints told a story, she had back-tracked in a hurry and taken off into the bush, something had startled her. I drove slowly forwards and came to where human footprints had come out from the thick bush onto the track. All were heading east in the same direction as we were; two sets of prints were large, suggesting man-size and two were smaller, probably two women, I thought. What caught my attention for a few seconds was that the two smaller footprints were more heavily embedded into the sand. This suggested to me they were carrying loads, maybe firewood – no. The red lights were flashing in my mind – few locals would risk walking through the bush, battling with its weight and the wait-a-bit thorns that cling to one's clothing. Firewood was in plentiful supply. A human would have to crawl along some of the wild animal tracks to progress through this dense area. These, there was no doubt about it, were poachers' tracks. It all made sense. The women were carrying their spoil back to their hide-out, somewhere in the thickets the snares had been reset, and the load was their catch.

I had three options. One, investigate further on foot, but I would need to be well armed. Most poachers carry poisoned arrows and will not hesitate to use them. Number two, stop where I was, switch off the engine and move a short distance from the vehicle as in ambush and conceal myself in a position with a view up and down the track, and wait. There could be other poachers around. My third option was to turn around, move out and head for the nearest Game Ranger Post for reinforcements. Unfortunately Sargeant James was on extended leave attending to a family bereavement; his father had passed away and there were inheritance complications to attend to.

First and foremost, I have to get a message to my trusted friend, Game Ranger Daniel.

I have always suspected that others in authority were turning a blind eye and were probably involved in this commercial venture of the bush meat trade. Corporal Daniel was at Keekorok Headquarters, some twenty miles south. The nearest tourist lodge to me here was several miles down river. All my plans for travel to Nairobi had to be shelved and Petal had hot-footed it to goodness knows where! It certainly had been a bad day at the office for both of us. I must get out of here and find Corporal Daniel, even if I have to go all the way to Keekorok in the dark to get him. I set off for the Mara River Camp; I knew the manager well and between us an unsuspecting, everyday communication radio message would indicate to Daniel that something was afoot. The manager was of the same opinion as I. He would radio-call Keekorok headquarters and have a message sent to Corporal Daniel to expect an old friend to visit him, before darkness fell, and could he offer me a bed for the night. Meantime, I set off for Keekorok, heading across country, taking a short cut that I know well – it would take six or seven miles off my road journey. Time was precious, if I could get Daniel and be back before nightfall, both of us would quietly check out the up-stream area, without raising any suspicions. I had my night-vision binoculars and with his cunning Maasai bush craft, coupled with his ability to surreptitiously nose into the bush meat cooking, between us we could creep in close to their hide and spy on their activities.

On arrival at Keekorok Ranger Headquarters, I first had to get the Chief Warden's approval to release Daniel. This would not be too difficult, for he was the one that had given me the authority to go ahead to bring up the orphan cheetahs in the wild. Anything connected with 'his project' would receive priority. I was able to report firsthand on the wild dog situation and my suspicions of the disease, the zebra snare incident and to add a little white lie that I required Daniel to help out with tracking Petal. He was proud of the fact that five orphan cubs had been raised by a human foster-father at his instigation, and it was a first time achievement, with a hundred percent wild cub survival to adulthood in the wild. This was a feather in his cap.

Corporal Daniel was eager to cooperate. On the return journey I was able to brief him on my plans. Daniel remarked, "You were right to keep it under the blanket." (The Maasai way of saying 'under wraps'). "There are too many snakes in the grass," he said. We both found communicating with each other easy, despite our different cultures. "These poachers are not Maasai," he said. "We live side-by-side with the wild animals and we do not eat or kill them, we are their protectors."

CHAPTER 10
POACHERS' HIDEOUT

Corporal Daniel was eager to cover for his kinsmen – I suspect he thought there might be local Maasai collaboration. "These poachers are from Tanzania," he said, "they also steal our cattle and rape our women." He was getting a little hot under the collar. "Corporal," I said. "First we must tread carefully and make our battle plans. We need to know who they are, which area they come from and how many. They could be in possession of firearms and poisoned arrows. If so, they will not hesitate to use them against us." He agreed, saying "You have the night-eyes, I will follow you."

We were now approaching the area, the evening light had long faded into the darkness and my night vision equipment was working perfectly, loaded up with spare batteries to cover almost twenty-four hours of use.

It's a very odd feeling to drive at night without headlights. I had earlier disconnected all lights, including the brake lights, and now having located the vehicle track leading to the forest area, it was now a matter of proceeding carefully. Petal's paw marks had been obliterated by the camper tyre tracks on my return journey coming out. My night vision and surrounding forest was now bathed in an eerie light green shade of colour. Corporal Daniel was sure the poachers would have set their snares an hour before dusk. Now it would be their dinner time. They would be cooking their 'nyama choma', a Swahili word for roasting venison over a spit. Vehicle sounds travel far at night, my Landcruiser vehicle had not the quietest of engines.

We agreed to abandon the camper just short of where Petal had turned back after sensing the presence of humans. I had only to look for the end of my tyre tracks and from thereon, follow the poachers' footprints. Tracking along the road was easy but our boots were overprinting the poachers. Our presence would be a give-away to any experienced bushman. Service type boot-prints mean that there are rangers about. We must not forget to each drag a branch to sweep out our prints, including the tyre marks in the soft sandy soil, on our way back from wherever the poachers' footprints took us.

Daniel believed the trail might lead us across the river. He knew the area well. There was a natural stepping-stone crossing about half a mile ahead, where the river flow was low. He had guessed right. It was hippo-grazing time now. At night, they are like silent giants with excellent hearing but poor night vision, often apparent by their blundering through heavy bush. They have no fear in attacking anything that moves within their striking distance. A hippo in four-wheel drive, jaws wide open like a mechanised construction grab, on land, can accelerate at a rate of speed that would out distance any athlete. Escaping over the bank into the river was not an option, except a sure way to die. Crocs, and there are huge and hungry ones here, are active at night. There is a fair chance that we could be confronted by one of these giants, either a hippo or even a croc. They too, sit in wait for the unwary on land; their activities are not only confined to water.

We arrived at the turn off to the stepping stones. Whoa! Not as easy in daylight with water flowing one way and my mind's gyro pulling the other way. Vertigo in green was also at work! Corporal Daniel held onto my trouser belt, moments later we had crossed, the poachers' prints were still visible on the well-worn hippo path up the opposite bank. I could see it was used as a human pathway too. Minutes later over the sounds of the flowing water, we could hear muffled voices, women's voices coming towards us about sixty yards distant.

Their leader was carrying a dim flashlight. Daniel and I slipped quickly into the thick cover. My pulse quickened as the thought crossed my mind that if they followed back across the river and along the dirt track that we had come, they would surely walk into the parked camper. Our cover would be blown. For the moment, I cursed my stupidity. To my utter relief all ten women, with a bowman in the lead, passed by some ten yards from us. The path they took continued straight on along the river's edge. Interestingly, some women were carrying heavy bundles balanced on their heads. They were tall and slender women, some had backpacks strapped onto their shoulders. Daniel was excited. "What can you see?" he whispered. "Wa na beba mziku" I replied. (People carrying loads.) "Wako ngapi?" (How many?), he asked. "Kumi (Ten)" I said. "Wanawake tisa na mwanaume moja mbele ana beba muchale." (Nine women and one male carrying a bow and arrows.)

We remained silent, allowing the carriers to pass us and distance themselves away from us. Maybe we were too late, was this the booty on its way out, and to where? As they passed, we both heard several talking quietly to each other in their language. We agreed it was a mixture of Kisii, a tribe from the south-west, and Luo, a tribe that lived near the shores of Lake Victoria. Their leader, guide and protector, was someone local. Though he never spoke, his gait was that of a Kalenjin or Kipsigis – a tribe that had recently moved into this area illegally. They were squatters intent on clearing the area of wildlife in order to have land to grow crops and build their mud hut homesteads. Most had been forced out of their tribal lands in the North by congestion and over population. Daniel was keen to follow their trail, at a distance, but finally agreed with me that we should locate their hide-out first. The odours of cooking were still in the air. Our plan was to get in as close as we dare, take stock and get out.

The coast was now clear and we moved forward. Ten minutes later a glow from a flickering fire could be seen through the thick bush, exaggerated by the night binoculars. I could see the scene as if in daylight.

Their camp was semi-permanent, with many low grass thatched shelters sufficient to accommodate some twenty individuals to crawl into. Others were made of clear plastic sheeting, resembling home-made bivouacs. I could clearly see some fires had large, steaming 'boil a missionary' type pots, being attended to by several women. Others could be seen huddled around smaller fires for warmth. I unclipped the night binoculars and strapped them

The Poachers' Kitchen
When it rained the makeshift roof was covered over with plastic sheeting.
Zebra and Impala steaks drying in the sun.

onto Daniel's head. He had never worn them before; he gave a gasp of incredulity. "Ni kama muchana" (I see them, like daylight), he said. Now it was his turn to brief me and the fact that everything was so near and clear, he began to instinctively move away. If one of us stepped on a dry twig, the pistol like crack might be heard and who knows what reaction would come from the poachers. We could be ducking a fusillade of poisoned arrows.

Daniel was quivering with excitement. He whispered to me, "We will need twenty Rangers to surround them, there are too many."

It was time to leave and retrace our footsteps. We had taken the precaution to remove our boots before crossing the river. Mine were tied by their laces to my belt; he had hidden his on the river bank. I would soon need my boots. The soles of my feet were soft and already hurting. Devil thorns were plentiful either side of the track, making it impossible for us to take a barefoot short cut; we had to stick to the well-trodden poachers' path. Devil thorns are seeds protected by spikes. They are smaller than pea size, shed by one of the family of comifora bushes. Birds will not eat them; if they do they will choke on the spikes. Barefoot humans with bicycles fear to tread these thorny patches that lie unseen on the ground in their

The Poachers' Hideout
Sleeping accommodation

thousands, waiting for fire and rain to propagate them. Predators, born of the cat or dog family, avoid these areas as do others, like the mongoose, squirrels, genet cats, snakes, monitor lizards and many more hunters that prey on the eggs of francolin, plovers and lesser bustards.

Beware, Nature has laid her carpet to protect the feathered variety that lay their eggs on the ground, among the sand and pebbles. Even elephants, hippo and rhino stay clear of the Devil's carpet. These mini spikes dig deep into the soft and padded soles of the feet – a quick way to bring lameness to all fours, Landcruisers included. With time and tread-wear, the broken off spikes make their way through to the inner tubes. Like 'siafu', the safari ants, they bite all at once, and it is a long way to walk to camp and there is no one I know in the safari business that carries four spare wheels and several hundred puncture patches. Beware of the devil's thorns. 'Shitani', (the Swahili word for Devil), lives up to its name.

It was Daniel who trod on the first one. "Shitani!" Hissing like a snake, he bent down to remove it. Trying to look down suddenly, with night vision binoculars and for the untrained, this action triggers vertigo, another sensation he had never experienced before. "Shitani ni mulevi" I whispered. (I said 'the devil is drunk' in Swahili). This comment tickled his sense of humour. He said it was time I took charge of the white man's magic. Daniel took hold of my belt once again, chuckling to himself all the way to the river crossing.

"The boots!" I said. I had no idea where he had hidden them and neither did he! In the pitch black of night everything around him seemed to have changed form; the bushes had moved their position. He was quite sure now that the Devil had taken up residence inside him. The white man's magic was strapped back onto his head again. Parts of the river bank were

Sun curing a cheetah pelt

steep, a fall of some thirty feet and more. I was taking no chances with him tumbling over and held firmly onto him and his rifle as he scrambled around on all fours. Now that he could see, he at last found one—the left boot—but no sign of the other. Panic! He began muttering nervously about appearing on parade with one boot; after all he was the Corporal of a Platoon with high expectations of being promoted to three stripes in the near future. Daniel's world was collapsing around him. We both knew instinctively who had stolen it (his one remaining boot). A hyaena—it must be. My imagination began to run wild, his too. He clapped his hands and, sure enough, from the bushes nearby out came a sub-adult hyaena in full flight. I asked Daniel in Swahili, "Was it empty handed" meaning just that. "Sijui" (I don't know) came his reply. I always carried a small pencil flashlight, a mini-Magna. I suggested he use it to look around and give me back the 'white-man's magic'. I would go and fetch the big Magna – this missing boot had to be found, no matter its state of disrepair – at least he would have a story to tell and the evidence to go with it, plus a good operational excuse to get a new pair from the Quartermaster's store. "Boots, size eleven are not in plentiful supply, in fact almost extinct." he said. "No one had flat feet like me." This was another give away for the poachers to admire if they noticed this spoor. If the bowmen were local they might even know the owner! All these little telltale signs make up the bush craft intelligence puzzle. I left Daniel to beat about the bush. My soles were reminding me I would be as lame as a duck soon – best wait until I crossed and put on my boots.

I arrived at the camper some ten minutes later. No other human footprints had passed that way, except it appeared my spotted friend had called. Her paw marks were all around the vehicle, but no sign of Petal on top. I located the Magna flashlight and set off back the way I had come. Something made me take a closer look at the prints I was following. They had gone forward of Petal's hurried turn around. I had duped myself – it was a hyaena's prints—that of a sub-adult. At a glance, both hyaena prints and cheetah prints are dog like and very similar. This chap had followed our trail and scent and then crossed the river and it was he who had stolen Daniel's boot. The hyaena possesses a highly developed sense of smell and tracking skill, more than a trained domestic sniffer dog. He had homed in to the Corporal's boots. I met a very relieved Daniel at the crossing. He had found his boot – well, most of it – the tongue and laces were missing! The rest had been bitten, but not chewed. Daniel disappeared into the thicket and returned with two brush-like branches. These were to be dragged behind us as we walked back to the caravan. Having covered our footprints, we would drive along the track as if a lodge vehicle, returning late to a lodge or camp up-stream, had passed this way. It was 8.30 p.m. in the evening and this would not raise too much suspicion.

To turn around where we were would only sound alarm bells if our tyre tracks were found by the poachers the next morning. They would venture out from their hide-out at dawn, to check their snares. The Mara Game Reserve's northern boundary was a good mile away to the south. The snaring was being carried out on a Maasai group ranch, bordering this boundary, undetected.

Petal had unwittingly brought me to this point where she had turned in her tracks; I would have been none the wiser and would have carried on. Now it was up to us. Daniel and I discussed the matter; the night was still young.

We will head for Buffalo Camp up-stream. I knew the German manager well; he had offered us an open invitation. "When in need – shout!" he had said. I decided to take up this offer. First, our plan – we must act fast. I would then radio-call the managers of Mara and Keekorok lodges and organise as many Rangers as possible from these outposts, and make up the shortfall with some young Maasai Morani, (Warriors). The Senior Warden at Keekorok was contacted and within the hour the arrangements were complete. The lodges had agreed to provide the transport and rendezvous with us at the Mara River Camp airstrip at 2.00 a.m. sharp, in the morning. The local Chief at Aitong was always willing to assist me and produced ten young Maasai Moranis with spears and machetes. Mara Buffalo Camp also had a Police Post with three policemen available to join us.

Nothing like this call to arms had occurred in North Mara, no one knew the reason except the Senior Warden, Daniel and I. Our meeting point was sufficiently far way from the poachers' hide-out not to arouse suspicion. The moon was in its third quarter to full, and was due to rise at 9.00 p.m. By 2.00 a.m. it would be lower in the western sky, throwing an elongated shadow off the trees, along the ground, for us to flit through into position around the poachers' camp. The moonlight would be clear enough for us to see without the use of flashlights.

There was one problem – the Maasai Morani would be barefoot and vulnerable to 'Shitani', the Devil thorns. I was able to get a message earlier to the Chief to acquire ten pairs of tyre-soled sandals, from the Aitong shoemaker, for the warriors. This valuable 'never wear out' footwear would be their reward for taking part. These young Maasai would trade their knobkerries for heavy-duty life long shoes. A pair would cost about three pounds, that's a lot of money for a Maasai warrior. Some had never handled money and knew little about its value, except that it might buy a young goat—not bad for a night's work. Three thousand shillings, about thirty pounds sterling, would come out of Petal's 'Friends of Conservation Fund'. Dollars and every other conceivable foreign currency were often donated to her cause by well-wishing tourists in the field, most of whom she had terrified out of their wits by jumping on their vehicle and spraying their windscreens. Petal had given them a story to tell, including pictures to show to their unbelieving friends back home. My plans for heading back to the big city were now on hold. The manager of Buffalo Camp invited both of us to dinner 'on the house'. The change of menu, sauerkraut and all its trimmings, was totally foreign to Corporal Daniel. He was so hungry, he claimed he could have eaten an ox – I believed him – he even had second helpings.

We set off by vehicle, in covert night-vision mode, to the Mara River airstrip to await the arrival of our strike force. Daniel was anxious about his tongue-less boot, the missing laces and his inevitable demotion to Private for destroying Council property. Would his commanding officer even believe his wild story? "No problem, Daniel," I said, "I'll tell him the story – you were so hungry you began to eat your boots." This sort of juvenile teasing appealed to his sense of humour.

The plan was that everybody would set off from the airstrip on foot; all following in double file, no talking, no flashlights but following Daniel and I. It would take about an hour's brisk walk to the poachers' hide-out. This exercise would punish all the over weights and overeating problems for many, including Daniel. For the Maasai warriors, they were in for a long journey that may take several days and nights away from their manyattas. After the showdown, the plan was that the warriors, as a one fast moving unit, would set off to track down the first group of ten load-carriers that we had seen. The instruction to the warriors was to send a runner back to us with information on their progress.

The policemen in our group would formally arrest the captured poachers and transport them to the Narok police headquarters. They would be prosecuted for trespass and hunting of wildlife, without a valid licence. With luck, a custodial sentence or a hefty fine may bring out their pay-masters. These are the people that we want. There is to be no shooting, unless in self-defence and no spearing the poachers to death, just plain arrests. Nothing is ever easy in the dark, especially when all hell is let loose with arrows flying and poachers running in all directions.

The final plan had to be simple. I would personally take three Rangers at a time and guide them, holding belt to belt, in single file and position them some thirty yards in a circle around the hide-out. There they must stay in ambush, silent, still, no coughing, no talking. All of us must defuel for obvious reasons before crossing the river en route to the hide-out. At the blowing of several short staccato whistles from a police whistle, (everybody knows the sound of a shrill police whistle, even the poachers.), the circle would quickly step forward to close into the centre and turn on their flashlights. Some poachers would try to break through the cordon, but on coming face to face with the spears and cold steel, there was little chance they would try and escape, even if they drew their machetes. One long blast, on the police whistle, would signal the firing of one shot by each rifleman into the air. Twelve riflemen and ten whooping warriors would be enough to scare the bee gees out of anyone, even if they were armed with conventional weapons.

The plan was now set and in place. It was 3.15 a.m. exactly. The poachers would be sleeping heavily at this time, but those with weak bladders would be nearing their defuelling time. I had no intention of waiting for that. I gave the shrill birdlike whistle of a nightjar, the signal for the three policemen to blow their staccato whistle. Everyone moved forward quickly. I planned for speed, surprise and fear. All were caught napping and gave no resistance. Every aspect of the operation had gone as planned. Not a shot from either side was fired, to my great relief. The poachers were all sound asleep in their makeshift grass and plastic covered bivouacs. The rangers dazzled the dosy sleepers with their high-powered flashlights. I was amazed when eighteen fully dressed women and two males were hauled out wide-eyed, blinking, blinded and stupefied by the bright lights and, of course, fear again played a big part. None had uttered a sound – they must have thought their end had come.

The women were much shorter and stockier than those Daniel and I had seen departing earlier that evening. This group, including the males, were all from the Kisii tribe, their reserve a small town called Migori lay some fifty miles to the west on the borders of Tanzania and Kenya.

Soon we would have the full story; the women folk were already talking. The party that had left earlier were mostly Luo. As we had thought, their guide was a local Kipsigis squatter. He was to take the group of ten to another in transit hide-out, some five miles away, on the edge of the escarpment, where another guide from Kendu Bay, near Lake Victoria, some seventy miles to the north west, would meet up and guide them through the forests and panya routes (smuggler routes), to Lake Victoria.

We gathered, from what we saw, that their operations had been in full swing for at least six months, with weekly trips back and forth, carrying load upon load of sun-dried venison of every description, zebra, wildebeest, impala, hippo, crocodile and skins. Not a vulture in the sky during the day to signal that here was a table where scraps of food were plenty. How was this possible? I asked myself. We were soon to find out. Petal had brought us to the very edge of a multi-million, illegal, wildlife slaughter house. The ill-gotten proceeds were carried physically into the western districts of Kenya, for sale in alleyway butcheries passed off, to the untrained eye, as domestic stock dried meat. The bones and other unnecessary offal and stomach contents were dumped into the Mara River to make the load lighter. The warriors were itching to go; dawn was an hour away, they would lie in ambush a mile down river, wait and capture the returning guide. He would soon talk. Never mess with Maasai Moranis; they have painful ways and means of making you talk. They helped us tie-up all the prisoners, hands behind their backs, and roped each poacher to the other, waist to waist, ready for the five mile eastward route march to Buffalo Camp, where the lodge manager and police would take them over and have them transported to Narok, to await their punishment by the local resident magistrate.

My party of five would stay behind and search every corner of the poachers' camp. There appeared to be no firearms, only several spare bows with poisoned arrows. We decided to retain one female and one male for further interrogation. The Morani were sent on their way with instructions to capture and bring back all of the meat carriers. This mission may take several days and more. These young men will never starve. By calling in at a manyatta (Maasai homestead), they will be given food and rest. It is when they venture out of their tribal bounds that trouble starts; they could be arrested as suspected stock thieves by the locals. Two young Maasai Rangers were attached to their group. Corporal Daniel was keen to go, but I felt it unwise; he was heavy in build and his age and fitness might hold back the fast moving youngsters. When hot on the trail, they will run for miles. The first meat-carrying group had many hours head start, but they would stop often to rest. Much of their walking time would be in the cool of the night and their progress would be slow. They may rest up for twenty-four hours at their number one hide-out on the escarpment.

I was beginning to see a possible flaw in my plans – maybe the Morani should have taken the remaining male poacher with them. I communicated my concern to Daniel; it would have made finding number one hide-out easier. "No!" he said, "there would be extra worry of having to watch his every move, and who knows, he could take them on a wild goose chase." The way he said it made me laugh aloud. "Huyu ata peleka hawa njia ya bata mujinga". (Translated into plain English: He would lead the Morani astray like a stupid turkey and they would kill him). Then! "Matata mingi." (Much big trouble.) "Our warriors will follow the trail like the hyaena that followed ours. They will find them maybe today, maybe tomorrow or the next day. They will find them for sure." Daniel was confident. I found his humour infectious.

Our two prisoners were looking sorry for themselves. Dawn had come and the poachers' den took on another scene of death and destruction. Piles of animal bones, crawling with safari ants, these black, pincer, pinching busybodies were already at work. They would pick the bones clean and the poachers would then dump them in the river.

The venison had been cut into thin steaks and spread among the top branches of the flat-topped acacia. Here, they would be exposed to the direct sunlight to dry out and shrink. "But what about the vultures?" I asked, "why don't they land on the trees and devour the meat?" Daniel looked at me and smiled. "Mzee" (old man), "did you not know that vultures will not eat meat placed in trees – only on the ground!" I was speechless. I had to confess to him that I did not know. "Why" I asked, "it doesn't make sense, what about the tawny eagles, the Marabou stalks, the flies, the ants". "No," he said, "you will not see one bird, but the only animal that sometimes gives them trouble is the leopard, but he cannot climb up onto the flat top of the tree. Flies do not fly to that height. That is why some lions climb trees to try to get away from the flies." That I knew. "But what about the ants," I asked. "If you look closely at the base of the tree, you will see why. It is covered, inches deep around the base, with fine, white ash from the camp fires." "But what about the skins," I asked, "zebra skins are difficult to dispose of." Daniel replied, "They are cut into strips, the hair is burnt off and sold as tie up straps for everyday use, but most skins are thrown into the river and rot. Zebra and wildebeest drown in their thousands, a few hundred go unnoticed and sink to the bottom and when the Mara floods, it all goes down to Lake Victoria."

Drinking water was collected from the cattle troughs and plastic sheeting spread over hollowed, saucer-shaped ground to catch the rainwater. The open-air food store contained posho (local flour made from maize meal), in plastic bags. There was sugar in plastic bags, teabags in plastic bags, all hanging from wires strung across like a washing line under a makeshift plastic cover. The toilets – well, head for the river! But back to basics, what is it about these meat steaks? How was it that they did not attract the feathered clean-up squad? Salt, thinly spread over each piece, was the magic ingredient used before being laid flat high in the trees, to sun-dry. Once dried, the meat loses its blood and water content by more than sixty percent. When required for cooking, place it in boiling hot water and in minutes your steak has once again returned to its normal form – tender and tasty. Birds, flies and other bloodsucking, egg-laying insects avoid the dehydration effects of salt. I learned this lesson first hand from Corporal Daniel, the Bush Master.

Meanwhile, our two prisoners had been debriefed. They seemed happy to have got rid of the anxiety that hangs over captured humans. Relief is instantaneous, the burden is shed. The interrogators gathered that the poachers' camp had been in existence for a year. Sixty tons of wildlife venison, per month, had been carried out of North Mara by a trail of some four en route hideouts; each hideout was designed to accommodate no more than ten. Where we were, at the main hide-out, thirty poachers/carriers could be accommodated. Business was booming in Migori and Kendu Bay and the 'fat cat' gang leaders getting fatter. The carriers were working in relays as each hide-out was vacated northwards. An empty handed group of ten, from the west, took over occupation allowing a full day's rest at each hide. Our hide, in the normal course of events, would be expecting a fresh group of ten any night and so their musical chairs played out its daily destruction of the wildlife. This was big money.

Our warriors played their cards right and located the first hide-out. They would lie in ambush for the changeover to take place, then pounce and, with luck, maybe net twenty in the bag and escort them back here to us at the main site. This operation would only work once. If the carriers did not arrive at number two, suspicions would be aroused, and poacher scouts would be sent back to find out why the incoming flow had dried up. All movement between hides took place at night. Their orders were strict. I calculated somewhere in the region of forty carriers were in operation along the trail, eighteen had been arrested, leaving some twenty at large. We would leave the steaks where they were. There would be less chance of them rotting in the sun and fresh air – no refrigerators here! The whole set-up works against our western principles of fresh and frozen meats that keep indefinitely? How the African half can live makes good sense to me.

'Enemies of Conservation'
A leopard snared by poachers.

It had been a long day; night was approaching. The Rangers and Daniel were happy to stay and have their meal cooked by the female prisoner, whilst the hapless male, with hands tied, was tethered to a tree. I was given time off to return to my camper for dinner and sleep. Daniel was in charge for the remainder of the night.

My anxiety shifted to Petal's safety. Snares had been set all around where she had bolted off the track, into the bushes. I must organise a full-scale 'operation snare clean-up'. This would be best done through the Chief at Aitong village and the Group Ranch management, though the latter was still in the early stages of formation. Several hundred Maasai members could be gathered from the surrounding manyattas, though I much preferred their warriors to search the area; they would volunteer without question. First, however, I must exercise patience. If I jump the gun here and move too quickly, I could blow the whole operation. I feared for Petal's life; the place was like a minefield, one mistake from her, the snare would trip and seize her by the neck or around her body. She would struggle to try and free herself, and then the noose would tighten. This thought was not the best nightcap for me to fall asleep with.

I slept fitfully, and in my waking moments my thoughts turned to a horrible and sickening incident which occurred on my friend's farm. A leopard had been decimating his calves; a metal cage and trap were set. Several days later, the herdsman came running with the news that a huge male leopard was caught in the trap. My friend and I rushed to the scene. Yes, the culprit was trapped in the cage, but it was very clear why this crazed and ferocious animal had created so much destruction and havoc amongst his stock.

How this animal must have suffered. The animal had broken free from a poacher's noose that was still embedded deep around its waist. The sight sickened me to the core; a photograph tells the rest of this horrific story. I had good reason to fear for Petal's safety and found myself listening keenly to the night sounds. I could sense death all around me; the hyaenas were busy, the jackals were calling and there were the sounds and growls of predators fighting for their pecking order over their snared dinner, dished up to them on a plate. A snared zebra or impala, unable to free itself would be easy meat for the predators. The Mara's wildlife was taking the brunt of illegal bush meat trade—the sickness amongst the wild dogs, the poaching menace—it was all having a disturbing effect on me.

The whole security system of wildlife management appeared to be collapsing. This may just be the tip of the iceberg, the rest was probably happening along the length of the Mara River, and the authorities were doing little to uncover this skulduggery. Tourist vehicles were being ambushed and robbed. Tourists being taken off into the Tanzanian bush and then made to walk three or more miles, minus their shoes, sore footed, lame and exhausted, back to their vehicles. By the grace of God, these terrified visitors avoided the elephants and buffaloes that could easily have despatched them to their Maker. Their tour drivers in most cases blaze the trail and get them safely back from over the border, into Kenya.

I awakened early; it was 5.00 a.m. The dawn light would be creeping into the sky in half an hour. A cup of tea and a few biscuits would fortify me. Breakfast would have to wait. As soon as it was light enough to see, and armed with my rifle, I began to look around expecting the worst behind every bush. It was not long before I tripped over a snare wire, attached to the end of it was a dead zebra. Snares and strangled wildlife were everywhere. This was almost too much for me to bear. I counted six zebras and three impala gazelles within an area of five acres. I lost count of the many other wire snares set ready to trap the unwary animals. I came across a zebra carcass; lion paw marks were clearly seen and hyaenas had been busy too. This was the cacophony of growls and snarls I had heard during the night. The 'King of Beasts' and his subjects had fed well.

I returned to the river crossing and followed the pathway back to the poachers' hide-out. It was the first time I had seen the approach to the hide-out in daylight – everything looked different – the green haze of the night-vision binoculars penetrated deep into the bush in contrast to my human vision which, in this clear light of day, went no further than the forest perimeter. The scene was totally different now it was daylight. I whistled my nightjar call sign to warn those in the poachers' camp of my approach. The call was returned, the 'all clear' was given for me to proceed.

To my surprise the Morani warriors were back, stretched out fast asleep on the ground around the fire. There were others too, tied by each hand to the other, nine women and one male. The warriors had surprised the group, in broad daylight, in their hideout on the escarpment. The carriers had surrendered without a murmur. They were caught sound asleep at 8 o'clock in the morning. It had taken the warriors three hours tracking on their initial run. They were all excited at having successfully carried out my instructions and captured every one—all ten! They were, however, unaware that another incoming group was due to pass through en route to the main hideout. Their captured carriers had not let on that there was another empty-handed group on their way into the main hide-out.

The warriors had returned with much of the dried meat. Fair enough, this would suffice as evidence for court, but how were we going to keep it in refrigerators – there was just too much of it.

I radio-called the manager of Buffalo Camp asking him to meet up with us at an up-river rendezvous with transport to carry ten prisoners (poachers), plus three policemen. We would hold back two women carriers who would take us through to hide number one, two, three and four. Corporal Daniel was insisting that he should lead the warriors and leave the remaining Rangers at the main hide, just in case the other carriers arrived by a circuitous route.

The logistics were becoming a little complicated. So far, we had netted twenty-nine poachers. Another twenty were somewhere between here and Lake Victoria, sixty miles away!

Daniel set off with the Maasai warriors, plus two women. Three policemen set off with the ten prisoners to meet up at the hand-over rendezvous with the Buffalo Camp manager. I was beginning to lose track of who was where! The rear guard had a job to do – that was my group. We had to cross the river, dismember the snares and destroy them. This was my responsibility. I had nine Rangers left, four would take up ambush positions in the hide, and five would come with me. The cutting edge of my heavy-duty pliers, used to free the zebra stallion, would come in useful again. No words could describe what the Rangers saw. I was prepared for the shock, having seen a little of the scene that morning, but the Rangers became genuinely and visibly upset as we combed the area. More and more carcasses were found, mostly zebra. Some wire nooses hanging from solid overhead branches intended for much larger and heavier animals, possibly elephant or hippo, were visible. These wires were stolen from the support stays which hold heavy wooden electric light poles upright and in place. Nothing but a hacksaw, supplied by our friendly lodge manager, could cut through the three-quarter inch pleated steel. By midday we had collected a truck-load of snares. All this would have to be transported to the Magistrates Court at Narok. The whole operation was destined to be time consuming, fuel consuming and tiresome, with bumpy road trips back and forth to give evidence to the court.

Impressive as all of this was, I knew full well that the Narok County Council's Exchequer was being plundered by their office bearers. Millions of shillings, the proceeds of tourist Game Reserve entry payments to the Maasai Mara, had vanished into thin air. The 'fat cats' had been fired and a few were prosecuted. Their replacements were soon back at the same fiddle. The till still continues to be short-changed. Friends of Conservation, a privately formed fund raiser organisation, specifically tailored to support wildlife projects in the Mara, came to the rescue. Its local representative, a gung-ho Kenyan cowboy, was somewhat embarrassed to learn of this drama and what was happening on his doorstep. We did not see eye to eye on matters of conservation. I was not alone in realising his jealously guarded position of local importance was being eroded.

Daniel had sent back a Morani warrior with the news that his tracker group had been side-tracked. They had received information from a 'friendly source', en route, that another poachers' hide-out was 'rumoured' to be in operation south of Governors Camp, along the Mara River, in the thick heavy forest, and that we should rendezvous at Paradise Camp, an unoccupied tourist and mobile camp site, used by an up-market camping safari outfitter.

Daniel's instructions were that we needed to be there by dusk. Time was running short. There were two hours before darkness would set in. The Corporal would be keen to try out the night vision equipment; this was going to be his show tonight and rightly so.

I bundled my group of five into the camper. They were most impressed with its layout, including the mobile toilet – how much did it cost, where could they get one? I knew what was coming, some would develop urgent nature's calls and any excuse to try it out!

We arrived at 'Paradise' by a roundabout route, taking a track over Rhino Ridge, avoiding the tourist game-viewing track, which ran alongside the forest edge and river. Who knows who might be watching us? My vehicle was well known and many associated it with having eyes and ears that contained some psycho 'mzungu' (white man), who walked with cheetahs. Cheetahs are categorised with the same family as leopards, 'Lo-ngwaro-ngeri' and when enquiring about the whereabouts of cheetahs with the Maasai, one has to specify 'the spotted one that runs with the speed of lightening.'

I get a real kick in setting the clock back in time with these fine pastoralists, unspoiled by civilisation. How will they preserve this fascinating culture in the modern world of today? Sadly, it will diminish as education and western influence changes their thinking. The march of time waits for no man, and should they fail to keep pace, they will become the 'aborigines' of Kenya. Some will survive to become the wealthiest of landowners in East Africa.

Corporal Daniel and his team had not yet arrived. Darkness had set in and the setting sun's fading orange glow had spread itself along the underside of the high cirrus clouds. The lights were about to go out and there was nothing else to do but sit silently and commune with Nature's nocturnal symphony. I thought it wise to keep the five Rangers in the camper for the time being. They would take the opportunity to cat-nap in preparation for a long cold night, sitting in ambush or maybe carrying out a plan similar to that which had been executed with surprise and success, two nights previously.

I had parked the camper in the middle of the Paradise Camp site; an empty, grassy glade within the forest. I could hear the rumbles and the occasional trumpet of a herd of elephants, up-wind from us. A colony of baboons had settled for the night in a large fig tree. The shrill and sudden shriek of a youngster, being punished for his mischief or for breaking some form of the baboon family law, gave me a start. I felt uneasy; was my sixth sense telling me something? The young Morani, the bearer of Daniel's message, was already sound asleep in the front cab with me. He had run non-stop for miles and was out for the count. The smell of rancid goat's fat, mixed with body odour of the highest order, combined with the fact that the camper windows were wound up to three-quarters height to keep out the cold and keep in the pong, triggered in me the urge to be violently sick.

The goat's fat taken from the male blackface-ram's bulbous behind, at slaughter, is a priceless Maasai skin conditioner. Young warriors go to great lengths to smear this fatty concoction over their entire body from 'top to bottom'. As a result, their light brown skin becomes smooth and soft as velvet. This condition lasts until middle age (a young thirty). As they begin to climb the pecking order ladder within their clan, their status changes to the bottom rung of responsible eldership. By the age of forty, their diet of blood and milk plays havoc with their bodies. Their skin gradually becomes darker and drier. Interest in the smearing of goats' fat is lost and the beginnings of old age and the wrinkles start to appear. At fifty plus, arthritis in its many forms, is noticeably present. The women folk become stooped at an early age, from the rigours of physical household chores, giving birth at regular intervals and carrying the loads of firewood and water containers on their backs. They are old at forty. Trade-ins for younger models are common practice amongst the older Maasai.

It was pitch black outside. The forest canopy blocked out the moonlight and the stars. I wanted time to think, plan and communicate with my sixth sense. I quietly stepped out into the cold; no one stirred, my posse was snoring peacefully. They had confidence in me and my alertness. Woe betides me if I let them down.

Recent clashes had taken place between our crack Police General Service Paramilitary Unit and well-armed bandits a mile down river. We were close to the 'border' of that G.S.U. patrol area. Ambushes by this unit were just that – ambushes! No questions asked or not even 'Halt! Who goes there?' It was a no-go area for anyone at night stumbling around, torches or no torches; particularly a rag-bag group of four spear-carrying warriors and one lead rifleman, coming in their night-vision sights—they would be dead meat in seconds. We were in a dangerous position; we were on the Game Reserve boundary, right on the edge of the 'no-go' area.

My senses were flashing red warning lights. I must find out where Daniel is. I called Governors Camp, two miles up river, on my hand held VHF radio. Had anybody seen him? Had he walked into their camp? Maybe he was in the tour driver's restaurant having a meal. Please check, and bring him to the radio. After an endless wait, the radio crackled into life. It was, to my great relief, Daniel speaking at the other end.

I had guessed right. "Mzee" (Old man), "I'm hungry" he said, "and so are my Morani— we're eating tourist chakula (food), kama mzungu" (white man style – knife and fork). "These warriors prefer to use their fingers; they are like the animals of the bush." This said in Swahili, "Wa na kula kama wanyama ya musitoni". This would touch any African's sense of humour, knowing that the Maasai claim the wild animals are their relatives! I was able to persuade Daniel, by using a subtle form of conversation that anyone overhearing our open radio message would not be able to make head nor tail of what was being talked about. I suspected some camp employees could be in league with these bandits. Tourist tented camps had been raided and tourists robbed on more than one occasion. I informed Daniel that I would have tea ready at the third hour, (the third hour after midnight, that's 3.00 a.m.), but 'Shitani' was waiting for him (the Devil) and he must use wheels.

A murderous ambush was in place somewhere. Who knows where? I could not take the risk that he would try and come to the Paradise rendezvous on foot – they must come by vehicle. At the mention of 'Shitani', he realised I was trying to tell him that danger was lurking in the forest. "I will come for tea—over and out."

Now it was up to me to pass the next five hours outside the camper. There was no way I was going back into the cab to join the stinky Morani – anything but that! I couldn't even light a fire for if there were poachers nearby, the flicker of the flames would give my position away. I didn't even have a blanket. This was too much; my warm sleeping bag was lying empty in the camper! I would have to wake up the Rangers, brief them about the plan, get my sleeping bag and find somewhere to sleep. What better than on top? – Petal's bed, perfect! Each Ranger would take an hour's watch on duty. All agreed. At least I might get the chance to have some sleep; I was beginning to feel very tired. Everybody paid their nature calls and dossed-down again. The baboons were unsettled and, sensing our presence, came to visit us. They were inquisitive and noisy. One of the large fig trees, with overhanging branches, became their grandstand and, of course, the bundle on top of the camper took their interest. My brilliant idea was about to be crapped upon. A few minutes later, it all came pouring down, splat, splat onto the roof, onto the sleeping bag and the smell was worse than two Morani put together. Much arm-waving and shooing shut them up, but the sh-t still kept raining down. Time to move, but to where? The on-duty Ranger just couldn't contain his mirth. Smart guy – when I climbed on top, he had surreptitiously crawled under the vehicle! Well, he was going to have company whether he liked it or not. Then I thought, 'What good was he to us, under the vehicle anyway?' Authority took precedence. "That is no place for a guard," I said. Mumbling and grumbling he got the message and moved out. I sensed that he would fall sound asleep wherever he moved to – not a satisfactory or confident situation for me to be in. So, it was I who had to catnap – with my rifle handcuffed to my left wrist and night-vision binoculars hidden in a get-at-able place in the sump-guard underneath the vehicle directly above my head. Oh! for a mattress, I thought – I must be getting soft. The ground was as hard as a rock. A bruised hipbone, with a sleepless night lay ahead. No wonder my mind strayed to the comfort of a hammock strung high up on the trees. I had two very up-to-date, state-of-the-art string hammocks that wrapped up the sleeper like a cocoon. There was no chance to tumble out! Actually, getting out of one requires a combined team effort—but no, the darned baboons, for sure, would dollop on me again.

I would recommend string hammocks to any bushman, they are compact and easily wrapped up in a sleeping bag or vice-versa. They are lightweight and there is no need for a mattress or blanket. Of course, one must not forget the insect spray can, guaranteed protection against any flying, dive-bombing, biting insects like mosquitoes, but if one is clever enough, one can always set up a little igloo-type mosquito net. They too, are light and compact.

A well-aimed squirt of the mosquito spray can, across the flame of a cigarette lighter, or a lighted match, produces a flame-thrower whooshing effect and makes for a satisfying burn-up against attacking ants, bats, snakes and particularly baboons with mischief on their minds.

For me, sleep was not on the menu. I just couldn't trust the night guard Ranger to stay alert. Africans seem not to be able to stay awake on guard duty, unless sitting by a charcoal brazier or a log fire. For myself, there is nothing better than falling asleep by a camp log fire, in two minutes flat. People talking around the fire, laughing and joking, seems to have a soporific effect on me. I have to struggle really hard to make conversation, particularly with clients all eager to hear the camp-fire stories – man versus beast. I have quite a few hair-raising ones, so much so that when 'hit the canvas' time arrives, most ask for an escort back to their tents!

The hour of midnight was approaching; the full moon had disappeared behind an ominous black cloud, a light wind was kicking up a bit of dust into my face and the baboons had gone quiet. The temperature was beginning to drop and all the signs of imminent rain were present. I was considering what best to do. Should I 'stay put' under the camper, or perhaps fix up the hammock and cover it over with a light-weight army poncho, with the ends hanging down either side? This would provide a safe and comfortable bed-rest, away from metals that might attract lightening strikes. Unless the tree receives a direct hit, you are pretty safe in a forest. Keep away from single trees out in the open, they are the dangerous ones that attract lightening.

I made up my mind, the storm was approaching—hammock it was to be. The Rangers and Maasai were still sound asleep in the camper. My interruption in extracting the hammock from its locker seemed not to bother them. Karanja, the on-duty Ranger, was shuffling around, stamping his feet, trying to keep out the cold. I offered him the empty driver's seat in the cab in exchange for some assistance in attaching the hammock, some four feet off the ground. A compromise was reached; he was now a happy boy, not fazed by his compatriot's rancid perfume. I too, was comfortable and ready to take anything the storm was intending to throw at me. And throw at me, it did! Thank goodness for the forest cover; it pelted down. In moments the ground was awash. No way would I have withstood the three inch deep rush of water now cascading under the vehicle towards the river. By 3.00 a.m. it was still pouring relentlessly. The plains and vehicle tracks would be flooded, impossible to navigate by vehicle before morning, and possibly not even then! We might be stuck in here for a day. There was nothing else to do, but wait.

I had enough emergency maize meal to make 'posho', the plum pudding type of Kenyan-African staple diet, gravy mix and baked beans, plus tinned veggies, to feed everyone, including myself. Chai (tea) and UHT (ultra heat-treated milk) lasted for months. The Morani would enjoy a break from his standard diet of blood for breakfast. A cup of tea with a tablespoon of sugar was luxury for them – that's how they take their tea!

By 6.00 a.m., water, water everywhere; the Mara River was now in flood. Those Rangers, back at poacher's camp number one, would be marooned; they had some food and poacher's steak to feed upon and no doubt, if push came to shove, they would seek food (posho) from the local Kipsigis, but then their cover would be blown. Radio hand-held communications have always been a problem in the Mara. The batteries run down, the transmitter sets break down and months go by while someone, a hundred miles away, tries to fix them. So, in general, everything was now in a beggar's muddle. This is Africa! Something would happen one way or another to kick-start our operation into effect once more. Just waiting was exciting – not boring, not for me, not for a minute.

By 9.00 a.m. the rain had ceased. There had been eight hours of solid non-stop rain – this is Mara. When it rains like this, communications and everything else goes haywire. Atmospherics destroy the transmission of the receiving waves and the hand-held radio goes into a crackling, spluttering, incoherent object of sheer frustration.

I wondered what the poachers would be doing to-day. One thing for sure, if they were on our side of the river, there would be no chance to cross for days. They would not go north towards Governors Camp, and the only way to go anywhere, even to poach, would be south and we were in the south and so was the General Service Unit ambush team.

I had no problem with cooking on gas in the camper or feeding the Rangers. After they were fed, we could quickly set up the points of ambush once again. The bird life was beginning to twitter, a sure sign that the rain was about to cease completely. The baboons were still quiet, save for the odd shriek from an infant being reprimanded. They would move off as we became more active – heading, no doubt, to the nearest Lodge rubbish heap. Yes, something had to be done about all that rubbish dumping.

Soon breakfast was served. Posho is easy to make. Fill a pan with boiling water, not too much; dump in the maize flour, add a little salt, mix and stir until it looks like solid John O'Groat's porridge, mix in the veggies, keep patting it until it is ready to up-end onto a flat surface and there is your steam pudding! Baked beans and gravy are separate entities to be dipped into. Take your portion of posho, roll it in a ball, about the size of a golf ball in your hand, press your thumb into it, fill it with beans and gravy and pepper, pop it into your mouth and eat it – it's delicious! Fattening? – Yes very. Energy making? – Yes, plenty, but beware the uninitiated, constipation lurks around the corner if you take too much. Prunes, if you are a westerner, 'brookey-laxy', 'Brooklax' if you are a local, wild figs if you are a baboon; all of these are worthy cures for constipation.

My radio crackled into life; it was Daniel. "There is no chance to come by road, the plains are flooded," he said, "the black cotton soil is too treacherous; we shall get stuck." The poachers' den was reputed to be somewhere between where I was, at Paradise, and Governors Camp, where he was, a matter of about a mile. He would set out on foot with his trackers, heading towards me. We would stay in ambush.

If the poachers bolted, they couldn't cross the river and there was only one way to go; that was towards us. We would be able to recognise friend from foe and hopefully take them on. This group could be well-armed and might be the ones that had banditised the tourists near Mara Bridge, a few days previously; stolen all the tourists' luggage and frog-marched them over the border into Tanzania, removing their shoes and sending them back, in the dark with their driver, to look for their abandoned vehicle. Their plan was timed to get well away from tracker combat forces who may take up pursuit, but Tanzania would not permit Kenya tracker units the privilege of hot pursuit into their territory, such is territorial co-operation in Africa.

An ambush was set; each Ranger could see where each of his colleagues was in cover. The Maasai Morani stayed with me, under control, mainly for their own protection. These Morani are frighteningly hot blooded, they have no fear and should there be a modern-day gun fight, it would be a little unhealthy for them to be dancing up and down, up-front amongst the hail of bullets. I had concern enough about Daniel's hit-and-run squad, now approaching, somewhere in the forest ahead of us. Every ear and eye was listening and looking out for a furtive movement or a twig cracking. It might be a frightened animal moving away, sensing approaching danger. Most wildlife has very acute hearing—eight times beyond the capability of a human. I have been blessed with excellent sight, hearing and smell, honed by living out in the open spaces. My long distance eyesight had perfected by zooming in on far distant objects. Take a man from a city, his distant vision is not trained, blocked continually by the closeness of the concrete around him. Place him among the plains of the Mara, without binoculars, and watch him strain to focus on distant objects.

The baboons were barking excitedly some three hundred yards ahead. This was a sure sign that someone, or something, was moving and had caught their attention. I re-issued a whispered instruction not to shoot unless they shot at us, if they were poachers. That included poisoned arrows. The thought alone sent a shiver down my spine – just a little nick and within minutes you die a painful death. One can survive with a bullet wound, but not the silent swoosh of a well-aimed poisoned arrow.

A single shot rang out; that was Daniel's .303 rifle. It was a sound I knew so well for I was trained to shoot with that type of service rifle. I could now break radio silence.

I called quietly, "Daniel, Daniel, this is X-ray Mobile (my call sign). Do you read?" "Roger, Effendi (Sir), mambogani." (What's your problem?) "I have found their hide-out," he said, "it's empty of poachers and their firewood is still burning." This told me that the fire had been kindled after the rain had stopped, only an hour or so ago. Daniel had fired the shot to scare them into running our way. Moments later, I heard the sound of an approaching aircraft; maybe he could help us with the search from the air. I switched over to the air-ground communication and called, "Aircraft in the vicinity of Governor's Camp, this is X-ray Mobile; come in please. URGENT!" The reply came: "X-ray Mobile, this is Papa Alfa Papa." I recognised the registration number and the pilot's voice. It was Mike Harries, a friend of mine. He was in the windmill making business and a lay preacher in his spare time, specialising in officiating at marriages and funerals. (This is Kenya, the world is your oyster – reach for the stars, if that is your wish!) He was also a reserve policeman and Padre to the Police Force.

Mike was a man of many talents, and right now I could use him. I asked, "Would you buzz the forest at tree-top level, as it would assist in putting more pressure on some poachers down here." "Roger, Dave, I will do that. I'll keep a close look out for you!" As good as his word, close it was. A low flying aircraft, thirty feet up, going like the clappers, at full chat, ten feet above the tree-tops, is scary for the unaccustomed, including wildlife. Bedlam had broken loose. A small group of five very large, old bull elephants, a coalition of short-tempered resident males, thrown out from the breeding herd by the Alpha bull, panicked and came charging towards our ambush positions. Moments before this, I had a smile on my face picturing the thoughts of those darn baboons dirtying their pants in sheer terror,—now it was a matter of every man for himself. These were huge blundering animals, the size of houses, trumpeting, head down, blindly crashing through the undergrowth. Anything and everything in their way was being flattened. Imagine five D10 bulldozers coming straight at you! There was only one way to go and that was up. Rangers' rifles were abandoned in short, sharp succession. It is incredible how a powerful shot of adrenalin can turbo-charge muscle, brain and limbs into a highly sprung machine, capable of incredible feats. The Rangers did not climb the trees—they seemed to fly up into the branches. The Maasai Morani had 'gapped' it on foot and sprouted wings; no emergency would part him from his spear. These elephants were in no mood to be messed with, nor was it their intention to stop.

I had visions of my Landcruiser and camper being reduced to a useless crumpled heap of metal and match-wood. It was no use trying to run into it for cover, or even underneath it—that form of escape was one click short of suicide!

My pilot was now making a return low pass from the opposite end; the place was like a 'break-out' from a zoo. I caught sight of one old bull buffalo heading for the open glade. I was well positioned behind the stoutest girthed fig tree in the Mara. I did not need a second opinion to tell me that this was definitely the best place to be. To add to the confusion, I fired two shots into the air, not that it would speed up the stampede, it was the return of the 'God-botherer' and his flying machine that forced the change of the elephants' direction. "Thank you, God. You came to my rescue in the nick of time." Inwardly, I promised to pay homage to his winged Samaritan later on when I got back to Nairobi.

The radio crackled once again, it was Daniel asking what all the commotion and shooting was about. I replied, "Keep coming, (Wako juuyamiti). (They're all up the tree). His chuckle spoke volumes. He had seen it many times before on patrol. We could hear shouting. "Simama." More shouting, another shot. "Usi pige" (don't shoot). My fearless Rangers had sheepishly returned to earth to collect their ironmongery. They too, had seen the funny side and were laughing and were itching to go into the fray ahead. One signal from me and they were off at the trot, but there was no sign of my Morani. This fire-fight belonged to the twenty-first century and they were staying out of it – wise guys!

I would stay with the camper until the mêlée sorted itself out. Daniel and his Maasai Morani had captured three male poachers, who appeared out of the undergrowth, hands held high and wide-eyed with fear. The Morani had been stabbing their spears into the thick clumps of bushes; the act of surrendering was a far better option for the poachers than being skewered.

"Mama amitoroka." (The woman has run away.) Smart lady! I sensed she had taken the opportunity to melt into the fresh air, whilst pandemonium was in progress. Daniel did not seem too upset over the radio. It may have been a deal to turn a blind eye and allow her to escape. Her information on the whereabouts of the number two poachers' hide-out was fair exchange for freedom. My long lost Morani turned up with an expectant look on his face. "Where **is** everybody?" he enquired. Jokingly, I said, "Up in the trees." My remarks sent him into hysterics. "And you, where did you go?" I asked. "I only fight lions not elephants." He retorted in broken Swahili. My question was answered, though I sensed he was insinuating that the Rangers had acted in a cowardly fashion. "Nobody, but idiots, throw away their protection." He was referring to the guns that the rangers had dropped in their scramble to get up into the trees. I had to admit that I agreed with him. I suggested we should both go forward to the hide-out. The courts would require photographs of the scene, the poachers and their booty.

Game meat was hanging from every branch, but the hide-out was not nearly as sophisticated as our number one. No shelters, except sheets of nylon that covered the bare ground where small portions of venison were spread out to dry. Whilst Daniel and several Morani were otherwise engaged in persuading the three trappers that it would be in their best interests to talk, the rest of us set about collecting the evidence for a group photograph. No way was it possible to take this fresh meat to court; it would all go bad in a matter of days. One of the more educated Rangers suggested that we take some samples and have them refrigerated in the Narok morgue. The Morani had a better idea – how about taking the poachers to the morgue and giving them the 'barafu' (ice) treatment! There was much laughter. It took a full hour to make a large bonfire. Every scrap had to be burnt—paper, nylon, old rags, worn-out boots—the lot. The funeral pyre sizzled and spat for several hours. Much of the game meat was from hippo and zebra. Anyone observing from several miles away would think that the Governors Camp cookhouse had gone up in flames. Rumours would spread like wild-fire.

All the pieces of the jigsaw had come together. This was all part of the number one gang, shuttling back and forth to Migori and places beyond. I estimated we had captured probably fifty percent of the carriers and most, if not all, of the trappers. The police would have to pursue the 'fat cats', whilst the trail was still hot. That in itself would probably fall by the wayside. Somewhere along the line, someone would pay somebody in authority to lose the tracks. It's a no win situation trying to bring to book the hierarchy involved in the illegal meat trade. The laying of red herrings shows cunning that we Westerners have yet to understand. The Arab ivory traders of old had long perfected this art of subterfuge in their forages through East and Central Africa. They taught the Maasai well. My young Morani said to me, "You, mzuungu (white man), have the brains, but we have the cunning, we know how to out-manoeuvre you." "You could well have a point there, but only in the bush," I replied. He agreed to that compromise. I began to like the chap; he had an interesting streak about his personality. "You," Mimi, (meaning; me), make good Morani," he quipped, in broken English. "You, hapana toroka!" (meaning 'did not run'). I asked him, had he ever been to school? "No," he said, "shule sitaki." (in Swahili) "School is not for me."

How would these young warriors take to standing in a Court of Law? If the trappers and meat carriers pleaded 'Not guilty', then all of us would be summoned to appear in Court. The offenders would give their plea and then be sent off to remand custody. A month could easily pass before the case was set to be heard. I inwardly hoped that the police prosecutors would see the sense in persuading their lawyer to present a plea of 'Guilty'. Anyone who has had a taste of remand prison for a month in a Kenyan jail will know it is better to plead guilty on a minor charge of trespass and trading without a licence. The fine would not be less or much more than a thousand shillings (about £10 sterling), or failure to pay, a custodial sentence and you would get one month's imprisonment. The 'fat cats' would soon pay the fine, and if the police had any sense, that would be the time to pounce; when they came forward to pay the fines for their employees. There would be many red herrings to discard. Might that be asking too much of the 'boys in blue'?

There was little point in hanging around. Those at the number one hide had to be collected together, with any other flotsam and jetsam that may have walked into their trap. All must be despatched to Narok Police Station.

As it was, no carriers had turned up. Word gets around quickly in the bush, almost as quickly as our modern telecommunications. We bade farewell to our band of warriors. A few hundred shillings each, that's about a couple of pounds in sterling, from Petal's fund, as a reward for their assistance, brought forth big smiles. Just how do they manage to get their teeth whiter than white? Simple, they say, brush them with a mukwajo stick, cut from the leleshwa bush. The Maasai call it the toothbrush bush. Its juice must have a cleansing property. Not only that, when its leaves are placed under the arm-pits, they make excellent deodorizers. This bush, the leleshwa bush, holds many secrets and has many uses.

Our obliging Buffalo Camp manager provided the transport once again. It happened that four months later, I was able to repay his generosity in another way. He was in the field with his vehicle, by himself, quietly taking photographs of a cheetah and her family when up rushed three mini-buses, full of tourists and undisciplined drivers. Uncaring as to where they drove their charges, three little cheetah cubs, hidden in the grass, escaped being run-over by a hair's breadth. My German friend went ballistic. His language was choice. The drivers, belittled by their folly, got out of their vehicles and forcibly dragged him out of his vehicle. He was about to have the daylights beaten out of him. My armed intervention brought instant shock and awe to the bust-up. My mood made it very clear that if they did not move their carcasses from the area in a cloud of dust immediately, twelve tyres would be shot out from underneath them—it was a long walk to their Lodge! Hans, the manager, was sure that he was going to die that day.

How this calibre of tourist mini-bus drivers ever got the job, beggars belief. Most are top-class drivers, courteous and well-read. I made a note of their vehicle numbers; they would soon return to the ranks of the kamikaze matatu drivers. Nairobi's privatised public transport from hell has bred a fearsome, drug-taking bunch of lunatic drivers, who have little control over the machines they drive. Seating only for ten! What is that? I have counted thirty extricating themselves from a mangled heap, so tightly packed are they that the tout, or conductors as we know them, are often seen magnetized to the outside of the vehicle, in total defiance of the rules of gravity. Many are scraped off the tarmac, having been swiped off by some crazy manoeuvre, by passing between two vehicles in their haste to climb the pavement, often taking out several traffic lights en route to get to the front of the traffic jam.

The traffic cops have a ball, relieving them of wads of 'kitu kidogo' (something small), better known as a cash transaction, to please their commander's blind eye. He can often be seen sitting in his squad car, parked behind a bush, either reading a newspaper or relaxing and enjoying the thought of his share of 'manna from heaven'.

A few of these 'get rich quick' coppers, fall victim to the eye of the television camera, caught in the act by the crafty zooming-in by the celluloid kings of the media. When displayed to the nation on the evening news at nine o'clock—oops! Fifteen years service and more—down the drain. Some don't even bat an eyelid. Fifteen years of 'manna' must have been profitable for them. Despite the continuous battle against these bent cops, the routine switches just a little further down the road for a repeat performance for next in line. It's a no win situation.

I love taking the 'Mickey, out of these traffic cops when stopped (for no particular offence). "Driving licence, please!" I produce my Kenyan driving licence, a red folding cardboard paperback, a 'never forget to carry' item, displaying up-to-date proof as to my sanity and competence to drive anything from a motorised lawn-mower to a kamikaze matatu. The driving license is the conveyor of the kitu kidogo. It is whisked out of your trembling hand with glee. By well-practiced sleight of hand, the crispy note disappears and unblinkingly the driving licence is returned. You will receive a heel-clicking salute. "Proceed" he says. One feels like the King of the Road, but surprise, surprise, my little ruse of half-a-dozen un-franked, hard to grasp, postage stamps flutter out like butterflies, flying hither and thither. Thinking this is their kitu kidogo, their reaction is to stamp on the worthless paper, whilst bemused passers by stand and clap in unison, at their tap-dancing performance in the middle of the road. One day their humour will run out, the penny will drop and I'll end up in the cooler!

Daniel was keen to return to his base at Keekorok. Unable to read or write, his account of the whole show would have to be recorded by his senior. I would submit my report to the Director of Wildlife in Nairobi, to include the suspected rabies amongst the wild dogs, and the necessity to act urgently in the matter.

In my report, I would also request a Commendation be despatched to Daniel, from the Director of Wildlife, for his outstanding efforts. Daniel would make an excellent Bush Patrol Commander.

It was time to head for Nairobi, but first I must seek out Petal in the Aitong Mountains. The plains had begun to dry out, though some of the tracks were still sodden and I must take care. I couldn't afford to get bogged down in this treacherous black cotton soil. I drove across the hillsides, keeping away from the lowland marshes. By nightfall I had arrived at Euphorbia Hill. This was our favourite meeting place, night or day, and maybe, with a bit of luck, she would turn up; it was worth the chance.

The evening sunset was spectacular. The rain clouds had passed over and the air was clean and washed of dust. The cloudless African night, in all its beauty, was about to engulf me in its magic; the myriad of twinkling stars, the wonderment of the heavens. Yes, there moving slowly south to north—was it a satellite? Could it be the space shuttle, or was it the International space station? This is man's creation in his first endeavours to explore the secrets of this vast universe. I often ask myself what this earth of ours will be in five thousand years from now. Just in my short life span, the changes, the scientific progress extending man's average life towards a full century, the wonders of communication, all continue to make it an exciting world to live in. Every day brings new pleasures. Yes, how lucky I am to be where I am, sitting right here, comfortable in my camp chair, communing with nature. Darn those mosquitoes! Why can't they leave me alone? I had forgotten to apply my 'Skin-so-Soft', a pleasant smelling and effective application that keeps these dangerous and vociferous biting insects at bay.

My stomach was reminding me that I hadn't had a decent meal in days. The odd posho ugali, (maize-meal pudding) had the usual effect on me. It had a habit of clogging up the works. Yes, dinner and an early night must be on the menu. I was tired; the last couple of days had been energy sapping. That enemy call 'stress' had been at work.

The night passed uneventfully. I must have slept deeply, sufficient enough not to have heard the commotion coming from the temporary Maasai night cattle-pen, half a kilometer up-wind. Apparently, some stock thieves had attempted to break open the thorn bush surrounds that enclosed their cattle. Maasai herders often use these night pens when grazing is in short supply. It permits longer and more distant grazing, from base, for their cattle; though the dangers of lion, leopard and cattle rustling break-ins increase the further they penetrate into the deep bush. On these away excursions, it is the young Morani's job to provide the night and day security. Most cattle rustlers are armed with modern weapons— they are more dangerous than poachers. When push comes to shove, the young Morani come off second best; but it can be almost guaranteed that the rustlers will leave a few of theirs behind, badly wounded or dead meat for the vultures. The Kuria tribe from Tanzania are born cattle rustlers. Their trek across from the Serengeti into the Mara can take several days and nights, but their exit is doubly fast. The cattle are chased and whipped into an almost constant canter. The weak collapse and are left behind for the predators. The herds are split up into groups of three to five, making it difficult to track them, their trails mingling with that of the wildlife.

The cattle rustlers had timed their getaway strategy well; the dawn was shrouded in thick fog, visibility was down to twenty meters. They could move freely without having to keep to cover. The Maasai posse would not get far, if anywhere, in trying to follow them. However, the Maasai 'alarm' would be raised. The young Morani runners would be sent out in all directions to spread the warning to other manyattas.

Petal had not carried out her usual turn-up-man-ship. The fog and poor visibility probably had something to do with it. I just could not leave for Nairobi without first locating her.

Most of the tour vehicles had not come out from their lodges – it was still a little early.

The tourists would probably have their breakfast first. The sun would burn off the fog by 9.00 a.m., and it was pointless to endanger lives in this sort of weather. A game-viewing outing would last well into midday, returning to their lodges by one o'clock, in time for lunch. Then an early afternoon rest, before setting off again after tea. They would then be on their way again at 4.00 p.m. until 6.30 p.m., followed by Sundowners in the bush.

I thought it best that I should stay put and let the tour vehicles buzz around. My hilltop position gave me a clear all round look-out post. My mind was in a whirl with all that had been happening. Concentration on the poaching issue had diverted my attention from any forward planning for the next few months. There was the planning for my Sanctuary home on the land that I had purchased, and most importantly, being present or nearby at the birth of Petal's cubs.

Added to this, there was my concern over the spread of rabies, the wild dogs and the looming court cases, that would take ages to process should those charged not plead guilty. Then there would be all the hassle that would follow if each case had to be heard separately, not as a group charge, but on an individual charge. My evidence would be required as a witness for the prosecution. I could see valuable time being wasted by waiting, hanging about Court rooms and corridors, whilst the inept Kenyan judicial and police process laboured its way through a labyrinth of unnecessary procedures. This is called the Western form of democratic justice!

The early morning mist had lifted and the rangelands were soon dotted with tourist mini-vans, their windshields glinting in the reflection of the morning sunlight. I could almost read their body language – they would meet up with the very early morning 4x4 Landcruiser squad heading back to the Lodges. The longer the stop, the more information was imparted. Then the mini-bus would take off at a pace – that meant lions – get to them before they disappeared into the bush as the sun rose, or maybe lions still eating their early morning catch. If it were the sighting of a leopard up a tree, down would come the roof hatch. When it came to a cheetah or a cheetah family, a vehicle encirclement would form. I have often had to break up these circles, for they are dangerous in the extreme for mother cheetah and her babes. Lions and hyaenas, the cheetah's most feared enemy, have learned that this is an opportunity for an easy snack. These predators use vehicles to provide cover for a stealthy approach and surprise attack that often catches the cheetah off guard. Panic strikes – escape routes are blocked by vehicles, the little ones scoot under the vehicles whilst mother, too big to crawl under, escapes by leaping across the bonnets and over roof hatches, a sure recipe for injury; all it needs is a misplaced footing. A broken leg; a scene of complete horror, too terrible to even contemplate will follow. I hope I shall never see such a scene. It has been close, but thank goodness for my portable fire extinguisher – the predator has never made it into the inner circle.

Yes, I saw Petal's mother killed. It was tragic, yet somehow I regard that incident as Nature's wish. Had I foreseen the happening on that fateful day, would I have intervened? I think the answer would have been 'yes'. The incident in which Petal's mother was killed, occurred on the border of the protected area. It took a matter of less than an hour for the clean-up squad to obliterate the traces of this tragic happening.

CHAPTER 11
SPITTING COBRA

A flash of light in the distance attracted my attention. A good thousand yards away, again it flashed, it was a beige, 4x4 tourist Landcruiser from the Mara Safari Club. Through my binoculars I could see he was facing me. I was being called. I grabbed my twelve-inch, two million-candle power, spotlight and flashed back three signals – Da-dot da-dot-da – an acknowledgment that I had understood his request. That would be Petal under the shade of her tree, I was sure.

I headed for the spot keeping the beige vehicle in sight. Doubts began to creep into my mind; those flashes had an urgency about them. Was it my imagination? Nothing, but nothing should happen to Petal. I was concerned for her safety. Where had the wild dogs gone? As I drew alongside, the concern on the faces of the tourists and their drivers, made my heart miss a beat. Yes, it was a cheetah. Yes, it was Petal, and yes, she was in trouble.

I could see at a glance that one eye was puffed up and terribly inflamed. The other, also, but not to any great extent. This I realised immediately was the work of a spitting cobra.

Petal was in pain. I had to do something! Would she allow me to attend to her predicament? A wild animal in pain will attack. Now the test was really on. Get a vet quickly, but how? It would take Petal's vet until tomorrow morning to get here. The incident could not have occurred more than half an hour ago as some of the venom was still clinging to her forehead and the side of her face. If she brushed that off and licked her paw, she would be in even more trouble.

I asked the driver to move ahead and give me some space. He obliged. I spoke briefly to his tourists and informed them that I was going to get out of my vehicle and attend to the cheetah. This was a moment when I would need Petal's total confidence in me. There was to be no talking or distraction.

Petal was hyperventilating—a sure sign of thirst and shock. I quickly prepared the karai and the plastic container of water, a damp cloth (it was my face cloth). I dived into the first aid box and found a small aluminium bowl, a packet of soluble alkaline powder, Vosene eye drops to ease the inflammation and a carton of long-life milk.

I knew I had to work quickly to save her eyes. I poured the water into the karai and offered it to her mouth. She started lapping. I found myself talking to her softly "It's OK, Petal, it's OK, I'm here to help you".

I took the damp cloth and gently wiped the venom from her face. She seemed not to

A spitting cobra had struck a few minutes before this photograph was taken.

Petal was crying with pain. I had to act quickly, remembering also, that she was heavily pregnant.

Petal's right eye took more than six months to heal and was prone to regular infections, during which time her cubs were born.

mind. The only thing on her mind was to quench her insatiable thirst. I quickly mixed a quantity of the alkaline powder with water in the small aluminium bowl, stirred it with my fingers, soaked up the solution with my face cloth and placed it over her puffed-up eye, gently squeezing the contents over her eyelids. I felt a sense of complete joy washing over me in her permitting me to attend to her in this time of need. I kept on sponging; soon she would stop lapping and move away. The alkaline solution was entering the eye as she blinked. I used the same procedure with the milk. She had stopped drinking now but continued to crouch over the karai. This amazing animal, whom I had purposefully avoided stroking, or even touching, was being the perfect patient. Tears were rolling down my cheeks. She allowed me to place my hand on her body; it was cold—the sign that secondary shock was setting in. Dare I try and squirt the anti-inflammatory Vosene into her eye? Anything that 'squishes' or resembles spitting or hissing sounds would send her into orbit. I unscrewed the cap and poured the contents over her eyelids. It seemed to help relieve the pain.

I had done as much as I could. The thought of a large spitting cobra somewhere in the grass nearby sent chills up my spine. These snakes can become vicious when disturbed. Petal was lucky not to have received the full frontal blast of its venom to both eyes. It appeared that most of the venom had missed its mark and had been fired from side-on at her. There was a wild animal track passing close by the tree. She would have been walking along this track, heading my way, when she passed close by her adversary in the long grass.

The minutes had passed so quickly, yet as always happens with fear, it seemed an age since I arrived on the scene. I could hardly stand up; my knees were locked into the kneeling position. Surely this embarrassing situation that so many people have experienced that happens just out of the blue was not going to afflict me now in my hour of pride! Petal's show had been exciting enough for my onlookers—now this? The only way I could handle my predicament was to roll over on my back and slowly stretch my legs. The cramp gradually wore off just in time. As I sat up along came another vehicle with tourists. I felt so stupid sitting on the ground, a cheetah lying down a few yards from me, and I surrounded by excited onlookers. Both groups seemed to know each other. I pointed to their tour drivers to move over to the other vehicle where the full story would be told. I had nothing left in me to summon up the energy to explain I was totally drained of emotion and felt quite sick. I realised this was a combination of stress and relief at work in me.

I walked over to where the tour vehicles were parked and let the tourists get on with their account of the incident. I spoke with both drivers. Their first concern was as mine, if Petal went blind, then what? Even with one blind eye this would greatly affect her hunting judgment when in full pursuit of prey at a speed of between sixty to seventy miles an hour both eyes need to be in focus. To prove this try driving at night on one headlight and you can sum up her problem very quickly. Even driving with one eye closed in daylight, at that speed, is an accident waiting to happen. Depth and peripheral vision is distorted.

Once again any immediate plans to head for Nairobi would have to be shelved. My place was with Petal. Now that her physical security was in danger and her sight seriously impaired she would find it very difficult to hunt and predators might easily catch her unawares.

I planned for a twenty-four hour guard over her and if her eye got worse the KWS Vet would have to fly in, dart her and give his verdict. She could have done without all this trauma with only a couple of weeks to go before giving birth.

Cobra venom burns and blisters the outer surface of the eye, the pain is excruciating, infection can quickly set in and blindness can follow. The next twenty-four hours would give me an indication how to plan the next move. One thing for certain, I would not leave her side.

My drinking water supply was plentiful but the fresh food supply was running low and my tinned emergency supplies could last for about two days but after that I would have to 'live on my hump'.

When the cool of the evening arrived maybe I could coax Petal to head for her initial intended destination—Euphorbia Hill. Once there she could take up residence in the leleshwa copse, away from the tourists and the heat. It would also be more convenient and less exposed for me to continue to administer the eye and milk wash procedure.

The tourists were clamouring for photographs and information regarding the story of Petal. Soon more vehicles would arrive and this place was about to become a zoo with no peace for my patient or myself. Word of the cobra drama would spread like wildfire.

Totally overwhelmed by the role of this lone bush-paramedic, the event had made the day for five overseas visitors and their driver who had witnessed it all. To my mind he was the hero of the day without whose timely appearance and call for help, Petal would certainly have lost her eye. Furthermore, in her pain and anguish her defences and alertness were impaired. Any hyaena or lion close by would have noticed and have seized the opportunity to attack her in her confused state.

Petal seemed more at ease and in less pain. The water had refreshed her and the spectators had moved along seeking further excitements of Nature's daily dramas.

I collected all the medical paraphernalia, and my face cloth, which I must not forget, to steep in boiling water and thoroughly hand-wash in detergent. That done the question of Petal's food came to mind. I would need authority to range-feed her and that meant 'shooting for her pot' a young gazelle every second day until she could cope with hunting once more.

The clearance would have to come from the Director of Wildlife himself, the controls for shooting wildlife were very strict and I had jealous and envious enemies of my own kind, several of whom I knew would love to put a spoke in my wheel, always watching and ready to make mischief—it would seem this is a British Colonial pastime that anyone enjoying apparent success and a little fame, the stops are pulled out to spread malice and then rejoice in the discomfort that poison brings to the individual.

Tourists often donated foreign currency for Petal's survival. I made sure this money went into her fund held by Friends of Conservation. The next thing I knew I had the Exchange Control Authorities on my doorstep investigating me. The controls were strict; all foreign currency had to be declared to the Central Bank and converted by that Bank into local currency. Somebody, and I knew that somebody, a busybody who was bad-mouthing everybody and any initiatives not of his own making.

Time will always attend to those who play that game of destruction. His safari outfit was short-changed by the local Maasai who ostracized him. It was time for him to move along.

I wrote out a report to the Director and gave it to a passing tour driver to hand over to the pilot of the next daily scheduled flight. My message and request for his authority to range-feed Petal, I knew, would reach him direct and the reply, in writing, would return by the same method.

The Director of the Kenya Wildlife Service, Richard Leakey, a household name in conservation, doesn't waste time nor does he suffer fools. The authority I wanted was back by dusk, copied to all those who required it. It read "Go ahead—range-feed—and keep me posted". For all his egotistic faults there was no one that could match Leakey for his efficiency and straight talking. I found he always gets the job done and will always stand by you warts and all. This type of character is poison to mischief-makers. Beware and be prepared to be torn apart if you show these trouble-making tendencies. He always had my loyalty.

The lone tree, which Petal chose to rest under, had lived through many years of varied seasons. Its weather-beaten branches bore little greenery to provide sufficient shade from the mid-day sun. Petal would have to move soon. If I moved back towards Euphorbia Hill, she might get the message and follow. Her right eye had now closed up completely; the other blinked repeatedly but appeared reasonably operational. I moved away very slowly—she was not asleep but in the lying-down, regal, alert cheetah pose. As I drove away I focused intently on the left wing-mirror. Come on, Petal! I was willing her to follow me. I am convinced that there is such a thing as thought telepathy. How often do we find ourselves saying to a friend or a colleague 'Funny, I was just thinking of you' in answering a telephone call from your friend or whoever, who had, at that same moment, decided to ring you up. Seconds later 'I was about to ring you, same here—what a coincidence'! These are the telepathic signals we humans have yet to understand and harness. I am sure it clearly connects into our thought waves as well as into those of our household pets, horses and wild animals.

Petal was not budging—I stopped, got out of the vehicle and walked around it, defuelled, looked intently at nothing in the grass; my curiosity tempted the cat to move. 'What was I looking at'? "Gottcha, Petal"—the ruse had worked. I drove on towards the hill and parked. I could see she was still on her way and taking her time. She would stop and sit on her haunches, look around trying to focus on her surroundings. The tunnel vision image was perplexing her. Then, flicking her tail, she once again commenced walking towards me. An inquisitive herd of Thompson's gazelles was running towards her, their tails working overtime like windscreen wipers. It is interesting to note how these gazelles sense the situation and can tell when it is safe to approach a predator.

The cheetah's body language says 'I'm not interested in you today', and so up they trot to within yards of her, snorting their warnings. This is a lesson for the young gazelles. Suddenly the herd scatters every which-way, some stomping, stiff legged, jinking, adding spurts of speed, practicing their 'get away' tactics, then stopping a short distance away, and returning towards Petal at a trot once more, en masse, for a repeat performance. This is cheek in the extreme, with contempt at its best, 'You can't catch me' written all over their faces! It is not often that these gazelles can get a close up view of their fleet-of-foot enemy.

Now, parked on the hill, I began mentally to prepare for a long stay—a day or two, possibly even more. The tour drivers would visit me to up-date, and in turn my hand-written messages would be forwarded by hand of pilot to my base in Nairobi. Tinned rations and fresh supplies of food would arrive the next day by the daily scheduled flight service, bringing in and taking out the tourists from the Mara. Neither Petal nor I would starve. Mail of urgent correspondence would come and go by the same free-lance courier method. The system worked perfectly. Added to this encouragement and cooperation from all sides fuelled my resolve to provide Petal with all the tender loving care she needed.

Word came through on my air-to-ground radio, that a vet would fly in by courtesy of Air Kenya early the following day. The whole of the Mara was rooting for Petal. Everyone knew her and that she had become the Queen Cheetah of the Maasai Mara, and quite rightly so. Tourists and the BBC wildlife photographers made her their priority viewing.

The question of the vet having to dart her bothered me. This he would have to do to make a closer examination and assess what damage the venom had done to her eye. Would the trauma, the immobilizer and the antidote be too dangerous to carry out? To imagine stillborn or even aborted cubs was unthinkable. There were only a couple of weeks to go before she was due to give birth.

We also had to consider how to go about the actual darting. Dart any cat once and then try again later, no matter whether domestic or otherwise, they sense and relate in the same way as any child. Fear and distancing comes into play. Petal might never allow me to be in such close proximity of her again. I must stand aside and not allow her to associate me with a situation that dispenses pain or disorientation.

There have been times in my life when animals, particularly my own domesticated cats, have sought help from me. I remember Princess, the young jet-black feral cat, with eyes like a panther. She always called on me for a tit-bit when her wild larder was in short supply. One early morning, at home, it was after 3.00 a.m. I was awakened by a meowing outside my bedroom window. I looked outside, shone the torch, and there she was. She had been savaged by a dog or a pack of domestic dogs on the prowl and had dragged herself goodness knows how far and from where. Both her hind legs were broken. I rushed outside in my pyjamas and picked her up. To my amazement she began to purr. I knew this was the end for this brave little cat. The pain must have been excruciating and there was little I could do. I laid her in a wicker basket and telephoned the vet, an Asian lady who had opened her practice only a few months before, in a rented surgery nearby. This was an emergency; sadly a one-way ticket for Princess, still purring, she was put quietly to sleep. My wish for her was for a merciful and peaceful end.

I support euthanasia. When the chips are down and all that is left is suffering, why on earth prolong terrible agony?

Petal lay down in the shade of a Euphorbia tree some fifty yards from where I had parked the camper. Nature permits this mixed up candelabra tree to flourish. Its branches appear to belong to the cacti family, but botanists claim this is not so. Most, if not all trees, have a purpose in the pyramid of Nature's wonders, but her reason for this indigenous monkey-puzzle tree is unclear. Within its flesh hides a very toxic and poisonous sticky white latex. A single drop in the eye will cause blindness and even a drop on the skin of a cow or wild animal often becomes a blister. The Maasai avoid this tree like the plague; they claim its poison, if placed in traditional medicine, can kill. The flowers produce abundant nectar and attract bees, but the honey cannot be eaten as it irritates and burns the mouth. Hornets, big and small, build their hanging honeycomb nests in its midst, and attack at the slightest excuse. "Hey, Petal" I could hear myself saying, "don't be a dumb kopf, you have enough bumps on your head without asking for more!"

There was a little madness in her purpose, for just below her resting place, was a small spring where the Maasai herders often watered their thirsty shoats on a hot day. Thompson's gazelles and their young also frequented this handy mud wallow to quench their thirst in the cool of the evening after sundown.

Petal had a plan; this could be an easy way to secure her dinner and save me the anxiety of a rifle shot ringing out and echoing all over the Aitong Hills. If I shot even a half grown gazelle it would be too much for her to consume at one sitting. Her present condition of pregnancy would not allow her to run any great distance, and with one eye closed completely and the other partially impaired, her chase would have to be executed over a very short distance. Maybe, between us, we could make this happen. It was well past the shoats drinking time and by now they will have all gone home. Petal has never shown any interest in killing sheep or goats or their young.

The same applied to the boys; I was proud of them too. Little had been heard of them or their whereabouts for a while but somewhere out in the vast spaces of the Mara or even in the Serengeti, I knew they would still be together as brothers, doing what they do best. Together they are a formidable group. Few other cheetah coalitions would ever dream of trying to unseat them. At present they are the top guns of the Mara. I often prayed for their safety and that, one-day, they would come back home to visit the place of their birth and call on their sister. God willing, they would. Might they have forgotten their foster father? I wondered.

If Petal continued to stay where she was when darkness fell that would signal her intention to lie in ambush near the spring. Soon a full moon would rise in all its splendour, appearing from behind the Aitong Hills. I defy anybody or any animal to pick out the form of a cheetah crouched in ambush on a bright moonlight night. With the white and yellow wash and black spots she blends completely into the immediate scenery.

Maybe I could participate and make the situation easier for her. It would be pitch dark between 7.15 and 8.15 p.m., before the moon was due to appear. During that time I would join her with my searchlight. It had a rheostat lever that increased or lowered the intensity of its light. When operated gradually, the initial dissipated light would concentrate into an intensive beam, temporarily blinding any animal whose eyes came into direct contact with it; disorientation then follows. All that Petal then has to do is to pad quietly up to her quarry, approach it from outside the beam, and then pounce. Another alternative we had successfully practised at night was for me to place a red darkroom photographic processing film over the front end of a powerful six-cell flashlight. Petal, under these circumstances, appears to see reasonably well. For her it must be like wearing night-vision goggles, I guess. The prey appears not to see the red beam. Often I have proved to myself that this is the case, having walked up to a gazelle on a dark night and almost touched it. So, two options were available.

I prepared my night-vision goggles, checked the battery power, and set the spotlight equipment on a tripod outside the camper under the mosquito-proof verandah. With a beer in hand and some cashew nuts to munch on, this bush living was definitely for me! Who wants cities or dingy, smokey nightclubs, belting out noise that's called 'go faster' music fit to scramble any right-minded brain? Boozing, getting drunk and becoming totally legless, what a way to live! No thank you, not for me! What others would give to live my life – I am truly very lucky and ready to tell the world.

Darkness had come. The cool of the evening had formed a thin layer of cloud above the Mara. Petal was alert and peering into the darkness. I could see her quite clearly near the edge of the watering hole. The night crickets were chirping their piercing staccato chatter, alternating in pitch according to their gender. Nothing else stirred. Several African hares were darting to and fro out of Petal's striking range. They could be a dinner possibility, but difficult to get close to. Their hearing is extremely acute. The African hare's long ears pick up the slightest noise, and off they scamper. A couple of frisky bat-eared foxes passed by the spring. Their bushy tails were held high, a sign that their mating season was approaching. They too, like the African hares and wild dogs, possess very acute hearing. Their saucer-like ears twitch and turn, here and there, cupped like a scanning dish picking up every detail of sound.

A single jackal barks behind the camper, alert to my presence. He is an unwelcome visitor. I throw a pebble in his direction and the startled animal takes off like a rocket. Jackals follow predators at night, often barking and yapping continuously. A hunting or resting lion, cheetah, leopard, or even a hyaena pack, gets the same treatment. Jackals tell the world that a predator is on the prowl in the vicinity. Petal cannot stand their presence and will take off after them, although more so in daylight. Her pursuit is aggressive but lacks the will to kill. They are not a physical danger to her, just a darned nuisance.

Time is running short and soon the moon will rise in the East. A half-grown impala with a young male come to the water's edge. Petal, though attentive, had not yet seen them. I triggered the six-cell infra-red. Yes, I could see the narrow light beam, through the night goggles, focussing on the pair. They were undisturbed and continued to cautiously circle the muddy hoof trodden edges towards the spring outlet where Petal had cleverly positioned herself. She must surely see them now coming towards her. Petal was standing up, head held down in the frozen 'stalk' position. My anxiety was focused on the lead impala; he had an impressive head with two very sharp juvenile six-inch horns. If Petal attacked, his first reaction would be to put his head down and Petal could impale herself on them as she charged. However, my anxieties were short lived. She took off after the younger one, tripping it up as it turned to run. The other male, in sheer fright, leapt high in the air only to collide heavily with an old fence post. The Maasai had built a barrier to protect the spring outlet from constant trampling by wildebeest, zebra, cattle and giraffe.

Petal had succeeded in capturing her dinner by herself, even though it was made possible by a red light. On reflection, that young six inch horned male impala certainly would not return for some days to seek out what it was that had almost knocked him unconscious in mid-flight one night—at his favourite pub!

I could see my patient was taking her time over dinner and I decided to walk down to join her by the light of my home-made infra-red torch. I was doubly pleased that I had found a state-of-the-art method of my own making to assist Petal's natural night blindness. Cheetahs do not see well in the dark, their photo light eye cells are quite different to those of a leopard. Nature has blessed the leopard with excellent night vision to assist in its nocturnal hunting. By day, she has provided it with a camouflaged coat that almost defies the best of eyesight to locate its presence in a bush or in a tree.

I approached her, whistling our bird like cheetah call, calling her name softly. The name probably did not mean anything to her, but it was the sound of my voice that she could decipher clearly from others. This fact was proven when surrounded by my clients chattering in their vehicles. I would call her name; she would look directly at me and clearly it was recognition of my features and voice. On other occasions, she would come right up to my door, I having not said a word. I felt goose pimples at the thought of her always giving me preferential recognition. It added strength to the growing bond of trust between us.

I sat down with her for a while at the spring, protecting her from any other intruder who might have ideas of stealing her dinner. She was comfortable and seemed not to be in pain; and was relaxed in my presence. The furtive and continual looking over her shoulder had ceased. However, those pesky mosquitoes were making their presence felt. I had forgotten to put on the 'Skin-so-soft' mosquito repellent – how stupid of me! This is the way to get the dreaded malaria; sitting by an ideal breeding ground where mosquitoes and their larvae flourish. This mosquito repellent seemed not to upset Petal's sense of smell, but after-shave lotion or a perfumed soap was a 'no-no'.

Petal had almost finished her meal; the bones, a few bits and pieces and the skin were all that was left. The pickings would be taken by the jackal that was, no doubt, somewhere in the vicinity, having scented the odour of death. It was remarkable how Petal had surgically removed the dead animal's entrails intact, and put them to one side. Many predators do this. Indeed, lions go further and attempt to cover the intestines by scraping up dirt with their fore and hind paws, burying underground the rich, odorous, tell-tale wafts that float in the wind, attracting hangers-on who are hoping for their share of crumbs from the King's table. Leopards have been known to disembowel and thereby lighten their kill before lifting the whole body into the fork of a tree. They know that prior removal of the digestive acids prolongs the shelf life of their larder. Nothing in the wild is wasted.

If I returned to the camper, Petal would be tempted to follow in due course. She had fed sufficiently well to last a day or more. In her present state of insecurity, she would probably stay with me to be *in situ* for the vet's arrival in the morning. I still had my dinner to heat up. Supplies were getting low and tonight's dinner would be made up of a bit of this and a bit of that, better known to me as a Heinz 57 mix-up!

It was well over an hour before Petal came home. As time wore on, I had become more and more anxious and kept checking with the night binoculars to ensure she had not wandered off in another direction. I thought I had lost her but, to my great relief, I found she had quietly parked herself, unannounced, in the netted verandah. The entrance was partly open with an escape route via a flap in the corner. She too was fed up with the mosquitoes! I poked my head out of the caravan window, softly talking about nothing in particular. I wanted her to hear my voice and to reassure her of my presence. With luck, it looked as if she would stay the night.

Tomorrow was shaping up to be an interesting day. The butcher, the baker, the doctor and the postman were all scheduled to arrive with something in kind. Before turning in for the night, I decided it would be a gesture of companionship to sit with Petal. This was not the time for aloofness; the closer the contact I displayed, the more bonus points I would earn, making her feel safe and welcome.

Tonight's vigil for me would be long, interspersed with short periods of cat-napping, wrapped in a warm sleeping bag, sitting in a deck chair. The situation could be a lot worse. I could dream that I was sleeping on deck, aboard a ship. I like the sea and I enjoy travelling on cruise liners, enjoying the sheer luxury of it all. World-class entertainment is at hand, the ports and tours are interesting. At night, sleeping in my comfortable cabin, I have television and telephone contact with the outside world, if needed. Then, during the day, relaxing, sunbathing and exercising and in the evening, excellent floor shows, comedians that make you laugh, meeting people, talking about wildlife, giving lectures, dancing and good food, all with nothing regimented. Yes, this is the best of both worlds, and I still have the wide open spaces to come back to. That is how I planned it, and that is how it will be.

Petal was sleeping fitfully, waking, and then lifting her head to see if I was still there with her. I spoke softly, my body language acknowledging that her security was my total concern; the periods of sleep became longer as her confidence grew in understanding that I was there to stay.

The night was uneventful. It was full moon and most of the nocturnal predators would be active, silently going about their business, until the hour just before dawn—the magical equatorial 5.00 a.m., when all their night's work is broadcast in vocal retreat, as Nature's creatures prepare to pull down their curtain on the coming day, others are opening their blinds to let in the morning light for the day ahead.

I had purposely refrained from attending to Petal's eyes. Nature's healing was at work. The right eye was weeping profusely and it would be unwise to dilute the healing tears that the system produces when the eyes come into contact with undesirable toxicity. I regularly bathe my eyes and find that drops morning and evening dispenses with the sandpaper graunching on waking. Blessed with excellent vision, my eyes are my life. I was once blind for many months following an air crash in the bush. The Lord gave me back my sight through the hand of an eye specialist. Sight is so precious; it is the light of life. I prayed it would be Dieter's hand that would save Petal's sight.

The morning could not come quickly enough. Petal must stay with me. I would try to keep any wandering Maasai away. At times when camped in the bush, they would come up to the camper asking for water or a mug of chai (tea). In return, I am given the local news and the whereabouts of any cheetahs. My signal of flying a small yellow flag, easily seen from a distance, advertises the 'Queen' is in residence nearby, so please keep clear! However, on the downside, this signal sometimes attracts the tour drivers who want to bring their clients to see the 'Queen'. They know she accepts tour vehicles as part of her scenery and something to climb upon with, I do believe, a mischievous glint in her eye. Today, however, it would only be tears for the tourist. Spear wielding Maasai are also definitely off limits for her as she does a disappearing act in double quick time when she sees them approaching from a distance.

Breakfast this morning consisted of a large bowl of cornflakes, with chopped up bananas, some long life milk, bread and marmalade, and a cup of tea. The larder had run out and tinned food stocks were very low. It was a few minutes before 8.00 a.m. when a beige tourist Landcruiser arrived. I was thinking it was a visiting tour group, but to my surprise it was not, and neither was it Dieter whom I had been expecting. A private pilot friend of mine had offered a seat to the weekend on-duty Kenya Wildlife Service Vet. This earlier-than-expected arrival would enable him to make the morning-scheduled flight back to Nairobi. The best I could offer the Doctor was tea and biscuits—I was completely out of food supplies!

Our patient had moved – she had stretched herself out on the warm Landcruiser bonnet and placed herself in a position to be darted from inside the cab, through the wind vent under the windscreen. Petal often sunned herself in the early morning on the bonnet of the vehicle, when the night had been cold and her body temperature needed heating up.

The vet was smuggled, with his box of tricks, into the rear portion of the camper. Good thinking! He had brought his 'blow' dart gun, a simple pea-shooter tube; the other pop-gun was too noisy. Petal would not hear the blow, but she would feel the prick. It would resemble a biting blood fly. These pestiferous insects live and move about under the hair all day and all night, pricking here and stabbing there. I was hoping an extra prick might go unnoticed. This would be Petal's first darting. Once the dart strikes home, the plunger moves forward at lightening speed, compressing the immobilizer fluid directly into the muscle.

Petal's rear was parked up against the windscreen. Ideal! Dr. Wambua quietly mixed the cocktail; bodyweight versus gender, taking into account her pregnant state. From my observations all of these procedures appeared to be by his eye of experience. With anaesthesia or any immobilizer there is always the risk of heart failure. I made my concern known. The doctor answered "It will be a very light dose, sufficient enough to put her to sleep for just a couple of minutes". I held my breath. There was a quiet 'phut'; Petal felt the prick in her bottom and flicked her tale wildly, sending the dart flying. It had a thin red marker flag to assist in its eventual location. She jumped off the bonnet and headed for the thick leleshwa bushes some yards away. "Do we have a problem?" I asked, "Has the full dosage penetrated?" All these questions would be answered in the next few minutes. The Vet was confident that everything was under control. So far the whole procedure had worked like a charm, far beyond my wildest dreams. The doctor, in his quiet and humble way was, I knew, impressed at the innovative idea and particularly the unobtrusive manner the darting had been carried out. Luck was on our side to-day.

The minutes passed; Petal had entered the bush and lay down in its shade. I could just see her outline and spots, now the pressure was on me. I had to time my approach to her correctly. Animals entering into the first phase of the gradual effects of anaesthesia show symptoms of fear at the gradual loss of control of their senses and limbs. Some try to fight the effects – some succeed and have to be re-darted. This is where major problems arise. The semi-consciousness can trigger a flailing attack on an approaching object. This is the wild automatic reaction of self-defence. The Vet and I accompanied by a very nervous tour driver, approached cautiously to within fifty feet of her. Petal was well into surrendering and was not fighting the effects. Philip, the driver, carried a tarpaulin to rest her body upon. It was imperative no dust or dirt should blow into her eyes. I carried the bowl of antiseptic eye wash and swabs, and the Vet brought the necessary magnifying equipment and antibiotic paste, similar to that which we humans use to cure conjunctivitis, but different, of course. It had healing properties as well. Our 'Queen' was now asleep, regal and beautiful in her pose at rest. We both lifted her gently onto the tarpaulin – I estimated her weight to be almost fifty kilograms. I closed my eyes; now we would know the worst or the best. I wanted so much for Petal to remain wild and have the wonderful freedom of sight. I had experienced that fear of darkness, the terrible thought of permanent blindness. I having known superb vision, then losing it, even for a short time, is terrifying. Wearing latex gloves, Dr. Wambua gently opened her eyelids; everything possible was being done to prevent infection. He didn't speak a word for a full minute, carefully examining the outer surface of her golden eye through the magnifying glass.

Dr. Wambua called for the eyewash and I poured it gently over her eye. Yes, the outer surface of the eye was burned on the side, which took the initial impact from the cobra's venom. The cornea luckily was undamaged. "You are a lucky cheetah", were the first words I heard. Those words brought me so much relief. It was magic! Standing to one side, the driver, Philip, son of the paramount Maasai Chief of the Mara, wore a great big smile that lit up his face – The 'Queen' was going to be OK!

The Vet quickly squeezed the lubrication over the bottom and top eyelids, leaving the lids to spread the antibiotic paste smoothly over the eyeball. The left eye was inflamed but no damage was seen. That eye too received an eye -wash. Now it was time for the antidote injection. Six minutes had passed since the darting and the Doctor and the driver moved away. I stayed with Petal, monitoring her steady heartbeat. Her breathing was regular, with no choking symptoms. Gradually the antidote took effect; Petal was waking slowly. I was calling her name, just the way it is when humans come round from an anaesthetic. You hear the nurse's voice, "Wakey, wakey David. It's all over." Those are such comforting words and so too, I hoped it would be for Petal. I was by her side when consciousness returned. There was no sign of fear, she had recognised my voice and probably thought that she was just waking up after a normal sleep. I hoped it would seem that way, albeit feeling a little drunk and a little thirsty. The sound of my fingers splashing in her 'karai' was my sign for her to drink a little, but I had no raw eggs to offer her as is always given to me to assist my recovery from anaesthesia! I learnt later that this was meant to make me throw up and feel better – it certainly worked for me!

The Doctor was satisfied her eyesight would be saved. A good sleep would throw off the anaesthetic effects, but it would be wise for me to stay with her until she regained full consciousness.

Her eye now fully
recovered, thankfully
without impairment.
Petal with Sprite and
Scamp at six months
of age.

The prognosis for the healing of her damaged eye was that it could take many months or more! Meantime, she would suffer from blurred vision for the next few days, but as the healing progressed, so her sight would improve. The burn was not deep but superficial, thank goodness. Time, that enemy of man was running out. The Vet had not eaten since his early departure from Nairobi this morning. His breakfast would be at my expense today. I felt my profuse thanks were inadequate, I wished I could do more, but the smile on both their faces was sufficient to tell me they felt satisfied and proud to have been of use. Petal had been the perfect patient and she was their star. Philip would take the Doctor back to the lodge and arrange for his pickup to the airfield. Meantime, my supplies should have arrived for collection and they too would be dispatched to me in due course.

'Bush cooperation' can move mountains. Everyone helps and asks for nothing in return. I find this so refreshing in the otherwise uncaring world of today, where only a few will do something for nothing.

CHAPTER 12
OUT OF AFRICA CAMP

MY plans for heading to Nairobi were once again scuttled. The camp staff would now be at the Nairobi base, attending to tent repairs and all the hundred and one things from repairing the cook's tent, to clearing blocked shower heads and fixing the five-ton diesel lorry and trailer that would carry everything back to my 'Out of Africa' camp. The crockery would need to be checked and the broken items replaced only when it had arrived at camp. It was a marathon task, but was made easy as each member of staff, down to the 'choo' (toilet) cleaner, knew his job and what was required of him. Each had a checklist and there was always Andrew, the cook! He thrived on his position and was proud to be the chief checker who checked the checkers! This is a system that must always be applied in Africa. No one interferes with Kibet's Landcruiser, except Nyundu, the mechanic.

All would have to be in place at camp, ready to receive guests before Petal's happy day. From the size of her tummy I was beginning to think I had miscalculated! I kept re-checking the dates of her honeymoon, like an expectant father. Ninety days is the magic figure. Not long now—only ten days to go.

The days passed quickly. Tourist vehicles came and went, and Petal's camouflage was just too good even for those with telephoto lenses. They clicked away, from a distance, hoping that when their photos were developed the 'spot' would mark the place. My welcome food supplies arrived regularly with mail and a few local newspapers. This would keep me from becoming addle-pated; there was also a pile of correspondence to deal with, as always. Paperwork seems to follow me everywhere despite being miles from nowhere. For some exercise, I took an occasional walk about within a five-second sprint to bring me to where Petal was. It was clear she had no intention of going anywhere.

Mobile safari operators from the well known Ker & Downey Safaris, passed by. They too, enquired after 'Queen's' health. In the distance, heading towards their forward campsite, was a group of horse riders enjoying the thrill and freedom of being able to gallop at full throttle. Zebra, wildebeest and giraffe were all gawping at these fleeing four legged objects – there was something different about them! I could hear the giraffe saying "Not our type!" There are dangers, particularly at night when the horses are tethered to a long rope. Lions, on the prowl, pick up the horses' scent. To them this is dinner served warm on a plate. The night guard has fallen asleep – the lions attack – and the scene is horrific. Does anyone fancy being tethered by the neck to a long rope, especially at night and particularly when there are lions about? Often I have found myself searching the Mara for runaway horses; the lucky ones that got away! My sadness and concern is for the poor animals that did not manage to break free and bolt. As for horse riding adventures in the Mara, the experience is unbeatable.

The African sunset was bidding us good-night, displaying a kaleidoscope of changing colours. It was telling me that tomorrow would be a hot and humid day, with little breeze.

I repositioned the camper and verandah netting closer to where Petal lay. When I hit the noisy Landcruiser starter button, it startled her a little, though it appeared to have the required effect in jolting her out of her stupefied sleep. I guess that is why nurses enjoy slapping their comatose patients around the face in the recovery room after an anaesthetic! Petal had several options; to stay where she was or come into the netted verandah, (this was my choice), or wander off into the night (her choice). In my opinion, she was not ready to check out of hospital and my care, but I, as the Queen's caretaker, could only try to entice her with home comforts and God's clean wine. I hoped she would not favour the animal polluted dung-based water that was on offer to lesser mortals at the spring! Petal continually licked the inner side of her right forearm, and brushing it across her eye, cleaning her face as every cat does. The soothing film of antibiotic paste, with its anti-inflammatory and pain relieving properties, was undoubtedly working. Under normal domestic circumstances, a plastic hood would be fitted, but in this instance it was an impossible option. After all, she was a wild cat with a difference.

Cooking was not a problem for me; my house cook, back in Nairobi had prepared in advance, my usual plastic multiple choice containers of meals on wheels! These were a most welcome break from real cooking, as no thinking was required!

As the evening drew to a close, I settled myself in a deck chair and slipped into my sleeping bag. To enable me to read my paper, I have a very handy spectacle reading light. At my right hand there was a glass of Tusker beer (made in Kenya), my night vision goggles and my fire extinguisher, all ready to serve as protection against any four legged or two legged intruders.

The art of survival is being aware and prepared for any eventuality, and always takes priority in my book. It has paid off both in the bush and at home in Nairobi, but more of that later.

My night specs are perfect for reading and they also enable the wearer to see into hard to get at places, such as vehicle engines, if you have a breakdown at night or have to replace a tyre in the dark. By toning down the intensity, I could look over towards Petal and she could see my outline. The light was not intrusive. I was her eyes in the dark and she was my ears. Petal was listening to the night sounds – between us and the African crickets 'our night guards', all security measures were comfortably in place.

Several hours passed and it was near to midnight. Petal sat up, stretched and yawned. I spoke gently to let her know I was awake. The dim fluorescent lights in the camper verandah were already switched off but there was sufficient moonlight to clearly identify outlines and objects. Petal had moved deeper into the bush out of sight. I guessed and hoped it was just for a defuelling break – an idea that appealed to me too! Unlike domestic cats, cheetah do not cover up their calling cards, neither do they leave them on their doorstep, except when Petal posts them on the bonnet of my vehicle. This is mail for her subjects to read, when on my round of her territory.

I read in one of Kenya's leading newspapers, an article on the poachers we had caught. Apparently all had pleaded guilty and were fined a thousand shillings, about ten pounds sterling, for trespass! The glory of their capture quite rightly went to the Mara Rangers. The paymasters paid the fine, the poachers were released to poach another day and their fat cats got off the hook. This sort of jungle punishment is not right. Our wildlife will not survive with this form of lenient justice.

I closed my eyes for a second, at least I thought I had, but found I had dozed off for some ten minutes. Petal was back in the same place; I had not heard her return. I am conscious that I snore but, luckily, this seems not to bother her, except that I have noticed when I awaken, she is always on guard. There is a pattern developing – each is looking after the other when we're together—this is good for my morale. Many little happenings are beginning to make communication sense between us, and this will stand us both in good stead when the children arrive.

Hopefully, I will be honoured with the custody and trust of her family whilst she goes off to feed herself, and later observe as the growing cubs are taught by their mother to recognise the 'no go' areas. It is important they understand that Maasai shoats are off limits and certainly off the menu. Most importantly, they must learn to give the Maasai, their cattle and shoats, a wide berth. The cubs must be taught to avoid lions, leopards and hyaenas, and other cheetahs, especially coalitions who may have other ideas in mind; also spitting cobras and other deadly snakes. Marshall eagles, the huge feathered aerial predators, can swoop down from the skies, with talons the size of a garbage grab, and whisk a five month old cheetah cub into the air, for several hundred feet, then let it drop—an easy way to kill a clawing, spitting, hissing, terrified cub in seconds. Cheetah cubs retain their needle-like claws until the age of ten months, and they know how to use them. There is much to learn. This knowledge will be so important for their survival if they are to fulfill their short lifespan of a little over fifteen years, in the wild. It is interesting that captive cheetahs have a longer life span of about fifteen to twenty years. Regular meals served on wheels, is probably the explanation for this longevity.

Tired and stiff from my 'one eye open, one eye shut' shifts throughout the bitter cold night had left me exhausted. At sunrise both of us would need a brisk walk-about to ease that deep, dull aching pain one gets when muscles and cold bones complain. Petal was content to inspect the surrounding area and to stretch out on the sun-warmed, rocky outcrop. I could see the swelling around her right eye had subsided considerably. Occasionally, she would open and blink this eye. I noticed her peering into bushes sniffing and scenting the night smells left behind by the nocturnal brigade.

Cheetahs pay careful attention to detail; they are fastidious creatures and always need to know what's going on around them. Just a darned inquisitive cat! In captivity, one can see their sadness; the eyes are dulled by boredom, their interest in life is mirrored in their body language. These cats need space, an ever decreasing commodity in today's world.

If I guessed correctly, Petal would not move too far from her present home comforts.

The spring was close by and here she could monitor her prey day or night, feeding when it became necessary.

I must make my decision when to return to Nairobi soon. The camp staff would be awaiting my arrival for instructions to proceed to the Mara. Petal's continued care, however, must take priority. Four days had passed uneventfully, during which my yellow flag was up and flying. I was pleased every passing tour driver waved acknowledgement from a distance, understanding the 'Queen' must be left in peace to recover. I was a little concerned about her nourishment. She had fed well on her first kill at the spring, and now was getting hungry again. The moon was on the wane with just sufficient light to hunt by.

The day, as predicted by yesterday's sunset, was hot and muggy. The oppressive energy-sapping weather builds up the afternoon storm clouds, thunder and lightening follow, and then there is a heavy downpour. Oh! The release of tension it brings to the wild animals. The Maasai cattle kick up their heels with joy and delight, and I enjoy the pleasure of watching Nature's happiness unfold. The birds sing, the plant life suddenly blooms, the air is washed clean and fresh, and my headache has lifted!

I looked again and Petal had disappeared. Now where had she gone? This phoenix had just vanished into thin air. I wandered around aimlessly, checking the surrounding area with my binoculars, surprisingly sharp after all these years; they are clear and still in focus in spite of having been dropped, run over and stood upon more times than was good for them! I needed more eyes to assist me. The yellow flag came down and I replaced it with a white one. This signalled that I required assistance. Some fifteen minutes had passed when two Mara Safari Club vehicles appeared. They were happy to search around whilst I checked out the thick bushes on foot, armed with my trusty fire extinguisher. Lions may have taken up residence in there during the storm – hence Petal's disappearance? Not an encouraging thought.

Twenty minutes later, a hoot from a vehicle was calling me; this signal suggested that maybe they had found Petal. I made my way out of the maze of bushes to the vehicle. The tourists on board were all wearing a wry smile – they asked me where the fire was! They just couldn't believe this fire extinguisher was my protection against lions, buffaloes and even tigers! Where was my rifle and all the necessary gear they had seen white hunters wearing on television? There was no mistaking where they came from – Texas USA!

The news was not that they had found Petal, but had come across a moth-eaten, mangy, scraggy adult male cheetah that looked as if it had been dragged up on skid row in downtown Dallas! According to the party joker, sitting in the rear and wearing a ten-gallon Stetson, "This was the meanest, down at heel, miserable-looking cat he ever sawd! Nobody would ever want to be seen dead with him!" That Texan drawl just blew me apart, I couldn't stop laughing. Even their tour driver raised his eyes to the heavens. He too claimed that he had never met such a wild bunch in his entire career to date – but they were fun! "Wako na raha sana", Kiswahili translated with an appropriate sign, suggested that 'Johnnie Walker' might have had something to do with their 'high spirits'.

Apparently, this creature was on the prowl just a hundred yards away – was this why Petal had been fastidiously sniffing around? I knew this guy! I had seen him several weeks before. He was a walking disaster covered in sarcoptic mange. The matter had already been reported to the K.W.S., (Kenya Wildlife Service). Unfortunately, Dieter was not their official vet. Our skid row 'leper' had been prowling around. Petal had sensed his presence and gone into deep hiding. Disaster had struck again; any physical or close contact between healthy cheetah and this decrepit animal is very infectious, even to humans. I have seen the burrowing mite under a microscope, and I can assure you it is the most incongruous looking, vile, bloodsucking, burrowing beast, with claws and spikes that makes for nightmares.

"Whaddya gonna doo, hunter man? I suggest ya shoot the durned ting – you'll be doin' him an' us a sure favour." The Texan was right in many ways. This infected animal could spread the disease like wildfire to every cheetah in the Mara. I toyed with the idea. As an Honorary Warden, I could put him out of his misery. Poor chap, it wasn't his fault, some domestic, mangy Maasai cattle herders' dog had passed it on to him. All it takes is for a few mites to brush off and transfer, and that is the start.

I wrote a note to the Manager of the Safari Club, asking him to get in touch urgently with the official K.W.S. vet in Nairobi. I would also pass the message, via my ground-to-air com, by 'voice of pilot'. It would be an impressive command to the Kenya Wildlife Service to get here quickly.

Meantime, 'this darned cat' would have to be given the 'git yer ass outta here' treatment. "Yer exterminator", said the bemused Texan, his eyes alight with humour, "squirt him until he suffocates in the mush. Hey man! I wanna get this picure for sure and show it to ma Fire Brigade buddies back home. They gonna know what to do with catterwallers. Let's give him the works!" And so we did. One well-aimed squirt produced the foam as expected, in a thick-pressured jet of ammonia that bowled him clean over, at five yards range, from the vehicle window. He took off like a scalded cat!

However, the show was not over yet – the wind direction had the last laugh. The spray came floating back at us with a choking vengeance. The sound of crashing gears, and we lurched away from this toxic cloud bearing down upon us, but not before a flurry of cussing and blinding issued forth from our Texan friend. "Holy cow! Whad sorta jungle juice have ya gotten in that doggone thing. He's gone supersonic!" That was the whole idea. Poor cheetah, nobody could love him in that state. If the K.W.S. vet did not appear soon and within the next twenty-four hours, there would be a lot of mileage and many days lost in looking for the 'leper'—this animal was well on his way to another planet!

The good humoured banter continued as I was driven back to the camper. The Texans were enjoying their freedom; their shackles and chains had vanished over the hill in a cloud of dust. It was their lucky day – such is the humour that abounds with friends on safari. The atmosphere of being free on safari brings tolerance and bonds people of all creeds together. Kenya's wildlife is certainly its best ambassador – long may it last!

Back at the campervan, the joke was on us. Their ladies had not 'disappeared forever over the hill'; they were patiently waiting for us, all eager to tell a story. Their wide grins and cross-chatter suggested something was going on. Had we found Petal? "No", was our despondent reply, "but we sawd a mangy superzonic cheetah goin like the clappers. We messed him up real bad, he's gonna need a psychiatrist." Our Texan joker was in good form. However, the ladies had observed 'radio silence' a one-upmanship game often played out by competing groups—who saw what and where, is only divulged by reciprocation, a little bit of give and take in exchange. A leopard is value for a pride of lions, a cheetah is value for another cheetah with babies, and so the bartering goes on. The tour drivers also participate and finally everyone gets to see and photograph.

In our case the story was different. We had been set up and were going to have custard pie slapped in our faces. Had they found Petal? "What do you think?" the ladies chorused in reply. "You're a bunch of drunks, you are all so piddled you can't see the wood for the trees." Our joker, in the rear, was never short of a quick answer. "Geeez, them cats of ours have got us cornered! What's the big deal?" he asked. The ladies replied, "The deal is that you all agree, as one, that men are no good for nothing!" Both drivers were now in complete hysterics.

Petal had returned to the caravan after her hide-and-seek with me in the bushes, whilst I was attending to the 'leper'. What better place for her to choose to view all the happenings than from 'on top'! When a cheetah lies flat, their wafer thin, streamlined body is difficult to see, particularly so when lying on their side, stretched out and head down.

The square top of the caravan, ten feet off the ground and measuring some seventy square feet in area, provides a blind spot from any angle. Also the skylight hump deceives the focus of vision when given only a passing glance from a distance.

Well, this was a triumph for the women. This would be a story that would be told many times by the ladies, over their dinner tables. "Walevi wata nyamasa sasa." chuckled their driver in Swahili. (The drunks will keep quiet now.) "Wanawaki yao wanawesa hawa kabisa leo". (Their women folk have proved their superiority today.) For once our joker was speechless. Petal, familiar and unphased by loud tourist chatter, flicked her tail as if to say, "Push off!" The drivers took the hint and drove off, the ladies waving and smiling, satisfied they were definitely the top cats of the day.

Dusk was now approaching. I climbed onto the bonnet, calling softly, and stood facing Petal on the camper roof. We were now both at each other's eye level. She raised her head in acknowledgement of my presence and looked straight at me. I held back a chuckle – one half opened very red eye and one fully open golden eye. It looked so bizarre and unreal. The puffiness around her right eye had subsided. This was such good news. She stood up, stretched both her hind legs and yawned; those teeth looked formidable. With fangs as good as any leopard, one chomp from that mouthful could cause a lot of damage. Sitting back on her haunches, she surveyed the scenery around her, lowering her head now and again to concentrate her focus on a distant object. I followed her line of sight towards a group of impala, some three hundred yards away. Her body language was suggesting the group might contain her dinner. If she decided to hunt at sunset, all Nature's favours of wind, cover and the setting rays, glowing directly behind her and towards the impala, was always a bonus for a successful hunt.

At sunrise or sunset most plains game turn their backs and graze away from the sun. Petal could stalk up almost unseen behind them, get in close and then make her dash from a short distance. The happy day was so close, she could not afford to injure herself or take a heavy tumble at high speed, a recipe that surely would injure her and the unborn babies. My intuition was correct. She came down from the bonnet, hardly giving me a passing glance, her mind already focused on her obvious plan of action. Now it was up to her hunting instincts and cunning. Petal had become a master of the art.

I followed her progress from where I stood on the bonnet, through my binoculars. I could see several very young impala, the ideal size to satisfy her hunger. One of these would be the target and if she succeeded, it would give me the confidence to dash for Nairobi tomorrow.

This expectant mother had her temporary disability under control much earlier than I expected. As the sun set, the colour of the Aitong hills changing from deep blue to gold, provided a fascinating picture. The group of impala was totally unaware that their vulnerable blind spot contained a stalking predator – until she burst onto the scene amongst them. The startled adults leapt yards into the air, as they do even to a sharp clap of hands, imitating a rifle shot. (These animals have a vertical take-off capability ingrained into their genes after years of being shot at by man.) Her prey, confused by youthful inexperience, fear and uncertainty about what to do next except run, Petal executed a quick 'trip-up' and the job was done. The 'Queen' will eat tonight!

I took my extinguisher as a precaution, and walked towards her. Hyaenas are dangerous scum in any cheetah's book; they are the thieves of the plains and will, without any hesitation or fear, relieve a cheetah of its meal within minutes of the kill. I was making sure Petal would not lose her dinner tonight. I found my adjustable shooting stick seat very useful, though for a while, it was looked upon by Petal with suspicion as a dangerous instrument. She eventually came to accept it as part of me. She had no qualms, however, about the fire extinguisher and was intelligent enough to know that it was for our protection. The extinguisher had become an ego booster for her and for some fun when her hated enemies, the hyaenas made persistent attempts to charge in and run off with her bounty.

On the dot of 7.00 p.m., the Mara mosquitoes appear as if programmed, bearing hypodermic needles designed by the devil himself, sharpened to penetrate most protective gear, particularly around the ankles. My boot leggings that cover my shins, just below my knees provide me with protection against thorns, snake bites, razor grass and biting insects. My leggings were designed by the devil's engineer himself just to beat these pests.

Satisfied that Petal had dined well, I returned to the camper hoping that this gesture would suggest she should follow me. If it worked, it would be another plus. God's wine, (clean water) was available at my table. I called her name and whistled our cheetah call as I walked away, hoping she would get the message. On looking back, through the night binoculars, I could see she had moved a safe distance from the remains of her dinner and was preening herself—all good confidence signals for us both.

Now the ball was in her court. If she came home for the night, fine. If not, then she would have made up my mind for me and I would be happy to head for Nairobi in the morning. I opened the top bunk window hatch. From my standing position over the gas stove, I could monitor her movements with ordinary binoculars. My dinner this evening would consist of cube soup, chicken, mashed potatoes, gravy, peas and garlic bread, followed by my favourite banana custard pudding, then later, a cup of hot Horlicks before turning into bed.

Tonight, I would sleep on the top bunk, where I could see any nocturnal wildlife wanderings through the observation window. This top bunk had only one fault, the space between the bed and the ceiling was about four feet. Sitting up suddenly in the dark could be a painful experience. There is some merit in being young and four feet tall! I always volunteered for the top bunk on trains and in cabin cruisers – despite the head banging there is something special about the top bunk when you are a child!

The moonshine cast a halo on the bushes, enveloping the camper in a warm glow. Beyond, the visibility was sharp and clear through ordinary binoculars. The night vision combat specials were a little cumbersome, so I elected to keep an eye on Petal with my 8x50 Bushnell's. The inevitable happened. I fell asleep and was awakened by a familiar grunt. I sat up and promptly hit the roof! Holding my head, I peered cautiously out of the bunk window. The camper was surrounded by lions. Two adult females were drinking from Petal's 'karai', the others; some six or seven sub-adults were generally being inquisitive. My deck chair had been bowled over and some young lions were about to have a tug of war with the verandah mosquito netting. I banged on the side of my cot and shouted "Yaaaa!" All scattered, each and every-way into the surrounding bushes. Petal would certainly have heard the commotion but was nowhere to be seen. Lucky! Lucky, I thought. If she had been on the camper roof, what then? Would she have had the courage to stay there out of sight, knowing I would protect her? One day it could just happen. Lions are inquisitive creatures. This pride must have been those that passed by towards the hills several nights ago. For such a large pride, they had not been vociferous. I remembered hearing their short calls most nights and early mornings. When the nights are dark, with little moon, they often roar in unison, establishing their presence in the area. When the moon is up full and bright, they tend to be quiet and move around more. Petal's disappearance was thankfully, in the opposite direction. She now would probably head for the safety of the hills, away from the lions, wild dogs and 'leper' area.

My plan of action was to pass by the Mara Safari Club to brief the tour drivers and the Manager. Should the K.W.S. vet arrive, they would point him in the right direction and attend to his needs. The 'leper' must be located and treated. I expected to be back within twenty-four hours. My camp staff would leave Nairobi ahead of me and set up camp. Meantime, all tour-driver eyes should be trained on Petal and her movements, in particular—not to harass, but to let her search for a safe place to give birth to her cubs.

The seven-hour drive back to Nairobi was hot and dusty. The road was full of deep ruts and potholes all the way to Narok. Broken down graders, in need of repair were abandoned along the route, adding weight to the grim, continuing story of corruption and misappropriation of gate tourist takings by the Narok County Council. In Narok town, County Councillors were strutting around, growing fatter by the minute. 'Status' in Kenya is determined by what type of vehicle you drive, and the bigger the beer-belly, the more votes you will receive at election time! Any grey matter between the ears is a bonus. To enhance this illusion, being chauffeur driven to and from the monthly fund raising rallies, is a must.

On arrival in Nairobi, I found the camp crew all present and correct, each anxious to know how the Queen was faring. Everyone had completed their check-lists, the trucks were loaded, diesel fuel bowsers and water bowsers would fill up at Narok. The gradual thousand-foot haul out of the Great Rift Valley to Narok tests the brakes and engines of any loaded vehicle. Tanker lorries regularly overheat their brakes, lose control, then jack- knife and overturn. It is not unusual to come across several of these terrifying mishaps en route, particularly on the rough tarmac sections.

Now it was up to the crew and convoy to leave home base at the crack of dawn the following morning. Kibet, the number two driver, Patrick, and Nyundu, the mechanic, carried the full responsibility to get through to the Mara. I was able to brief them on the rough road conditions off tarmac. If the roads were wet and the eighteen-inch dust- filled ruts turned into mud by heavy rain, their journey would take on the nightmare situation we last encountered coming out. This time they were on their own. I admired their courage and their keenness to take on the elements; they were, after all, intrepid trail-blazers! The true and no doubt colourful stories told back home in their tribal reserve, would give them prestige and status amongst their friends and neighbours. This challenge had to succeed.

Whilst I was away from Nairobi, my paperwork backlog always had its attendant problems with bureaucracy. Added to this was a disappointing message from Jamie, explaining that a long vacation, accompanying her husband overseas, had put a spanner in the works. Thankfully, Stan, a good Kenyan friend, recently retired from a neighbouring country's Game Department, offered his temporary services to plug the gap. His many years of experience in the field of wildlife conservation would be invaluable.

The safari bookings chart was looking good. The personal touch and 'word of mouth' certainly beats any media advertising. Sadly for all, Stan too was planning for a new life in Australia. Maybe, I could persuade him that he would miss the African wild so much, and that this stop-gap could turn into a happy and fruitful retirement job for him. Stan was a Godsend, knowledgeable like Jonathan Scott, but somehow a very different personality. Employing youth and inexperience as a tour guide is a recipe for total disaster in this professional field of tourism. In my humble opinion, five years tutelage under the eye of a true professional is a minimum training requirement for a safari guide. Hands-on wildlife management, a pilot's licence and good communication skills rank high on the wanted list. Many overseas fly-by-nights come and set up as bulk outfitters; their product is usually sub-standard, back-packer material that does little to enhance the image of Kenya's tourism under canvas.

Lawyers, as always, were dragging their feet over my sanctuary title deeds. Fading and ragged documents of Maasai family ownership entitlements, handed down over generations and kept under the titular holder's cow-skin bed underlay, have to be examined and checked thoroughly for forgeries and unapproved alterations of boundaries. A complete re-survey, with beacons placed for government approval and records will further delay the transaction. Maasai elders are not used to this type of modern law. They much prefer a nodding agreement and the parting with some livestock as a purchase contract to seal the deal, with an added understanding that the grazing of those cattle may continue on the purchased land, as a neighbourly gesture! I would have to break the bad news that modern law and title deeds provide for legal ownership, total tenure and privacy for the purchaser on a willing buyer, willing seller basis. The deal would be cash, not cattle. I wanted nothing but wildlife in my Sanctuary. They would be my cattle!

My friend, the old Maasai elder, acknowledged my warning of the expected drought that follows the El Nino floods. I persuaded him that he must sell all his cattle immediately. The drought continued unabated for about a year and wiped out thousands of cattle. Those Maasai stock-owners that did not heed the signs paid a heavy price. I was invited to bring my camper anytime and camp on the Sanctuary land, for as long as it took to complete the transfer. A substantial cash deposit to the old boy permitted me to store building materials and quarry blocks, and to generally lay out the design for 'Sanctuary Place'

This is what I find so satisfying in Africa, any personal effort and initiative is amply rewarded and restrictions can be overcome. It is said all that is required is an honest understanding between parties! Sometimes you get lucky – I got lucky! Some of the old Maasai traditions still prevail. A deal is a deal and woe betide those that do not uphold their principles. The younger Maasai of today have lost these principles. The new world teaching and values are frighteningly different. Our insatiable greed for riches has become the primary ingredient surrounding our Western capitalistic values.

I spent two days encamped at the Sanctuary. At night I could see the distant lights of the city of Nairobi some fifteen miles away, across the sprawling acres of the Nairobi National Park, with its teeming herds of wildlife—zebra, eland, wildebeest, some forty lions, ten cheetah and a number of leopards, plains game aplenty and rhinos, all sixty of them! This was my life's wish – this was paradise. Between the Mara and here my ambitions had been totally fulfilled. I had visions of finding another 'Queen'. Could there be another cheetah like Petal out there? I doubt it.

I had visitations from lions at night. They roared just a few meters from my camper window. This was a regular occurrence during my stay. Were they objecting to my intrusion on their territory? They knew nothing of the deal and my unfenced boundaries. This was my own little plot of land in Africa. Did I detect defiance in their tone? Somehow, I must prove to them I would do them no harm. After all, this was their sanctuary; they were free to check out any additions within their territorial boundary. However, I pleaded, "Please don't chew up my tyres!" Wild animals with sharp teeth, long fangs and jaws like vices, seem to have a preference for rubber, like I have for chocolate! Yes, this was to be my new home, away from the stench of diesel fumes, gridlocked traffic and pollution from human congestion.

The local Maasai were friendly – actually, too friendly! Pre-printed cards began to arrive on my doorstep inviting me to their fund raising functions for a church, a school, donations to buy a wheel-chair for a mother crippled with polio, a medical clinic, etc. Funds were required to address all of these issues. The community consisted of about fifty families, bringing the population to some two hundred residents. There was no electricity, no proper toilet and washing facilities and kindling for cooking came from foraging dead wood along the river. Acacia trees were ring-barked so that in a very short time, the tree would dry out, die and break up into ready-made firewood. The off-take was becoming unsustainable and the riverside forest was fast diminishing. The drought was forcing the Maasai to night-graze their livestock in the park. Strict regulations forbid the grazing of domestic stock within any of the Kenyan Parks. The wide-open spaces have their problems. I had chosen to try to do something about solving these.

The ugly head of human/wildlife conflict was staring me in the face. The Park lions would be the first to come into the firing line of the Maasai spears. The lions' larder was migrating out of the Park, heading for greener pastures well to the south. Some lions, with young cubs, would remain behind to feed on the Maasai cattle that grazed in the Park illegally at night – others would establish new territories within the Maasai group ranches bordering the Park. For lack of prey, they too would attack the cattle left behind in the Maasai night-holding corals. Soon many lions would die a terrible death. The Maasai are tolerant people, but anyone or anything that interferes or attempts to destroy their walking 'bank balances', is asking for a load of trouble. The Kenya Wildlife Service and the government must move quickly to establish, with the Maasai Elders, a community conservation education plan before the matter gets out of hand. The only other options—an unthinkable idea at present, but a necessary requirement if this unique world-renowned wildlife park is to survive the expansion of uncontrolled human settlement—is to fence the Park and manage it from within, or form the whole area including the Park, into one large Maasai Group Ranch. Everyone would then benefit from good wildlife husbandry, tourism and domestic livestock ranching in easy reach of Nairobi's main abattoir

I was pleased to read in the daily newspaper that the Maasai Mara group ranchers in Petal's territory had held an urgent meeting to discuss the removal of illegal squatters in the area responsible for poaching wildlife. This was encouraging news for me. The illegal squatters were accused of complicity in the poaching, and either way, they were bound to find themselves between a rock and a hard place.

Petal's magic intuition had drawn my attention to a conservation matter that required to be dealt with urgently. These latest developments would please 'Her Majesty'. It would be interesting to see whether Petal would ever lead me back to that area of death and destruction.

CHAPTER 13

A GOOD OMEN

REGULAR daily radio communication with my 'Out of Africa' camp was now established. The crew were in high spirits; they had survived the long journey with no mishaps. However, more importantly, 'Queen' had paid them a fleeting visit at midday by walking, unconcerned, through the camp. Construction came to a halt whilst she inspected the area where my tent was always erected, a little to one side at the secluded end of the campsite. The staff were apparently in absolute awe. To them this was a good omen. I felt a surge of excitement. I remembered experiencing that same wonderful feeling as a child at Christmas; the moments of expectation just before the arrival of Father Christmas at the annual gathering of the Railway Club Christmas function. Father Christmas always had a present, not only for me, but for all the other children too. It was a special function for the five to ten year olds. Many long lasting friendships were made there. The growing up together formed a strong bond of comradeship as we progressed through our excellent colonial primary and secondary school education, carrying on into our adult life attending reunions to exchange and relive the stories of our past experiences. There were few failures; each had carved out a good life here and abroad. Many attained high profiles in all walks of life. Africa's climate and the freedom to build and succeed in establishing an outdoor career brought forth many colourful characters later to be portrayed on the world's cinema screens and TV documentaries.

These were the masterpieces, 'Born Free', 'Out of Africa', and for the animals, 'Where no Vultures Fly' and 'The Serengeti Shall Not Die'. These films and more to come, will find an honoured place in the archives of man's memories of how it was in the early pioneering days of British colonial rule in East Africa. Today the winds of change are shaping a different Kenya, eroding a once flourishing East African community that was committed to quality. Now, handouts, from the world's 'caring nations', have accelerated a development process that requires a substantial and regular monetary input to maintain the structure of the hungry beast it has created. One day, I am sure, Kenya, Uganda and Tanzania will return to form the 'East African Community' that worked so well during Colonial times, but was sadly dismantled as each country gained their independence and self-government. Now no longer self-sufficient, the error of their ways are becoming more evident each day.

Despair and disrepair, in times of world recession, continues to fuel the fury of many of Africa's strife torn countries of today. I say let nature take its course; it has all the tools. Humanity has become the spanner in the works, and man is determined to survive over all the odds. I often question that forecast, for I know that nature holds the trump card – it will play its hand when the time comes. I stand firmly on the side of conservation and will always protect its natural world.

A game warden friend of mine had recently returned from Malawi and was looking for stop-gap employment. Here was the ideal opportunity presenting itself to fulfill Stan's requirement. The Maasai Mara beckond once more. Petal has not been seen for several days and Stan was soon preparing to meet and escort the first group of clients to the camp. There is no question about his capabilities; he has a retiring, gentle nature, with an infectious chuckle and a sense of humour that makes his company enjoyable. He understands that clients who pay good money will ask for nothing less in return. Stan alone is value for money and combines a wealth of knowledge to back it up. As for myself, I shall play second fiddle, my priority will be to protect Petal's first born and promote the interest of her cause as my own hands-on project. Difficult as it may be, I must not allow it to trespass on Stan's preserve. Petal will become her own ambassador for her kind, and I will be her support.

The camp crew greeted my arrival with enthusiasm. They had worked hard to please me, knowing my standards were high. It was an 'inspection parade', everything had to be closely examined from crisp, sun-dried towels to freshly ironed sheets and pillow cases; blankets and bed covers properly aired, there must not be a hint of mothball smell or storage mildew; mosquito proofing must be intact—clients worry about holes in them for good reason; grass (the mosquitoes haven) must be cut in and around camp; toilets clean and sweet and shower roses that work.

Then to Andrew (the cook with a flair for showmanship) and his kitchen. Heath Robinson as it may be, with his tin trunk as his magic oven, he never fails to produce the best meals that can otherwise only be found in top-class restaurants in Nairobi.

Cleanliness is paramount, from the air conditioned dry stores facility to the kerosene freezer, all built into a water-tight, rat proof, insect proof, modified caravan on wheels. The dining room tent, large and spacious with kerosene lamps hanging from the canvas roof with a difference. No smell of acrid kerosene fumes comes from the array of coloured, solar powered light bulbs inside them. This is Africa's bush electricity of the future for heating all manner of things, thus saving the destruction of the environment for firewood.

The camp staff were well organised and fresh supplies came in by air every second day. Kerosene deep freezers took care of the perishables and all dry stores were locked into hyaena proof metal boxes. The man of the match was always the camp cook. Andrew was a true magician; sumptuous meals were produced from a tin trunk set over charcoal, the right temperature being obtained by rule of thumb, by placing coals around and on top of the box. Not only did he cook the western style of fare, but also delicious African dishes, some of which appeared on the guests' table just to taste. Favourable and genuine comments made the variety of choice worth his effort. Dinner time was always a special occasion on safari when later, under a full moon, by the camp fire listening to the distant calls of hyaenas and lions on their hunt; an occasional belly rumble from elephants nearby communicating with their kind, and to top it all, a chilled wine of your choice—yes, this is the true African safari experience.

There is nothing to surpass the pleasure of being in Nature's paradise and we her honoured dinner guests.

The Mara will always hold a unique safari adventure with boundless wildlife of every description providing the true and exciting African experience under canvas.

The Maasai Mara is Kenya's undisputed wildlife wonder of the world; the startling variety of its landscape is awesome. In my opinion it has so much to offer; the climate is perfect and there is little need to seek further adventure elsewhere. To travel along dusty and pot-holed roads to get there is, in my opinion, a waste of quality time—fly; it's safer!

The camp passed muster. I was the only guest and the dinner served was fit for a king. After a hot shower, I fell sound asleep to the faint singing of the camp crew. They were happy and content that their hard work and attention to detail had been appreciated by the boss. Stan was due to fly in with the clients on the following morning's scheduled flight—Kibet would meet them at the airfield. I would set off at dawn and meet up with the Mara Safari tour drivers to seek out information on 'Queen' and check out her last seen whereabouts.

If the babes had already been born, Petal would seek and locate a regular water supply to keep up her milk flow. Day ninety was today – three months to the day – I was cutting it fine! She had been seen two days ago, looking heavily pregnant, near an open ended steep-sided gully about two kilometres from the camp. Both she and I had often walked through here; with its high sides it offered her several almost inaccessible, thickly covered, over-hanging bramble sites.

This could be her hidey-hole, but water was only available in the gully during the rainy season. The nearest water was two kilometers away at the 'donga' pools that were fed by the Euphorbia Hill spring near the camp. This distance was quite a long way, but there could be method in her choice. No water, no animals equals no predators – good thinking! I believed she was here, in hiding.

I parked the camper at one end of the gully, out of sight, then watched and waited. Petal's aluminium water 'karai' was placed alongside a faint track made by light-footed African hares. I also spotted several hyrax perched on a rock. They would be good sentries for Petal; she would not harm these four-footed, grey in colour, furry and feisty guinea-pig look-alike chaps—allegedly related to the pachyderm of the Pleistocene age, which holds scientific claims that are hard to believe – apparently its skeletal framework bears a similarity to that of an elephant. Their enemies are leopards, eagles and pythons, all of which would not be welcomed in the gully. For certain they do not trumpet, but for sure they have a good set of lungs that makes the tearing of calico sound as if your hearing aid has tuned itself into another solar system! The advance or presence of any enemy is vocally publicised by these creatures.

Petal had built up a layer of body fat over a period of several weeks. With little food and little exercise, the storage facilities in her body were now available for her to draw upon in lean times. This puppy fat would disappear quickly if long hot journeys to water were made early on in the immediate period after birth. Her 'karai' of water, close to hand, would ease her stress. She would not hunt nearby for fear of the smell of her kill attracting feathered undertakers from the sky, and other meat eaters. My presence would also give her confidence that her security was in place. It was midday and a cool breeze was blowing gently through the gully. There were no trees to offer shade for my camper, so I opened up all the windows and rear door, to keep the temperature down. I questioned my gut feeling. Was I right, or was I in blank territory, making friends with a couple of rock hyraxes? They would be the ones to warn me of any movement. What did they do for water? Was I about to be given a lesson in desert survival? The hyraxes were stretched out, belly down on the ledge of the rocks, not quite asleep, but just catnapping in the sun. It was a pied crow that first squawked a warning.

My binoculars were focused on the bird to see the angle of its gaze. It was peering into the undergrowth below. I could see nothing but obviously something was attracting his attention. The crow kept moving its position and peering again into the bushes, cocking its head to get a better view.

The hyraxes were alert looking downwards, then suddenly the scene came into focus. There was Petal crouched down drinking from her 'karai'. I had not seen her approach but the crow was still squawking and peering into the undergrowth—that would be where the lair was. Damn that bird! He was dangerous but his size would not allow him in through the tangled creepers. The African pied crow will peck the eyes out of any new born. My sudden appearance at the camper door, waving the kitchen towel, spooked him and the hyraxes too. They all vanished in a flash.

Petal gave me a knowing look but did not venture in my direction; she was slim and elegant. My calculations had been spot-on; the birth, I sensed, may have taken place the previous day. As she walked away, I noticed dry blood stains on the inside of her leg. I was surprised to see her take the faded path out of the gorge and, much as I wanted to follow her, it was too early to distract her attention from the job in hand. I would have to be patient. Petal would come to me when she was ready. A few moments later she reappeared walking along the ridge above me, then disappeared down into the undergrowth out of sight, slightly forward of the camper kitchen window. It was nowhere near Mr. Crow's last position, but Petal's camouflage was so good I could not identify any form or sign of her. There must be a cave or hollow of sorts accessible only from the ridge she had walked along.

I turned down the radio-call volume to muffle the hiss. I was close enough to hear any squeaks or sounds of Petal's mothering, but maybe it would be more audible at night when sounds carry further. However, since crickets set up a high pitched whirr during the early hours of darkness it could be difficult to identify the sound of baby cheetahs.

How I wished I had the latest photographic night technology and gadgetry, now coming into fashion, to home into her den. The overseas TV cowboys, as they were rightly called, had huge resources but were loathe to part with their technology unless they were given the kudos and the run of the credits. Certain of their presenters in the field used Petal on many occasions, giving her different names at each presentation, never revealing the true story behind her struggle for survival and the manner in which she became the most celebrated cheetah in the Mara.

When tourist harassment became intolerable for Petal, we both moved off into inaccessible areas, far from the crowd of minibuses. Those days and nights away were our golden moments in togetherness. I was so looking forward to being part of her new family!

Stan had arrived in camp after a low-level, bumpy flight from Nairobi. His clients were unfazed. They had thoroughly enjoyed flying in Air Kenya's fifty year old DC3 (Dakota). The pilot, Ian Cowie, an old friend of Stan and myself, provided the personal touch by inviting all

Petal in her den

Priority was always given to grooming the cubs. Petal left to hunt, leaving me in charge of her five little babes.

ten, one by one, into the cockpit on the forty-five minute flight. They just happened to be, according to a star struck Stan, ten of the most beautiful Swissair flight attendants he had ever seen! Here am I, stuck out all on my own in the sticks – how unlucky can one get!

This first group was to be the forerunner of many more years of a happy Swiss family business relationship with them; they were delightful people and the airline crews brought their mothers, fathers, brothers, sisters, girlfriends and boyfriends. Children less than fifteen years of age were not permitted. AMEN! Few children have the discipline to keep still or quiet for more than thirty seconds, particularly so when 'still photography' means still photography! Children soon become bored and resort to attention seeking. Having successfully achieved that, Plan B is selected for action at the very moment when Leo decides to perform his matrimonial duties. The video and soundtrack records only the cries of cross-legged agony from the wretched child, calling for an immediate defuelling stop. Not surprisingly, Leo releases his fury at the interruption and the nearest vehicle takes the brunt of it. There have been many close calls and for this very good reason repeat clients have the option to demand the exclusion of children – and the right to live to see another day.

I continued regular radio contact with camp from my home on wheels. It was critical I should stay alert with Petal to give her the freedom and security to leave her cubs and hunt. A cheetah mother seldom kills close to her den when nursing. To retain their body fluid mothering cheetahs prefer to hunt in the early morning as dawn breaks. I was prepared to continue the vigil night and day for as long as it took. Cheetah young grow quickly. They are born blind and helpless, as are domestic puppies and kittens. After five days the opaque film covering their retina gradually fades and for a short period the clear reflection off a cloudless blue sky brings out a pale tinge of blue that makes them irresistibly photogenic.

During the next four days Petal drank copious amounts of water at regular intervals, leaving her den on two early morning sorties to hunt, returning within an hour to drink once again. On the fourth day it appeared she had fed well and spent some twenty minutes with me, resting beside her 'karai'.

I took the liberty of following her closely down the centre pathway and up along the ridge. She was undisturbed by my presence; I detected a calm but controlled excitement in her body language as she stopped to look over the rocky outcrop along the side of the gorge. There, some fifteen feet below, in a small clear sunny spot were five tiny cheetah babies; one in particular was looking up and trying to focus on me. I took a snapshot. Petal then moved gently down through a maze of brushwood to appear in the open spot. Her den could not have been better chosen, making access difficult for any lion, hyaena or even leopard. She really had chosen well; the surrounding area was covered in a thick bramble entanglement allowing the cubs to escape into, out of harm's reach and away from any predator attempting to dislodge them. Even a heavy rainstorm giving rise to a sudden flash flood would not prove hazardous. Their home was secure and well above the waterline.

Petal spent much of the day in her hide; she became active at dawn, and at dusk came up for air to watch the African sunset with me. We shared those wonderful moments together and, as darkness fell, she would retire downstairs to her den once more.

Ten days old
Petal's den could not have been better chosen. Their den was almost impenetrable.

As each day progressed I took 'time off' to revittle my stores, take a welcome shower at camp and to meet the clients before they returned to Nairobi. Most, indeed all, were keen to return on their next flight layover just to come and see the 'Queen' and her little family. By then her children would be at their most playful stage, their world would be all brand new and exciting.

Several heavy downpours had laid the dust and soon the herds of Maasai cattle would seek out the flush of early green grass shoots after rain. Petal would have to move. Maasai herders' dogs leave no stone unturned. If she stayed, my presence would still provide her with security, but it would be necessary for me to convince the local Maasai chief and the ranch owners to allow me the sole privacy of the gorge from prying domestic dogs and their young spear-wielding herders.

The cubs were growing fast; they were ready for their first dangerous venture into the outside world. They would be at the mercy of hyaenas, lions and jackals by day and night, not forgetting the feared Martial eagle, which predates on the unwary cheetah young. A mature eagle has a lifting capacity of three to four kilos of captive body weight; their wings can span the width of a human's outstretched arms. Petal would be well aware of the danger, having seen a capture attempt by a 'Martial' on one of her siblings. It was Prickles, aged four months, who scrambled up a nearby thorn tree when the eagle's first misjudged attempt to grab him failed. The rest of the family scattered in every direction – luckily for them the area they happened to be in was made for a quick shin-up the long trunked, three metre umbrella ('Oltepessi', Maasai) acacia. This area, known as 'Tiri-Tiri' became very popular with Petal and her brothers. For each one hundred square metres there was a 'shin-up' tree available for any young cheetah cub to escape from a predator. After the age of eight months, their needle like claws begin to retract slowly and their vertical shin-ups become more difficult. However, at this age Nature has already given them the agility and speed to out-distance any predator on four legs. As for their feathered aerial enemy, the Martial eagle will always be on the lookout to swoop down and grab an unwary four-legged little 'lunch box'.

Three weeks had passed since their birth and Petal's cubs were now becoming adventurous, moving quite freely in the undergrowth. By the sounds of their plaintiff squeaks and growls they had begun to put their pecking order into place. As far as I could observe the litter comprised two females and three males. One female was much smaller than her siblings; she would be the runt of the family and the first casualty nature would weed out. The wild animal world has no place for the weak.

Twenty-eight days had now passed and there were still no apparent signs of Petal preparing for a move. I had been given the privacy of the gorge by the Maasai Paramount Chief, Ole Ndutu. The cattle, shoats and herders had kept their distance. The grass was still green, but water was scarce. Some plains-game, including Thompson's gazelles and impalas, had moved in accompanied by their newly born fawns. The wild dogs had moved south— what was left of the pack. There was only one alpha male and two females that survived. Rabies had demolished the rest and the Veterinary Department was still confused. Soon after being inoculated many died. Something went very wrong; questions were being asked about the vaccine – had it been responsible for the deaths? No answers; somebody was covering up – there was no doubt it was rabies.

Petal made her move and set her sights in the direction of Tiri-Tiri; the five babes followed her in a single line procession over the two-kilometre stretch. I took several photos of her leading the babes through the foot high green grass that threatened to swallow up the five little midgets. It was a slow process, even after fifty yards, the effort in having to make little leaps at each step exhausted them. They would seek the shade of any nearby cover—as the sun rose the heat would be just too much for them.

My eyes were constantly searching the skies and every bush along the trail. This time I was ready for any eventuality from the ground or the air. I had my trusty fire extinguisher at the ready and, as back-up, my auto-shotgun was loaded with the right dust cartridges at the ready that would modify the tail-end of any feathered predator that might just have the idea of attacking the cubs on the first safari into their new and dangerous world.

The cubs became more adventurous, bolder and stronger as the weeks went by. Petal made her move. She set her sights in the direction of the 'Tiri-Tiri'. I was ready to modify the tail feathers of any aerial predator that had ideas of attacking the cubs.

I was relieved that Petal had chosen the 'Tiri-Tiri' area situated opposite my camp. She would teach her children how to take care of themselves in the event of any attack. The area was perfect for bringing up her cubs, the grass was short, there were trees that provided plenty of shade and trees to 'shin-up'; plentiful impala and gazelle and watering holes were all available close by and just a quarter of a mile away was my tent, with her foster-father sitting there on his verandah watching over her with his binoculars.

For the next three months Petal stayed within the three thousand acre 'Tiri-Tiri' and never a day passed without a vehicle from the camp visiting her. Clients were overcome with joy at the antics of her brood. Petal often surprised them by leaping onto the bonnet of their vehicle. Many times she jumped right on top and lay on the flap of the open hatch; anything for a half-an-hour's peace from these tail pulling, playful little tearaways! The proximity of her presence on the roof just blew the clients' minds, some were brave enough to pop their heads slowly through the roof hatch and be photographed within inches of this beautiful wild animal by clients in another vehicle.

There was to be no touching, sneezing or coughing, otherwise the penalty was torture from a thousand tickles with an ostrich feather! Any other crime, like screaming or crying with fear, would result in an immediate dumping overboard and walk the rest of the way home alone! Joking aside, everyone knew that what they were experiencing was awesome, that a truly wild cheetah was prepared to share with them her happiest moments and her most precious things in life.

Stan surprised me by announcing his readiness to leave for Australia; I had hoped this would not happen. He was happy and jovial, loved the job like nothing on earth, but something 'down under' in his soul was bothering him. His marriage to a local girl in an adjacent country had broken apart. He had taken full responsibility for the two young children and was going to stand by them as a single parent but he wanted them out of Africa for the sake of their future.

My twenty-four hour security cover for Petal was weakened. I took over Stan's job of leading the clients on safari each week. This meant travelling to and from Nairobi by air and road with them – this was part of the deal. Aircrew, on no account, must be stranded away from their base. Imagine a full Swissair aircraft sitting on the Nairobi airport apron with no crew to fly it! It must never be allowed to happen! As a back up, I had an all-weather twin engine ten-seater aircraft on standby in Nairobi every day between 4.00 p.m. and 6.00 p.m., the time the crew would fly back to their base from the Mara, a full twenty-four hours before their duty flight take-off. There was always a possibility that the daily commercial flight schedule might have a technical fault or be hit by bad weather. Visibility in the Mara could turn into 'QBI' (a pilot's abbreviation for 'Quite b——- impossible') weather to land. The twin engine, instrument-rated, ex-Flying Doctor bush pilot, with a much lighter aircraft, would put down on a chosen strip almost anywhere we could get to by 4x4 vehicle. Bog rolls (toilet rolls) soaked in diesel make good runway markers at dusk in an emergency; this was never used, but we came very close to using them on several occasions. The DC3 pilots from Air Kenya were top class; they never once let us down, even when the wild geese had stopped flying. They always got the reliable old war bird down somehow. Pride with professionalism in the face of beauty has its advantages!

One early morning a message came from Kibet at camp. One of Petal's children (Watoto) had gone missing. Kibet claimed it was a female. "The little baby of the group," he said. This was what I had feared; Nature would weed out the weak in her own time. Now Petal's family had suffered its first casualty. Unable to keep up with the pace, the weakling may have been abandoned or fallen prey to a jackal or an aerial predator.

Two days later, I returned to Mara with clients. Kibet met me at the airstrip; he was not his usual smiling self. My group consisted of eight flight attendants, all eager to see the 'Queen' and her children. I sensed there was something wrong – I could read Kibet's face like a book. Everyone was asking, "will we see 'Queen'? "Are the babies all right"? I held my breath; he could sense my anxiety. "Yes," he said. "Queen is alive, but one of her babies has been stolen." "Stolen!" I gasped. "Yes, stolen," he replied. "How? Why?" I choked. "A Maasai herdsman saw a vehicle stop and take one. It was a white man driver," came Kibet's troubled reply. My mind flashed back to Hackles and his disappearance; that too was the work of a white man, but he was returned to the family fold in a roundabout way.

Then came another blow. Kibet was now talking in our local language, Swahili, as he did not wish the 'wageni' (visitors) to overhear the bad news he was about to tell me. We moved to one side. The clients were now busy loading their cameras; their excited chatter indicated expectations of an adventurous start to a 'safari with David'.

"The Queen is showing signs of a terrible sickness, but she appears to be strong in body" Kibet said, "her coat has small round red patches of lost hair the size of a shilling and oozing blood." Kibet was visibly distressed. I was in a state of agitation and dared not transmit my feelings to the clients.

We would drive direct to the camp in two vehicles and unload the baggage. It was 10.30 a.m. and plenty of wildlife would be around to whet the visitors' appetites and keep the camera shutters working at full speed. My brain shutters were working overtime too. What was this disease? It had to be mange of some sort—for Petal's sake, surely not the killer canine distemper that many of the local Maasai dogs were dying from – could it be? This was scary; the cubs could be infected too. I told myself I must not panic although I had every reason to do so! Not only had the wild dogs died of rabies, but some had been diagnosed with this killer mange.

The route to camp seemed to take an age yet it was only half an hour. Without even taking a look at Petal for confirmation, I hit the camp radio transmitter button to Nairobi. It was Friday, the start of a weekend and not the best time to get a vet. Why should all this happen when Dieter was away in Tanzania? Murphy's Law was at work! Murphy's Law was invented by an Irishman: 'Anything that can go wrong will go wrong.' The world knows it; it is the same in any language. I like the one: 'No matter how long or hard you shop for an item, after you have bought it, it will be on sale somewhere cheaper!' Murphy was an optimist and I was about to wring his neck today.

A message was passed to the Kenya Wildlife Service roving vet. It read: 'Urgent, from Drummond. Get to Mara a.s.a.p. by whatever means possible. The 'Queen' is sick – bring Ivomec.' I hoped that message would advertise the urgency of the matter even more so than the slow response they (K.W.S.) gave to attending and looking for the 'leper' which had, to date, never been located since it came face to face with the fury of my fire extinguisher.

The clients were keen to head out into the Tiri-Tiri area. It would be an opportunity for me to obtain a first-hand, close-up view through my binoculars. Petal would be resting – the sun was high and it was hot. I explained we would pay a quick visit but would not disturb her. The best time to re-visit her would be an hour before sundown, about 5.00 p.m., when it was cool and her cubs more active. Everyone was in agreement.

Petal was located close to where Kibet had seen her in the morning, nursing her four cubs, (one female and three males) under an acacia. I circled the tree to get a clear sight of her back. I could see the two red patches Kibet had described. This was not the sign of distemper, but a burrowing mite that was causing the bleeding. This was sarcoptic mange without a doubt – the same disease that debilitated the 'leper'. I noticed the tips of Petal's ears were also showing signs of bleeding. 'Ivomec', the one shot miracle drug injected subcutaneously, would clear the dreaded disease within ten days, but what worried me most was the effect of darting her. Would she go down with the first shot? Knowing Petal, she would fight like a tigress to overcome the effects of losing consciousness, particularly when she had cubs. The body has a way of producing high doses of adrenalin that provides the willpower to fight the effects of the tranquilizer. Subsequent darting could induce heart failure. I was already questioning the capability of the team. Had they any experience of darting cheetahs, particularly a nursing mother? They were qualified, yes, on paper, but did they have a hands-on track record? I was having doubts. It was going to be another sleepless night for me.

The aircrew were in a jovial mood. All eight of them were good-looking mature flight attendants and I was the envy of the Mara tour drivers. Their grinning smiles and knowing looks spoke volumes. They were lovely, bubbly, intelligent ladies and I was truly proud to be their guide. They were so keen to learn about nature, the questions never stopped. Kibet was up to it! He impressed them with his gentle nature and vast knowledge; birds were his speciality and he had a pleasant way of making this subject interesting.

Kibet joined us at the campfire before and after dinner. He preferred to eat 'black man's food the way the black man eats it.' "This white man's food no good, makes for embarrassing noises especially in motor vehicles." The way he said this brought forth peels of laughter.

Our first game drive produced a male leopard in a tree eyeing us with interest. I guess he was showing the blondes his bedroom eyes, so beautiful and enticing. We also saw a large herd of elephants near the swamp about five miles from camp. They were grazing and moving in our direction. I held my position as they advanced, unconcerned, towards our vehicle and passing either side of us. Thirty-five huge elephants, some with little babies, wriggling their trunks and making mock squeaky charges at us, ears flapping just like Daddy does it. And, Daddy was big – he was gigantic! Nobody, but no one questioned his authority as he ambled past us without even a sideways glance. Our girls were silent, scared and very, very impressed. He had all the tools of his trade on display. Interestingly, these are breeding males. This is Nature's way of producing the biggest and the best, nothing less. There are also males that fire blanks! Giraffe by the dozen with their young just fascinated the ladies—so close and looking disdainfully down at us from a towering fifteen feet. What was it about these beautiful animals that intrigues women? "Look at those long eyelashes, David. How we envy them their lovely long, slender necks; they are so graceful in their walk; so sensual and so gentle. And look at their children's hairstyles, they are so cute!" They were referring to the tuft of black hair, resembling an eagle's crest, on their forehead. I shared their enthusiasm – but then Daddy giraffe came along. Now it was my turn! He was seventeen feet tall, if an inch. "Look at the bumps on his head, battle- scarred from defending his harem." My observation brought forth hilarious and ribald comments about how their husbands might learn a thing or two on safari. I was always amazed how few male crew members took part on these short safari stop-overs. The ladies had the answer; the men were making 'body beautiful' in the sun at the swimming pool in Nairobi!

Lunch and an early afternoon rest was called for. Tea at 4.00 p.m. and out once more at

4.30 p.m. was the schedule. Andrew's kitchen was inspected while he strutted his stuff in full cooks' regalia – long white hat with all the trimmings; and dwarfed by beautiful women! Photos galore were taken and he just had to have a copy 'for his wife'. I think perhaps more likely to impress the boys back home!

We drove over to Tiri-Tiri. Petal had moved and there was no sign of the cubs, not that she would have left them unattended for one minute. "She must be around here somewhere," I said to a rather perplexed Kibet. Those that had binoculars scanned the open spaces. "There she is" one called out. "Where?" "No, sorry, false alarm, it's a gazelle lying down". I turned off the engine; it was time to think this one out. Unless something had spooked her she just couldn't be far away! Kibet drove over to me, that wry smile on his face. "She's given us the slip, Kibet," I said. "Wapi kwenda?" (Where has she gone?) "Na potea," (She lost us) came the reply. "Water, Kibet, that's where she has gone." "But not with her babies" was his simple, sensible reply. "Start looking in the trees." So, off we went again, each taking an area to search. Sure enough there they were all four of them high up in the umbrella of a Tiri-Tiri tree. It was Kibet who spotted them with his eyes like those of a hawk. "How did we miss them first time around?" I asked. We had passed within fifty yards. Our vehicle tracks were still clear.

Now, where to? Which direction? To the water, of course! I was talking to myself. We coursed up and down the lugga but there was no sign of Petal. Two female lions were sprawled out asleep under a leleshwa bush; she wouldn't have come this way! After some picture taking, we patrolled either side of the lugga, up stream towards Euphorbia Hill and the spring. Still nothing! I kept looking back towards the tree, which was now some six hundred yards away.

By keeping the sun on my back, objects become very clear. Suddenly, there she was, three hundred yards away walking back disconsolately in the direction of her tree-borne cubs. Petal had taken time away either to hunt or drink. I flashed my headlights towards Kibet; he had parked himself on Euphorbia Hill and this was our signal that I had located her. Returning to just short of the tree, I positioned the vehicle with the sun still at our backs. Petal's oncoming track would pass within a few feet of us. I prepared her 'karai' of water and placed it at a convenient point for the best photography. To my surprise she looked at it, sniffed it and walked on! I could see she had not eaten, her hunt had been in vain.

The babes came scuttling down from the tree, romping excitedly towards their mother. Then, turning them round, Petal brought them to where I was standing; the 'karai' was at my feet. The babes were a little unsure about this human at first, but a throaty call from her calmed their natural fear. This was my first close meeting with them; she had brought her cubs to me for their first drink. Petal lapped, encouraging them to do the same. Several times their noses touched and felt the clear clean water, then their little red tongues appeared, lapping, slapping and slurping and not quite in control of how to cup the water. In less than a minute all tongues were under control. I had slipped several fizzy tablets of soluble vitamin C into the 'karai'. It would help to firm up their bandy front legs and provide some immunity against disease.

Petal was standing close by me in a supervising stance. I could now clearly see the festering sores and the serrated red skin on the outer edges of her ears. It was clear both were being eaten alive by the burrowing mites, but thankfully the cubs seemed clear of them. I was elated and thankful that help was on its way. She would have to be darted, given the drug and the wounds attended to. Gentian violet and Picric, a yellow disinfectant that adheres like glue and is very effective, would need to be generously applied. Our 'Queen' was going to look like a modern day yuppie hippie.

The crew were fascinated as the cubs inspected their new partner. I was now kneeling on one knee but still towering above them. Their little faces showed intense curiosity but seemingly they understood that I was part of the furniture; their mother's presence had confirmed that. Petal was purring contentedly but constantly twitching her ears. The mites were burrowing and driving her to distraction; she lay down, stretched and rolling on her back, began wriggling to get at that itch! The babes were inspecting the vehicle tyres, scurrying under and around, playing tag and then returning to pounce on their mother and tug at her tail. If they hadn't yet got mites they would; the condition is contagious.

That night my shower at camp contained a strong dose of permanganate of potash, a disinfectant crystal that turns a dark red colour in water; it is excellent for washing hands and dishes. In each clients' basin and shower bucket there is a hint of potash; it gets rid of any spore that may have come into contact with the hands or skin and is known as 'Granny's cure' for most skin infections! It is mandatory that all the kitchen staff and tent attendants use it. The camp rule 'wash your hands' was one never to be ignored at any time!

We still had time in hand before sunset for a quick back-track to the two female lions we had seen earlier. Though it was difficult to pull away, Kibet decided to go ahead first, inching slowly and safely away from the 'playground', leaving us with the cubs and the 'Queen'. Not long after that she jumped onto the bonnet of the vehicle to look across to where Kibet's vehicle had stopped further along the lugga. She knew the lions were there. Her instinct confirmed that fact.

My radio com. crackled – it was Kibet talking to the camp or vice-versa – I couldn't quite pick up the whole story, but from what I understood of the conversation the K.W.S. vets would not arrive until the next day. In the meantime, did I know where to get some Ivomec? Their stocks had run out – this was typical! My wife worked for an international organization researching into domestic animal diseases, mainly cattle. They surely would come to the rescue. Some of their scientists had been on safari to my 'Out of Africa' camp and had met Petal; they knew the background.

The second transmission was from Kibet to me. The lionesses had four little cubs that we had not spotted on our first encounter. Obviously they had been hidden away by their caring mothers. Further observations established only one lioness was a mother and the other an 'aunty'. Lionesses have a very social, good housekeeping management policy. Aunty is a lioness a little younger, just short of her first oestrous. Her attachment to the older lioness is for several reasons: firstly to be taught the art of child care and regularly act as nanny when mother goes hunting and then to bring the cubs for all to feed when mother calls them. This is a fairly regular pattern operated by a single lioness that has no pride or extended family to assist her. More often than not, they are strangers to the area and seek to avoid resident female territorial non-acceptance.

Petal had captured the hearts of her admirers by placing her front paws on the cab roof and leaning against it, with her hind legs firmly placed on the slip-proof bonnet. She was looking eyeball to eyeball at the startled clients now standing shoulder height through the viewing hatch. "Don't smile, don't show your teeth, and don't stare, don't sneeze or cough and above all try to be subservient." These were the instructions that issued thick and fast from me whilst I stood outside the vehicle observing Petal's antics.

The Maitre de Cabine of the group was always quick off the mark and never short of a humorous, ribald answer, added "I've just peed in my pants!" This aptly timed remark prompted calls for an urgent pit stop. Kibet had timed his return perfectly. We could now leave – but Petal's presence on the bonnet was so uplifting it was too good to disturb. Her cubs lay under a tree close by, exhausted after their runabout antics.

Fifteen minutes to sunset – that magic moment for all of us was approaching – willpower and brakes must be applied to all bladders until after sundown. The excitement was electric; they could not move away and were prepared to agonize cross-legged for the next half-hour.

Both our vehicles were facing each other, some twenty yards apart. The cubs were still resting quietly at the foot of the acacia tree on the opposite side to where we had parked, allowing Petal an unrestricted view from the bonnet of my vehicle or from the other one if she chose to move. I took the opportunity to walk slowly back and forth from my vehicle to the other, passing close by the cubs. The idea was for them to become used to my presence and to identify me as a friend and trusted companion of their mother. My constant appearance, in my khaki safari outfit and wide brimmed safari hat would establish and cement an early recognition code in their minds and the fact that their mother tolerated and accepted my company sealed that trust. From this moment on I was accepted and recognized as part of her new family. Petal never accepted any other human on foot or out of their vehicle.

Some white safari tour guides had tried hard to emulate my routine, but failed miserably, to their embarrassment. As they got out of their vehicles to show off their fearless talent, Petal and family scattered in all directions. Their clients labelled them as mad, egotistic gofers! These impostors were unaware of the built in recognition codes, the cheetah whistle, the 'karai', the clothing and the voice. Never once did I hear of an African tour driver attempting to impress his clients in this manner. Even Kibet, who knew all of the secret codes, respected the need for Petal, her brothers and her offspring never to become confused, uncertain or domesticated.

It was a glorious African sunset. Petal treasured these moments close to her new family and we, as her admiring guests, savoured the profound peace it brought within ourselves by sharing an association of togetherness with a wonderful wild animal.

We said our goodnights and headed back to camp.

The two lionesses had moved closer downstream towards our camp. The fact that they were less than two hundred yards away provided another sense of excitement. Lions and their young often visit campsites during the late night hours, usually when most sensible humans have gone to bed. Everybody, including the guests and staff had a whistle by their bed and, in the event of any incident or disturbance, they raised the alarm by blowing it. The rule was 'stay in your tent.'

From my vantage point I could see the whole camp through my night vision optics, anybody or anything that moved would be seen and appropriately challenged. Only wild animals had admission and right of way, even elephants. Never have I experienced any problems with my 'big five', elephant, lion, cheetah, leopard and hippo. Hyaena and buffalo were not welcome and were chased from the precincts day or night by the fire extinguisher. Our resident pack of some twenty banded mongoose kept snakes, rats and other creepy crawlies at bay. Nothing escaped their attention. They had the run of the camp and showed little fear of the human residents. The staff nicknamed them 'The Securicor'.

We arrived back at camp to find welcome hot showers awaiting us. Also, ready for consumption were cashew nuts, lovely hot potato crisps and a sundowner of choice, around the campfire. This added a wonderful ambiance to the pre-dinner atmosphere.

A safari leader has to be a good raconteur. This is a necessary qualification for stories of daring, some true, others a little embellished, a guitar, a camp fire and a little strumming from a music-minded staff member, provides the after dinner entertainment. Andrew, the cook, had excelled himself again; he appeared at the dining tent ready to receive well-earned compliments from his satisfied diners. The food was excellent, presented in the best tradition of English fare – the plates were never cold!

Nearby grunts from our two lionesses reminded us we were not alone. Distant hyaena whoops were interrupted by the crackling call of a tree hyrax, objecting to the melanistic genet cat feeding off the scraps put on the bird table. The night had come alive. Nature's nocturnal squad was awake, for this was their breakfast time, as we prepared to turn out our lights. A goodnight radio call from base in Nairobi informed us that Petal's one shot 'Ivomec' cure had been donated by a scientist and that the K.W.S. veterinary team was expected to arrive by mid-afternoon the next day.

There was more good news! The missing cub found abandoned near Euphorbia Hill was picked up by a caring 'Ker and Downey' safari tour leader and taken to the Nairobi animal orphanage. This little no-hope bundle was the runt of Petal's family, unable to keep up; it was left to die in the wild. The Maasai herder had spoken the truth; I must not forget to reward him. Hopefully, with tender care and the will to live, this emaciated little female, in her weakened state, would find the strength to recover, but sadly, may spend the rest of her life behind wire. I really could not allow this to happen! *I had an idea.....*

Fate intervened in the life of this little cub. The bizarre way in which it presented itself will forever be etched in my mind.

On arrival back in Nairobi I went straight to the Wildlife Animal Orphanage where this little bundle lay, and found her in a pathetic state of health.

I could see that an intensive care regime would have to be introduced immediately to save her life. I knew of a young recently qualified vet whose domestic problems had left him alone and confused—his business had failed. 'Petal's Fund' had some money left in it to pay for 'care and attention' and would help to ease the psychological strain that had beset both the cub and her appreciative carer.

The cub gradually pulled through and over the following month grew quickly—the spectre of its complete domestication began to trouble me. The cub had, in a way that only animals can do, brought her foster father out of his terrible depression that humans suffer at the loss of a loved one or partner, to whatever cause.

After completing a couple more weeks of rehabilitation my idea was to re-introduce the cub back to her siblings and mother, Petal.

The project would be a challenge in timing the re-introduction before her domestication became irreversible. I had not bargained for the reply I received from the cub's carer. He refused to part with the cub. Her loving nature had found a place deep in his heart and she had become a lifeline for his continued therapy in helping him to overcome his severe depression.

I had to consider in favour of the humanitarian angle; his state of mind was certainly going through a roller-coaster situation bordering on the suicidal. I found myself between a rock and a hard place. 'Let it be, let it be'—that familiar voice was talking to me again. Petal's cub is helping her foster father to get his life back into perspective in the same manner that Petal had done for you when your world was turned upside down with grief when you lost your daughter.

Eight months passed—it was time to revisit the cub.

Fate was to intervene once more—this time it was drastic. News was flashed to me in the Mara that the cub's carer had taken his life and had been found, days later, by a close friend who had called in to see him at his home. The cub had not eaten for several days though food had been thoughtfully left out for her.

I knew of a neighbour who owned a twenty thousand-acre ranch near Nairobi. His cheetah pet had lived an adventurous sixteen years on his fenced in ranch, terrifying the workers children, by pitching up at the door of their mud huts. All the workers on the ranch knew of 'the big duma' and his mischievous ways, but the presence of this domesticated animal wandering about their premises was too much for the faint hearted Mums and their children.

Duma had passed away and once again Petal's 'baby' was destined to play another role of healing the sorrows of human grief.

I was amazed how similar in appearance and temperament Petal's youngest was. It was if she were the twin of her mother. This cool cat was given the name Chala by her new owners, named after a picturesque lake that is fed by the clear and cool waters of Africa's highest mountain—Mt. Kilimanjaro.

I was elated. Here was another Petal in the making—she would be free to roam within the 20,000-acre ranchland without fear of being attacked by predators that she had never known or understood were her enemies. The owner of the cattle ranch had diversified into part-beef cattle and part wildlife-venison in the main the ungulates of the plains. Conservation by utilization was his forte by applying practical science balanced by controlled wildlife cropping.

It fell to me to teach Chala to hunt for herself and to understand that 'home' was for 'coming home' to provide a bond to the family that offered her the freedom to live her life in a semi-wild state.

One day she gave me the slip—like her mother, the phoenix could vanish into thin air. Chala did just that. I had left her in the charge of her minder whilst I flew to the Serengeti to be with a group of special friends from the USA for a few days.

In mid-flight during conversation with my pilot, he recounted that whilst in the flight dispatch office at the airfield in Nairobi he met two scared-looking British Naval Helicopter pilots on a three-day navigation exercise from their ship that had docked in the port of Mombasa three hundred miles away.

My Pilot recounted their experience to me. Both were suffering from 'Montezuma's revenge' and were forced to put down their helicopter in the bush and relieve their agony. None were more surprised than they when this 'spotted panther' came out from the bush to investigate their predicament. They were literally caught with their pants down and could not recollect much about what happened next—except their one aim was to get the blazes out of there. They did remember, however that it had a green collar fitted with a transmitter around its neck.

I asked my pilot—"did they indicate where?" Thinking to myself they had landed within the ranch boundary. "Yes", he said "fifteen miles south west from Stoni Athi Station on the Mombasa to Nairobi railway line"!

I knew the area well—this was miles away from the fenced-in ranch! Chala obviously had 'escaped' from her minder; found a hole in the fence and gone on a long adventure heading towards the foot of Mt. Kilimanjaro. She would have to cross through dangerous and unfriendly territory to get there and knew no enemies—not even man.

I never joined up with my friends, but made a 180-degree turn and flew direct to the ranch, which had an airstrip. All the ranch staff were still out searching for Chala. She had gone AWOL (absent without leave) that previous evening and so had her minder—he went on a bender after I left.

Would the radio direction finder pick up her transmitter bleep? I drove the caravan to the nearest hill some five miles away and to my relief I heard several faint bleeps and took a bearing. Two hours later, driving over rough territory, I arrived at where Chala was sitting on her haunches surveying the countryside with a 'what's all the fuss about' look on her face, or was it a 'where the hell am I' look?

The local squatters living in the area had already armed themselves with sticks and stones and were planning their attack. None so surprised as they when I walked up to Chala and coaxed her into the back of the camper. Had I arrived ten minutes later she would have been dead. A close call!

Chala lives on—happy and content and has caused no more heart failures. At ten years old and with freedom to roam her patch at will she may well live to a ripe age. I so wanted Chala to meet her mother so I could record the encounter. Would they recognize each other? But Chala and Petal were some one hundred miles apart—it was too much of a risk. If things went wrong, then what? Her human family would disown me.

Chala and her admirer—my wife
I had an idea to return Chala to her mother (Petal) and family in the Mara,
but realized she had long passed the point of no return to the wild.

Chala, in her semi-captive state seldom showed a yearning to seek a mate. Her oestrus cycle never became strong or fully active. Something was missing in her make-up.

Male cheetahs seek out Chala at regular intervals at her night-time residence (a large chicken wire cage) at the Ranch House. Yet these nocturnal visits by her wild suitors seem not to trigger any desire or interest in firing up her libido. It may be that easy access to domesticated living outweighs her natural wild urge to procreate, or has early domesticity beyond the point of no return to the wild something to do with her lack of awareness to preserve her species? Or just plain 'if you don't use it, you lose it'?

When in camp, I sleep lightly; half my mind seems to fall into a deep sleep, the other floats gently on the surface of light sleep, tuning into any movements around me. At 5.00 a.m. I awake rested, with none of those exhausting city dreams that make you feel you have been climbing Mt. Kilimanjaro all night. I put my good sleep down to a fresh, unpolluted, re-oxygenated night air wafting through the mosquito-proofed windows. The forests have washed and recharged the Mara night air with their perfume, a welcome relief from the stink of Nairobi's diesel fumes.

The pouring of hot water into the basin outside the tent and a gentle tap on the canvas signals 5.00 a.m. has arrived. This is the wake-up call. Wheels will be turning at 6.00 a.m. after morning tea and biscuits at the campfire. Breakfast will be served in the bush on Euphorbia Hill; lunch will be taken back at camp, with all bags packed ready for the final game drive to the airstrip for a mid-afternoon flight departure to Nairobi.

There is always plenty to do; time is precious and late starters can get left behind though this hasn't happened yet. It is all go. Andrew and his crew have already left with the trailer laden with camp tables, camp chairs and all the necessary kit to set up a five star 'cooked in the bush' breakfast.

When clients stay for several nights, a dinner under the stars in camp by candlelight is always a popular request. Our resident wildlife hyaena and lion band play their music, serenading us free of charge. When the curtain falls, more often than not they come and inspect Andrew's kitchen. He never fails to receive a handsome tip from his satisfied patrons; he calls it the 'danger money' for the Hyaena Orchestra. Without his humour and expertise we would be lost!

The man is full of cleverly thought out mischief. I remember once in camp a group of fifteen clients came for a three-day, four-night stay. All the kitchen services were stretched to the limit; Andrew was working at full speed, the pressure was on. We were operating at five people over the limit and the emergency cook had gone sick! During the vital hour of preparation for dinner, a large, single male lion, unfamiliar with the camp layout, walked calmly through Andrew's territory uninvited! Andrew being Andrew, seized upon this opportunity to 'state his case' for a rise in wages, or at least overtime 'danger money' at double time rates!

It took myself and the rest of the clients an hour of hard monetary negotiation to get him to come down from the nearest tree he had shinned up for safety. It was a very realistic show of sheer fright or very clever acting. He was presented with his promised 'OSCAR' in cash which he accepted with bows and hand-clapping from a delighted audience at their farewell dinner. Andrew had once again pulled off a spectacular coup. Despite his talent for extracting money from the rich, he had not the faintest idea how to save money or how much the money was worth, and above all he knew not how to count a cent. He had never attended school and never let on where or how he learned his trade. I became his trusted accountant and banker.

The day passed too quickly for the Swissair crew. We found our two lionesses and cubs cowering in the lugga! The resident female pride of six had picked up their scent and was searching around for the intruders. If they found them the cubs could be killed. This is the territorial law of the wilds. The lionesses must move to the hills with their cubs and soon – like tonight!

Maasai herdsmen reported seeing three large cheetah males some ten miles south of the camp; we would head in that direction. Could they be the three boys coming north to visit us? If we found them they would be keen to smell around the vehicle for any scent of Petal.

Before heading off to look for the boys, it was necessary to have breakfast. Andrew had prepared it well, the tables and the setting were just perfect, and of course, the time and place to make good that eight o'clock bush stop feeling. There was urgency in the air – not a minute must be wasted. Breakfast completed – off we went. Ten o' clock had come and passed and lunch would be at two o'clock, so we had to get the skids on.

We saw giraffe, wildebeest, eland, more lions and a den of hyaenas with their puppy-sized cubs. We also came across a hippo in the open heading across from one river to another. He was certainly taking a chance, but luckily there was sufficient cloud to provide him with some cover from the hot sun, otherwise, within several hours, if he didn't get to water or shade, he would be sunburnt and die of dehydration.

We stopped and enquired from Maasai herdsmen for news. "Lions, plenty," they said, "they are bothering us." These Maasai were always willing to have a joy ride on the mudguard to show us where. I asked about the cheetahs—they called them 'calf killers'. "No", I said "the special ones." They seemed to know and acknowledged my keenness to find them "Drymon's (Drummond's) Lo-engwarungeri (calf killers in Maasai). "Yes, we hear from others they have been seen south from here", they said with pointing of spears and puckering up their lips, from which a good tracker would guesstimate at least two to three miles away. But first they asked "Maji, maji?" (Water, water?)—We obliged. This is good interaction and we knew they would not cheat us.

Now it was cheetah hunting time; everybody was to scan the horizon each time we stopped. Fleeing wildebeest would be a sure sign of a lion, hyaena or cheetah chase. We passed a herd of cattle; their accompanying Maasai dogs looked mangy and underfed.

Early tomorrow morning would be the best time to attend to Petal. The vets would arrive after the clients had departed. I wondered where Namibia, Petal's prince, had gone? Nothing had been heard of him. He would have been pleased to know he was a daddy, but what would the boys have to say about that? Namibia would have to keep clear of them even though he was big. Three strong cheetahs would be too much for him to tackle. We could see vultures gliding down from the skies. "That will be them" I said, "they've made a kill." Sure enough, the three boys were busy having their breakfast when we arrived. I had not seen them for months – almost six months, I think. They were in fine shape. I wondered if I dared make my presence known—how would they react?

We still had a little time in hand. The 'karai' of water may do the trick; water was not close by and the boys would be thirsty. The vultures, high in the sky, were now homing in on the carcass; their time to feed was yet to come. Other predators would see these signs in the sky and head this way too. The hyaenas, were already on their way – we could hear their distant whoops.

Hackles looked superbly fit—he was big and muscular; Whispers and Hopeless were slick, lightweight and sporty, they were the sheep dogs of the coalition. Hackles was capable of bringing down a sub-adult wildebeest or even a zebra. I once saw him leap onto the back of a sturdy young zebra at full speed. The sheer size and weight of him toppled the animal. Could these three musketeers cope with the pack of five hyaenas now approaching their kill? I doubted it! It was not my territory to interfere; they were very capable hunters, well fed and could dine whenever they wanted. Petal, alone with her cubs, was a different matter.

The hyaenas arrived cackling, hooting and howling aggressively at the three cheetahs — Hackles held them at bay. Four of the hyaenas were young adult males, in the company of one large female, probably their mother. She was the more experienced aggressor. The others held back, heads held low, baying for blood but playing cautious. Hackle's resolve was being tested. Meanwhile, Whispers and Hopeless had their faces bloodied as if they had fought a ferocious battle in the boxing ring.

Hackles was standing tall, his ears pressed right back alongside his head, with hackles raised. He was a formidable and fearsome sight. I had often witnessed him present this stance, positioning his hulk towards me when he wished to reinforce his number one pecking order. When we were alone, I never felt totally comfortable with him, nor him with me. We both had respect for each other – at a distance. Yet at times, particularly at night, he would come right into our fold. However, he was forever watchful of my movements and he eyed my fire extinguisher with distaste, knowing that was where my strength lay. I was thankful for that!

The hyaenas snapping jaws convinced the trio there was no contest. They had fed sufficiently well, now it was time for the scrum. The cheetahs moved away and the feathered squad moved in, fearless of the hyaenas. Vultures too have an 'armour-plated' beak and claws that flail. It was pandemonium personified; within seconds the remains of the carcass was torn apart. Each hyaena took his share and trotted off, head held high to eat in peace and return again to repeat the performance. The clients were impressed and so was I.

The cheetahs had moved well away by now, to rest and watch from a distance. This was my chance to present them with the familiar 'karai' they knew so well. Storm water was not close by and they would be thirsty. They had not forgotten me – Whispers and Hopeless came forward, drank and returned to their shade.

I refilled the 'karai' and took it towards Hackles. When he growled, I knew it was time to put it down; I was only a few feet from him. I walked slowly backwards, keeping a subservient posture, looking away but keeping him in total focus out of the corner of my eye. I had purposely filled the 'karai' to the brim. If he attacked when I was carrying it to him, the deluge of water thrown at him would take him by surprise. Cats hate to take a bath; I was just being extra cautious for my own safety. Hackles lapped contentedly, showing no signs of stress. However, when he looked up, our eyes met and I looked away, muttering to myself, "No contest, my boy, no contest." Whispers and Hopeless came over to join him. They had watered well, but their interest was centred on the 'karai'; they were sniffing the brim and sides.

I never subjected this aluminium bowl to a scrubbing or used any form of disinfectant. It was kept in Petal's cupboard in the camper, along with her flea powder. The boys knew this was the family bowl – minutes later all three were inspecting my vehicle tyres, front bumper and spare tyre holder and Kibet's too. Our vehicles were being given a thorough going over. They were in fact reading the latest update (cheetah style). Unfortunately, Petal had not dumped her newsletter on the bonnet of my vehicle for some days.

The clean-up squad had left their table clean, leaving to one side for marabou storks, the stomach contents of the unfortunate beast. Now a red patch on the short grass was the only clue left to show that the hunters of the plains had been here.

The hours passed quickly, the cameras and videos had worked overtime and most were about to run out of video film! Murphy's Law then took hold. "We've got a puncture", I announced. There was a deathly hush. "What do we do now?", they asked anxiously. "We all get out and help change the wheel", I said. "You're joking." quipped their leader—for a fleeting second her quick-witted flair for humour had deserted her. Then she announced "Volunteers wanted, you, you and you." Came her authoritative, but joking reply. "This is your Maitre de Cabine speaking. Attention please! In the absence of the Captain, I have taken charge here. I shall supervise the operation from the safety of where I now sit, thank you. Now ladies, get on with it." A flatter than flat wheel change, on safari, surrounded by wild animals—how the Maitre de threw her brood to the lions is a photo and video record that the flight attendants would die for!

This was their finest hour. They all wanted photos of each other with the appropriate spanner in hand, but the idea behind the group picture had a mischievous twist. I believe it appeared in the Swiss airline magazine with the caption 'Whose afraid of the big bad wolf?' Hackles and his mob could be seen in the background with the Maitre de conducting operations from the safety of the roof hatch!

We passed by Petal on the way to camp. The lionesses and cubs were seen moving cautiously through the swamp towards the hills and the resident pride had now taken up a high point overlooking 'Tiri-Tiri'. The Queen, her cubs and the boys must stay alert. Territorial supremacy in the area had now been re-established by the lions.

Our group of intrepid hostesses was still chattering excitedly about their 'daring' escapade in changing the tyre as Maitre de, now nicknamed 'Mother Hen', ushered them aboard their flight to Nairobi. Andrew, the cook, insisted he too should come along to inspect their aeroplane – he had never been close to one – he just had to touch it! Thunder in the hills warned that a heavy storm was approaching and it would be a bumpy ride home in the DC3. The pilots wasted no time in getting airborne. I could see a waving hand at every window as it passed over us.

I suddenly felt very deflated. How would the veterinary team cope with the waterlogged road through the hills? Would they possess the resolve to make it through? I was doubtful.

The weather was turning against us and Petal must be attended to first thing tomorrow. I would stay with her throughout the day to ensure she recovered fully from her darting; in fact I had already planned in my mind to take the camper and stay the night with her. This would be her little family's first experience of a true Mara electric thunderstorm and they can be frightening. The huge cumulonimbus is pumped up by the updrafts from the hills to heights of fifty thousand feet and more. I personally find the fork and sheet lightening quite scary. On a night like this the wildlife takes to the open plains away from trees and forests; they too sense the danger of lightening strikes.

I carry in the camper a large twelve-foot square piece of waterproof tarpaulin that acts as a roof covering for the awning of the verandah shade netting. Placing the tarpaulin flat on the ground and then parking on top of it, keeps the soil and grass underneath it dry. Once the storm is over I drive off, remove the tarpaulin and 'hey presto' there is a dry patch for Petal to lie on. If the signs are for a night of miserable drizzle I drive back onto the dry patch. Petal knows the form and will, on most occasions, take cover under the vehicle. Just a little thought and care for her cubs would be appreciated tonight!

The plan worked. The three hour storm abated at about 9.00 p.m., but a light drizzle, the fall out from the towering anvil above us, was to continue well into the early hours of the morning. A late radio call to camp confirmed my fears: the veterinary team had not arrived! This was not surprising. They would have taken refuge en route or spent the night in their vehicle and, most likely, be stuck somewhere in the hills. The camp mechanic Nyundu, Patrick the number two driver, and two members of staff were instructed to leave at dawn and back track through the hills, locate them and escort them direct to where I was. Petal was soaked when she arrived at the camper about midnight, with four bedraggled cubs in tow. The lions or hyaenas would not bother her tonight, the black cotton soil surface becomes too slippery and resembles a skating rink; this does not encourage predators to hunt.

It would not be wise for Petal to feed again before her tranquilizer. It appeared she had consumed a small meal whilst we were at lunch in camp, most likely a Thompson's gazelle fawn. I had noticed several vultures in the 'Tiri-Tiri' tree, plus another picking up scraps from the ground not too far from Petal's original rest point.

It was a fitful night's sleep for me. I was unsettled and anxious about Petal's forthcoming 'medical'. I kept questioning in my mind – was the veterinary team proficient and experienced in darting cheetahs? They are delicate creatures with a big heart and surprisingly small lungs, which limits them to short bursts of high speed and the need for prolonged panting and rest, to run down their turbos after a two hundred metre, sixty-mph chase. Petal, I knew, would try to fight off any feeling of unconsciousness in her mothering state. Might it be possible to try to set up the same 'on the bonnet' blowpipe dart scenario that worked so successfully with Dieter? Petal might not cooperate this time! She had not shown too much inclination to jump on the bonnet since having her cubs.

I soon realized I was crossing my bridges before I came to them. It was mindless trying to plan too far ahead.

Kibet had instructions to set off from camp at dawn to seek news of the 'leper' and try to locate his whereabouts. It would be pointless curing Petal and not him. I suspected it was he that had infected her. But for certain, I knew that 'supersonic cheetah' would avoid going anywhere near the three boys. If they found him in their territory, they would kill him.

I had just finished a late breakfast. The sky was clear and Petal had moved from underneath the camper with her cubs to her favourite umbrella tree. The sun had appeared over the hills, its rays burning off the silvery dew. During the night a heavy, dense mist had enveloped the whole of the ground area around us; as the sun rose higher the mist began to rise as steam to form once more into low cloud. I forecast another night of drizzle.

Out of the rising mist appeared a white Land-rover covered in mud. It occupants looked bleary-eyed and hungry. This was the Kenya Wildlife Service veterinary team; they had spent an uncomfortable night in a ditch! The rescue team had found them sound asleep. Their only choice was to wait until the sun dried out the track, but help had arrived first and the search crew had winched them out. It was 9.00 a.m. My instructions to the team were to get the job done and then go to camp, have a meal and wait there for news from Kibet. They may have another darting job to do.

Any chance of enticing Petal onto the bonnet was out of the question. She viewed the arrival of the white Land-rover with suspicion. Though she had never set eyes on it before, she knew instinctively, like all domestic dogs and cats, that 'this was a Doctor'.

I questioned the team closely. Had they darted cheetahs before? What was the dosage, how long before recovery? If she didn't go down first time then what? Would a second shot of tranquilizer be safe? Was there a danger of overdosing, thereby inducing cardiac failure? The standard reply to all of this was, "It will be okay." This did not convince me. "Who tutored them", I asked? "A vet from London" they said, pointing at the vehicle – a donation from a caring Zoo.

I retreated some one hundred yards to observe the darting through binoculars. I wanted a videotape of the whole proceedings and a blow by blow record of my comments. If anything went wrong heads would roll and they knew it. The team manoeuvred their vehicle into position to about fifteen yards from Petal, lowered the window, took aim and fired; there was a sharp crack. Petal jumped up and ran, the cubs scattered in every direction each looking after their own safety to get away. Two came towards my camper and hid underneath, the other two I saw running far apart some two hundred yards away. Petal turned to come to me having seen her two cubs safe with me; she hesitated, looking anxiously in the direction the other two had gone. The first dart had struck home; I could see the red dart locator flag high on her front shoulder. Five minutes passed with no sign of any effect; she seemed stunned but was still standing. A second dart struck home. I began to panic inwardly. This was what I did not want to see. A member of the veterinary crew started running, his overall tails flapping, chasing after the two other cubs; the scene was beginning to get chaotic.

The cubs underneath my vehicle panicked, seeing the coat tails flailing, they too took off in the opposite direction. This was all going pear shaped and horribly wrong. My immediate reaction was to go to Petal, but first I must get a line of sight on the directions of all the cubs. They had disappeared into the mist. I sent out a blind transmit emergency call for Kibet to hurry back, we required urgent help. No reply! He must be out of range. I spoke to the camp and told them to keep calling Kibet and to send Patrick out to me here ("Mambo imiharabika hapa") –"Things have gone wrong here"!

Petal was fighting off the tranquilizer effects; the 'Queen', as predicted, was not going to submit. Then there was a third 'pop'; that was it, no more! I was fuming, inwardly cursing to myself that I had even contemplated letting this team act on Petal. The whole show, so far, had been recorded on video. All hell would soon hear about this, including the Director of KWS. This was a botch up from beginning to end. These guys were total amateurs.

Petal was now staggering and looking dazed, yet somehow managing to summon every bit of strength she had in her body not to succumb. Another ten minutes passed; she flopped down, but was not out.

The third dart had finally put her to sleep. A small wedge was cut out of her right ear for further laboratory tests. This nick in her ear became her recognition marker for life.

Sarcoptic mange at its worst. Petal's body was covered in these suppurating sores. The mites were eating her alive.

Kibet and Patrick arrived and could not believe what was happening before their eyes. Kibet, in his usual controlled and gentle way, went forward to the head vet and spoke. "You have seen and learned something today, my friend, a cheetah mother with cubs like this has the power of God behind her to protect her children. Kill her and the people of Mara will banish you from here forever." This was Kibet showing his true anger.

I walked up to Petal, calling her name and for the first time in our association, I stroked her along her back, still talking gently to her. She recognized it was me. Petal was crying, the tears rolling out of her golden eyes; I felt sick and angry at the whole incompetent show. If she survived this trauma, would she ever be the same gentle beast again. I would have to prove my loyalty to her by locating her cubs and returning them to her personally.

After what seemed to be an age, she lay down on her side. The third tranquilizer had finally put her to sleep. Kibet had driven off with Patrick in their respective vehicles to search for the cubs. In my anxiety at Petal's state, I clean forgot to ask whether he had located the 'leper'. It was of little importance at this moment.

Petal's body had half a dozen reddened suppurating sores and the tips of both ears also showed signs of being eaten away. The 'Ivomec' injection was administered and the sores treated with gentian violet, (a purple liquid antiseptic) mixed with yellow Picric – another liquid disinfectant. A small wedge of flesh was cut out of her right ear for laboratory analysis, for official confirmation that the disease was indeed sarcoptic mange. This wedge became her recognition marking for life, a chink on the tip of her right ear; her beauty now ruined, but for a good cause.

I was clock-watching and counting her heart rate, which was slow, but regular. Her body temperature had dropped alarmingly; the antidote was given and I continued to vigorously massage her body all over. I wanted to be alone with her when she came round from her anaesthetic; if animals can have bad dreams, this was to be Petal's worst.

The vet and his assistants drove off to camp, nothing more in their heads but food, leaving one of their team somewhere in the bush, still looking for two terrified cubs. Kibet soon arrived with a big smile on his face. He had found the missing assistant up a 'Tiri-Tiri' tree, trying to coax the two spitting and snarling cubs to give themselves up. By placing the vehicle right under the tree, Kibet was able to stand on the roof hatch and stretch upwards and pluck them out from underneath the top of the umbrella tree. "Eh kali sana." ("Very wild") he said, showing me both his hands in a shredded, bleeding state. I could see who did the capturing; the vet's assistant was unscathed. The capture of the cubs was a great relief for me. Petal was still very woozy. I took the two cubs, one at a time, and presented them to her. They were no longer spitting, fiery little creatures and lay down nervously, but quietly at their mother's side.

Many female cheetahs bring their cubs into the 'Tiri-Tiri' area opposite my camp where these trees are plentiful. They provide a quick and safe getaway for their little cubs from most predators, even leopards. The thick umbrella is almost impenetrable.

During all this commotion, I had mentally pictured the direction and the area where the other two cubs had fled from underneath the safety of the camper. I drove towards a clump of bushes and found them huddled together. They allowed me to pick them up, making no attempt to run away. I placed both of them in the passenger foot-well of the vehicle cab next to me and drove back to where Petal and her other two cubs were resting.

I opened the passenger door to let the two little cubs see for themselves where their

The 'Tiri-Tiri' tree

mother lay. Out they hopped, as if it were a regular happening, full of confidence and ready to play with their siblings.

Kibet set off once again to look for Patrick in the other vehicle. Again, I forgot to ask him about the 'leper'! 'Queen' was still struggling to keep awake, though she had only partially recovered her senses. The initial trauma, three doses of tranquilizer and her refusal to submit had sapped her energy. She was totally exhausted, comforted only by my presence, knowing I would take care of her babes. They too surprisingly, after their 'up the tree capture', were happy to settle down beside their Mum, their little minds accepting my presence close to their mother as part of family in this, their new world.

I was very aware of the dangerous implications of planting the seeds of confusion into the cubs' instinctive reactions at this early age. Petal and I would teach them 'the code' of recognizing me and my approach to them. I taught Petal and the boys, at the early age of five months, the dangers of 'Morani' cattle herders and other humans approaching or passing close by on foot. It was a simple experiment. I arranged for Maasai cattle herders to participate and offered them two hundred shillings each (approx. £2.00), to take part.

Petal was still very woozy from her anaesthetic
I took the two cubs, one at a time, and presented them to her. They were no longer spitting
fiery creatures. Later I located the other two cubs and brought them to their mother.

The idea was for the Morani to creep up on the four cheetah cubs when Petal and I were
at rest, wearing their tribal red shukas (wrap-around), and war paint, then charge out of the
bushes directly at us, whooping, brandishing their spears and throwing their knobkerries wide
of the mark. The loud 'whoosh, whoosh' of those weapons travelling at speed with a
vengeance through the air is frightening. There was only one such attempt made; it was
extremely well acted by the Morani and took us by surprise. All the ingredients of an actual
hunt were present. Had it been a 'real' attempt, I would have been the first casualty!

The cheetah family outdistanced me both in reaction and speed. We never forgot that
lesson. Petal always made sure to keep plenty of distance between her and the Maasai cattle
herders. She too had been taught the hard way by her mentor. 'Give the Maasai a wide birth';
this was imprinted in their minds at every opportunity by me whilst out walking with them.

Passing tour drivers stopped by to enquire about Petal's health. They too had heard of
the shambolic way the veterinary team had displayed their professional incompetence. The
drivers brought good news about Petal's brothers. 'The boys', all three of them, had been seen
on Euphorbia Hill that morning. I was keen to see them too and dispatched Kibet, via camp,
to drop off the hungry and exhausted assistant, then proceed up to the hill and locate their
whereabouts. My plans were to stay the night with Petal, leaving nothing to chance, until she
was fully recovered. The boys would be seeking out their sister very soon!

I would be on hand for the safety of her cubs and to ensure no more traumas occurred to this confused and terrified family. The situation must be calmed down to re-establish their trust and confidence in me. I must continue to prove to the family that I was not a participating individual in their latest 'ordeal'. The doctor and the white Land-rover were now pictured indelibly in their minds as an object to fear. As a parallel to this, our domestic pets can be seen to tense up as they are driven down 'Veterinary Lane'. They too recognize 'this is the road to pain and suffering'.

Kibet had seen the boys enter the thick leleshwa bushes at Euphorbia Hill. They would rest there until sundown and then make their move. Petal too just might head for the hill. The leleshwa bushes would provide cover for her but it would not be a safe place for her cubs. 'Tiri-Tiri' offered tall trees for her cubs to shin up. My bet was that she would stay and hunt in this area for the coming weeks.

I did not sleep well, my mind was troubled. I lay awake for hours listening to the sounds of the night; the moon was full and bright. From my bunk I could see Petal cat-napping with her four little cubs snuggled up together; would the boys harm her cubs? For sure they would meet up. The cubs were sired by Namibia, a lone ranger out of his area. He was poaching on their prey and committing a crime by pollinating the flowers in the boys' patch! This was reason enough for Hackles to kill him.

I would need to be alert and prepared to counter this hazard. Though Namibia was a big, fine male cheetah he would be no match for Hackle's brute strength and aggression. No doubt, in any confrontation, he would be assisted by Hopeless and Whispers. Namibia's chances of surviving and escaping from a three pronged attack were very thin. Kibet had returned to camp with a promise to be with me at first light. He too was aware of my anxiety and realized that the cubs could be harmed.

Short sharp gusts of wind had rocked the camper in the early part of the night and soon after midnight the weather returned to a cool and calm breeze. Now, free from the jerking motion of the camper, I fell asleep for several hours. When I awoke, Petal and her cubs had moved. Nothing as far as I could sense had disturbed her. Sometimes she would move a little distance from the camper at night, knowing that inquisitive hyaena and sometimes lions are drawn towards an unfamiliar object or odour in their territory; a different smell of wafting roast beef or whatever for them is always worth checking out! I cook and eat dinner early to avoid the odour that humans often find pleasurable. For me, newly baked oven bread never fails to entice me, sometimes just to walk in and enjoy the smell; then my willpower fails me! I'm tempted to buy and, with butter knife in hand, the damage is done!

I hurriedly turned on the spotlight, a searchlight by another name. The two million-candle power stabbed the darkness. I stood on the bonnet gradually moving the five hundred-yard beam through a full three hundred and sixty degrees. There was nothing I could see resembling a cheetah or a pair of eyes reflecting from ground level. Cheetah eyes are very sensitive to excessive bright light and only a fleeting glimpse of a yellow tinged reflection is seen before they either close their eyes completely or look away. Lions' eyes at night will only give a brief yellow flash.

I doubled up my distance acuity by putting on my night binoculars. My field of vision lit up like another Milky Way. Most wildlife grazer's eyes reflect like sparkling stars at night. I could see a herd of wildebeest on the move, mingling among the Thompson's gazelles and impalas leaving no chance for me to distinguish any predator, let alone a well-camouflaged cheetah and her cubs! By driving in circles in the Landcruiser I could start a stampede; this must be avoided when baby cheetah are around. Something was disturbing the wildlife! Caution would have to be carefully exercised. There was insufficient moonlight to see clearly with the naked eye. I switched off the searchlight and returned to the night binoculars. These would not disturb or panic the wildebeest and hopefully all would then return to normal – but that was not to be. A pride of lions had spooked the huge herd of several thousand animals. The ground trembled with thundering hooves; first moving in one direction, and then changing to another, back and forth. The scene was chaotic and terrifying. For Petal and her cubs the safest place would have been under the camper, but she had vanished.

I was helpless with no other option but to stay where I was and weather the dust storm until morning. This was truly a stampede of stampedes; the dust was so thick the night vision binoculars could not penetrate the brown curtain. The morning would turn this nightmare into reality. I was sick to my stomach. Had Petal sensed the danger of the impending stampede and quickly moved with her cubs out of harms way? The hours and the minutes to the equatorial dawn that brought the first light rising into the eastern sky seemed to be wearing lead climbing boots.

It was 6.00 a.m. and still too dark to see any distance with the naked eye. The night binoculars helped a little but the green transparent flare they produced within their focus did not provide the clarity I required to scan into the distance. God's precious light, clear and bright daylight, has no substitute. Minutes later Kibet arrived as he had promised, spot on time. I related the night's drama to him and my concern for the cheetah family's safety. What could have caused such chaos? "Only lions," I said. "Maybe it was the boys on a night's hunting spree," he replied. I hadn't even considered that possibility. "At night?" I questioned, "Hardly likely I think". "Labda ni hawa tu", Swahili for "Possibly it's them." Kibet had a gentle but endearing way of making his point. He would never think of putting his view over by uttering a forceful or blunt statement. To do so was not in his nature, he was a gentleman and always acted with mature and considered tact.

The kettle was boiling, tea was on the make and taken with a couple of digestive biscuits, it would temporarily satisfy our pangs of early morning hunger. Kibet and I decided to split our search effort into two parts. I would take the northern sector of the 'Tiri-Tiri" and quarter it, traversing the breadth in square sections. Kibet would take the southern section and traverse its length with one hundred-yard spaces between turn around. We were to radio each other and report any fresh carcass finds, then examine them and decide which of the predators was responsible. A trained eye can usually determine the killer by the evidence left behind.

By this time several tour vehicles offered to help us in the search. They were given carte blanche to roam at will so as to speed up the search process. We were not on the same safari radio link as the Mara Safari Club vehicles and so anything interesting would be 'flashed' to us by headlight bush Morse code. A long flash means 'Come quickly', short flashes 'We have found a kill', hazard lights 'Lions are here', indicator lights 'Nothing yet, we're still cruising'. This is an extremely quiet and efficient way of instant communication avoiding the crackling blasts of loud radio voice transmissions that can be carried on the wind and heard for almost half a mile.

Kibet was searching the Euphorbia Hill area. He was following his hunch. Half-an- hour passed—no flashes, no communication, nothing from anybody. I was getting seriously worried. Then I saw what looked like four lions resting at a distance on the open plain. I broke off my search and drove directly towards them. My find turned out not to be lions but the three boys, and who should be there with them – their sister with only two cubs! Neither Petal nor the two cubs, one male and one female, were in a happy state. Was I too late? Had the boys killed or chased away the other two little cubs? Something very serious had happened. I called Kibet to come to me and I sent out a long flash to the tourist vehicles. They were almost out of sight, a mile away and may not pick up my signal. I got out of the vehicle and walked slowly over to Petal, quietly whistling our cheetah bird like chirp. Suddenly, I remember that Hackles and I had never settled our differences. This could be his chance to even up the score with me. I hesitated and decided to return to the camper for the fire extinguisher, returning once again to where Petal was cowering with her two babies. The boys were spread out with Hackles positioned closest to her. His eyes were firmly fixed on me, watching my every move. I could see he recognized me by my khaki safari outfit and made no aggressive moves, on the contrary he seemed placid but very alert to his surroundings. Hopeless and Whispers were grooming themselves and remained unconcerned about their foster-father standing amongst them.

By this time Kibet had arrived with a knowing look on his face. "Ni hawa tu," he said, "It's them all right that caused the stampede." This was a statement which could be taken several ways. Yes, it was the boys; there was no doubt about that. Secondly, he was sure it was they who caused the complete uproar in the semi-moonlight – not an unreasonable suggestion. I began to think his intuition was right. No fresh carcasses had been found and no lions were near about. Without further instructions, Kibet proceeded to drive around us in ever widening circles. I was hoping against hope he would not come across two little carcasses or bits of cheetah cubs.

Despite a complete and thorough search that continued for several days, no signs and not a hair of the two cubs could be found. The lack of any evidence proved nothing either way, or any way, that Hackles had been responsible for the cubs' disappearance. Petal was very nervous of his posture when he approached her in my presence. He too was cautious of the fire extinguisher. He recognized its presence as my deterrent from the past, to counter aggressive behaviour from any wild animal, including himself that decided to attack Petal or me.

Hackles chose to approach both Petal and me. He was intent on smelling and sniffing the air and the short grass around where the cubs lay and also took a keen interest in Petal. I knew he wanted to check out who was the 'father' of the cubs. Petal had set up a long, high-pitched whine. I had never heard this before, it was almost the same sound and level as a domestic cat makes seconds before entering into a caterwauling spat. Hackles was nervous of Petal and her show of fangs suggested, 'one step further and I'll latch on to your nose, my dear brother.' Hackles backed off. I wasn't quite sure what he had in mind but I felt his intentions were not honourable. I believed that he was probably going to try and panic Petal or the cubs to scatter them, and from there one would see what his true intentions were. This whole twenty-four hour drama was turning into a total disaster; months of preparation had gone into ensuring the 'Queen's' safety during her pregnancy. With several near-misses with poachers and now this—two precious bundles of fur had vanished! I was gutted.

Two keys to part of my project had gone missing forever, at a very early age. To have assisted another five wild cheetahs to adulthood would have been an achievement in itself, remembering that one cub, the runt of Petal's first litter, was alive and improving in health under the care of a private veterinarian in Nairobi. My hopes were to return her to the wild to be with her siblings, Sprite and Scamp. This in itself was another aspect for the continued survival of this family.

Hospitalized cheetah cubs released back into the wild, without linking up to their former existing wild family, have little chance of survival. Captive breeding and their subsequent release into the free range wild is also a dead end project. South African cheetah breeding stations have learned this the hard way. The same does not apply to their release into fenced areas. Here they can survive, provided there is lots of space and many acres with plenty of prey. This is the key to their continued, controlled survival. Where the free-range cheetahs' prey is decimated by legalized culling and the illegal bush meat trade, the sheep and cattle farmers will suffer great losses and few will tolerate the cheetahs' presence. Farmers will eliminate them for they have no value outside the protected areas on shoats and cattle ranches other than those bordering Game Reserves or National Parks.

Calls for compensation for wildlife predators chomping on domestic stock, is becoming the clarion call of today; overtaken only by the claims for heavy compensation for the loss of human life from encounters with elephants, hippos, crocodiles and other wild predators.

Where will the funds for compensation come from? The wildlife itself, of course! How will this be managed? This is the major problem, which the Kenya government has yet to come to grips with, let alone support a system through its wildlife forums. They are losing the battle as poachers decimate the pockets of wildlife that survive, by the grace of the cattle farmer, who has now become isolated and surrounded by burgeoning populations of humans, eking out their survival on semi-arid land that turns into desert at the slightest whiff of a drought. Famine follows – the population has to eat to survive and so the wildlife takes a hammering – the predators' wildlife food chain then crumbles.

I was keen to observe the interaction between Hackles and his two brothers, their sister and her cubs. This was a coming together of the original family, minus Prickles who died of recurring intestinal blockages. 'Fur balls', the curse of the cat family, are a common malfunction in the intestinal tract following long periods of feeding on African hares and other furry creatures. Whispers and Hopeless were good friends – they just tagged along as back up to Hackles. He was the Alpha male in scientific speak and his body language was law,

I was witness to this incomprehensible attempt at incest and coalition rape
Petal reacted with such speed and agility, even the camera shutter-speed failed to 'stop' the
action. Petal fought them all off and the cubs ran towards me for safety.

even in my presence. Their hunting skills had been honed to perfection through brotherly
team spirit. Hopeless was really not so hopeless anymore, he too was a fine athletic specimen,
much lighter than the heavily built Hackles. Whispers too was built like a greyhound, for
speed. Both had that happy-go-lucky carefree attitude that is important to coalition harmony
and a definite asset for longevity, especially when there is a 'control freak' in charge!

Although the boys treated Petal with guarded respect, they were curious about the cubs,
in particular the little male. Hackles became overly investigative again. The evening light was
fading and darkness would soon be upon us. The rising moon would be coming over the
Aitong Hills within the next twenty minutes.

Hackles' attitude now had changed to a much bolder and aggressive mood towards Petal.
Within a split second all hell was let loose. Hackles attacked Petal; Whispers and Hopeless
backed him up. What on earth was going on? Petal fought them off. The two cubs ran to
where I was standing. Petal rushed towards me and took refuge underneath the camper, as if
to say to me, 'there's trouble on the way; you take care of one cub and I'll look after the other'.

The moment of truth had arrived. I held my flashlight beam full into Hackles' face as he

Order and calm was restored
The petrified cubs returned to their mother. Hackles, by the look on his face, knew that my presence was to protect Petal and her two cubs.

approached me, head down. The light was blinding him. In my left hand was the portable fire extinguisher which I intended to use at the first sign of any attempt by Hackles to snatch or kill the cub now shivering uncontrollably between my boots. 'Don't even think of it, Hackles'. I said to myself. 'You are about to get something to remember for the rest of your days'. The cub, petrified and whimpering with fear, peed all over my boots. That was the true defuelling ticket that Hackles was searching for. This was the clue to the intruder's identity. Namibia's picture would be posted all over Hackles' territory – 'WANTED—DEAD OR ALIVE.' The pressure was lifted almost immediately. I was shaking – my adrenalin had been working overtime too. Hackles, now satisfied, returned to where his brothers were waiting some twenty yards away. His problem had been solved; it was time to move on and hunt down Namibia.

The moon was now up. I was sad to see them disappear into the darkness. Would I ever see them again? They were a tough trio, set to roam the hundreds of square miles of the Mara and Serengeti plains. I sent out a silent prayer to Namibia. 'Don't mess with these guys; stay away, stay safe, but don't forget to come and visit us one day soon.'

Petal and her two cubs stayed the night under the camper with me. It was a sleepless night for all of us. I dared not leave her for a second; I wouldn't put it past Hackles to return! Were my suspicions valid? Was I becoming paranoid? I believe I had reason to question Hackles' motives.

Wildlife has its principles – it is called 'natural instincts'. Let us not try to interfere with this sensitive balance too much. Rigid, laid down scientific procedures permit no leeway to stray from the norms of the law of science as we know it, or rather, that method which we have been taught is right and believe must be followed. Our American allies in wildlife research have become much more liberal in accepting the undisputed value of unfettered hands-on projects, where many discoveries have resulted through unconventional observation which would otherwise have bypassed the vital missing pieces of Nature's jigsaw. So much research has been documented on wild cheetahs; many researchers, seeking their PhD's, have spent many hours studying the behaviour aspects of this beautiful and gentle predator, at a distance. They have been led by the principles of the methodology of scientific evaluation. In fifteen years of being permitted and accepted into the 'inner sanctuary' of the wild cheetahs' mind, and being led by their principles and practices in the free wilderness, is something that cannot come out of research, a laboratory or fenced enclosure. The cheetahs make the rules and I follow them. A captive born adult male cheetah, released into the wild, is like throwing your child overboard into the jaws of the first predator it meets. Streetwise, it will never be, and will not survive.

It is a well-recorded fact that infanticide occurs among lions; was this what Hackles had in mind? Yet moments before the trio left on their journey, Hackles allowed the male cub to sit with him. Petal, all this time, was in a high state of anxiety – calling her cub continuously to come to her. My finger was glued to the extinguisher trigger throughout this ordeal.

Captive-bred cheetahs will survive within the fenced ranches without their predators, lions, leopards, hyaenas and wild dogs, but the survival of the wild free-range cheetah, maintaining their wild instincts and man lending a supportive hand, under their rules, is to my mind the key to their future survival. Let molecular science and DNA come into the equation to try and eliminate the faults in their genetic paucity of variation caused by inbreeding. This to my mind is the way forward. Wild cheetah females are choosy. It is not just any male cheetah who rocks up that the female will agree to mate with.

Namibia was wild and came from afar. For him it was a long journey that took weeks of trickery, on my part, to finally escort him to his bride. His tenacity and his will to follow her sack cloth that she unwittingly urinated upon and sat upon during oestrus, showed it must have contained the full chapter of an invitation to him that she was his mate. I had fulfilled my dream and a photograph proves it, taken on the day Namibia chose to walk right up to my Land-rover door, look me in the eye, clamber all over the fender and bonnet and say 'I'm here, I've made it. Where is she?' My matchmaking had worked a treat – dragging that sack-cloth over many kilometres and days, had paid off.

My fear is the damaging result of incest amongst siblings. Some of it, just a mere click short of coalition gang rape, is a matter that has yet to find an accepted place in my mind. I see now why the female cheetah sends out her body signals 'You are not for me!' Natural instincts come into play; 'your blood line is too close; it is my offspring that will suffer the consequences.' As in humans, it is against the law. As in nature, it is against their instincts too, but it does happen. The three boys once tried to mount Petal before her first oestrus, she fought them off tooth and claw. I interfered and became Hackles' 'bete noir'. From then on my crime was never forgiven. I had dislodged his pecking order as top cheetah. The law of the wilds amongst males of territorial status is death to those who dare. I knew that I was on Hackles' death list and I had to be constantly on my guard.

Kibet continued his daily relentless search for the two cubs. Every tree and bush was carefully examined. The Maasai cattle herders and tour drivers were all briefed. It became a matter of national Mara importance to seek for clues as to what had happened to the two remaining little cubs. Petal herself did not seem to show any upset or loss in any form; nothing really that I could detect. She was still communicative and comfortable with her two remaining cubs and my presence. Female cheetahs seem not to be able to count. Lions can and will search and search, calling and showing distress at the loss of their cubs. Petal gave me little feed-back on her loss. I thought, on occasions, I could detect a little of 'what will be, will be' attitude. My gut feeling was that the stampede had panicked the cheetah family; the two cubs had become separated and had been hoofed into the ground and their little bodies pulverized. The cause of the stampede lay at the door of the cheetah coalition. I had witnessed before, several daylight examples of 'let's cause a stir amongst these clowns of the plains that forever follow us, snorting and telling the world of our presence!' The boys were very capable of doing just what mischievous boys do best—together they create hell amongst the pigeons!

Kibet reported seeing several Nubian vultures overly bloated, too heavy to fly any distance, sitting near a patch of blood on the ground in the vicinity of where the stampede occurred. His examination failed to reveal any clues.

Petal, as forecast, stayed in the Tiri-Tiri area for almost five months, within sight of our camp. Our airline clients came, they experienced the highlights and they returned again and again to watch and enjoy the progress of the two remaining cubs growing up. Regular updates were printed on their airline staff news circulars. The special safaris worked like clockwork and news was spread around the world to air travellers in casual conversation with passengers, telling them of exciting places to travel to and experience. The Mara North lodges flourished. 'Queen' was becoming a legend in her own right.

As time progressed, each of the cubs developed their own characters; a fitting name for each would have to be found. Soon it was clear the female cub was very sprightly, wide-awake, sharp and intelligent. I named her 'Sprite'. The male was a perfect pest, cheeky, mischievous and a scamp. I named him Scamp. He had a heart of oak, but pester me he did. When given the chance, Scamp would come up from behind and playfully claw into my trouser leg and trip me up when out walking – he enjoyed seeing me stumble in my tracks! His favourite lookout-point was the top of the camper; he would neither let his mother or his sister occupy his vantage-point. They were consigned to the Landcruiser bonnet. Scamp was intelligent; he

Sprite at three months old

Sprite learning to climb up the shin-up trees in the 'Tiri-Tiri' area.

Amazingly Sprite was capable of chasing, tripping, capturing, throttling and retrieving. She took great pleasure in presenting her catch to her mother to incise and prepare her dinner.

Scamp, the male, would trip up his prey but was then unsure of what to do with it.

Scamp, the lion-spotter!
Not even Petal was permitted to sit on top when he was on duty watch.

had exceptional eyesight and used the height advantage of the camper top to warn us of any dangers ahead. Lions in particular were his speciality, he could spot them from miles away, letting us know by growling and looking continually in their direction. Sprite was a young lady, quiet and respectful and a joy for Petal. Mother and daughter often played tag together whilst Scamp looked on as referee. Occasionally, he would tear into the frolicking duo, sending them sprawling into the dust. Petal would return the compliment by cuffing him lightly around the ears.

During these playful times Petal permitted me to introduce my ball game in which I could participate in a little fun with the cubs. The 'Queen' did not take part but lay to one side looking with keenness and pleasure at her children leaping high into the air, in an attempt to catch the bouncing ball which, when thrown vertically into the air by me, returned to earth to bounce back up again and again. It was made of solid compacted rubber purchased in one of the fun game shops in Nairobi. There was method in this game; it taught them the art of honing their lightening reactions by making them look up and timing their leap to cuff and down the ball on the upward stroke. Both would then pounce on it.

Friends of Conservation
Scamp, Petal and Sprite

They became very proficient in startling and capturing both guinea fowl and Francolin for our dinner. Petal approved and so did I! It was a pleasant change from dry British army compo rations. An American embassy friend of mine, who once came on safari, was able to provide me with a taste of their army rations. It was like eating out at the Savoy, with a choice of breakfast menu that definitely provided a kick-start for the gruelling walk ahead.

The cubs grew quickly. I watched with interest as their mother taught them how to avoid the dangers of walking into situations that could cost them their lives. Lion scenting and observing their movements was paramount at every wild animal crossing which we crossed, where lions or leopards could lie in ambush. The crocodiles in the Mara River were monsters, true craftsmen of their trade floating practically submerged, with only a pair of eyes and snout visible above the water, waiting motionless to pounce on any hapless creature that attempted to make a crossing. Petal often chose a safe point on the river bank to rest with Sprite and Scamp, never allowing either to approach the water's edge, even for a drink. Some of these giant creatures would crawl out of the water and sun themselves, jaws wide open, displaying sets of teeth that any dentist would have taken a month to extract.

This open mouth posture is designed to assist in slowly releasing the pressure of gasses that build up within the crocodile's stomach. It also assists in the process of fermentation and, in some cases, permits the fearless black and white feathered wagtails to clean their teeth.

Petal, Scamp the Lionheart, and Sprite would watch in fascination from a concealed vantage point. On one such occasion a young, lone male Thompson's gazelle chased out of the herd by the dominant male, thought he would make good his escape by running into the shallow river crossing in an endeavour to make the other side and safety. He had taken only a mere step or two into the water when this huge reptile, aware of the developing situation, slipped quietly and smoothly from his sun-bed into the water. In seconds it was all over; a grizzly and sudden end to the gazelle's life, watched by the pursuer and the cheetahs. Even Scamp could not hide his fear. A lesson had been learned. We moved away from the river with Sprite and Scamp looking over their shoulder with an expression that hardly required translation. 'Is that horrible monster following us?'

At ten months the cubs were becoming wise to the dangers within their Tiri-Tiri territory. Soon their mother would introduce them to a much wider world outside the terrain they had come to know so well. I too, learned the safe short cuts to their favourite rest up points and knew instinctively where to seek them out after weeks of my absence from the Mara. Sometimes they found me, and came to know my places of habit. This form of 'communication' was a constant source of amazement to many of the tour drivers who, after days of looking for 'Queen', would come to me in total frustration and ask for directions. I, in turn, bartered my information for the whereabouts of other cheetahs and leopards, including the three boys. Gradually a picture formed in my mind on the general whereabouts of these predators and their territories. Forewarned was forearmed, and something to pass on to Petal—that this human was not all baggage—whilst accompanying them in the bush.

Cheetahs' paws and black cotton soil do not fare well together, particularly after rain; the cheetahs soon become footsore caused by the hardening of the pea-size clods that stick to the hairs between their toes. Black cotton dries and hardens in a matter of hours and chafes against the soft skin on the inner side of their toes.

Alternate rain showers and sunshine makes for a black sticky gum-like surface that clearly imprints the cheetah's direction, a blessing for trackers to decipher other cat paws that during the wet season can be confused with the criss-crossing of hyaena and leopard prints. The cubs were very grateful when I offered them my chiropodist skills! When lameness set in, there was instant relief for them after removing the clods and applying some petroleum jelly to the chafed parts. This was rewarded by a reciprocating slurp to my ear. Their sandpaper tongues can remove human skin just like paint stripper, in seconds!

Several of the adult female cheetahs that Petal had introduced me to before her pregnancy, had taken up residence on the group ranches. Two were heavily pregnant and two had brought their young cubs with them. Rather than give them an impersonal number in my record album, I gave them names as I had done with Petal and her siblings. Now Petal's cubs had names too for my record. The tour drivers also cottoned on to the names and were able to identify the newcomers when describing the area where they had been seen on their game viewing drives.

It was important to check Scamp and
Sprite for early signs of sarcoptic mange.

Extracting a thorn from Sprite's toes.
I received a thank-you slurp for my efforts.

Open clinic!
The cubs were keen to participate in the weekly clinic.
They were always appreciative of any running repairs to their footwear.

The female territories were contained within a twenty-five square mile radius that sometimes overlapped each other. Astra was first introduced to me by Petal as a single female when Sprite and Scamp were about two and a half months old.

The extraordinary video I have of this scene took place near my camp. Astra had come in from the cold, taking her chance of being accepted into Petal's domain and when confronted by Petal, displayed a body language of total subservience to her. The 'Queen', regal in her dominant stance, accepted Astra, making it plain who was in control of this area. I was standing some fifty yards away, filming the whole proceedings. Moments later, Astra passed within a yard of me; my presence did not seem to bother her. I was transfixed by what I had seen. She acknowledged my presence in passing, confident that I would not harm her.

Astra, to my delight, showed signs of heavy pregnancy and, from what I could judge, was only days away from giving birth. I recalled that Astra had been seen in the vicinity after Namibia had mated with Petal, but had disappeared from the 'Queen's territory until now. There was a good chance that Namibia was the father of her expected offspring. I was overjoyed that her retreat into some very thick bush was within my camp perimeter.

News of another female cheetah with four cubs filtered in from the tour drivers' information network. This time it came from the head driver of Buffalo Camp, situated some five miles down river. Kamau had taken a keen interest in developments of the cheetahs in our area. Always willing to go the extra mile in search of our cheetah families, more often than not he was successful and passed on the news.

My camp became a regular 'stop by' to check out the latest 'Cheetah news bulletin.' Kibet had been given the visual co-ordinates of various trees, a large rock, a rocky crossing, a ravine and copse. The two drivers who passed this information gave it over to us in code. For example, in Swahili the code name for a cheetah was Madoa doa (spotted one). The Tiri-Tiri area was where the tall trees were in the three-thousand acre area. Bila shaka (without fail, in Swahili), was another forested area. An area where lions can always be found, and mawe ya chui (the leopard rock) and so on. The female cheetah with four cubs had been seen near Leopard Rock that morning. This was good news for Kibet and Stan. Their ten Swissair clients would be arriving by air at around 11.00 a.m., all eager to see the 'Queen' and her babes, plus Astra who had now taken up residence in the camp copse, occasionally appearing around midday, drinking from the 'karai' (bowl) of water that I had placed in a convenient viewing spot not too far from my tent.

I know that cheetahs drink copious amounts of water for some twenty-four hours before giving birth to tank up their milk supply. Also the proximity of water to their lair is important in avoiding long sorties during the heat of the day, thereby losing precious body fluid in the effort. Several days pass prior to and after the birth before they consider a quick dash out to hunt for food, returning by a roundabout way, seldom tracking back along their outward-bound route. This method of criss-crossing throws off most predators that, like the jackal and hyaena, have a well-developed and efficient tracking sense of smell.

The disappearance of Petal's two cubs several weeks ago in the stampede remains unsolved. Their chances of survival had long passed. Stan and Kibet located the new female and her four cubs; both remarked how unusually dark they were. All had clear-cut Plimsoll lines of dark hair as if they had waded through a muddy swamp up to and beyond their bellies. The mother was light in body structure and previously unidentified by Kibet or Stan. Kibet was of the opinion that she had come from 'very far'. Her cubs were about three months old. Their mother showed a tolerance for vehicles but the cubs were timid and suspicious, preferring to keep their distance from tour vehicles. I was intrigued by this information, went to check for myself, and sure enough the description was correct.

This was a new cheetah to the area. I too had never seen her before nor did she appear on any of my photographic records. These were encouraging signs that the North Mara Group Ranch land was becoming the breeding ground for the Mara cheetahs; it certainly looked that way. I named her Polo, a name that came to me out of the blue. So, all in all, the female count to date was Petal had two cubs, Astra I hoped, would produce four cubs, Polo with four cubs in tow, Hackles x three (that's the boys!) and Namibia, all breeding males. The tragedy that befell us was that of Pearl; another newcomer. She lost all her cubs to a leopard near Leopard Rock.

Pearl was a young first-time mother. She gave birth to three little cubs in a donga (dry river bed), within three to four hundred yards of a resident leopard's lair. Kamau had reported seeing the cheetah mother carrying one cub into the donga and, through his binoculars, he was able to see another two newly born ones not too well hidden. It would only be a matter of time. An hour later the leopard was seen emerging from the donga and the cubs had been eaten. Pearl also died in an attempt to defend her little ones. By the following morning her body had been consumed by the night clean up squad. This and the loss of Petal's two cubs was the tragic count to date. Nature's rules, if broken, have no mercy.

Much of my time was taken up with Petal, Sprite and Scamp. They were now growing quickly into their teens and, at eleven months old, were beginning to flex their muscles. However, tail chasing and attempts to hunt at speed were easy to achieve, but their lack of speed control and misjudgement ended up in disaster. They often collided with bushes that seemed to step out into their track, sending them sprawling in a cloud of dust! A look of dazed amazement suggested a little more than 'I got it wrong!'

Petal now appeared ready to leave the Tiri-Tiri area despite the security it offered to her cubs. It was time to take them out into the big world; secondary schooling was about to start.

For me this was a dream coming true. I prepared my rucksack with only the necessary essentials. Water purifying tablets were first on the list, compo rations (American army style preferred), paper water filters, a Swiss army knife that had so many gadgets to cope with every situation, my trusty light-weight fire extinguisher, of course, a square meter of light plastic sheeting, midget camera, mini first-aid medicine kit, spare pencil batteries for my walkie-talkie, flashlight and night vision binoculars, a light-weight waterproof sleeping bag, light-weight binoculars, a ladies handbag mirror, magnifying glass, mosquito special 'bug off' spray which Petal hated, my micro stove with odourless fuel sticks, tea bags and plenty of them. It was important that my waterproof back-pack remained as light as possible. Oh yes, mustn't forget my ostrich egg water bottle. Its thermal qualities and durable shell would keep water cold or

Petal walking her territorial boundaries
Sprite always positioned behind her mother and Scamp behind me. We spent many
days and nights out together.

Scamp was always up to mischief, trying to unseat me
We often growled at each other for fun. Scamp would reciprocate by playfully attacking me.
Scamp took great delight in tripping me up, cheetah style, on our walking safaris.

Cobra encounter!
About an hour after sun-up, we all set off on a walking safari with Petal leading the way.

Walking with Petal, Scamp and Sprite

Me running without cap
Earlier my adrenalin had run high when a huge three-metre long black cobra appeared from nowhere, ready to do battle with me.

A Cobra
I threw my red cap towards it to distract it's attention whilst I took to my heels.

hot, dependent upon my need at the time. A fishing line and several hooks were always handy too. The Mara River is full of edible fish; I expected to vary my diet with guinea fowl too. I must carry the rubber bouncing ball to keep the children happy! Another essential was flea powder, an efficient executioner for the bloodsucker flies and tsetse fly that bother cheetahs. I protected myself with the 'bug off' when passing through infested tsetse or horsefly areas. Petal would refuse to sit near me. She was allergic to the smell and sneezed continuously. I had to move a short distance down wind of her or be ostracized from her favours!

Later Kibet following at a distance by vehicle came across the same cobra, whilst searching for my cap. The snake suddenly appeared again and attacked the front wheel of his Landcruiser. The Canadian couple who took this photograph had visions of the reptile attacking them too. They, like I, were pretty shattered by the experience. My cap was recovered some fifty yards away from where I met the snake. Lucky for me the cobra was momentarily distracted by this red object. I needed those extra few seconds to put distance between us. The black cobra's venom is deadly. If bitten you have little chance of survival! I came across quite a few on our walking adventures with Petal and the cubs. It would be impossible for a fit human to outrun one if chased. These reptiles can reach a speed of almost

Crested Cranes!

I often thought about what it was that triggered this unusual aerial performance by the crested cranes when they spotted cheetahs. The cranes followed us for miles. A herd of some twenty Thomson's gazelles were so fascinated by this unusual scene that curiosity overcame their fear. The herd came towards us to take a closer look and Petal struck.

The end of a long walk
Resting under a tree having completed some ten miles!

fifteen miles per hour, and more. The beady eyes of that creature behind the hood personified the power of Nature. I must confess the sheer awesome strength of this reptile gave me the shivers. Thank goodness for the fire extinguisher. I often used it to good advantage on some of these occasions, when fired, it has a temporary blinding effect on snakes, but on that day I was not carrying it. It was due for a service pressure fill-up awaiting my attention. I had used up all the pressure the previous night when a herd of inquisitive elephants, some thirty strong in number, mistook my box on wheels for a toy to play with.

My excitement was already in high gear. However, there was one big 'but'! I had bet my last penny that Astra would decide to give birth on the very day Petal chose to leave the Tiri-Tiri area. Astra did not fail me – she did just that!

I was torn apart with indecision. Murphy's Law was at work again but my walking safari must go ahead! I planned for five nights out, with one night back at camp to revittle, have a welcome shower, and generally keep in touch with the stressed out world of pressure, politics and people. Kibet would park the camper in the area of our walk-about. I could then pick it up and drive to camp in my own time, day or night. I prefer to be totally free and flexible working to the cheetahs' schedule. I made no decisions for them except when they came into harms way. I was riding shotgun for the family. This they seemed to understand though sometimes my heavy footedness did give them cause for concern. I held back from their

Elephants on the move

The next day I was amazed to see not only thirty elephants as I had at first thought, but the complete herd that had made fun of my 'box on wheels' the previous night. I counted more than a hundred. They were moving silently. It was an awesome sight.

stalking lessons, lying low and watching through my binoculars. When the lesson was over, or they had blown their concentration, as children do, Sprite and Scamp would head back to where they left me. I tried to hide but it was a pitiful effort on my part; I was soon uncovered.

It was interesting to see, when they were at a distance, that my cheetah call carried well on the wind. It made them stop, listen, then change direction towards me. It was important not to compete with Petal or confuse them when she called. Petal returned my call on occasions when she was out hunting, particularly when the children were left in my care, but now they were old enough to accompany her it was important that they listened and acted on her command. It was a great thrill for me to see the cubs' excitement whilst sitting on their haunches, at a distance, watching their mother hunt; their ears tuned and awaiting her call to come and dine on the kill. Once the signal was given, they would tear off towards her at speed. At other times they would just amble along in their own time. Their hunger level controlled their energy and temperament.

Petal had made her kill and called for them to come. I was amazed at the distance – almost three hundred yards. Their sensitive ears had picked up their mother's whistle. She had downed a half-grown Thompson's gazelle, sufficient for all to feed on. This was hyaena country and they would be watching. Sometimes, hyaenas follow at a discreet distance and when the cheetah has made the kill, they steal it. This is why cheetahs gulp down their food; it is almost 'direct ingestion' for this very reason. 'Eat whilst you can and quickly before dinner is lost!' Yes, the clean up squad had been watching and my arrival at the kill was timely. Three hyaenas were approaching at a lope from three different angles. The look of disbelief I saw on their faces when they stopped some twenty yards away was hilarious. 'What is this?' They began moaning and whooping, calling for reinforcements. This show of aggression bolsters their courage when intent on stealing the kill. Hyaenas in numbers can be dangerous.

My surprise trump card gave me the advantage. Their confrontation was fearsome. Now with tails held high and heads lowered they mock charged us, baring their vicious looking teeth. I held our ground; Petal and the cubs were confident the situation was under control and that I would do the necessary and scare the pants off the marauders. I had to earn my keep this way, but there would be other similar situations where I would not get involved. The cheetahs must learn not to be lulled into a false sense of security by my presence. The family gradually came to know that when I was with them, their security was in place. When I was not, it was their lookout. Sprite and Scamp learned very quickly. Often I kept well away and out of sight. 'You are on your own Jack!' Those were the chilling words my flying instructor said to me as he stepped out of the aircraft, on the runway, and sent me on my first solo flight, and so it was for the cheetahs. The adrenalin pump starts the turbo, the mind and body muscles go to full alert. Right now it was all happening again to me. Fear triggers the body's adrenalin mechanism, that raw power surges through your system and blocks out all reason and pain. Instinct and training then take command of one's actions. I have been there many times. I acted quickly and fired the extinguisher directly at all three hyaenas now facing me. It had the desired effect, so good in fact that the large, aggressive, lead female hyaena toppled 'backside over kettle' with fright, in her desperate attempt to get away. Petal took advantage of this organized chaos, and mock charged them for a short distance in their hurried flight. It made her feel good to give them some 'stick'. Female cheetahs will seldom fight to retain their kill; they prefer to retreat gracefully and abandon their catch.

Having fed well the family moved some distance away from their kill to a shady single tree. That would be their resting place for the remainder of the day. They had over indulged and now sported magnificent pot-bellies.

This was my chance to take my leave of them and head off back to camp, via the area where Polo and her four very dark cubs were last seen. I spent several hours searching; the wildlife gave me no clues to follow, most of the gazelles were resting, unconcerned, under the low short acacia. Nothing much stirred. High noon was approaching and the equator heat mirage was already dancing its way across the plains, making it difficult to spot or distinguish the distant actions of the wildlife. I thought, I might as well go to camp and enjoy lunch with the clients. It was important too that I showed my face there; they would be keen to hear of my encounter with the hyaenas this morning.

Stan had delayed his departure awaiting his clearance for Australia. I appreciated his offer to continue to help me out with these safaris.

On returning to camp I gave Kibet the coded reference area of where Petal and the cubs were resting for the day. Kibet and Stan would be game viewing in that area this evening. More importantly, I wanted news of Astra. "Was she still taking water from the 'karai' near my tent?" "Had she been seen at all?" I asked. The only evidence was that the water level in the 'karai' was down and had to be refilled. The signs of cheetah paw prints were there too. The camp staff were sticking to my strict instructions not to disturb or walk near where it was suspected Astra's hiding place was. I would make use of the afternoon rest period to investigate, when clients were taking their afternoon nap before setting off on 4.30 p.m. game viewing drive. Tea and cakes at four o'clock was always a winner. This is a traditional safari custom at all lodges and camps. Our ten clients were all mature Swissair female flight attendants; the male variety had been left behind, making brown the body beautiful beside the swimming pool in a five star Nairobi hotel.

Once again it was a pleasure to be in their company. They were as keen as mustard to know all about nature, the wildlife, its wonders and 'The Queen' of the cheetahs. No mention had been made to them of Astra—that would come later as a surprise once I had confirmed her presence, but that plan was soon scuttled. Moses, the given name of my new young, very religious Christian tent attendant, came into the dining tent with eyes almost popping out of his head. He had actually seen the chui (leopard), drinking water near my tent. "It was a very big one, as big as a lion! It had many black spots, like this lady's spotted shirt," he said, pointing to one of the flight attendants sitting at the head of the table.

Leopards and cheetahs are one and the same to many young Africans who have only seen pictures and postcards of these beautiful creatures, despite the fact that most of their working lives are spent in remote areas. The 'chui' is known for its cunning and fierceness, particularly when cornered. Many a Maasai herder, defending himself or hunting to kill them for decimating their shoats, has been severely disfigured. This animal can kill if wounded and has the speed of an arrow when it attacks. The leopard is number two on my list of the most dangerous African wild animals. The buffalo is number one. A lone male buffalo will stalk a hunter down or wait in ambush for the right moment. Yes, I have been there too, and so lucky on each of my many unprovoked encounters with both of these cunning killers.

The diners were now electrified. "What is a chui?" they asked. "Leopard," said Stan. I chuckled. "Near our tents?" was the question most were asking. "No" said Stan mischievously, aware it was Astra, but not letting on to the clients. "Moses, where did you see this dangerous animal," Stan queried. "Near the boss's tent," he said. All eyes were now on me. "Maybe he was thirsty and wanted to drink my shower water," was my nonchalant reply. The girls were wide eyed. "But are you not going to do something like chase it away?" they queried. I replied "a leopard is too dangerous to mess with"!

I was beginning to think I had overstepped the drama act. Stan was in near hysterics and Moses had already taken off at high speed to warn the kitchen staff and Andrew the cook, to take cover! "It's up to you Dave", said Stan with a twinkle in his eye that clearly read as 'you started this buddy, now you finish it!' "Oh" I said, "let it be. We want our visiting wildlife to trust us. Wild animals have right of way here. We are their guests, so we treat them accordingly and always welcome them." This age-old patter of wisdom is never queried. Everyone settled down, excited at the thought that they were sharing this lovely 'Out of Africa' camp with the wild predators of the Mara. Nobody wanted to head for their afternoon siesta; there was a sense of expectation in the air. I excused myself and made off towards my tent. I felt many eyes boring into the back of my head as I walked away. Stan would keep the secret, and as he said, it was now all up to me.

I approached my tent cautiously making the cheetah whistle call. I looked over to where the 'karai' lay and there, a few yards further away in a sunny clearing, lay Astra quietly grooming herself. She had already taken her fill of water and was momentarily relaxing. I continued to my tent, still quietly whistling. She appeared not too concerned, but watched intently as I disappeared into my tent. Once inside, I went to the window and peered through the netting.

My immediate thought was to contact Stan on the camp emergency intercom. I called softly, "bring the crew to my tent via the front path." This route would hide their approach from Astra's view. It worked. The excited group were able to view Astra from some fifteen yards – but not one came with a camera. Mine was in the camper and there was not a video between us! Astra completed her grooming and quietly slipped away into the dark shadows, disappearing into the thickest part of the copse. Our new guest, I hoped, would stay a while.

Astra had given birth, of that there was no doubt. She was now slim and sleek and very hungry. Tomorrow she will hunt well away into the Tiri-Tiri. I planned to take the chance of her absence and listen for the tiny squeals that would direct me closer to her den. Petal and her cubs would be on their own tonight without me.

I planned to position the camper outside the copse, wake early and watch for any movement. By 10.00 a.m. that morning I had seen or heard nothing. Maybe Astra had given me the slip via an unseen route out?

Moments later, I spotted her returning downstream towards camp. As in our first meeting (through Petal's introduction), she passed within feet of where I was standing, by the front bumper of the campervan. Unconcerned at the camper or myself, she took little notice of my presence. I was amazed. Astra was showing unusual confidence on our second date – our first was now some three months ago.

It was important that the kitchen staff left no litter, food or disposable kitchen waste around the camp. All of it had to be taken away to our incinerator a mile away. Unwelcome scavengers are drawn to open rubbish pits.

I was surprised that Astra had decided to establish her lair so near to human habitation. It was true there was this link I had with Petal and her first litter of cubs – other than this there was no 'family' connection – Astra had come in from the 'cold'.

This time I was closer to the area of her lair. She had fed well, but was not too distended. Yes! I could hear the squeals of her little ones coming from the thicket. This was not the time to intrude or disturb her. I left quietly and unobtrusively, sensing she knew I was not too far away. I went to my tent, leaving the camper parked in the copse for the rest of the day, returning after a sumptuous camp dinner, to spend the night in the camper. It was important for Astra to smell and feel my presence close by as a friend and protector for her and her new family.

My caring attitude was rewarded six weeks later when Astra left the precincts of the camp and took up residence in the 'Tiri-Tiri'. The area provided a safer haven for her cubs to escape from predators. The 'Tiri-Tiri' tree provided a getaway as it did for Petal and her offspring.

I was out game viewing for the day with a television team interested in filming a documentary about cheetahs. "The Queen of the Mara" was about to appear on television, but she was suffering from stage fright! We searched and searched; Petal had gone to ground somewhere with Sprite and Scamp. In my frustration, I headed for the 'Tiri-Tiri' and found Astra with her four little cubs.

Now was my big chance. Would she allow me to approach her and her family? I had briefed the television crew; this could be a scoop for them. Either I would be ferociously challenged, or Astra would take off over the savannah at high speed. The moment of truth had arrived for me to prove my worth. It was midday, the equator sun was hot and the dry air made one's lips dry and crusty. I carried the 'karai' to the shade of a nearby tree and poured the contents from my yellow plastic five-litre water can into it. Astra, still quite relaxed, was some twenty yards away from me; her cubs were with her, watching my every move. Their instinct, I could see, was to run; they were looking about furtively just one click away from panic. I moved back some ten feet from the 'karai' expecting all the family to come together to drink. However, it was only Astra who ventured towards it, leaving the children in a quandary as to what to do next. I saw or heard no instruction to 'stay' given by Astra to them. She lapped contentedly, occasionally taking a breather and looking around and once again, paying little attention to me.

This was my cue to move forward to within a few feet of the 'karai'. There was still no reaction or sign of fear from her. I was wired to the television crew by a small walkie-talkie transmitter – they joked that my heart was pounding so loudly it was interfering with transmission! Moments passed, and then Astra made two short sharp calls, the same bird-call I use with Petal. Now four little thirsty mites joined her. I could feel a surge of adrenalin through my system, a wonderful feeling, identical to that one experiences when winning a sport gold medal or accepting your degree at University, that first kiss from your first love, making you want to reach out to the stars and touch them. This was my breakthrough. I knelt down and gently touched each little one on the forehead. Astra was in an attentive, crouched, but relaxed, posture nearby. I wanted to cry with joy as each one I touched looked up at me. I prayed the television crew were filming and getting this action without the presence of Petal. Astra had obviously remembered her first introduction to me by the 'Queen'. Now this was her way of returning the favour by introducing me to her little family. I was ecstatic. The cubs lapped and lapped, I did not want them to stop drinking, but stop they must for their little tummies would surely pop.

Finally, the spell was broken, Astra rose and walked back to her tree and her cubs

Astra!
This was my first encounter with Astra and her litter of four two-month old cubs.

followed, each looking back at me, as if to say 'Well, come on, you are one of us now.' Yes, the television crew had filmed this amazing happening. They too were over the moon; the two assistants were spellbound and open-mouthed. They had witnessed something quite extraordinary. I too was on cloud nine, unsure whether this was all a dream. Indeed, for me it was a dream come true.

The film crew were scheduled to move on to another camp several miles across the plains. Their next adventure was to take a hot-air balloon flight across the Mara; the wildebeest migration, one of wildlife's most spectacular events, was now in flow. The vast herds were congregating to cross over the Mara River into the Maasai Mara plains. The advance wildebeest party had pioneered the route several months back. That fateful night had taken the lives of two of Petal's cubs. I could think of no other reason for their disappearance, they had just vanished with no trace.

I stayed with Astra for the remainder of the day. She was content to rest and feed her cubs, dozing off into a light sleep and then waking and nodding off again. As the day progressed she became more confident that my presence was there to serve as her security guard. She slept soundly in half-hour shifts, a form of deep sleep cat-napping as seen in our own domestic cats. Soon, too soon, sundown was almost upon us, a time for savouring the colourful setting and its euphoric glow. It was the cheetah's prayer time and for me too. I thanked the Lord for another incredible day. Today was made for me to remember – it had been a perfect day.

The two males of this litter survived to adulthood, establishing a new territory some five miles south of their birthplace outside the game reserve in the Olaro-Orok valley. Astra moved away towards the Siria escarpment of the Mara Triangle, crossing and re-crossing over the Mara River Camp bridge. She often came back to visit Petal's territory near my camp. I was happy that Astra always remembered our first introduction. I treasured her trust in me.

This new development with Astra required me to take stock and think hard where this communication and close contact would lead. The cheetahs, both Petal and Astra, were calling the shots and I was going along with them. "Jubatus", their scientific name has a long history of past association with man. Cheetahs were the regal pillars of the Emperors. They graced their halls and provided an unusual hunting pastime for royalty of centuries ago. I was once invited to the Palace of the Emperor, Haile Selassie of Ethiopia, in the late 1960's. There, sitting upright either side of the palace entrance pillars were two of the most beautiful cheetahs I had ever seen, dressed in resplendent hunting regalia. They were strikingly proud of their

I was always fascinated by Astra's body language.
She displayed such superiority. I felt humbled in her presence.

royal privileges. My thoughts turned to questioning their past association with man. Was I witnessing their dormant genes now manifesting and seeking man's help in arresting their slide towards extinction? I was almost convinced it was.

Research and science had not yet ventured into this wild phenomenon that I was experiencing. I was touching on something which, even I, was unsure of why all of this was happening? I could understand Petal's reactions as 'paying homage' in another way to her foster father, but Astra was in no way 'related' to the 'Queen' or me.

My anxiety was centered on me overstepping the mark and leading them into domesticity. This would be fatal for them and their cubs. They would present no 'fear' of humans and not realize there was a bad side and killer element within the two-legged Homo sapiens. There was sufficient prey around in quantity, thus avoiding the need to predate on the Maasai calves and shoats. However, an aged or sick cheetah will take advantage of an easy catch in the field, where young Maasai herders have fallen asleep under a bush, and one bad apple spoils it for the whole cider chest, making double trouble for all the other law abiding cheetahs.

A plan finally evolved in my mind; I should concentrate on protecting Petal, Sprite and Scamp, observe and record their new ventures as they progressed to adulthood and beyond. I planned to 'hold back' on Astra and her family, permitting her the full freedom in deciding her future. I would be there to arrange medical assistance, if necessary, and to continue the precious contact by providing tender loving care and water, when they needed it.

Stan's days with me had come to an end. The authorisation for his relocation to Australia had finally come through. Jamie's departure had been delayed and she offered to assist. She was not in a position to match Stan's professionalism, but was keen to assist me with Petal and particularly, Sprite and Scamp. This young lady had passed her bush driving trials with flying colours and possessed that very necessary ingredient of 'communication skills' coupled with a sense of mature responsibility. This was fertile and intelligent ground to work with.

Jamie's husband's overseas posting had turned into retirement so her days with me in the field would soon be cut short. I jumped at her offer to come into the fold once more, albeit for a very short period of time. To find maturity combined with wildlife experience and the right communicating skills would not be an easy task. Those that have any potential had already been snapped up, or had established their own safari business. The pioneering spirit of the early twenties through to Kenya's independence belonged to the women. They were the rock that supported their settler husbands and partners in many ventures that saw hardship, toil and tears, particularly in cattle and agricultural farming. The film 'Out of Africa' portrayed the life of Karen Blixen so perfectly, a tribute to the actors, Meryl Streep and Robert Redford, and the film director Sydney Pollack. A brilliant Universal/Pollack production that immortalized the scenic beauty and the life of Kenya's early settlers filled with tragedies, triumphs and lost love. I was proud to have played a small, unnamed part in the flawless film, even though I was just one of the crowd!

Much as I wanted to stay with Astra and her babes, I knew I must return urgently to Petal. It was important that I follow her trail and note the marking of her territory. Her 'beacons' were now being revisited and the children shown the extent of her patch. This was to become theirs too, approximately fifty square miles scribed with a circle paralleling the Northern Mara Reserve boundary. Seldom did she enter the Game Reserve – there were too many lions, too many hyaenas and lots of hassle from tourist mini buses. She preferred to stay within the group ranches where the few lions there kept a low profile for fear of retaliatory measures from the Maasai Moran.

It would be interesting to see where Astra would stake out her claim and whether it would overlap into the 'Queen's' territory. Time would tell and I would know in about four to six months.

These cats require a sizeable territory to survive. Bovine tuberculosis and feline aids are becoming a problem threatening African lions. We must develop contingencies with the few options that are now left. My observations to date reinforce the absolute necessity for an action plan to conserve the large cats of Africa.

Bad news always comes like a bolt from the blue; no sooner are things looking rosy than something is bound to happen. News was passed to me by the bush telegraph. 'Queen' was in frenzy. One of her cubs had been injured by a tourist vehicle and was lying in pain, in a wooded copse, unable to move. Her other cub was missing. These were the bare details that were given to me by one of the Mara Safari Club tour drivers. My alarm bells were ringing – which cub was hurt and which one was missing?

I drove at breakneck speed to the given coded, visual reference to a place called 'kivuko mbaya' (the bad crossing), referring to a stony dry river-bed crossing that passed close to a wooded copse. The twenty-minute journey felt like an hour. On arrival, Kamau, the faithful head driver from Buffalo Camp was waiting. He pointed to the copse. "I think it is Spritey that is badly hurt. Scampy cannot be seen anywhere, and Petal has gone to hunt for food." Kamau was upset and unsure of what had happened, but he was able to confirm the story that it was a 'rush around' tour bus that was responsible, other than that he knew no more. He had not witnessed the incident.

I went into the copse barehanded. Yes, it was Sprite. In her pain and anger, this beautiful beast was transformed into a snarling, dangerous cheetah ready to bite anybody or anything that dare come near her. I was momentarily taken aback when I realized I may not be able to control her and that I could be the target upon which she would unleash her fury. If only I had a tranquilizer gun! Unfortunately, firearm regulations and the Kenya Wildlife Service were unwilling to let anybody, except a qualified wildlife vet, of their own choice, attend to any wounded or problem animal. It is a short sighted and expensive policy to bring a vet by air all the way from Nairobi. Several days might even pass before anyone arrives.

I had to work fast. I radioed a passing aircraft and asked the obliging pilot to contact Nairobi and do the necessary – get a vet here by yesterday – fast! Meantime, I could not just sit there and do nothing. I had to get through to Sprite. Yes, the water 'karai'! She was in shock. Hurriedly, I collected the 'karai' and plastic water-can container and returned to where she was, calling softly to her in our cheetah whistle. I poured out the water into the 'karai' and walked purposefully towards her. The charm worked; she tried to sit up to drink, but collapsed back onto the ground, crying out with pain. I tilted the 'karai' under her chin and thankfully she lapped. By stroking her body in long, light, gentle full palm movements, she began to relax. I could see her right hip joint was dislocated, but thankfully, no legs appeared to be broken. A broken limb in the wild signifies the end. Like a horse, it has to be put down.

Dr. Wambua of K.W.S. Veterinary Department had answered my call. He had given me his word after the Petal darting disaster that he would personally attend to my emergencies. True to his word he was on the afternoon inbound flight, now due in an hour. Kamau would meet the aircraft at the airfield and bring him direct to me. Dieter was otherwise engaged in Tanzania – I already knew that. The hours dragged on as if all the clocks had all stopped.

I must stay with Sprite and not leave her for a moment. It would be impossible for her to defend herself against any predator that could be lurking in the forest nearby.

Kamau had set off to the airport, but soon came back to tell me that he had found Petal. She had made a kill and was eating a half-grown impala male, sufficient for her and Sprite. Scamp's whereabouts had not been located. All of the North Mara tour drivers were out looking for him. I was unable to come to any valid conclusion what might have happened. What sort of 'accident' was this?

Sprite was totally exhausted. Fortunately, my gentle caressing and presence had given her courage; I understood her fear of being unable to protect herself. Now she was in a shallow sleep; this could mean the shock had passed and warmth was now returning slowly to her body. Dr. Wambua arrived. Kamau, in the meantime, was dispatched to locate Petal once more, and reported back that she was on her way, struggling to carry the remains of the impala. There was not much of it, but enough for Sprite to eat. I went to assist Petal. Sprite was not happy at my departure and protested loudly.

My son and daughter-in-law, John and Catherine, had arrived from England to spend a little time with me. This was going to be a day for both of them to remember. Dr. Wambua felt it prudent to keep away from Sprite until my return.

I eventually found Petal, struggling down an animal track almost half a mile away. She was in a tangle with the loose ends of her kill, and not in a very good mood but permitted me to carry her burden and followed close behind. My son had the presence of mind to videotape the proceedings.

I had abandoned the camper whilst I took a short cut across to where Sprite lay. Both mother and I had brought food for her. This was a joint operation and it was manna from heaven for Sprite, attended hand and foot by the 'Queen' and her foster father. Sprite ate voraciously; she was hungry. I sensed this 'accident' was not of today's date but probably twenty-four hours old and whoever was responsible would have got out of town by now. We required to know more: what had happened to Scamp? Was he lying somewhere injured and unable to move? Would Petal, once Sprite was able, help us to look for Scamp? We could only wait and see. Sprite ate well and took another drink of water from the 'karai'.

It was now time to tranquilize Sprite. Dr. Wambua attended to the syringe and dosage and I was to apply it. Petal was uneasy at Wambua's presence, continuously eyeing him

Sprite lies injured
Pain had transformed her into a snarling dangerous cheetah ready to unleash her fury on anybody that came close to her.

suspiciously from a distance. Any suggestion of a dart gun or even its 'pop' would send her into orbit. It had to be by the syringe.

Being the son of a cattle rancher I was well trained in the art of injecting cattle and sheep. This was not new to me, but nothing must be hurried. I went back to the routine of stroking Sprite, pinched her now and again to get her used to a slight prick—after all those darned blood flies were doing the same. I took the opportunity to use the flea powder and spread it around her underside, the blood flies were soon abandoning ship to escape the effective pyrethrum powder. The prick was quick and placed intra-muscularly into her rump. I believe she hardly felt it, for she looked at me with an expression that said 'What was that?' and went back into a light sleep.

I was relieved, Dr. Wambua was impressed and my photographer son thought I was totally mad! A few minutes later the drug began to take effect. Her eyes, now fully open, began to stare and became glazed, her head lolled about on her shoulders; seconds later Sprite was out for the count. Wambua moved quickly. Petal was still eyeing us from the bushes some thirty yards away. He placed some petroleum jelly into Sprite's eyes and covered her head with a cloth. Then, between us, we gently maneuvered her right pelvis hip-bone back into place.

I took my rifle and set off with them
Petal walked at Sprite's pace for an hour. Darkness was almost upon us and Sprite decided
she could go no further.

    The job was done. A good body check for any external injuries was carried out but none were found. The Vet applied the antidote and we both moved away so Petal could return to Sprite and be there when she recovered.

    This was a slick operation that worked a hundred percent from start to finish. I could hardly believe it was not a dream, and even today, as I write to remind myself of the incident, I have to marvel at the sheer chance that it all went according to a hurried plan. Both Kamau and Dr. Wambua were smiling as they waved good bye on their way to the airport. They knew we had succeeded in handling a difficult and unusual situation.

    Several hours passed and dusk was approaching when Sprite, still 'groggy', was being persuaded by her mother to move out into the open and away from the wooded area. I was surprised by the move. Why?—it seemed a good safe place to stay the night. Then I realized it was the remains of the carcass smell that might draw the attention of a leopard or hyaena. Good thinking, Petal! I took my rifle this time and set off with them, leaving my son and Kibet to take care of the camper and await further instructions.

    Petal, walking slowly at Sprite's pace, continued non-stop for almost an hour. The moon was up and I was wearing my night vision binoculars. Once out in the open and well away

Two heads better than one
I left them snuggled up to each other. The night had turned bitterly cold and Sprite would
need all Petal's body-warmth. This is how I found them the following morning.

from the forest, Petal 'camped down' for the night. Sprite was once again at the point of exhaustion. I left them snuggled up to each other. Sprite would need all of Petal's body-warmth; the night had turned bitterly cold.

On my return journey through the forest, I came across a small herd of buffalo, about ten females with young calves. Female buffalo with young will charge blindly at anything and everything that moves, particularly at night. Many of my close friends have been killed by these cunning beasts. Having the advantage of being able to see in the dark I was able to circumvent the herd by tracking downwind.

A hot shower, a tasty dinner and several stiff whiskeys, in pleasant company, put paid to a day when Murphy's Law met its match. We had righted the wrongs for a change. I spent the rest of the night with Petal and Sprite, parking the camper some fifty yards from them. She must have been feeling bewildered at the disappearance of Scamp. I too was gutted. In a little under twelve months, we had lost two of her family with no clear-cut cause for Scamp's disappearance, and now her daughter having come within a hair's breadth of being maimed for life, was a little too much to stomach. However, with the whole of the Mara out looking for Scamp there was still some hope that we might find him.

Most days Petal continued to walk about her patch with Sprite, each day adding a few more kilometres to their trek. Sprite was badly bruised and rested often. Days went by, sometimes she never moved from where she lay whilst her mother went off to hunt.

The problem was the distance from where Petal's kill was made to where Sprite lay so, having feasted sufficiently, Petal permitted me to take the rest of the carcass, dangling from the front fender, back to Sprite. Petal followed in due course at her own pace, sometimes taking several hours, with bush stops and catnaps en route. Her world of 'no hurry' really appealed to me!

Stan had packed his bags—it was a sad farewell but I admired him for putting his children first. I could see, etched on his face, the deep disappointment of leaving a job that most people would have 'killed for'. The call of the wild is a very powerful drug; it gets into the system. One is drawn back again and again to Kenya just to feel it's magic and the peace of the wilds.

My time with Queen and Sprite grew less. My clients and business had expanded to a point where the camp crew and I could hardly cope having recently lost the services of both Stan and Jamie. To farm out the clientele would have been disastrous. Many safari operators volunteered their services and transport when their business was lean. Some offered their personal services free of charge, but I could sense the order of their ploy was not in my favour. The intent was to try and poach the repeat clients.

Astra was coming along fine. She was an excellent and caring mother and her four cubs were growing fast. She too was ready to establish her territory and was due for her big walk-about with them. Astra was easily identified by the three-dot triangle on her chest.

When I wore my 'identikit' recognition khaki uniform Astra displayed an outward calm which she transmitted to her cubs. Any other clothing would not be acceptable and she would bolt.

The 'Queen' was restless; She had lost Scamp. He was too inexperienced to have gone off on his own, neither was he fully capable of hunting for his own food. A sighting of a young, single, hungry male cheetah was passed to me. Kamau took it upon himself to investigate, but came to the conclusion that this animal was from the 'Serengeti', well out of his range and in unfamiliar territory. Other unconfirmed sightings were bandied about, but the sources of information were those herders who could not differentiate between a leopard and a cheetah. Scamp was never found or seen again.

Petal, Sprite and I spent many nights out together they having walked me off my feet! Today I was just too tired to trek back to the camper, but happy that Kibet was standing in for me entertaining the clients. He was very popular. His gentle, kind and considerate ways, plus his expertise at being able to recognize any bird and quote hook, line and sinker, the page number, the place and related patter, left me wondering where his photographic mind had been developed. Leslie Brown and Don Turner, authors of 'The Birds of Africa, were Kibet's mentors at one time in the past. They were well respected by international bird-watchers that were besotted by any LBJ (little brown job) with a feather sticking out of its bum! I did not have the patience to sit there and discuss the virtues of 'birding'!

CHAPTER 15
LEUKAEMIA STRIKES

MY annual flying licence medical, my 'MOT' as I called it, was due. I hated giving my blood to the blood-sucker department, but my GP insisted. Malaria, of the worst kind, was rife in the Mara. I did not take prophylactics until I really felt the early symptoms coming on – then I would take the cure. Two tablets – no, not quinine – but Metakalfin, an effective single-dose cure. I had been feeling tired and washed out, but put this down to the heavy physical workload. My GP, a brilliant and ancient gentleman could spot trouble a mile way. After what seemed like pints of blood had been sucked from my body, the lab prognosis was not good. My PSA was very high and this suggested I was heading for a major prostate or big C problem. My world was shattered. How could this be happening to me? It only happens to others.

I took the next plane to South Africa for another major check-up. I wanted a second opinion. Sure enough, there was something wrong. My PSA turned out to be normal for a man of my age, but my platelets were shot. In layman's terms, the count was low. The factory in my bones was producing low quality, immature blood cells, characterized as myelodisplasia, in medical terms, a form of smouldering leukaemia. Worse still, there was no known cure. This blood disease was considered life threatening. My world went upside down. "How long?" I asked, "Months? A year?" This disease could accelerate, it might plateau or it could explode into full-blown chronic or acute leukaemia. How had this happened? "The cause is not known," was the physician's reply. Panic stations set in. I had to get back to peace and quiet to think! The shock played on my mind day and night. I had been to the red line before, on several occasions, in particular a horrendous air crash which left me struggling, for almost three and a half years, to find equilibrium in body and soul. I, like some of the injured Battle of Britain pilots, was pretty well smashed up physically and mentally. My saviour was the expertise of the plastic surgeon, Sir Archibald McIndoe and his special nursing team at the world-renowned Queen Victoria Hospital at East Grinstead in England.

Here I met many brave men. They were the remnants of the badly burned and injured fighter and bomber crews that survived the Battle. Personalities, like Wing Commander Douglas Bader, the RAF flying ace and others took me under their protective wing. They made sure I did not let go of my precious life.

Now, once again, the fight to survive was on. I felt the tiredness in my bones and in my body, but I had no medical tools to fight the enemy. I would have to dig deep into my soul and communicate with my maker. Somewhere, beyond the distant stars, I knew I had a guardian angel looking after me. I knew her voice and it was that of my wonderful mother who died painfully of cancer at a young age.

On one occasion, it was her voice as clear as day, that navigated my aircraft with me at the controls, through the clouds above the Voi mountain range. My single engine Piper-Cherokee Six had driven a piston through the cylinder head. With a dead engine I had nowhere else to go but down, and fast, it was only the wind beneath my wings that kept me afloat for seven kilometers. I could see nothing ahead; the instruments had shaken themselves into a stupefied flurry of useless crazed information. I followed the familiar voice. "Turn left, now turn right, place your match box under the flap, it will give you the correct degree of flap. Watch your airspeed, it's too fast; slow down and keep her floating a few clicks above the stall. When the stall-warning screams, put the nose down and trim out gently." All of this information came from a lady who knew nothing about flying aeroplanes. My mother was a white-knuckle flyer of the first order. She maintained 'if man was to fly, he would be born with feathers'. "When you break out of cloud – act fast – turn hard left; there's a mountain a few hundred yards ahead." True to her word, there it was an all-blue and ugly sheer face of rock. Was this all going to end up again in East Grinstead and another fractured marriage? My first had gradually drifted apart during my self-rehabilitation in struggling to return to my original status quo. Counselling, as we know it today, was not understood.

Months and years of pain wears down the fuse of patience and tolerance, there are character changes that few seem to understand. At that time modern-day counselling did not exist. My children still do not understand the changes this incident created in my personality. I had pulled down the steel shutter—a long lasting sub-conscious protection against pain and suffering.

I quickly glanced across at my passengers, Madame Dard, a beautiful French lady was sitting next to her eighteen-year-old daughter, even more beautiful—and single! I realized I must bring this machine to earth in one piece. The voice had left me and I was in clear skies. I was trained to fly at Kidlington, a wartime British RAF airfield. The RAF instructor took me to hell and back when out of the classroom. He made me fly that 'training crate' as if it had no wings or engine. We practiced stalls, spins, engine failures and loops upside down, in cloud. 'Crazy attitudes' he called them, and at the end of all that when I thought I could control the brute in any situation, he said "When in doubt, just let go, it will come out itself!" "Thanks," I replied. "After all that madness, you tell me now?" That madness saved my life and the lives of my passengers. My effort was rewarded. I received a personal letter from Wing Commander Mac Mackenzie, DFC, AFC and author of 'Hurricane Combat', a brilliant account of his daring experiences in the air during the Battle of Britain. I treasure that letter. He was an ace pilot and knew well the skill required to survive this complete mechanical failure. It read, "Well done, David! I congratulate you on your dead-stick landing. Good luck for the future, you live to fly again."

I thanked my instructor in silent prayer. "You trained me to fly and to listen to good advice, never fly by the seat of your pants in thick cloud and always believe in your instruments." Unfortunately, I had no instruments to believe in! It was my guardian angel that saved me.

Chronic Leukaemia was now knocking at my door. The time had come to consult my higher authority once again. Her presence, I feel, is always close to me. I never need to speak; only think of her and the voice of advice is there. "What must I do now, Mum?" I asked. Her words came through loud and clear. "Face reality, my son, sell your business, set up a wildlife sanctuary of your own. That is what you have always wanted in life." But what will happen to Petal and her family, Astra and Polo and their families, the boys? I could not bear to leave them. Namibia! His Queen would like to see him again as well. The voice was firm, "But first, David, do as I say—there will be time later to visit the Mara."

Petal was due to come into oestrus in a month's time. Sprite would not stay around too long. After learning the ropes she would be on her own to face a life of solitary wanderings, hopefully with a new family. Who would be their lucky father? Not Namibia, I hoped! The blood-line was too close. But how was all this going to help me beat this leukaemia? How was this therapy going to benefit me? These were some of the questions I asked myself.

After several months I sold my safari company and my beautiful 'Out of Africa' camp. I had found and purchased the sanctuary on the edge of the Nairobi National Park. The deal was all done and dusted. My mind became occupied with its construction and planning. I had my own team of tradesmen. This was a complete diversion – the thought of leukaemia went on to the back burner. My enthusiasm was at full charge. Then came the day when my body was telling me, 'Hey, rest a while, go away and touch the stars with your 'Queen'. I did just that.

My camp staff continued working with the new owner. Kibet had gracefully returned to his tribal home and Jamie left with her husband to parts far away over the seas. In my heart I knew all of this was to prepare me and help me to get my house in order.

The Kenyan people were also preparing. Their house was in disorder. Elections were looming and a change of guard seemed necessary. They were tired of rampant corruption. Judges and magistrates became involved in scandals and backhanders. The worst forms of injustice had now taken hold and corruption had seeped into the very seat of Parliament. It had to be seen to be believed—there was neither law nor order.

The elections came and went with hardly an incident. This was a complete surprise to everyone. The bets had all been placed on the side of violence. The pundits were wrong. Almost a year has now passed and the battle to get to grips with the embedded corruption continues with little progress. Yes, there has been a change in the guard, but will they deliver? All of these cast a shadow over the Kenya people and what is left of Kenya's wildlife heritage. Some of the fertile savannahs of the Maasai Mara have been turned into wheat lands. Should Kenya's tourism fail, the burgeoning Maasai population, where the average life expectancy has recently increased by twenty-five percent, will extend its pressures into the game reserves. The large cattle herds now appearing, as a result of profits from Group Ranch tourism, will lead to overgrazing. Cattle grazing will also overflow into the game reserves. This is inevitable. Wildlife will always lose out on this front. Cattle, wildlife ranching and controlled tourism must merge. This is the only way forward now for the Maasai Mara

News is filtering in from the arid lands of the north. These vast acres of bush land, north of the equator, are home to many species of wildlife that nature has adapted so they can survive in dry and hot conditions. The desert is encroaching from the north at a frightening pace and the sands are marching southwards. Climatic change may halt or hasten this phenomenon, but upmarket tourism is thriving on the large, privately owned ranches. The local Samburu tribe, blood brothers of the Maasai now see great potential in these new ventures on land previously thought to be of no use except for sheep and goats. If this destructive element of domestic browser can be phased out of the equation, then these lands will become a haven for wildlife.

I knew I had arrived at the crossroads of my life. Prior to this the road ahead had always been clear in my mind and the traffic lights were always green. Suddenly, they had turned red. The major road that lay ahead had only two options, and only one of these was right. Should I go north to the U.K. or to South Africa in search of medical attention? The ailment had no known cure. Progress in research to understand its many forms was slow in the U.K. Scientific trials were bogged down by fear of the unknown effects of certain drugs. However, South Africa and the U.S.A. took a more positive and direct stand. In China and in particular Japan, scientists seemed convinced that solar radiation and the fall out of radiation from the atomic bomb had much to do with the possible cause of myelodisplasia.

Surprisingly, offers to purchase my wildlife sanctuary and my Nairobi home came in from several quarters, at a time when Kenya's economy and the value of property was at an all time low. The market was dead, with little sign of any recovery on the distant horizon. The offers were very reasonable and I accepted. The inevitable and expected delays by lawyers never materialized; in fact, all the legal and required transactions for both sales were completed within six weeks – a record by all accounts. I was now free and happy to feel the wind under my wings once again, heading south I left Kenya behind, but not its memories.

The long and tedious search for a cure could be likened to being a door-to-door salesman; doors were shut in my face. Nobody wanted to buy my wares and nobody seemed to care. I joined the rat race of numbers, not a human anymore or even an individual, but just a number among many numbers. Everybody else had a problem; they wanted to tell theirs, but were not interested in mine. I realized those of us that have lived a life in the wide-open spaces of Africa and seen the broad horizons, clear and clean, speak a different language. We see things from a different perspective and we go about them in another way. The direct way—get to the point. Second opinions were sought in Johannesburg. There was hope this blood disease could be beaten! Much of the cure had to come from within myself. There was always a helping hand in each South African Hospital that I visited. They were up-to-date, efficient and very professional but they did not have a medical cure for myelodisplasia.

Britain's health service was in a mess, overloaded with spongers from poorer nations. It was not my wish to add to the numbers game and so I settled for an 'Island in the sun', from where I could reach any destination if I so wished. The wrench and translocation was almost unbearable, but the sea came to my aid. I cruised in the Mediterranean and the Indian Ocean

Sanctuary Place—my dream home
My own African artisans, trained, tried and tested under my supervision, built sanctuary place.

and was terribly seasick in the Bay of Biscay. I lectured and gave wildlife talks to the many well-read people who filled the cruise liners lecture theatre to listen and see the extraordinary videos of my years with the 'Queen of the Mara'. Many passengers were charged with the urge to visit the Mara; others flew the air safari from the port of Mombasa to see this incredible animal. It was the highlight of their safari. The 'Queen's' fame began to spread like wildfire on the high seas.

My life had suddenly changed. The combination of the locks that held a possible cure were being slowly unscrambled by the boffins, but it would all take time – even years. The bottom line was that my life could be prolonged with platelet and blood transfusions when the time came.

Sanctuary Place, although sold was still available for me to occupy as and when I required a roof over my head. There was also a small cottage for my personal use. I therefore had a base in Kenya and the camper for safaris to the Mara. When the chips were finally down my home in the Channel Islands was available and medical attention was near at hand.

I was the architect, designer and problem-solver. It was a joy to work with them. Each took great pride in ensuring that every aspect of its construction was to the highest standards. The Nairobi Game Park stretches as far as the eye can see from the viewing platform. Wildlife of every description can be seen throughout the day. It is wonderful to hear the lions' roar echoing through the valleys at night. It broke my heart having to sell it. This was my very own piece of Africa.

The problem I faced in Africa was the risk of contracting aids. How could I be sure my blood infusions would be one hundred percent screened and clean? My circle of Kenyan friends would all gladly help out, but sooner or later they would run out of blood when my need became a weekly requirement!

A year went by as if it was only a month. I kept myself busy, traveling and setting up a new home, making new friends and keeping in touch with old ones, visiting doctors who stuck needles in me. I was beginning to feel as if I had a hedgehog for a bed companion. The platelet blood count was dropping alarmingly; time was running out for me.

I must make my final visit to Petal. Her fourteenth birthday was approaching and now she too was on borrowed time. Word filtered back to me that she had been visiting my old campsite and had been seen close by my tent on many occasions, looking old, thin, arthritic and unsettled. It was definitely her; the chink in her right ear was the marker. The call of the wild was beckoning me. Petal was calling. We both had unfinished business to attend to. It was a year since I had been to the Mara. Would she recognize me? I had no doubts. The 'Queen' had always been faithful to her one and only foster father. She allowed and trusted no one else to come close to her. Others had tried to impersonate my image and tactics without success.

One morning I awoke feeling very unsettled with a sensation that something was wrong or about to happen. "Go now, go today." It was that familiar distant voice I knew so well. I packed my bags and, with ticket in hand, I took the next plane out of Jersey. The Channel Islands had become my new home.

The flight was long and boring, with not an empty seat to allow for extra comfort. The guy next to me took full advantage of the free liquor and put himself out for the count before we hit the turbulence of the Pyrenees. Like the Bay of Biscay, it can be rough and bumpy. Maybe I should have done the same! Instead, I was white-knuckle flying, visualizing all sorts of disasters. We were literally flapping our way across the Mediterranean to Africa. How do these wings stay on, let alone the engines? The marvels of aircraft construction these days have always impressed this old bush pilot.

On arrival at Nairobi International airport familiar faces greeted me. Immigration and customs officers smiled and shook hands with me, 'What have you brought us?' stamped all over their faces. They were hesitant to push their luck with this man who had a reputation for locking up those corrupt civil servants that lined their pockets by confiscating excess 'duty frees' and re-selling at a three hundred percent profit. A single visitor's visa paid in dollars or pounds and fake-receipted was worth a dinner for four at any five star hotel in Nairobi. I refused to agree to any of this corrupt nonsense.

With the formalities done and dusted and a genuine three-month visitor's visa stamped in my passport, I was on my way. The taxi driver promised me that I would arrive safely at my destination, and for a few extra shillings he would 'fill up' at the nearest petrol pump. The fuel gauge had seen better days as the needle pointed to somewhere which suggested that the only fuel in his vehicle was in the pipeline!

We left the airport in a cloud of white smoke, only to find the front left tyre was one pound short of pressure from being a complete flat. The spare tyre—what spare? That was being 'fixed' at some joint down skid row! The look on my face suggested that he should light the taper and run. I was ticking like a time bomb. Other taxi 'hopefuls' must have been watching from the wings. How the bush telegraph works in Africa! Suddenly, I had the choice of two within minutes; both were telling me their chariots were full of fire and rearing to go.

I proceeded to carry out an inventory check. I had been caught out many times and this time I was going to check everything; fuel gauge (half full), wheel spanner, jack, spare tyre fully inflated but no tread, road licence, valid, or was it? Insurance was on a week to week hand to mouth payment. The check-list seemed unending. I had to make a choice. My old trick was to ask "Have you change for a 200-shilling note?" The first one to say 'yes' got the job. The moral behind the question was that at least he had money in his pocket. Most of the others had spent theirs at the airport bar and reeked of the 'go faster changaa' (60% proof home brewed alcohol drink) that fired up their system into 'African overdrive'!

With many pedestrians seen heading for the ditch on the way, this 'shock absorber-less' monster eventually arrived at its destination. The fare had already been agreed and the driver told there would not be a penny more, so there was little need for him to 'meter cheat' by taking the long way around. Short cuts can be either over the roundabouts, off road, or up one way streets. The shortest distance between two points is "Direckt, Bwana."

My Suntrekker Toyota camper, conveniently stored at my friend's garage, was ready and waiting. A supply of food and fresh vegetables was always obtainable along the road to the Mara. The Land cruiser was fitted with twin fuel tanks and a hundred litre water tank. Fuel and water would best be taken on board at Narok, halfway to the Mara, and the last filling station before the great Maasai Mara game reserve. It would take the best part of a day to make Euphorbia Hill by dusk. I would then shut down for the night, shake off the jet lag and hopefully wake up to a bright sunny morning, refreshed and eager to search for Petal. I must have been dreaming to expect her to perform her 'turn-up-man ship' after almost two years of my absence from her scene, but I couldn't help hoping!

It was now six days since I arrived. Every cattle herder and tour driver for almost two hundred square miles knew I was desperately looking for the 'Queen'. She had not been seen for several months. The camp was closed for the 'off season' and the tents stored away in containers. Astra, Polo, Namibia, Sprite and the boys were nowhere to be seen. The cheetah population of North Mara had disappeared. What had happened I asked myself?

Kamau had been transferred and many of the tour drivers, whom I met from the surrounding lodges, were new to the area. The area recognition codes had changed. I felt like a stranger, a newcomer in my old home range where, at one time, I could recognize almost every blade of grass. Tourism had collapsed; the lodges and camps were feeling the financial pinch and running on skeleton budgets.

In America, September 11 had taken its toll; I wondered who would be next. The ugly face of terrorism and its associated religious beliefs had turned the world upside down. I was in at the beginning in Aden in 1972 and realized we were in for the long-haul against formidable and radical assassins.

A few of the old tour hands from the Mara Safari Club bemoaned my disappearance, saying that the cheetahs lost their friend and had gone away. Maybe there was some truth in this. The daily search continued; I could not believe there was not a sighting, not a word, not a cheetah. It was all very ominous and empty.

I had sent for Kibet, via the bush telegraph. His home in Litein was only a few hours away by road, even less as the crow flies from where I stood. Kibet, the old faithful duly arrived, looking thin, gaunt and much older. He had fallen on hard times having spent all his retirement savings, and from what I could see much of it on the bottle. How many lives, families and tragic happenings has this curse of the western world wreaked havoc? The Muslim abstinence from alcohol has much to be said for it. Their religion will survive and so will their people. I have my doubts about the English people's faith. Its children of today hardly know the church and the Christian faith it preaches. Yet, in Africa, Christianity flourishes and grows day by day. The churches are full to bursting point.

I wanted a miracle. I wanted Petal to turn-up again and surprise me as she had done on many occasions when I returned to the Mara. I was at a low ebb; my morale was at rock bottom and I was not a happy bunny!

Kibet had fixed up his accommodation with one of his old buddies at the Mara River Camp. The idea was that I would collect him each day, he would drive and I would be on lookout and vice versa. This way, we hoped, would reduce the chances of a missed sighting. Driving and looking at the same time is a recipe for slipped discs and broken springs. Hit just one ant-bear hole and you are guaranteed to leave the vehicle suspension and your intestines solidly in the hole.

Today was day twelve – could tomorrow be my lucky number? I had already taken Kibet to his camp; here too there were no tourists. We arranged to meet in the morning, an hour after sun up. This is cheetah 'walk-about' time. Prior to this most cheetahs are still curled up, keeping out the night's cold. I had parked the camper on a hilltop with my bedroom window facing east. Like the cheetahs, the warmth from the morning sun, would kick-start my day.

It was pitch black outside. As I stepped out of the cab, my international mobile phone rang.

I stumbled back into the camper, fumbling in my safari jacket pocket. This, my only contact with the outside world was playing 'Scotland the Brave' with bagpipe accompaniment, in the middle of the Mara! I promptly dropped it. Any predator close by, with intent on an easy meal, would have stopped in his tracks. This robust machine kept on wailing from somewhere underneath the camper. Once found, I was in business.

I had forgotten about any dangers that might be lurking around me when I heard the voice at the other end.

"How are you getting on out there?" It was my wife phoning from Jersey. "Have you found Petal?" she asked.

"No, not a sign, nothing, maybe she is dead", I replied.

"Well" she said, "I had a dream last night. It was so clear. Petal is alive, she is looking for you and you will find her close to a small lake, with an island in the middle of it. Stay a while when you find it. She will come to you."

"Are you crackers?" I asked.

"No, it was so clear I just had to phone you. The dream was so very, very clear," she insisted.

We spoke of other things, the fog and rain in Jersey, but all the time my mind was racing.

I asked myself where this place could be, where is this lake with an island? It could be anywhere. It was certainly nowhere I knew in the Mara. I began to dismiss it all as just a dream, which it was, but my wife's insistence had a ring of the supernatural at work. After all tomorrow was the thirteenth day of the month, my lucky number!

'C'mon, David, let's roll at first light!' It was 6.00 a.m. and Kibet appeared bleary eyed from his roosting place when I knocked on his hut door. "Shauri gani?" (What's wrong?") he asked. I lied. "I've had a dream; we must look for a lake with an island on it."
Kibet looked at me not sure whether I had gone crazy or was joking. "The only lake I know that has an island in it is Lake Victoria, a hundred miles away," said Kibet. "And they put madmen on it to keep them away from society!" His message was plain and clear to me. I had to chuckle, even at this hour of the morning he still had a sense of humour.

I relented and told him the full story of the phone call I had received from Hilary, my wife. Kibet looked puzzled but not dismissive of the idea. "Pengine ni haki." (Maybe it's true.), he said. Like me, he knew of no lake with an island in the Mara. Only in the wet season could one take one's pick of many.

I made him a cup of tea whilst he dressed. 'Brunch', the bush word for breakfast and early lunch, would be the feeding order for the morning wherever or whenever we felt hungry.

We met several Governors' Camp tour vehicles on their early morning game viewing drive. An old guard was at the wheel of one. We asked if he knew of such a lake. For a moment he pondered. "Yes, it could be a large murram pit dug out over several acres by the Council bulldozers when they carved out the Game Reserve boundary road several years ago." He confirmed, "It's full of water and the wild geese have made their resting place on it". "Asante-sana" we chorused. (Thank you very much), and off we set, following his pointing finger to "Somewhere out there, about five miles away."

Kibet and I looked at each other. Could this be it? We located the road, much of it washed away and in disrepair. This was something new to us, a deep scar on the landscape that had formed into a large ten foot wide ditch that takes all the surface water off the thirsty land in one swoosh. We bounced along for a good half-hour in this gully in four by four drive and came to a recent burn. The new bright green grass shoots make it look like a twenty-acre billiard table! There was the lake and there was the island, host to a pair of noisy Egyptian geese that objected to our presence. Was this the dream coming true? I just had to take a photograph. Thompson's gazelle and their young were scattered about, grazing peacefully. A group of banded mongoose was investigating an anthill and some were sunning themselves on its slopes. Everywhere looked too cool, calm and collected, yet both of us knew instinctively if there was a cheetah around, this would be the place to find it. Our instruction from 'on high' was to wait here – and wait here we would until whatever happened.

Kibet, in his usual way, got out of the vehicle and took a short walk armed with his binoculars. One eye-piece was missing but they were nevertheless workable. His three- year-old from his third wife, a young eighteen-year-old, had between them done the damage! Africans, especially Maasai are drawn to this 'spy glass'. Everybody wants to look through them, even if it is the wrong way around. Their surprise at what they see, close up or far away,

The pond with an island
My wife's dream that defies explanation. This was exactly as she had seen it
in her dream. In the distance the tree where Petal was found resting in the shade.

seems to unbalance their inner ear! They stagger around, laughing as if drunk. Try it yourself sometime, it can be most unsettling, like vertigo in reverse!

In the meantime, I set about making the breakfast. Kibet was quite accustomed to western food. A few minutes later, he appeared at the door of the camper asking if he could borrow my binoculars. Mine were still in good shape, though somewhat battle scarred having endured countless drops, rough landings and mistreatment at the hands of many young Maasai herders.

Kibet indicated he had seen lion and hyaena spoor and was sure some looked like a cheetah's paw marks in the mud close to the far edge of the lake. So far, the prognosis looked encouraging. I found myself talking aloud. 'This has got to be it!' I had no more cards to play. Moments later, Kibet was back at the camper door. "Iko kito chini ya miti", (There is something under a tree). The only tree was about five hundred yards away. I climbed onto the bonnet and took a steady look. Yes! There was something, pale in colour, lying down and too far away to really identify it clearly. The mirage from the morning heat was blowing left and right, then boiling upwards. We would wait a while; have breakfast, then go over and take a look before the old guard arrived. The driver of the Governors' Camp vehicle obviously knew we were on to something special, but his first choice was to attend to his client's demand that he find a leopard; the carrot was a monetary reward for doing so. Breakfast was a hurried affair for us, eaten between alternate viewing through the binoculars, in particular at the object under the tree, lest it should disappear. If this happened we would never be certain what it was.

The Egyptian geese had brought their three little chicks out from under the island foliage overhang. Kibet was fascinated as always. Birds of any feather were his true forte, a most unusual trait in an African. But what an expert he was, a true bird-brain with a photographic and computer-like mind. I admired his outstanding professional approach to all of nature's beauty.

We drove cautiously towards the tree; as we neared it we recognized it was a cheetah; an old and tired cheetah. But unmistakably, it was the 'Queen'. She was desperately thin. I stopped and switched off the engine; my hands were trembling. I had found her at last.

Water was the next thing that came to mind. I got out and stood momentarily at the side of the vehicle. I was dressed in my khaki safari clothes; this constant factor was so important for her recognition of me. The cheetah whistle and all the communication reactions of our past encounters came flowing back. I retrieved the 'karai' and plastic water container from the back of the cab seat and poured out the water. This was the signal that always triggered an approach. Petal rose stiffly – arthritis had taken hold. She was desperately hungry. The last few years had cast a shadow of suffering on her gaunt face.

The 'Queen' came to my feet; Kibet was still sitting quietly observing from the inside of the cab. He knew this was a very personal and emotional moment for me, and totally understood my feelings. Petal sniffed at the water but was not thirsty; hunger was in her sunken eyes. She attempted to leap on to the bonnet but did not have the strength so lay down under the camper. It was obvious she was incapable of hunting for a fair sized meal, and was probably surviving on newly born gazelle fawns and the odd African hare. Months of malnutrition had weakened her and this had not passed unnoticed by Nature's death squad. Several hyaenas were close by, keeping her under surveillance, waiting for the right moment to kill her. My presence had given her the security she required to sleep in peace knowing I would protect her.

CHAPTER 16

FAREWELL DINNER

KIBET and I were in a fix, unable to move, unable to seek help. I was not carrying a firearm; it had been handed back to authority when I left the country. Kibet suggested we buy a lamb, a sort of sacrificial last farewell dinner. I thought this was a brilliant idea. Armed with a tyre lever and 500 shillings (£4) worth of small change, he headed off across the veldt, picking up the boundary road. He had earlier spotted a Maasai herding some shoats on the group ranch bordering the game reserve. His purchase would have to be brought back alive and, depending upon its size, he would either have to carry it or walk it back to the camper. After he had gone I realized this was a plucky but crazy idea. What if a predator, a lion or leopard, decided that creature was to be its lunch? There would be nothing Kibet could do except drop it and run. I suddenly remembered the fire extinguisher – of course! What was I thinking of? I chased off after him. A herd of gazelles were stomping a stiff-legged warning, alerting all and sundry, of the two humans in their territory. Kibet heard my shouts and turned back towards me. He was highly amused and jokingly chided me, saying I had forgotten he was of the Kalenjin tribe that feared nothing and whom the Maasai had great respect for as cattle thieves! Such was Kibet's humour – he really was a gem. He took the fire extinguisher and handed me back the tyre lever.

Petal had sensed my absence and was awake and alert on my return. The angle of the setting sun provided an eleven o'clock shadow off the camper. I was able to sit comfortably in the shade, with my back resting against the rear wheel. For the first time I stroked her neck gently; the soothing effect soon brought on a deep sleep. Each time I stopped she stirred, awakening for a few seconds and falling asleep once more. These were precious minutes for us; her days of life were running out and she must get something to eat. I was breaking one of my commandments; a lamb was something she had been taught was not on her menu. To become a sheep killer would have meant death by cold steel. The Maasai do not tolerate any predator that predates on their livestock. Would Petal kill this lamb? Would she even consider eating it? I was relying on her hunger to overcome those inbred instincts that I had driven home to her so often. Kibet had disappeared out of sight, but the resident gazelles had come in closer to have a better look at this four and two legged phenomenon; snorting and squeaking their warnings to each other, with tails wagging furiously like windscreen wipers.

I had time to reflect on the past twenty-four hours. It was a truly amazing occurrence, indeed it was hardly credible, but the facts were all there, ready for any 'doubting Thomas' to question. This animal had sent out her call for help on a wavelength totally detached from mine, and yet somehow, the wonders of telepathic dreams still remain an unfathomable mystery.

It was now almost four o'clock in the afternoon, some five hours had passed since Kibet had left on his journey. In the distance, I could detect a moving figure coming towards us, but with nothing in tow. His arms were hooked over a stick across the back of his shoulders, a common method of long distance, relaxed, cross-country walking configuration used by most pastoral tribes. Was it Kibet? Had he dumped the fire extinguisher for a stick? No way! Yes, he was carrying something tied to the stick across his back but I couldn't see what it was. I assumed he had purchased a lamb.

Petal would not tolerate Kibet's presence, so somehow I had to create a diversion and signal that he should approach us from within the blind spot of the front wheel. Petal continued to sleep as Kibet, hidden from view, walked up to the vehicle quietly. The bleat from his burden was not the fatted lamb I had expected – it was a young impala fawn! The story would have to come later. Right now Petal was awake and highly suspicious that something was afoot. Kibet then released the hapless fawn from its strapping and it ran off at high speed cutting across the front of the camper into Petal's sight. This was all that was needed. She took up the chase and with several bounds the matter was over in seconds. It was obvious she had not eaten for days, if not a week or more.

Kibet had slipped quietly into the rear of the camper. His safari had not been as expected. The Maasai herder only had fully grown shoats, not lambs. However, on hearing Kibet's story, he volunteered his two dogs, for a price of 500 shillings, to hunt down a fawn from the nearby herd of grazing Impala. It had taken a little time, but between them they had run the chosen fawn to ground. This is how the Maasai feed their dogs, though many swear blind they buy their dogs' meat from the local butchery! Kibet was happy to part with the money, not the few pounds in sweat, which he could ill afford to lose! At one time, in his prime, he could be described as a portly, well-fed gentleman!

Now it was a matter of keeping the hyaenas at bay. I elected to stay with Petal whilst Kibet chased the two hyaenas away for almost a mile or more, in the camper. They were determined beasts, using every ruse to double back towards us again. They wanted more than just the leftovers of Petal's feast.

It was now turning dusk and over the horizon, as expected, the old guard appeared. He had guessed, as I thought he would, that we were up to something. His client was delighted to have found a leopard, but now a cheetah on a kill, with a human sitting on the ground close by, with no mode of transport in sight – his world went camera flash mad! He too wanted to be in the 'picture' sitting beside me. His mentor and guide had quite a task explaining, in broken English to his German client, who understood little of that language, what the matter was all about. Thankfully, Kibet arrived back in the camper and the scene took on a less bizarre and more acceptable place in our visitor's mind. He was totally astounded. The Der Speigel newspaper back in Germany, was in for a great story, a coup of the first magnitude! He had seen Tarzan no less!!

As 'Petal's tree' became silhouetted against the setting sun, I sensed the last hours of the Queen's incredible life were coming to a close. I had not bargained for the dramatic manner in which it finally came to an end.

I suddenly remembered I had not seen Kibet return with the fire extinguisher; his hands were full carrying the young trussed-up impala. "Kibet, wapi moto toto?" This was the amusing name he gave to this important piece of my personal equipment. "Where is my fire baby?" I asked. "Oh, I forgot," he responded, "it's with the Maasai herder. He said it was too much to handle with the struggling impala." I asked the German tourist whether he would kindly take Kibet in his vehicle to see the herder. For this effort, Kibet and his tour driver would organize a photo, free of charge, with him standing with this young warrior, spear and all. The deal was done and off they went on another exciting adventure.

The problem was that dusk was approaching and the herder would be well on his way back to his cattle boma (corral), hopefully still clutching the fire extinguisher. My mind boggled at the thought that if, as young Maasai do, he fiddled with the trigger mechanism the thing would 'fire', sending him and his shoats into a coughing, choking, spluttering melee of sheer panic. The safety catch was easily triggered into the fire mode. The pressurized smelling-salts were a mighty powerful deterrent!

It was necessary for me to stay with Petal for the next few days. She required care and protection and it was the least I could do for her. Kibet would get a lift with the Governors' Camp driver to their camp and return here first thing in the morning. His old buddy would look after him. There is always a bed in the bush and there is no need to go hungry.

Petal had consumed every morsel; there was just nothing left, nothing for the hyaenas or jackals, only a picking for the vultures in the morning. The meal had revitalized her, but my concern was her general state of health. I had asked Kibet to contact the warden stationed at the north entrance gate and request a ranger patrol to range feed her to get her strength back. I would provide the necessary security for her, around the clock. The meal Petal had eaten would last twenty-four hours at the most and another feed the next evening would be necessary.

Age and Nature's countdown had taken control. Fifteen years, if she is very lucky, is the lifespan of a female wild cheetah. The 'Queen' had already passed her sell-by-date. Feeding her now would extend the precious hours that were left for us to be together. Petal had given me all her trust and with it had sown a golden thread through my heart forever. Now, knocking at death's door, she had used her telepathic powers to call me to her side to be with her in her last days. What more could I ask of this elegant, wild animal that permitted me into her kingdom and bestowed on me the honour to be one of her subjects. I felt so very humble.

She gave me the freedom of her territorial palace, the pride to walk with her and the privilege to share the joys of her little family. Petal had provided the key to me being accepted by her other subjects, Astra, Polo, their children and her Prince, Namibia. The three boys too had accepted me. Hackles had earned his place at the top of the pyramid. His sheer strength of character and dominance will one day be challenged and as the years of his useful breeding life span grow old; another unrelated dominant male will take over.

This story of Petal, the cheetah, Queen of the Maasai Mara and Queen of my heart will reach out and touch the very souls of the many tourists that saw her. They too had a silver lining sown into their hearts; their joy and the safari memories will never be forgotten during their lifetime.

It was nearly dark when Kibet and the old guard returned with the German tourist. He had his picture taken with the Maasai Moran just at sundown. The fire extinguisher had been located, having been speedily abandoned when, according to the only witness, it had become bewitched and started frothing at the mouth and letting off bad smells after he, the herder, had taken charge of it. All of us guessed correctly what had happened! They left a very confused but happy herdsman out there, fired up having thought he had made a fortune out of some kindly tourist who had paid him generously. His day had been unusually profitable, but that fire extinguisher—he could not understand why it had behaved so badly!

My concern was now directed at the Queen's survival. The hyaenas were whooping, calling up their reserves. I sensed they were drawing up their battle lines. Tonight was going to be a long one. If Petal held her nerve and stayed with me, she would survive. Without my protection in the dark and being unable to see any distance at night, her chances of living to see the dawn would be slim. My 'moto toto' had lost pressure and liquid at the hands of the young Maasai herder. The pressure I could boost up with an ordinary foot pump, other than that I would have to dismantle the whole system, refill and pump it up again and time was running out. Nature's scavengers were under orders to seek and eliminate and they were now coming in our direction! The whoops and their calls were getting closer. I sat near to Petal, talking quietly to her in a tone that might indicate not to panic. I was in control. We had faced hyaenas like this before, two, three and four, but this time they were a pack of at least six. My spotlight picked out six pairs of eyes ahead and several pairs behind us. Petal could see them illuminated in the spotlight and was growling nervously. She would have no chance to outrun them in this total darkness, crashing into bushes; even trees would only injure her and her stamina might not hold the course now that the cards were stacked against her.

I remembered I had several thunder flashes and some Christmas thunder-flashes in the camper as a deterrent or diversion if I was attacked by poachers, whilst parked or asleep in the bush. Using them for this occasion would scare the living daylights out of the 'Queen' and everything else for miles around. It was an option, the very last option; further it would probably set the Mara on fire and send an anti-poaching unit in my direction.

There was no alternative but to wait and stand our ground. I moved over to the camper in the hope she would follow and take refuge under it. This was a tactical mistake on my part for, without my presence close to her, she panicked and bolted into the darkness. Now more problems arose. If I turned the spotlight on her to give her a clear path of light to follow, it would only illuminate her direction and give away her position. Wearing my night vision binoculars, I could cause a diversion and add confusion and distraction by driving at the hyaenas flashing my headlights at them.

For the next hour, I charged at everything I came across, wildebeest, hyaena, eland, impala, Thompson's gazelles and jackals, scattering them in all directions. Round and round I went until I realized I knew not where North, South, East or West was. The thick cloud had covered over the moon and stars. My buzzing around in circles had landed me in a saucer like area, blotting out any distant lights, which I knew and could use as a direction reference. For the second time in my life I was lost in the Mara, without a compass. The first was allowing myself to be caught out alone in a thunder-storm that lasted most of the night. The storm flooded the gully and landscape. The reflected mirror headlight image, at night, can only be described as driving across ice in the arctic. Everything becomes featureless. With no other cards to play, I shut down for the night and prayed that the diversionary tactics had thrown a spanner in the hyaenas' works and given Petal a head start to get away. For much of the night, confusion reigned in the dark as each group of animals that had scattered returned to status quo.

I was awake and ready to move as the dawn broke, half expecting to find Petal had found her way back to me, but no such luck. It was now a matter of watching and checking out the surrounding wildlife body language that might give me a clue. Number one priority was to locate the hyaena pack. Some individuals whooped during the night, but nothing worth noting. The calls were mainly locator calls and families communicating their positions. They were not the cackling type of call that brought groups to feed on a carcass or assist in a kill. By afternoon not one sighting of a cheetah had been made. Kibet arrived with the old guard and his German tourist. They too joined in the search. The Council Rangers turned up, but lacked sufficient fuel to undertake a thorough search. Two days passed and still there was no sign of Petal. The 'Queen' had vanished. I made a point of contacting the Maasai herders to keep a look out for a cheetah and to let any passing tourist driver know of their find.

The young Maasai herder, despite his encounter with the bewitched extinguisher, had tasted the fruits of easy money. He was willing to participate in the search on condition that he and his mongrels were hired out for a daily fee of 1000 shillings (£10). Overnight he had become a businessman, a far more interesting job than tending his father's shoats! I offered a substantial reward for any sighting of a lone cheetah, 'Cash on the nail.' This would trigger the bush telegraph into action. I kept asking myself if the 'Queen' had managed to escape? If so, where and in which direction had she gone? Indeed I asked myself where had she come from and was that the likely place she may have returned to? Only Petal knew the answers.

In hindsight, fitting a radio collar would have solved the problem, but bureaucracy would definitely require an application, in quadruplicate! The days and nights passed with not a hint or a clue coming my way. Fuel and food was low, and so was my morale; it was literally scraping the bottom of the barrel. Five days later, a snippet of information was passed on by an old Maasai elder. He had been walking his way to a friend's manyatta in the hills, had come across a cheetah's carcass some seven kilometers from where Petal had left me. The message came to me third hand. Now it was a matter of looking for an old man 'somewhere in the hills'.

Both Kibet and I set off with a heavy heart, following an old and overgrown vehicle track that would lead us through the rocky lugga crossings to the foot of the Aitong hills, some ten kilometres away. We could be looking for a needle in a haystack with just the flimsiest of information. An old Maasai man going to see his friend in the hills! Despite all of this, by dusk we had achieved the impossible. The old man was known by the locals and in true African spirit, no information was volunteered until 'kitu kidogo' (something small), had passed into the hands of the informer. He would gladly take us there the following morning, but for an added fee! He claimed he was the young Maasai herdsman's brother! They certainly learn fast, these guys! I was now expecting to hear the old man was his father! Wrong, when I inquired I was told the old boy was his uncle! Was this all really a family coincidence? Kibet was shifting uneasily, but not letting on his discomfort to me. He too was probably imagining something along the same lines as I. Could this all be a red herring, a smoke screen of some sort, hiding the real truth, but now sold to us in a way that made custard look like chocolate mousse? This is the African cunning at work and the only people who can match it are the Arabs.

We decided to head for our old 'Out of Africa' camp, now called Kicheche camp. (Kicheche is the Swahili word for mongoose). Why of all things, did they change the name? We would find accommodation, fuel, good food and could spend the night there.

It was now dark. We drove in total silence, each pondering over the 'family' coincidence. The urge within me to break the silence between us was overpowering. I blurted out one word, "Mbwa", (the dogs). Kibet knew I was not talking about wild dogs; they had all died of rabies. He looked across at me and nodded his head gently. "Is it a conspiracy of some sort, Kibet" I asked. "Inaonekana ni hivyo" he replied. (It looks that way). We were both on the same wavelength. The jigsaw was beginning to fall into place in my mind. It wasn't a pleasant one. Tomorrow, Kibet would deliver his own judgement in his own time. It would be carefully considered and on the mark.

The following morning, having slept fitfully, but well fed and refuelled, we set off soon after dawn to collect the brother 'for a fee'. He would then guide us to the uncle who would take us. 'for another fee' no doubt, to the spot. This was all getting too commercialized. The route to 'uncle' turned out to be a bundu bash, no road, no track, but a steep climb in low 4x4 drive. Sometimes the Landcruiser teetered at an impossible slant and any misjudgement on my part would surely send us toppling over and rolling down the hill.

We came to some cattle tracks. They, unlike the wildlife tracks, went straight up and down, not along the contour of the hill. Cattle are the very worst at eroding the landscape; the tracks become mini furrows and when it rains carries all the topsoil downhill.

At last we arrived at the manyatta and were set upon by a horde of young Maasai children. "Sweet, sweet." Surely not, I said to myself; how did the Americans get here? The children were all dressed in their blue school uniforms and ready to walk, as a group, to their school three miles away. The American tourists had brought them loads of candy to their school. "What have you brought for us today?" they asked. Not satisfied with my answer they all wanted to pile into the camper for a free ride to school – I felt like saying 'only for a fee, fee, fee!'

The old man was located, and as predicted, he required a little something to help him think when and where it was he saw the carcass. Several bottles of large Tusker beer, Kenya's number one best seller in the beer line, helped to loosen his tongue and kick start his addled brain. Even for the hardened drinker, two of these beers, on an empty stomach, before breakfast will make the world go around and is a sure-fire way of setting off on a merry-go-round in circles to who knows where, in search of a carcass that was now into its seventh day! Nature's aerial clean-up squad, plus its super efficient ground work force, will have ensured their job was well done.

We set off down hill, this time straight down! The 'brother' guide was dumped for he was no longer of use. Now the old man was holding on tight, sitting between us in the front cab. Heavens, I thought, when did this man last have a bath – it smelt like never! His sheep fat 'Eau de Cologne', he called it his skin moisturizer, had gone rancid years ago!

The track we were following on the straight and level savannah began to take on a familiar pattern. It was not long before we crossed our tracks from the previous day. We latched onto these, soon coming into what we now knew to be the 'uncle's' nephew, herding his shoats. The jigsaw was almost in place. The three mongrel dogs were there, looking reasonably well fed on the butcher's shop meat! There was much jabbering with directions given in coded Maasai between the old man and the herder. The 'uncle' it would appear had 'only heard' but had not 'actually seen' the carcass himself! Both Kibet and I gathered this from piecing together the bits of conversation and gesticulations that were coming from the two.

The old man returned to the vehicle and off we went, not surprisingly, without the young Maasai herder. He was not meant to be in the know, but I knew that he knew more than he was willing to tell us. It was he, I am sure, who found the carcass. Kibet and I would soon know for sure if the old man dithered or became suddenly confused by the surroundings. This would signal another ruse to get more money out of us.

1987-2002
Petal's grave. Nature blessed her with a living wreath of such beauty.
I shall miss her dearly each time I go to visit her descendants in the Mara.
The memory of this very special wild animal will come flooding back.

We travelled south for a mile towards a large single sausage tree. The seed-pods are shaped in the form of a large sausage. The unripe fruits are poisonous but have medicinal properties for treating skin rash. When sun-dried and with the seeds shaken out, the remaining skeleton becomes an efficient and durable 'loofah' – good for removing 'dead' skin from the body! Nature has provided an excellent back scrubber free of charge.

As we came to within yards of the tree, I noticed an intensely bright red, beautiful cluster of flowers, commonly know as the Pin Cushion. This 'marked' the spot. We stopped and the old man walked over towards it. It was here, he remembered this flower. The trained eyes of Kibet and I could make out the discolouration on the grass. The fur, the colour of a cheetah and its skeleton had been spread around. Evidence of vultures, hyaenas and jackal were easy to see. I could not, at first sight, be sure this was Petal or how the cat had met its end. There was no sign of a struggle. All three of us fanned out, looking for evidence, in particular facial skin attached to a skull that I could easily identify as the 'Queen'. We had almost given up when the old man found the identifying clue. It was a piece of skin and attached to it was an ear, the right ear. The Queen's trade mark was clear. The 'V' shape that Dr. Wambua, the K.W.S. veterinarian had cut out from her ear was plainly visible. Petal's life had tragically

'As the sun sets over your grave
I will always remember our golden moments together'.
Petal, Queen of my Heart.
Rest in peace.

come to an end at the spot where I stood.

I knelt down in solemn prayer. I prayed she had found happiness in her new world that she so richly deserved. Knowing her as I did so enriched my life and gave me the courage to fight this dreaded leukaemia.

Now the story has come to an end in print, a full year of endeavour to record this into the archives of the true and extraordinary stories of reciprocated trust and understanding between a wild animal family and their human companion. The doctor's report today gives me some hope that this life threatening disease that came from nowhere five years ago, may have been beaten. Time would tell if my guardian angel would again work her gracious spell for me.

Without my being aware, both men had stood well aside and had seen me kneeling in prayer, sobbing my heart out. I had an obligation of honour to the old man and offered him my reward of five thousand shillings in cash (the equivalent of fifty pounds sterling). None was more surprised than I, when he refused to accept it. Instead he promised that each time he walked by this way he would stop and stand in silence at the red flowers and offer a Maasai prayer for my special cat. The old man wandered off, returning with some gnarled wood. This he placed around the flowers to protect them from harm. This was his way of marking the grave. Neither Kibet nor I will ever know how she died. Was it at the jaws of the hyaenas, or was it the Maasai herder's dogs that killed her?

When the TV field presenters came to know 'their friendly cheetahs' were some of the five adult orphans of the Mara they decided to give them different names which they felt most suited their documentaries. Petal, Queen of the Mara, had already become a legend and did not take kindly to being stripped of her title and given the commoner name of Amber. For this dastardly crime the Queen invoked a smelly curse on the perpetrators. She decreed, by common consent, that they, the presenters, would be 'dumped upon' and defuelled upon' from on high by her successors. Her daughter, Kike, 'star of the current Big Cat Diary series', enacted the curse.

The Queen's pride and dignity has now been avenged.

Open roof hatches of the BBC Big Cat Diary vehicles are now hurriedly and firmly battened down when Kike approaches their vehicles.

The moral of this true story is:

'Give credit where credit is due.
The truth of the beginning is now out!

Petal's progeny and their successive generations continue to bring joy and pleasure to many visitors from all over the world. They promise to return again to witness Nature's amazing spectacle unfold its daily dramas in the heart of Kenya's wildlife wilderness.

EPILOGUE

KENYA'S wildlife is under siege. Soon it will be completely decimated and destroyed by the burgeoning illegal bush meat trade. This commercial plunder and poaching has now reached alarming proportions.

Without its wildlife attractions Kenya will lose its magical appeal.

It is my hope that the many television documentaries and the caring few who have dedicated their lives to conservation and preserving our Natural World, will continue to touch the hearts and minds of the less fortunate people of Africa. It is vital for them to protect their precious heritage so that we—the human race as one—can become the driving force in conserving Nature's master plan.

Pollution of the air, land and sea by the world's population is destroying the very legacy that Nature has entrusted to us. If we fail, she will not guarantee our existence on this planet.

GLOBAL WARMING
IS
NATURE'S WARNING!

Jomo Kenyatta
1st President of the Republic of Kenya

The Pledge

The natural resources of this country ? its wildlife that offers such an attraction to visitors from all over the world, the beautiful places in which these animals live, the mighty forests that guard the water catchment areas vital to the survival of man and beast ? are a priceless heritage for the future.

The Government of Kenya, fully realising the value of its natural resources, pledges to conserve them for posterity with all the means at its disposal.